Lucy Thurston
and
Linda Arvidson

Photograph of Lucy Thurston taken in the late 1860s or early 1870s during the last years of her life.

Photograph of Linda Arvidson taken about 1913 for a movie magazine called *Moving Picture News*.

Lucy Thurston and Linda Arvidson

Two Unforgettable Memoirs about the Early Days of Hawaii and the Era of Silent Movies

SPECIAL EDITION
Edited by Gary Brin

LIST OF TITLES USED FOR THIS COLLECTION

Life and Times of Mrs. Lucy G. Thurston was originally published in 1882. It was reprinted in a second edition in 1921 and a limited third edition in 1934.

When the Movies Were Young was originally published in 1925. It was reprinted in a special edition from Dover Publications in 1969.

BOTH TITLES CAN BE FOUND AT THE SITE LISTED BELOW
www.nancyhankslincolnpubliclibrary.org

Spelling errors and visible publishing mistakes found in the original versions listed above were corrected or slightly adjusted whenever necessary for this edition. Original text was left intact to preserve the historical accuracy of the writings.

BOTH BOOKS USED FOR THIS EDITION HAS BEEN REFORMATTED FROM THE ORIGINAL 1882 AND 1925 PUBLISHED VERSIONS.

Images of Lucy Thurston and Linda Arvidson displayed in this book are courtesy of the Library of Congress. Both photographs were digitally restored for this edition.
Cover design and book layout © 2022 by Standish Press
Compilation © 2022 by Standish Press

FIRST EDITION

ALL NEW MATERIAL AND CORRECTIONS
Copyright © 2022 by Standish Press

All rights reserved. No part of this book may be reproduced by any means whatsoever without written permission from the publisher.

For more information about reprint rights please visit
www.standishpress.com

ISBN—978-1-945510-10-6

Library of Congress Control Number
2022944586

MANUFACTURED IN THE UNITED STATES OF AMERICA

In Remembrance of

Lucy Thurston and **Linda Arvidson**

They left behind lasting historical documents with their recollections of the times they experienced and the events they saw happening which changed present-day history.

This book is also dedicated in memory of

Robert Taylor Thurston and **Robert Harron**

Two young men with so much to live for before their lives were cut short by tragic events in 1874 and 1920.

Contents

Page 11
Foreword
Page 13
Lucy Thurston
Page 217
Linda Arvidson
Page 394
Afterword
Page 397
Additional Notes
Page 406
About the Series Editor

Foreword

    When books are written and published, the last thing that occurs to the writer or the publisher is that sometime in the future the material found in the pages of a particular book will eventually be considered worthy of being preserved because of its historical content. Such is the case for the memoirs of Lucy Thurston and Linda Arvidson. Books can be written for various reasons such as money and fame, but usually when a book is written simply as a look back at history it proves more valuable because it captures events that occurred which as decades slip by become harder and harder to be written accurately by so-called historians who think they know more than they actually do.

    Lucy Goodale Thurston was born at the end of the eighteenth century and seemed poised for a forgettable life until the story of Henry Obookiah caught her attention. Obookiah was a Hawaiian youth who ventured to New England and became associated with a group of Christian missionaries. Tragically, he died before he could fulfill his dream to return to Hawaii. Regardless, his dream didn't die with him and a year after his death plans were underway for his missionary friends to journey halfway around the world. Upon landing in the Hawaiian Islands, Thurston began keeping a record of her exciting experiences and through the decades that followed—her words captured many historical accounts that today seem more like a movie than actual reality. Considered one of the most important memoirs of life in the Hawaiian Islands during the nineteenth century, her words still holds us spellbound as if it were happening presently.

    Linda Arvidson never assumed her goal to be an actress would give her an in-person eyewitness view of the early years of motion pictures in the United States. Her account about her association with famed director and secret husband D. W. Griffith leads one to relive what it must have been like to see history unfolding as movies became a part of the American fabric. She also writes about the everyday lives of such silent screen greats like Robert Harron, Dorothy and Lillian Gish, Mabel Normand, Mae Marsh, Jack and Mary Pickford, Blanche Sweet, Wallace Reid, Thomas Ince, Florence LaBadie, Mack Sennett, Richard Barthelmess, and Charlie Chaplin as well as their many foibles long before they became film royalty which few biographers have bothered to write about. Arvidson's memoir was one of the first books written by someone who worked alongside future legendary stars and despite the passage of a century it has remained one of the most important works from Hollywood.

    Both Thurston's and Arvidson's memoirs offer a look back at the past, written during a time that seems so long ago, but of which we can still relate to. Books such as these make reading worthwhile, and maybe, just maybe, lessons can be learned.

Gary Brin
Series Editor

Lucy Thurston

Life and Times of Mrs. Lucy G. Thurston
An Autobiography

Part First—1819-1840. **ARTICLE 1** Hawaii was first discovered to the civilized world in 1778. In the same year, Kamehameha fought, a soldier, under his uncle, Kalaniopuu, King of several districts on one individual island. In the year 1810, all the islands of this group became one united, kingdom under Kamehameha. In the same year, in America, [Henry] Obookiah became theoretically the first Hawaiian convert to Christianity. They both lived after this, the one eight, and the other nine years. Kamehameha in his last sickness, asked about the white man's God. But in the language of the narrator, "*They no tell him.*" "Obookiah" died young, with a hope full of immortality. His prayers, tears, and appeals for his poor countrymen, as described in his memoir, [*Memoirs of Henry Obookiah*] did more for them than he could have done in the longest life of the most devoted labors. The church was newly aroused to send a mission to those who, for long dismal ages, had been enshrouded in all the darkness of nature. **ARTICLE 2** (To Mrs. Persis Goodale

Parkhurst, Plainfield, New Hampshire) *Marlborough, West Parish, September 11, 1819*. How shall I address my own dear best beloved sister? Our corresponding ages, pursuits, sentiments, and feelings, caused Persis to be more peculiarly mine. We commenced and traveled together the journey of life, together tasted the delights, and culled the flowers of spring, and when, by reason of the way, our hearts have sunk within us, we have set down together and mingled our tears. Ever precious will be the recollections of those days and years, spent beneath a father's roof—never to be forgotten the period, when by assuming a new relation, you bade farewell to the paternal abode, thereby causing our future pathways in life to diverge. Our Mother—gone. Persis—gone. Wonder not when I say, that the depths of my sorrows were revived, and that I more than ever felt myself an orphan. The dear solitary chamber that I occupy witnessed my grief, while I walked it from side to side, or watered my pillow with my tears. I applied to the fountain of all grace and consolation for support, sacredly devoting all my leisure hours to the study of the will of the Supreme. Here my sorrows were assuaged, and my heart comforted. But I emphatically feel that earth is not my rest. *Your loving sister, Lucy Goodale.* **ARTICLE 3** *Marlborough, West Parish, September 18, Saturday*. Three weeks have elapsed since the departure of my sister Persis. Yesterday, during my noontide intermission, I received, at my boarding house, an unexpected call from cousin William Goodell. He gave me information that a Mission to the Sandwich Islands was to sail in four or six weeks, dwelt upon it with interest and feeling, and notwithstanding his efforts to assume his usual cheerfulness, now and then I saw the tear start in his eye. His conversation and appearance made me tremble. At length, having prepared my mind, the proposition was made, *"Will Lucy, by becoming connected with a missionary now an entire stranger, attach herself to this little band of pilgrims, and visit the far distant land of Obookiah?"* Now I feel the need of guidance. Oh, that Persis were here! Never did I so much long to see her. The gentleman proposed as the companion of my life is Mr. Thurston, member of the Senior Class, in Andover Theological Institution. He had recently become an accepted missionary of the American Board of Commissioners for Foreign Missions, soon to sail for the Sandwich Islands. This has all come suddenly upon him. Now that he knows the situation he is called to fill, he has no personal knowledge of one who is both willing and qualified to go with him to a foreign land. Some of his classmates were admitted to his private confidence. One of them, in passing back and forth, had been entertained at Deacon Goodale's. He spoke of his daughter Lucy, as being fitted for such a position. It proved a hinge to act upon. They knew that Goodell of the Middle Class was a relative of the family. They admitted him into their counsel to speak of the missionary qualifications of Lucy Goodale. Most closely and seriously, during the last year, he has pressed the subject on my consideration, of personally engaging in the missionary enterprise. In his very last letter, recently received, he wrote thus, *"When I say I hope cousin Lucy will be of the next company that go to the heathen, instead of imputing it to any desire of never seeing her again, she will rather think, that I believe her to adopt from the heart the favorite language of Spencer—'Where He appoints, I go.'"* The result of the whole matter was, that William Goodell was appointed to obtain permission for a personal interview. So here he was, delivering his message, adding, *"Rebecca said, 'I will go.'"* What could I say? We thoroughly discussed the subject, after which I gave permission for a visit. Next week on Thursday is the anticipated, dreaded interview of final decision. Cousin William walked with me, and, as we approached the schoolhouse, bade me goodbye. I immediately entered the school, but how I longed to find my chamber, that I might give vent to the feelings of an almost bursting heart. Last night I could neither eat, nor close my eyes in sleep. *September 21, Tuesday*. The subject has been to my mind utterly overwhelming, and I all alone during this season of conflict. Situated six miles from my father's, I have no confidential friend near me to whom I can unfold my feelings. William Goodell fully informed my family that the waters were troubled. During the week, my two sisters from home, Eliza and

Meliscent, called on and comforted me with their sympathy and affection. I have received, too, communications from my father. But they all leave me to myself, to act agreeably to my own judgment and inclination. Dear to my heart are my friends and country. Yet, all this side the grave, how transient! The poor heathen possess immortal natures, and are perishing. Who will give them the Bible, and tell them of a Savior? Great as must be the sacrifices, trials, hardships, and dangers of such an undertaking, I said, "*If God will grant his grace, and afford an acceptable opportunity, Lucy and all that is hers, shall be given to the noble enterprise of carrying light to the poor benighted countrymen of Obookiah.*" After this decision, I could contemplate the subject with a tranquil mind and unmoved feelings. *Home, September 22, Wednesday.* This afternoon I returned to the paternal abode. I have, with the most perfect freedom, conversed with my family here on the subject. They left me alone to breast the billow. But, when I came among them with composure and serenity, buoyed up by a noble purpose, they gave me their full sympathy and approbation. *September 23, Thursday.* The close of this day brought our expected Andover friends, William Goodell and Mr. [Asa] Thurston to our door, and established them in our parlor. That was a strictly private family interview. I returned home, and alone entered the house the night before. Our dwelling was completely isolated from neighbors, and not a word had been dropped of expected company. We were alone in our little world. There were my father and my two brothers and their wives, all belonging to the house. There, too, was Uncle William Goodell, (cousin William's own father) who had lived with my father for several years, and who was in sympathy and confidences as one of us. William Goodell had now accomplished his mission. Under the most favorable circumstances, he had opened the way and brought Mr. Thurston to Deacon Goodale's, brought Lucy to her father's house to interview the stranger in the bosom of her own family, amid a band of six close confidential friends, where no prying eyes or ready tongues were admitted to give intelligence to the outside world. The early hours of the evening were devoted to refreshments, to free family sociality, to singing, and to evening worship. Then one by one the family dispersed, leaving two of similar aspirations, introduced at sunset as strangers, to separate at midnight as interested friends. *September 24, Friday.* In the forenoon, the sun had risen high in the Heavens, when it looked down upon two of the children of earth giving themselves wholly to their heavenly Father, receiving each other from his hand as his good gift, pledging themselves to each other as close companions in the race of life, consecrating themselves and their all to a life work among the heathen. And it came to pass after that decision, that there met together a committee of Ways and Means. The first thing to be fixed upon was a programme. That was Friday, September 24th. September 26th, October 3rd and 10th, would furnish three Sabbaths for publication. Then the 11th was Monday, not a convenient day, but the 12th, Tuesday, was fixed upon as the day of the wedding, and after the ceremony, the party was to proceed directly to Boston. According to this programme, letters to friends in different places were written, and directions given to the town clerk in Marlborough, and to the town clerk in Fitchburg, Mr. Thurston's native place. It was afternoon before letters and messengers were dispatched. *September 25, Saturday.* The very next morning after the decision, William Goodell and Mr. Thurston started for the ordination at Goshen, Connecticut. I rode with them six miles, as they passed my school, in order to dismiss it. *September 28, Tuesday.* The candidates, [Hiram] Bingham and [Asa] Thurston, were examined at Goshen. September 29, Wednesday, they were ordained. During these exercises at Goshen, Connecticut, brother Nathan and myself in Massachusetts, hastened to Boston to obtain my outfit. Miss Frances Irving assisted me to accomplish my business. Nathan accompanied us, paid bills, and carried the parcels. After returning to Marlborough with all this abundance of material, we made a long table across the middle of one of the front rooms. Lucy Howe, Susan Witt and Sophia Rice, three friends, came and cut garments by dozens and by scores. When the gentlemen returned from the ordination, William Goodell was an untold blessing to me in his activity and zeal in finding persons to make some of the cut garments. Just before giving the parting hand, when the two gentlemen passed on to the ordination, William Goodell said to me, "*Now, don't regard the barking of little dogs.*" In one week, a cousin and his wife arrived to pass the Sabbath with us. His father was a clergyman, but he himself was an Attorney at Law, and an openly avowed, active infidel. Had he set his artillery in motion it would have been a lion's roar. Mr. Thurston, too, spent the same Sabbath with us, and preached for Mr. Bucklin, our minister. At intermission, as we were returning to the second service, Mrs. Bucklin remarked, "*After leaving your country, you will never again hear the sound of the church going bell.*" Our cousin highly commended the services of the day, and conversed with me of my prospects with tender encouragement. When he retired Saturday night he took my album with him to his room, and returned it Monday morning. Within he had written the following lines, containing strange sentiments indeed to come from *his* pen, "*And art thou called to visit distant lands, to teach the heathen God's divine commands? Then go, sweet cousin, cross the foaming sea, thy God will bless thee wheresoever ye be, soon thou wilt see Hawaii's fertile shore, and settle there to see thine own no more, there build thy cottage by the rising flood, and tell the natives of their Savior, God. His life, his sufferings be thy fruitful theme, while faith and hope will in their faces gleam, thy social hearth will flame with love divine, and all will bless thy steps and all that's thine. Oh, may He fill thy soul with sovereign grace, and bless thy partner in his charge and place, bless all his labors, bless his little flock, and bless thy children from our Goodale stock. In memory's favorite hour wilt thou remember me, full often our prayers shall ascend for thee, long shall we dwell on this farewell to you, and long shall memory linger over this last adieu.*" [Ten years after this, I received a parcel of black pepper, done up in a newspaper, from our Secular Agent. The first thing I did was to pour the pepper into a bowl, and search the paper wrapper for intelligence. It contained the following [sermon], REMARKABLE

CONVERSION. One instance of divine grace exhibited the winter past in my immediate vicinity, and which fell under my own observation, I will, with permission, relate. The subject of this change was an Attorney at Law, the son of a clergyman. He had been emphatically the son of many prayers, and his childhood had been endowed with all needful moral and religious instruction. But as he grew up and went out from the government of his father's family, he apostatized from his early education, and became a terror to those who would do well. At this time, he entered into an agreement with a brother, by which they were mutually bound, that the first called from this world should return and inform the other of the invisible state, if permitted. The brother, not long after was drowned in the Connecticut, and as soon as this survivor received the intelligence, he hastened to the place where the deep and dark wave still rolled over the lifeless body of his brother, and there in an hour of retirement, he called aloud, and the voice echoed from bank to bank, for that departed brother to fulfill his engagement, but there was no voice, nor any that answered. And he relates that he repeated the same over his brother's grave, after the body was found. He remained unshaken in his infidelity. Being a popular advocate in his profession, he, in a few years, accumulated a large estate, but he had no bowels of compassion, no breathings of benevolence. About eighteen months ago, his father desired him to carry his annual contribution to the Treasurer of the Board of Foreign Missions, which he did, and said to the Treasurer, "*I bring you fifty dollars from my father to aid the objects of this Board, but I would rather throw it into the sea.*" It however pleased God the last season to take from him a beloved child by death, and for the first time in his life did he realize that this world is shadowy and evanescent. The impression grew upon him, and he soon felt that all would ere long be taken from him, and nothing remain but the ghosts and penalties of millions of sins, sins of the most aggravating kind. He strove to conceal his distress, but strove in vain. He, at length, confessed his condition, and sought the prayers of those people, whom he had so lately despised. For some weeks he bowed like the rush, and his mourning was like the mourning of Hadadrimmon in the valley of Megiddon. But the hour of release came, for he was a chosen vessel unto God. He bowed to Prince Emmanuel. He became as a child, and openly and fearlessly espoused the cause of him whom he had persecuted. He gave public declaration, that if he had defrauded any man in the course of his business he would make them amends to the amount of fourfold. At this time he recalled his saying to the Treasurer of the Board of Foreign Missions. He could not rest until he had made a written confession to him. In that letter the Treasurer found a hundred dollar bank note. A reformation succeeded this conversion, which spread through the town, and many have been added to the cause of Christ. The description of this individual so answered to the cousin, whose lines I have just recorded, up to the time of his religious convictions, that I immediately wrote and asked him if he had become a Christian. (In due time, we received the following reply. *January 24, 1830. Dear and Respected Cousins*, years, eventful years, have rolled away, since first we met, since last we parted. You have left all the dear scenes of your childhood and youth—your father's land—and gone to the sea-girt (surrounded by water) islands where all is comparatively dark and dreary. The Indian hut, the Indian manners, the savage life and accommodations surround you. But what hath God wrought! Did I say all was savage about you? I mistake. The Lamb of God is there, and has taken away the savage heart, the heathen life, the untutored Indian, and given you brothers and sisters dear in the Lord. O, bless His great and excellent name, all ye His people, all ye His lands, all ye His islands of the sea! I often recur to that hour when I bade you farewell. Like Balaam (prophet), I wrote blessings on your head when I had no heart to bless. I looked on the tents of Israel. I saw them spreading from sea to sea, and filling all the plains and islands with a happy race, praising the Lord our God. I saw you building your cottage on the shores of Hawaii, and then I saw temples rise dedicated to the living God. I saw the natives hang around you, and like children receive the word of eternal life, and I could not but say, "*then go, sweet cousin, cross the foaming sea, and God go with you wheresoever you be."* Yet I was a very infidel at heart, and how, on recurring to what I wrote in that album of yours, I could write so, I know not. It was a wonder to myself. I, who scoffed at the Bible, at its miracles, its revealed contradictions and absurdities, as I then thought, how could I speak of your teaching that Savior's love, which I thought an imposter? But so it was, and like Balaam, when I would have cursed, I could only bless. Now, I thank God, I trust I can bless Him too from my heart. I do believe I do love, as I humbly trust, that dear Redeemer, who died for sinners, who tasted death for us all. The white, the red, and the black man, too, encircled in His arm of love and mercy, all may lie on His bosom, like the beloved John, all may lean on His breast and live forever. O, preach Him, proclaim Him to all lands, to all people, blow the gospel trumpet over all the Islands, an angel blast, and let the heathen hear and live. But I wander. I meant to speak of the years we have been separated. The same kind Providence that has always blessed the ungrateful has ever continued to bless me and mine in all these years. Two of our children sleep side by side under the green turf of our graveyard. They were lovely boys, both born in March. Both lived until August of their second year—and then died. We could not save them, nor, do I now repine their loss. I trust they are happy. We had been insensible of all God's mercies, but when He laid his hand on our little ones, it brought us to bless His holy name. May praise be His forever. Your father and my father have also gone to their last home. I trust they are now perfect in Christ. It was good to hear my dear father express his earnest hope and belief that God, for Christ's sake, had forgiven all his sins.] **ARTICLE 4** (Mrs. Persis G. Parkhurst to her sister, Mrs. Lucy G. Thurston) On the night of the 23rd of September, the very night of your first introduction to Mr. [Asa] Thurston, I was transported in a dream to the home of my youth. You were not there. I saw the house surrounded with carriages. Within was a large collection of people, many of whom were strangers. The doors seemed opened from room to room, and whichever way I turned, I was surrounded by numbers, some walking to and fro, and others standing in solemn, fixed attention. I saw nothing transacted, heard nothing said, but thought the occasion was your wedding. Though never in the habit of thinking much of dreams—this took strong hold of my feelings. It cost me many tears. Every succeeding day I wept, for I could not divest myself of the idea that my dream referred to your death. A letter from home was put into my hands. It was not superscribed by you. I was overwhelmed with an undefinable dread that you had dropped the pen forever. At first I could not open it. At length I summoned resolution and broke the seal. I read the lines traced by your pen. You were not dead, but destined to cross the ocean, and spend your days in a foreign heathen land. On the 12th of October your marriage was solemnized in our father's home. In one hour after the rite, you gave your parting hand to all, entered the carriage at the door, with your new-found husband, and, attended by cousin William Goodell, parted forever from the friends and scenes of your youth. When the sound of the carriage wheels ceased to be heard, I looked, and behold, both in the house and in the yard, a most perfect representation of my dream. *Your loving sister, Persis G. Parkhurst.* **ARTICLE 5** A brig was about to sail from Boston to the Sandwich Islands. Previous arrangements had been made, and a voluntary company there assembled, whose language to the Prudential Committee of the American Board of Commissioners for Foreign Missions was, "*Here we are, send us.*" There were two ordained preachers and translators, Mr. Bingham and Mr. Thurston, and their wives, a physician, Dr. Holman and wife, two teachers, Mr. Whitney and Mr. Ruggles, and their wives, a printer, Mr. Loomis and wife, a farmer, Mr. Chamberlain, wife and five children. Three converted native youths, partially educated, Thomas Hopu, John Honolii and William Kanui. *October 17, 1819.* These seventeen individuals were organized into a distinct Missionary Church, to be transplanted to the Pagan Islands (Hawaii) of the Pacific. It took place in the vestry of Park Street Church, Boston, beneath the auspices of the Prudential Committee of the American Board, among whom Dr. [Samuel]

Worcester, first Secretary, and Jeremiah Evarts, first Treasurer, were prominent. On the same day there was a large gathering in the body of the church, in the middle of which that company of consecrated ones were placed to receive the public instructions of the Prudential Committee. That revered father, Dr. Worcester, was their organ. From fifteen printed pages, the following few detached paragraphs are a specimen of the whole. *Dearly Beloved in the Lord*, you are now on the point, the most of you, of leaving your country, and your kindred, and your father's houses, and committing yourselves, under Providence, to the winds and the waves, for conveyance to far distant islands of the sea, there to spend the remainder of your days. You have given yourselves to Christ for the high and holy service of missionary work. You have made your vows and you cannot go back. If it be not so—and if this point be not fixed with you immovably—stop where you are, nor venture to set foot on that board, which is to bear this holy mission to the scene of its labors and trials, and eventual triumphs. Whatever of earthly privations, or labors, or sufferings awaits you, they are comparatively as nothing. You may glory in them all. You may count them all joy. Other things, dearly beloved, are before you. Your mission is to "*a land of darkness as darkness itself, and of the shadow of death without any order, and where the light is as darkness.*" You will find Jesus in Hawaii, as you have found him in this land, a sun and shield. His gracious word, "*Lo I am with you always,*" was sufficient for the first missionaries of the cross, and it will be sufficient for you, sufficient for all the purposes of safety, of support, of guidance, of consolation, of strength, of courage, of success, of triumph, and of glory. Abide fixedly on this word, and you will have nothing to want, nothing to fear. You are to aim at nothing short of covering those Islands with fruitful fields, pleasant dwellings, schools, and churches. Mr. Bingham and Mr. Thurston, the world has not an office in its gift which is not annihilated when compared with that of a [Protestant] Christian missionary, not a crown that would not fade into utter obscurity in presence of that of Paul. The seraph nearest the celestial throne might esteem it a distinguished honor, to execute in a manner befitting its nature and design, the trust committed to you. Be not high-minded, but fear. You are but earthen vessels. All your sufficiency is of God, and the whole glory will be His. To you, jointly, is committed this consecrated mission, proceeding from the bosom of Christian and of heavenly love. The beloved females of the mission are not to be forgotten. There is no law of Heaven for excluding the sex from the participation for which the same sovereign goodness has fitted them, in the toils and perils, the joys and glories of recovering the common race. When the Son of God was on his mission, woman, many women testified the deepest interest in it, ministered to him of their substance, attended him in his journeying and labors, and even followed him when his disciples forsook him and fled, and earth and Heaven were in dismay, followed him out to the scene of crucifixion. These favored daughters of Zion (Jerusalem) then, who, with so much tender cheerfulness, have given themselves to their Savior and Lord for this arduous service, are not without warrant for thus leaving the world to its own opinion and pursuits. Beloved members of the mission, male and female—this Christian community is moved for you, and for your enterprise. The offerings, and prayers, and tears, and benedictions, and vows of the churches are before the throne of everlasting mercy. They must not be violated, they must not, cannot be lost. But how can you sustain the responsibility? A nation to be enlightened and renovated, and added to the civilized world, and to the kingdom of the world's Redeemer (Jesus Christ) and rightful sovereign (king)! In His name only, and by His power, can the enterprise be achieved. **ARTICLE 6** The next day after these preparations, from various parts of the New England States, a concourse of the friends of missions assembled at a farewell meeting. Mr. Thurston, one of the numbers about to embark, delivered in Park Street Church. *[A PARTING ADDRESS—AN EXTRACT]* Permit me, my dear friends, to express the sentiments and feelings of this missionary company on the present occasion. We would express our gratitude to the Great Head of the Church, for the provision he has made for the souls of men, and for the evidence which he graciously gives us, that we are severally interested in this great salvation. We bless God that we live in this interesting period of the world—that so much has been done, and that so much is still doing to extend the blessings of the Redeemer's kingdom to the ends of the earth. The present is emphatically styled a day of action the Church is opening her eyes on the miseries of a world lying in wickedness. Her compassion is moved, and her benevolence excited, to alleviate human sufferings, and to save the soul from death. We have felt that the Savior was speaking to us, and our bosoms have panted for the privilege of engaging in the blessed work of evangelizing the heathen. We have voluntarily devoted ourselves to this great object, and have been set apart to go forth and labor for its accomplishment. In a few days we expect to leave this loved land of our nativity, for the far distant isles of the sea, there to plant this little vine, and nourish it, till it shall extend through all the islands, till it shall shoot its branches across to the American coast, and its precious fruit shall be gathered at the foot of her mountains. **ARTICLE 7** *October 23, 1819*. We embarked from Boston on board the brig *Thaddeus*, with Captain [Andrew] Blanchard. We cut loose from our native land for life, to find a dwelling place, far, far away from civilized man, among barbarians, there to cope with a cruel priesthood of blood-loving deities, and to place ourselves under the iron law of kapus requiring men and women to eat separately. To break that law was death. It was death for women to eat of various kinds of food, such as pork, bananas, coconuts, and etc. It was death for her to enter the eating house of her husband. The choicest of animal and vegetable products were reserved for the male child, for the female, the poorest. From birth to death, a female child was allowed no food that had touched her father's plate. It was death for a woman to be caught looking at an idol's temple. When she passed one, she was required to turn her face another way. Such were our prospects during our long voyage of more than five months across the ocean. Our only hope and trust was in God. Although we set our faces to pass beyond the pale of civilization, yet the animating prospect was held up before us, that we might communicate with our American friends once a year. The whales of the Pacific Ocean, and the gold mines of California were then unknown. Intelligence of the arrival of our mission at the Islands, reached the United States seventeen months after we left Boston. **ARTICLE 8** (Letter to Persis Goodale Parkhurst, Eliza Goodale and Meliscent Warren Goodale) *Dear Sisters*, the season has again returned, which, in its last revolution, brought with it such scenes of sorrow, connected with our mother's death. That time I seem to live over again. Every event of every day is called up afresh, as it were but of yesterday. Nor is this all. The kindred tie has again been severed, another, dear to me as my own soul, I can no more find in the domestic abode, no more behold on earth. Never perhaps were sisters more tenderly attached. You know the similarity of taste, of sentiment, and of feeling which existed between us, of our habits of intimacy, and how much we loved. It is needless then to say, that the separation is inexpressibly painful. Often does the thought rush upon my mind, *"Lucy is gone, and I can see her face no more."* It requires all my philosophy, and all my piety, to enable me, at some moments, cheerfully to acquiesce. But when I can calmly reflect upon the subject, I do indulge better feelings. Yes, I can then rejoice, with all my heart, I trust, that God has given her opportunity and disposition to go and tell the perishing heathen that Jesus died. **ARTICLE 9** (To Abner Goodale and His Family in Marlborough, Massachusetts)—Brig *Thaddeus, December 20, 1819. Dear Father, Brothers and Sisters,* soon after we put forth to sea, ere we lost sight of the American shores, sickness obliged me to repair to my couch. To this I was confined two days and nights. The rest of the [extended] family were in similar circumstances. Chests, trunks, bundles, bags, and etc., were piled into our little room six feet square, until no place was left on the floor for the sole of one's foot. Two-thirds of the way they were built up considerably higher than the berth—and for a space they extended to the height of the room. With such narrow limits, and such confined air, it might well be compared to a dungeon. This was with me a gloomy season, in which I felt myself a pilgrim and a stranger. The third day the whole family met on deck. Could you have beheld the scene exhibited, while you pitied, you must have smiled. Beside a boat, hogsheads, barrels, [bath] tubs, cables, and etc., with which the deck abounded, there were to be seen a dog, cats, hens, ducks, pigs, men, women and children. Our whole family—with the exception of the natives—were all under the horrors of seasickness, some thrown on their mattresses, others seated in clusters, hanging one upon another, while here and there individuals leaned on the railing, or supported themselves by hanging upon a rope. When the hour for refreshment arrived, a container of soup was brought, and placed on deck. A circle gathered around it, and seated themselves like a group of children. Those at a distance were not neglected. Look which way you would, and all were sipping broth or picking bones. In this rude manner we were obliged to eat several days. We had entered a new school. It was among the very first lessons taught us, that all ablutions, of whatever kind, must invariably be performed with salt water. Most of our number soon recovered, when we were introduced to a well regulated table. We have family devotions in the cabin morning and evening, Sabbath forenoon, a religious service in the cabin, and at noon, when the weather allows, public worship on deck. The monthly concert of prayer is observed. The interesting situation in which we are placed, separated from the Christian world, and engaged in such a work, renders this a season doubly precious and animating. In concert with our American friends, too, we observed December 2nd, as a day of thanksgiving to God. At no time have I thought so much and so tenderly of my dear relatives. The idea that I could no more make one in your associated circles, produced in my mind sensations inexpressible. But though my place evermore, remains vacant, yet you will affectionately remember, you will daily pray for your absent Lucy. If it will be any gratification to you, I will tell you upon what we dined. We had not that rich variety which crowds the boards of our American friends on such occasions, but we had enough of that which was good, etc., roast pork, meat pie, biscuit and cheese. Our little room is vacated of everything not essential to every day comforts. I have often thought, would that I could tell my dear friends that Lucy is contented and happy. I can reflect with satisfaction on the rugged pathway I have entered, viewing it as selected by my Heavenly Father. No trial or privation which I have experienced, or now anticipate, has ever caused me to cast a lingering look back to my native shores. If I may best contribute to the happiness and usefulness of one of Christ's own ministers, of assisting in giving civilization, the Bible, and letters, to one of the tribes of men in utter darkness—it is enough that I bid farewell to everything my heart so late held dear in life, and subject myself to all the trials, privations and hardships of a missionary life. It is to me a source of no small consolation, that my present undertaking met the approbation of my father and friends. *January 25, 1820*. After having been out ninety-four days, and witnessing nothing but floating barques like our own, some monsters of the deep, the expansive ocean and the widespread Heavens, I cannot describe to you the joyful emotions which the sight of land has this day produced. We have a fair view of Tierra del Fuego on the right, and Staten Land (Isla de los Estados) on the left. The Captain has this evening heaved to, viewing it as dangerous passing the strait in the night from the liability of meeting a gale in this tempestuous region. *January 27*. Yesterday we entered the Le Maire Strait, fifteen miles wide. The scene before us was interesting and sublime. On either side was a long continued range of mountains. The tops of some were covered with snow, while others reached to the clouds. There the naked eye could discover forests, trees, grass and sandbanks. But what interested my feelings most of all was the discovery of a smoke on the island of Tierra del Fuego. Through spyglasses, two men could be discovered near it. Whether they were natives or shipwrecked mariners we knew not, nor could it be ascertained without much labor and danger. *January 29*. By a strong wind we have been driven fifty or sixty miles east. Sails were taken down and we were carried before the wind. The incessant and violent rocking of the vessel keeps me here laid prostrate upon my couch. Oh, the luxury in feeble health of reclining on a bed with tranquility and ease! But I must not, I will not repine. Even now, though tears bedew my cheeks, I wish not for an alteration in my present situation or future prospects. When I look forward to that land of darkness, whither I am bound, and reflect on the degradation and misery of its inhabitants, follow them into the eternal world, and forward to the great day of retribution, all my petty sufferings dwindle to a point, and I exclaim, what have I to say of trials, I, who can press to my bosom the word of God, and feel interested in those precious promises which it contains.

February 21. Several things respecting the mission appear in a much less favorable light than when I contemplated the subject in my native land. The circumstance which appeared so auspicious of the king's returning with his influence cast in the scale of civilization and Christianity—now appears in the following light, that George Kaumualii is the illegitimate son of a chief. One reason why he sent him abroad—was to save him from falling victim to the malice and jealously of his wife. On his return, he has serious apprehensions that his life will be sought. It was said that Kamehameha, the king, was wishing that instructors might be sent there, promising to be a father to them. Poor man! Age has carried him almost to his grave, and his decease presents the prospect of a civil war, to decide which of the chiefs shall be his successor. I inquired of the Captain a few days since if he thought there would be any danger of our lives being taken at the Islands. He said, aside from intoxication, to which they were addicted, and which sometimes led them on to make bold assaults, he thought not in any other way than by the use of poisons. When they conceive a dislike, no intimation is given, but by these means they secretly seize on the first opportunity to accomplish their fatal purpose. Theft among them is a most common thing. I will mention one instance of this as a fair specimen of many. The Captain once visited the Sandwich Islands, having in his possession twenty-four shirts. By the time he left the Islands, the number was diminished to three. As we approach the field of our anticipated labors, the officers, to prepare our minds for future scenes and trials, kindly draw aside the veil which conceals their pollution and depravity. I will not yet draw a picture of their degradation and impurity.—Enough for the present to give you some idea of the prospect before me.—The nearer I approach those savage shores, the more I reflect on the subject, the great work magnifies, and I exclaim, "*Who is sufficient for these things?*" *March 11*. This afternoon, as the vessel lay becalmed, one of the officers, Mr. Bingham, Mr. Thurston, and two of the native youths went into the water to bathe. Only one hour after they came out, a shark was caught. When first observed it was approaching a sailor who was painting the outside of the vessel, his feet hanging down in the water. He was ignorant of his danger, until he received the alarm from one of our family. When caught, it seized hold of a hard stick of wood so violently as to break out several of its teeth, and continuing its grasp, by this means suffered itself in part to be drawn up into the vessel. A large bone was found in its stomach, thrown overboard at the time our friends were in the water. Its extended jaws, sufficient to embrace a man's head, are now hanging up in a conspicuous place. How it makes the blood thrill through my veins when I think of the danger to which our friends were exposed. But as a matter of encouragement, amid all the perils which may await us in a savage land, may it strengthen my faith and confidence in Him who has this day been their preserver. *March 20*. When I gave my hand to Mr. Thurston, and came out from my father's house, to go far away to a land unknown, I felt assured of the care and friendship of one precious friend. But my expectations have been more than realized. To be connected with such a husband, and engaged in such an object, in the present state of the world, is, of all situations in life, what I choose. Farewell, my dear friends. May the prospect of meeting you all in a world (heaven) where trials, separations and sins shall be known no more, soothe the feelings, and animate the hopes of your affectionate and far distant daughter and sister, *Lucy G. Thurston*. **ARTICLE 10** (Islands of Hawaii Sighted) After sailing one hundred and fifty-seven days, we beheld, looming up before us, March 30, 1820, the long looked-for island of Hawaii. As we approached the northern shore, joy sparkled in every eye, gratitude and hope seemed to fill every heart. The native youths were all animation, scarcely seeking the refreshment of either sleep or food. Thomas Hopu, though he was up all night that he might enjoy a glimmering view of Mauna Kea, after eating half a meal at breakfast table, begged to be excused, that he might go and see where his father lived. **ARTICLE 11** To learn the state of the Islands and the residence of the king, the captain sent a boat on shore with an officer, attended by Hopu and John Honolii. Nearly three anxious hours we waited their return. Every minute seemed to whet our eagerness for news. Then, as Mr. James Hunnewell hastily came over the side of the vessel, we gathered closely around him. Quickly, with agitated lips he said, "*Kamehameha is dead—his son Liholiho is King—the kapus are abolished—the images are burned—the temples are destroyed. There has been war. Now there is peace.*" After the death of Kamehameha, Liholiho, the young king, and Hewahewa, the last idolatrous high priest, cautiously approached a dangerous subject. Priest—"*What do you think of the kapus?*" King—"*Do you think it well to break them?*" Priest—"*That lies with you.*" King—"*It is as you say.*" And in this way, endeavoring to penetrate each other's sentiments, they were led to the expression of their own thoughts. Keopuolani, the king's mother, urged the king to violate the kapus (rules), setting the example herself by eating with his younger brother. Kaahumanu, in authority associated with the king decidedly told him that she would cast aside his gods. To this he made no objections. Between them matter were arranged for the further development of their designs. He then smoked and drank with the female chiefs. A feast was prepared after the custom of the country with separate tables for the sexes. When all the guests, including many foreigners, were in their places, the king rose up and said to Mr. [John] Young, "*Cut up these fowls and this pig,*" which being done, he suddenly started off and went to the women's table, where, seating himself by the queens, he [Liholiho] began to eat with a fury of appetite, requesting them to partake with him. The whole native assembly was struck with horror and consternation at the sight, and looked to see him fall down dead. But no harm to the king ensuing, they at length cried out with one voice, "*The kapu is broken, the eating kapu is broken.*" When the feast, indulged in indiscriminately, was ended, the king issued his commands, that all the idols should be overthrown, the temples destroyed, and the priesthood abolished. It was last October that the flames were lighted up to consume the sacred relics of ages. The high priest, Hewahewa, was the first to apply the torch. He said, "*I knew that the wooden images of deities, carved by our own hands, could not supply our wants, but worshipped them because it was a custom of our fathers. They made not the kalo to grow, nor sent us rain. Neither did they bestow life or health. My thought has always been, there is one only great God, dwelling in the Heavens.*" He was cordial in his welcome to his brother priests, as he styled the missionaries. **ARTICLE 12** There was another pagan priest who tenaciously adhered to the idols. In the presence of the king he was brought to the test of renouncing the system of idolatry by being required to eat some poi (Hawaiian food) from the women's calabash (gourd). He would not do it. As a consequence, the king required him to drink a whole quart bottle of whiskey. The natives then placed him perpendicularly by the body of a tree, and lashed him to it with a rope, in such a snug manner, that in a short time it squeezed the very life out of him. He was no farther care to them that night. In the morning they took down his lifeless body, tied a rope to his heels and drew him about the village. When weary with that sport, they put the body on board a canoe, carried it out to sea, and threw it overboard. **ARTICLE 13** Simultaneously with these strange events on Hawaii, last September and October, a new and powerful impulse was given to missionary enterprise in the New England States. There was a deep interest and feeling, an extended moving and melting of heart. Hasten, hasten, was the watchword that went from church to church. Mr. [Samuel] Whitney, pursuing a course of study in Yale College, being in his sophomore year, was impelled to go to the heathen at once. Captain [Daniel] and Mrs. [Jerusha Burnap] Chamberlain, of independent property, surrounded by every comfort of a New England home, with five children, were impelled to go at once, taking their whole family with them. Ladies were ready to go, leaving "*Home, and ease, and all the cultured joys, conveniences and delicate delights of ripe society, in the great cause of man's salvation.*" Six marriages were solemnized, two missionaries were ordained, a band was gathered from four different States, and a dozen different churches, to go forth as messengers of the churches, to the far distant land of Henry Obookiah, having hold of the strong cable, of leaving the church on her knees. Obookiah from on high saw that day. He saw the darkness fleeing away from Hawaii, and that that Mission Family, so hastily fitted out, was going forth to carry the Bible to a nation without a God. But we return to brig *Thaddeus*, sailing along the western coast of Hawaii. **ARTICLE 14** Soon the islanders of both sexes came paddling out in their canoes, with their island fruit. The men wore girdles, and the women a slight piece of cloth wrapped round them, from the hips downward. To a civilized eye their covering seemed to be revoltingly scanty. But we learned that it was a full dress for daily occupation. All was kapa (fabric), beaten out of the bark of a certain tree, and could ill bear washing. Kamehameha I, as well, understood how to govern, as how to conquer, and strictly forbade foreign cloth from being assumed by his large plebeian family. As I was looking out of a cabin window, to see a canoe of chattering natives with animated countenances, they approached and gave me a banana. In return I gave them a biscuit. "*Wahine maikai*," (good woman) was the reply. I then threw out several pieces, and from my scanty vocabulary said, "*Wahine.*" (woman) They with great avidity snatched them up and again repeated, "*Wahine maikai.*" Thus, after sailing eighteen thousand miles, I met, for the first time, those children of nature alone. Although our communications by look and speech were limited, and simple, friendly pledges received and given, yet that interview through the cabin window of the brig *Thaddeus* gave me a strengthening touch in crossing the threshold of the nation. **ARTICLE 15** Approaching Kawaihae, Hopu went ashore to invite on board some of the highest chiefs of the nation. Kindly regarding the feelings of the ladies, he suggested that they put on garments. So they prepared for the occasion. Kalanimoku was the first person of distinction that came. In dress and manners he appeared with the dignity of a man of culture. He was first introduced to the gentlemen, with whom he shook hands in the most cordial manner. He then turned to the ladies, to whom, while yet at a distance, he respectfully bowed, then came near, and being introduced, presented to each his hand. The effects of that first warm appreciating clasp, I feel even now. To be met by such a specimen of heathen humanity on the borders of their land, was to "stay us with flagons, and comfort us with apples." Kalakua, with a sister queen next welcomed us with similar civilities. They were two out of five dowager queens of Kamehameha. They had limbs of giant mold. I was taught to estimate their weight at three hundred pounds, and even more. Kalakua was the mother of three of the wives of the young king. Two wives of Kalanimoku followed. They were all attired in a similar manner, a dress, then the pau (skirt), which consisted of ten thicknesses of the bark cloth three or four yards long, and one yard wide, wrapped several times round the middle, and confined by tucking it in on one side. The two queens had loose dresses over these. Trammeled with clothes and seated on chairs, the queens were out of their element. They divested themselves of their outer dresses. Then the one stretched herself full length upon a bench, and the other sat down upon the deck. Mattresses were then brought for them to recline in their own way. After reaching the cabin, the common sitting room for ladies and gentlemen, one of the queens divested herself of her only remaining dress, simply retaining her pau. While we were opening wide our eyes, she looked as self-possessed and easy as though sitting in the shades of Eden. Kalanimoku dined with our family, eating as others ate. The women declined sitting with us. After we rose from table they had their own food brought on, raw fish and poi, eating with their fingers. From Kawaihae the chiefs and their large retinue all sailed with us to Kailua-Kona, where the king resided. They all slept on deck on their mats. While passing in the gray of evening between two rows of native men in Hawaiian costume, the climax of queer sensations was reached. Kalakua brought a web of white cambric to have a dress made for herself in the fashion of those of our ladies, and was very particular in her wish to have it finished while sailing along the western side of the island before reaching the king. **ARTICLE 16** Monday morning, April 3rd, the first sewing circle was formed that the sun ever looked down upon in this Hawaiian realm. Kalakua, queen dowager, was directress. She requested all the seven white ladies to take seats with them on mats, on the deck of the *Thaddeus*, Mrs. [Lucia] Holman and Mrs. [Nancy] Ruggles were executive officers, to ply the scissors and prepare the work. As the sisters were very much in the habit of journalizing, everyone was a self-constituted recording secretary. The four native women of distinction were furnished with calico patchwork to sew—a new employment to them. The dress was made in the fashion of 1819. The length of the skirt accorded with Brigham Young's rule to his Mormon damsels (have it come down to the tops of the shoes.) But in the queen's case, where the shoes were wanting, the bare feet cropped out very prominently. **ARTICLE 17** Kalanimoku was prime minister of the king, and the most powerful executive man in the nation. He was sometimes called the "Iron cable of Hawaii." Last January, while we were in the region of Cape Horn, a rebel chief usurped kingly power, to sustain the idols, and caused the blood of the last human sacrifice to flow. His party in favor of the idols was opposed by the king's force, led on by Kalanimoku, who proved victorious. When about to join battle he thus addressed his men, *"Be calm, be voiceless, be valiant, drink of the bitter waters, my sons, turn not back, onward unto death, no end for which to retreat."* Now the great warrior was among us, learning the English alphabet with the docility of a child. He often turned to it, and as often to his favorite teacher, Daniel Chamberlain, a son five years of age. *"And a little child* *shall lead them.*" [Six years after this Kalanimoku was called into the spirit land. He lived to receive and to *love* the "glad tidings of great joy."] **ARTICLE 18** *April 4th, Tuesday, AM*. One hundred and sixty-three days from Boston, the *Thaddeus* was anchored before Kailua-Kona. The queen dowager, Kalakua, assumed a new appearance. In addition to her newly-made white dress, her person was decorated with a lace cap, having on a wreath of roses, and a lace half neckerchief, in the corner of which was a most elegant sprig of various colors. They were presents we had brought her from some American friends. When she went ashore, she was received by hundreds with a shout. Captain [Andrew] Blanchard, Messieurs Bingham and Thurston, together with Hopu, went ashore and called on the king in his grass-thatched house. They found him eating dinner with his five wives, all of them in the free, cool undress of native dishabille. Two of his wives were his sisters, and one the former wife of his father. After completing their meal, four of the wives, with apparent sisterly affection and great pleasure, turned to a game of cards. As was the custom, one wife was ever the close attendant of her regal lord. Hopu then introduced Messieurs Bingham and Thurston as priests of the Most High God who made Heaven and earth. The letters were then read to the king from Dr. Worcester of Boston, and from the Prudential Committee, and the object for which they came to live among them was explained. The visitors then retired, leaving the subject for royal consideration. **ARTICLE 19** April 6th, the king and family dined with us by invitation. They came off in a double canoe with waving kahilis [feathered object] and twenty rowers, ten on each side, and with a large retinue of attendants. The king was introduced to the first white women, and they to the first king, that each had ever seen. His dress on the occasion was a girdle, a green silk scarf put on under the left arm, brought up and knotted over the right shoulder, a chain of gold around his neck and over his chest, and a wreath of yellow feathers upon his head. We honored the king but we loved the cultivated manhood (image) of Kalanimoku. He was the only individual Hawaiian that appeared before us with a full-civilized dress. After dining with the royal family, all were gathered on the quarterdeck. There the Mission Family, the captain and officers sung some hymns, aided by the bass viol, played by Kaumualii, a young native chief returning with us. The king appeared with complacency, and retired with that friendly aloha that left behind him the quiet hope that he would be gracious. **ARTICLE 20** The next day several of the brothers and sisters of the Mission went ashore, hoping that social intercourse might give weight to the scale that was then poising. They visited the palace. Ten or fifteen armed soldiers stood without, and although it was ten or eleven o'clock in the forenoon, we found him on whom devolved the government of a nation, three or four of his chiefs, and five or six of his attendants, prostrate on their mats, wrapped in deep slumbers. **ARTICLE 21** The king had just put down one religion. In doing it, his throne had tottered. It was a grave question for him to accept a new one. Hopu, who was apt to teach, had told them that our religion allowed neither polygamy nor incest. So when Kamamalu, the sister and marked favorite out of five queens, urged the king to receive the Mission, he replied, "*If I do they will allow me but one wife, and that will not be you.*" His royal father had twenty-one wives. Nor did the King seem to understand about learning what kind of a thing it was, and whether it would be good for his people. He asked a missionary to write his name on a piece of paper. He wrote it "*Liholiho.*" The king looked at it and said, "*It looks neither like myself nor any other man.*" **ARTICLE 22** After various consultations, fourteen days after reaching the Islands, March 12th, permission, simply for one year, was obtained from the king for all the missionaries to land upon his shores. Two gentlemen with their wives, and two native youth were to stop at Kailua-Kona. The rest of the Mission were to pass on forthwith to Honolulu. Such an early separation was unexpected and painful. But broad views of usefulness were to be taken, and private feelings sacrificed. At evening twilight we sundered ourselves from close family ties, from the dear old brig, and from civilization. We went ashore and entered, as our home, an abode of the most uncouth and humble character. It was a thatched hut, with one room, having two windows made simply by cutting away the thatch leaving the bare poles. On the ground for the feet was first a layer of grass, then of mats. Here we found our effects from the *Thaddeus*, but no arrangement of them could be made till the house was thoroughly cleansed. On the boxes and trunks, as they were scattered about the room, we formed a circle. We listened to a portion of scripture, sang a hymn, and knelt in prayer. The simple natural fact speaks for itself. It was the first family altar ever reared (erected) on this group of islands to the worship of Jehovah. Flat-topped trunks and chests served admirably in accommodating us to horizontal positions for the night. Honest Dick, a native who had been with us while lying in port, sat within, and the king sent soldiers to keep sentinel without. Notwithstanding all, the night proved to be nearly a sleepless one. There was a secret enemy whose name was legion lying in ambush, or rather we had usurped their rights and taken possession of their own citadel. It was the flea. Thus, the night passed. But bright day visited us with its soft climate and gentle sea breeze. **ARTICLE 23** In the morning the two Hawaiian youth walked away to see the gentry, and having an eye to influence, they put on their best broadcloth suits and ruffled shirts, their conspicuous watch chains of course dangling from the fobs of their pants. Their hair was cut short on the sides and back of the head, but left long on top, to stand gracefully erect. Their style was just the same as if again about to enter the capacious drawing rooms of Boston where they had been received with so much eclat. The two American missionaries rolled up their shirt sleeves above their elbows, and went to work in good earnest, removing from the house all their effects brought from the *Thaddeus*, conveying away all old mats and grass, giving a thorough sweeping to the thatch above, and the ground below, spreading down new grass and new mats, putting up two high post bedsteads of Chinese manufacture, lent them by Kamamalu, the queen, and bringing in such articles as would be a substitute for furniture. A large chest in the middle of the room served for a dining table, small boxes and buckets for dining chairs, and trunks for settees. We had block-tin tumblers, which answered well in receiving hot tea, and likewise served to impress the mind with the philosophical fact, through the lips and tips of the fingers, that metal is a good conductor of heat. We trimmed the high post bedsteads with curtains—then added one from the foot corner to the side of the house, thereby forming at the back of each bed a spot perfectly retired. The two native youth were added to the king's retinue. In twenty-four hours we found ourselves in circumstances comparatively neat and comfortable. For three days the king's steward kept three pewter platters liberally supplied with fish, taro and sweet potato, cooked in the native manner. For several days we received calls from the queens and their whole train of attendants, three or four times in a day, and at each time were solicited to hear them read. When the queens were at our house, we sisters were "Marys," when they were away—we were "Marthas." **ARTICLE 24** Three days after landing, King Liholiho (Kamehameha II) gave us a large circular table of Chinese workmanship, having six drawers, which became a very eligible dining table. In that manner it was generally used for twenty years, until a family of children had risen and been dispersed. Since which time it has thirty years graced a parlor, every year becoming more and more valuable for its antiquity, and as having been a royal present at one of the most interesting periods of our lives. **ARTICLE 25** Three days had not elapsed after landing when the wife of our associate invited me to a private conference. It was secured by going to a mud-walled storehouse nearby. Having entered, we closed the door to exclude the scores of natives hovering about. But in so doing we shut out the light of day. On two of our number "Tekel" has been written. They had been weighed in the balances and found wanting. The wife said she never would be willing to exercise that degree of self-denial which was called for by a situation among this people. In three months they left the station assigned them by the Mission, and branched out into independent plans, to terminate in returning to their native land. Mr. Thurston, in writing for more aid, thus describes the character of persons wanted, "*We want men and* women who have souls, who are crucified to the world, and the world to them, who have their eyes and their hearts fixed on the glory of God in the salvation of the heathen, who will be willing to sacrifice every interest but Christ's, who will cheerfully and constantly labor to promote His cause, in a word, those who are pilgrims and strangers, such as the apostle mentions in Hebrews, 11th chapter." **ARTICLE 26** *April 29.* For two days we heard one continued yell of dogs. I visited their prison. Between one and two hundred were thrown in groups on the ground, utterly unable to move, having their forelegs brought over their backs and bound together. Some had burst the bands that confined their mouths, and some had expired. Their piteous moans would excite the compassion of any feeling heart. Natives consider baked dog a great delicacy, too much so in the days of their idolatry ever to allow it to pass the lips of women. They never offer it to foreigners, who hold it in great abhorrence. Once they mischievously attached a pig's head to a dog's body, and thus inveigled a foreigner to partake of it to his great acceptance. The above-mentioned dogs were collected for the grand feast which is this day made to commemorate the death of Kamehameha I. The king departed from his usual custom and spread a table for his family and ours. There were many thousand people present. The king appeared in a military dress with quite an exhibition of royalty. Kamamalu, his favorite queen, applied to me for one of my dresses to wear on the occasion, but as it was impossible for her to assume it, the request happily called for neither consent nor denial. She, however, according to court ceremony, so arranged a native cloth pau (skirt), a yard wide, with ten folds, as to be enveloped round the middle with seventy thicknesses. To array herself in this unwieldy attire, the long cloth was spread out on the ground, when, beginning at one end, she laid her body across it, and rolled herself over and over till she had rolled the whole around her. Two attendants followed her, one bearing up the end of this cumbrous robe of state, and the other waving over her head an elegant nodding fly brush of beautiful plumes, its long handle completely covered with little tortoise shell rings of various colors. Her head was ornamented with a graceful yellow wreath of elegant feathers, of great value, from the fact that after a mountain bird (Palila) had been caught in a snare but just two small feathers of rare beauty—one under each wing—could be obtained from it. A mountain vine, with green leaves, small and lustrous, was the only drapery which went to deck to cover her neck and the upper part of her person. Thus this noble daughter of nature, at least six feet tall, and of comely bulk in proportion, presented herself before the king and the nation, greatly to their admiration. After this presentation was over, her majesty lay down again upon the ground and unrolled the cloth by reversing the process of clothing. **ARTICLE 27** The first time that Mr. [Asa] Thurston preached before the king through an interpreter—was from these words—"*I have a message from God unto thee.*" The king, his family, and suite listened with attention. When prayer was offered, they all knelt before the white man's God. The king's orders were that none should be taught to read but those of rank, those to whom he gave special permission, and the wives and children of white men. For several months his majesty kept foremost in learning—then the pleasures of the cup caused his books to be quite neglected. Some of the queens were ambitious, and made good progress, but they met with serious interruptions, going from place to place with their intoxicated husband. The young prince, seven years of age, the successor to the throne, attended to his lessons regularly. Although the king neglected to learn himself, yet he was solicitous to have his little brother apply himself, and threatened chastisement if he neglected his lessons. He told him that he must have learning for his father and mother both—that it would fit him for governing the nation—and make him a wise and good king when old. The king brought two young men to Mr. Thurston, and said, "*Teach these, my favorites, Ii and Kahuhu. It will be the same as teaching me. Through them I shall find out what learning is.*" To do *his* part to distinguish and make them respectable scholars, he dressed them in a civilized manner. They daily came forth from the king, and entered the presence of their teacher, clad in white, while his majesty and court continued to sit in their girdles. Although thus distinguished from their fellows, in all the beauty and strength of ripening manhood, with what humility they drank in instruction from the lips of their teacher, even as the dry earth drinks in water. [After an absence of some months, the king returned, and called at our dwelling to hear the two young men, his favorites, read. He was delighted with their improvement, and shook Mr. Thurston most cordially by the hand—pressed it between both his own—then kissed it.]

ARTICLE 28 For three weeks after going ashore, our house was constantly surrounded, and our doors and windows filled with natives. From sunrise to dark there would be thirty or forty at least, sometimes eighty or a hundred. For the sake of solitude I one day retired from the house and seated myself beneath a shade. In five minutes I counted seventy companions. In their curiosity they followed the ladies in crowds from place to place, with simplicity peering under bonnets, and feeling articles of dress. It was amusing to see their efforts in running and taking a stand, that so they might have a full view of our faces. As objects of curiosity, the ladies were by far the most prominent. White men had lived and moved among them for a score of years. In our company were the first white women that ever stepped on these shores. It was thus the natives described the ladies, "*They are white and have hats with a spout. Their faces are round and far in. Their necks are long. They look well.*" They were called "Long Necks." The company of long necks included the whole fraternity. It was the custom of a chief to have a personal attendant to carry a spittoon, a fly brush, (to protect the extensive surface of bare skin) and a square cloth for a covering, folded and borne upon the shoulder. The highest point of etiquette among illustrious Hawaiians was, not to move. So, court form, in receiving the most distinguished foreigner, was, to keep the seat. An American lady, the active wife of a missionary, could not be measured by such a yardstick. And thus it was, that in superintending at the cooking stove, in order to place civilized dishes on her husband's table, that she early became classed, by the people, in the category of cooks, whose special realm was the ship's caboose. Those were the only foreign cooks they had ever seen. The idea was natural enough—the Captain's cook—the Missionary's cook. Our stove was necessarily placed outside at a little distance from our front door. There was no back or end doors to native houses. The principal point of attraction in our village lay in full view, but a few rods from us. There were hundreds of natives, all ages, of both sexes, and of every rank, bathing, swimming—floating on surf boards, and etc., nearly or quite in a state of nudity. We could command only green brushwood, brought two miles on the backs of men, for cooking and heating our one iron, for smoothing all our light, thin, tropical dresses, which had been so abundantly prepared for us. But to such dresses we were limited. Every quart of water was brought to us from two to five miles in large gourd shells, on the shoulders of men. The natives were too ignorant to wash without superintendence. A new article was sent to be washed at the fountain, but five holes were made in it by being rubbed on sharp lava. We had entered a pathway that made it wisdom to take things as they came—and to take them by the smooth handle. **ARTICLE 29** King Liholiho, the royal family, and a large retinue called upon us. The last urchin of the party entered the house, and crouched upon his heels within the royal presence. Seventy heads were counted whose feet crossed that threshold. Soon the king's steward entered with a bearing that showed how well he understood his responsibilities. He bore in his hands a large tray, the contents of which sent forth an aroma, which, to the initiated, was as if the pleasures of a full cup were poured out to them. It was a baked dog. He placed it on the table, tore it in pieces with his hands and teeth—then passed it around, each of the grandees taking a piece. For reasons not necessary to mention, the representatives of America, did not, as usual, partake of the regal repast. **ARTICLE 30** It was evening twilight. I was behind the screen in a side room. From the outer door into the sitting room, proceeded these words, "*Good evening, Mr. Thurston.*" It was a voice never to be forgotten. We were newly transplanted exotics. We had not then taken root. We were in the heart of the nation, shut up to a strange dialect, without associates, and without foreigners for neighbors. English words, in cultivated tones, fell with strange power upon the ear, and upon the heart. So it was when an American vessel visited our port. We heard words, and experienced deeds of kindness. God bless mariners. They are the links that connect us to the fatherland. The white sails of the ship were again unfurled to the breeze, and the only vestige around us of civilization had passed away. Then a whole sisterhood, embracing fifteen or twenty, assembled and took scats in a conspicuous part of the village to display themselves. Before the arrival of that ship, they were simply attired in native cloth. After her sailing, each one was arrayed in a foreign article, obtained from that very ship. Their own relatives and friends, perhaps fathers or brothers, or husbands, had paddled off that whole company of women and girls, to spend the night on board that ship, especially for the gratification of its inmates. When they returned, each one flaunted her base reward of foreign cloth. Thus it was that when these children of nature first came in contact with a superior race, they were quickly led to follow a course, which in their view, won distinction and honor. **ARTICLE 31** It was a rule of the Mission, in the first years of sojourn among the heathen, not to expect it of a man and a wife to live alone at a station without the protection of a second family. The rest of the Mission at Honolulu, learning that by the withdrawal of our associate, we were thus situated, in the very heart of the nation, immediately dispatched a deputation of one, Mr. [Samuel] Whitney, to make a trip of more than a hundred miles to bring the isolated ones to share in each other's protection. That visit was to us like the visit of an angel. After long conference, he asked for a decisive answer to the invitation he had brought. Mr. Thurston said, "*I wish, for the present, to remain at this post.*" Turning to me the deputy asked. "*And what do you say?*" I replied, "*My feelings are expressed in the wishes of my husband.*" After a long pause the response came, "*I believe you were made to be missionaries.*" Under such a despotic government, it was all important that those in authority be taught and Christianized. It was forging a key that would unlock privileges to a nation. The house which we then occupied was, at the time of our landing, the best in the land, and was appropriately called the king's palace. It was distinguished from all others by having two doors. On the front side, close by the corner, was one, two feet and a half high. But the state entrance was in the middle of one side, where was a rudely constructed frame of a door, three and a half feet high. It was duly poised on hinges on one side, and connected by a hasp and staple on the other. Two very narrow boards would have reached from hasp to hinges. But the board next the hasp was left off, that the door might be unhooked with the same ease on each side. So, there was no means of fastening the door, either day or night, when at home or abroad. Thus situated, we could not both leave the house, and suffer our effects to be carried off—neither could I go out without an escort. Thus the lack of a lock kept me as with a lock for four months from passing beyond our own dooryard, and the lack of eyes in the back of my head, gave opportunity of having property taken in my very presence. Thus situated, so often alone, having no protection whatever against the admission of evil, I stood in my lot, strengthening myself to the inglorious work of looking after the stuff, while my husband looked after the people, and the angels looked after me, for in my perilous position, not a hair of my head was singed. **ARTICLE 32** One day Mr. Thurston attended a religious meeting. He had no sooner gone from the house when a company of natives, perhaps a dozen, excited by strong drink, advanced and stationed themselves outside the fence of the dooryard. The gesticulations of their naked arms were frantic, and the house was made the target for the fiery glances of their wild eyes. Within that slight pole fence, stood our slight grass-thatched hut, where, from the door, everything met the eye at a glance. I cautiously closed the doors, and justly feeling the perils of being alone, stood for an hour, peeping out at a crevice, to note whether the house was to be invaded or simply besieged. An hour contains sixty minutes, and a minute sixty seconds. But at that lone fearful post of observation, a second seemed to become a minute, and a minute an hour. Mr. Thurston's return was a signal for that inflamed party of natives to go their way. Anxiety and apprehension were washed away by the soothing waters of safety and peace that swept through our humble dwelling. **ARTICLE 33** I was at my dwelling teaching the young prince who had half a dozen attendants with him. A pagan priest of the old religion, somewhat intoxicated, entered, and with insolent manners, divested himself of his girdle. Before I was aware, every individual had left the house and yard. The priest and I stood face to face, alone. As he advanced, I receded. Thus, we performed many evolutions around the room.—In a retired (secluded) corner stood a high post bedstead.—He threw himself upon the bed and seemed to enjoy the luxury of rolling from side to side upon its white covering. On leaving it he again approached and pursued me with increased eagerness. My tactics were then changed. I went out at one front door, and he after me. I entered the other front door, and he after me. Thus out and in, out and in, we continued to make many circuits. The scene of action was next in the dooryard. There, being nearly entrapped in a corner, having a substantial stick in my hand, I gave the fellow a severe blow across the arm. As he drew back under the smart, I slipped by and escaped.—Loss and pain together so enraged him that he picked up clubs and threw at me.—There we parted, without his ever touching me with a finger. In my flight I swiftly ran through the crowd, just as I was, straight toward the palace where Mr. Thurston was teaching, quarter of a mile distant. Under ordinary circumstances it was an imprudent pathway, the beach being lined with hundreds of the king's soldiers, retainers, and other idlers. I had not proceeded far, however, before I met my husband. The prince and his attendants, being frightened at the appearance of the priest, ran to tell Hopu. He quickly communicated it to Mr. Thurston, and so it was that he hastened to the rescue. As long as action was required, my strength, courage and self-possession were equal to the emergency. But when I sat down in my own dwelling, safe beneath the protection of my husband, there was a mighty reaction. Then came prostration, trembling and tears. In fifteen minutes the house was filled with scholars and their numerous trains of attendants. The queens were very sympathizing. With tears they often tenderly embraced me, joined noses and said, "*Very great is our love to you.*" The priest soon returned. His standing among the people was formerly very high, so that at his presence they all fell prostrate. Now he was commanded to retire from the dooryard. Refusing, he was walked out off the premises with a muscular strength that no common man could resist. Then, from an apprehension of his resentment, by applying a torch to our combustible house, two of our devoted pupils, John Ii and James Kahuhu, for a fortnight slept beneath our roof, with deadly weapons by their pillows. According to advice from foreigners, the king would have put the priest to death, but Mr. Thurston restrained him. We had been made to feel that it was imprudent for a lady to go abroad unattended, but now it was found that a protector was necessary to make even home a safe asylum. [A few years after, this same pagan priest visited a missionary. He penitently acknowledged his sins in general, and this in particular, and professed to have embraced the Christian faith. As far as is known, this is the only instance where a missionary lady ever received insult from a Hawaiian.] **ARTICLE 34** After spending the first seven months of missionary life in Kailua-Kona, the government removed from that place to Honolulu, in the latter part of the year 1820, and we were directed by the king to go too. We were to have accompanied him, but the vessel was so completely filled with natives as scarcely to leave room to recline in any position. So we remained, with the prospect of following them in five or six days. However, after having everything packed ready to put on board immediately, we were obliged in that state to remain three weeks, every few days being on the point of going. At length, for the first time, we embarked on a native vessel for Maui. When on board, I was, at first, conducted through the crowd down into the cabin, not expecting again to set foot on deck till called to land. Mr. Thurston assured me that he did not think he could find a vacant place sufficiently large for me either to sit or stand, excepting in the cabin. But sickness and oppressive heat obliged me to make the trial, when I was kindly furnished with an eligible situation on the top of the companion way. Mr. Thurston stood at a little distance upon a ladder. Men, women and children, from gray hairs to the infant that had just seen light, were disposed of in almost every position that the mind could conceive. Four hundred and seventy-five souls were on that brig, and with the exception of a few individuals, all were then above deck. Several hundred calabashes, containing poi, fish, water, and etc., provisions for the passage, occupied not a little room, while a large number of dogs, with here and there a nest of puppies, served to fill up the crevices. The officers were obliged to keep watch most of the time, and to proceed from place to place on the sides of the vessel. We were treated with a great deal of kindness, being presented with fruit, vegetables, fresh meat, and etc. My hands, fingers, nails, and every part of dress, were examined and felt of with the utmost minuteness. They were all good, very good. Then they asked about my dear father, brothers and sisters in America, and contrasted the skill of the people in that land with their own ignorance. **ARTICLE 35** In reaching Maui, we went ashore, and at the distance of half a mile from the beach, were received into a retired new thatched house built by Kalanimoku. It was under the care and occupied by an English sailor, who had been cast upon these shores, and who had previously been in our family at Kailua-Kona a fortnight. An own brother could not have given us a more welcome reception, or done more to render our situation comfortable and pleasant. The very next morning after our arrival, in a fit of intoxication, the king was off at the other side of the island, followed by all the scholars and the whole tribe which came from Kailua-Kona. Here we were again in a posture of waiting for more than four weeks. For two months before leaving Kailua-Kona, I had not the means of washing garments at all. Now when the finest streams of water were running at our feet, our dirty clothes were in the vessel's hold, at the other side of the island. When I ultimately obtained them at Honolulu, more than two months after I put them on board at Kailua-Kona, most of them were soaking wet, and had so long been in that state, as to be nearly or quite ruined. **ARTICLE 36** Having obtained permission from the king, who was still on the other side of the island, to proceed to Honolulu, we went, one evening, on board the famous barge *Cleopatra*, by invitation from the captain. It had a spacious cabin elegantly ornamented. As we approached the shore at Honolulu, our hearts were gladdened by seeing Mr. Bingham on the beach waiting to receive us. Then rose to our view a village of thatched huts. It was bare of trees save groves of coconuts on the margin of the shore. Beyond stretched out an extensive plain, open on one side to the sea, otherwise hemmed in with an amphitheatre of mountains, some of the nearest as naked of trees as the village. But the more remote were dressed with nature's richest, most verdant robes. After walking half a mile, followed by a crowd of natives, we reached the wicket gate of the large kapued (forbidden) enclosure of the missionary establishment, which was dotted with new thatched cottages. We were conducted into a large room, with seats of plank around its sides. There the whole family immediately assembled, and gave us a cordial welcome. A circle was at once formed, who united in singing. Then all knelt in thanksgiving and prayer to Him, who, during our separation, had been our preserver, granted some degree of success to our efforts, and was opening up before us prospects of increased usefulness. A little cottage of one room was given up to our accommodation, and we were again reinstated in the bosom of the Mission Family on December 21st, 1820. **ARTICLE 37** After spending several months in passing from place to place, the king, Kaahumanu, and the rest of the royal family, came to reside at Honolulu. The very next morning after their arrival, the king called on the Mission Family. He, with his queens, visited every family cottage, the schoolroom, the cookhouse, and examined the well. An improvement of window frames and wooden shutters had been introduced into our own personal cottage of one room. Into the window shutter on the east side of the cottage, one pane of glass had been admitted. It was probably the first pane of glass through which the sun ever pierced its rays into a dark Hawaiian hut. The walls of our dwelling were lined with fine mats. To a common dining chair, the only one we possessed, Mr. Thurston had attached rockers, arms, and a high back. He had, likewise, with a saw, broadaxe and jackknife, made a settee, which had been trimmed with furniture calico. Trunks and chests, liberally placed around the walls of the room, answered the double purpose of receptacles and seats. There was a tier of shelves, containing a library, and a table with two writing desks upon it. A good-sized traveling looking glass, opened and firmly suspended at a due distance above a toilette, which, with a high post bedstead, was trimmed with white throughout, curtains, valances, and spread. Then, to the severe simplicity of the room, was given a touch of decoration, by vines of mountain evergreen. Our royal visitors examined every part of the room and every piece of furniture in a most critical manner. All was pronounced to be very good, and the hands that prepared them very skillful. The king felt the bed. Finding it a mattress, he sought farther and entered another cottage. There the featherbed had just been stripped. Unceremoniously he threw himself upon it and rolled from side to side in a jovial manner, that he might the more fully experience its soft delights. In passing out they met with our hand cart. The king took a seat in the bottom of it, and thus backwards was drawn by his servants with speed to the village. A large retinue of attendants, his wives, and an armed guard, all scampered across the Plain to keep up with his majesty, their loose garments flying in the trade wind. We had little more than time to adjust our things after this company left us, before another of fifteen distinguished characters approached our establishment. They came in solitary grandeur, destitute of a retinue to carry shawls, spittoons, fly brushes, and guns. They were the commodore of the Imperial Russian Navy, his aged venerable chaplain of the Greek Church and thirteen of the officers, all in their appropriate uniforms. The chaplain wore his long sacerdotal garment, his white beard reaching down and nearly covering his bosom. Again our little hut was completely filled. Only two of the gentlemen could speak English, but they were none the less social for being unacquainted with our language. They belonged to an exploring expedition, and they seemed well-pleased to explore our premises, our cottages, schoolroom, the meat of our table, the sitting of our Mission Family, the attendance of our native boarding scholars, and our manner of ministering to those who sat at table. In the schoolroom, lessons first recited in Hawaiian, were translated into English, then into Russian. In their splendid uniforms, these officers again came on shore, and sat with us at the frugal board of our united band. Our dining table was sufficiently long to seat twenty-five, and was encircled by benches without backs. It stood in a long open piazza which connected three cottages by the gable ends. Bushes were spread for the feet. A colored cloth was the table's accustomed covering, while salt beef, sea bread, kalo (taro), coffee, tea, a small portion of goat's milk, and two molasses bottles well-replenished, were seldom known to fail. On gala days, the somber covering of the table was exchanged for white damask. Molasses bottles, too, might give place to the more refined sweets of brown sugar. Our steward was unwearied in his chance efforts to obtain what was so very scarce, a pig for roasting. What was more, it was the second year in the history of Hawaii, that woman might either partake of baked pork or sit at table with her noble lord. Two priests headed our table. The one saw to it that all piously turned their thoughts to the living bread, the other, that each received a portion of the bread that perisheth. **ARTICLE 38** A house had been sent out by the American Board to their missionaries who asked permission to put it up. The king decidedly said, "*No, in that respect I wish to follow the policy of my father. He never allowed foreigners to build a house but for the king.*" It was in vain to tell him that one of our young mothers had suffered a severe illness, the result of living on the ground, saturated with flooding rains. Some time elapsed, when two of the missionaries, accompanied by their wives, called on the king and again made application for erecting their house. But the reply was a decided negative. While the missionaries were retiring and saying *aloha* to the numerous members of the royal household, one of the ladies stepped to the elbow of the king. She would have said, "*If we have found grace in thy sight, allow the foreign ladies who have come to serve thee, to save their health and their lives, by living in such a house as they have been used to.*" But the grace of idiomatic language in that new dialect was wanting. She spoke necessarily in feeble, broken language. Yet the king was quick to discover and appreciate her want, and immediately replied, "*Yes, build.*" Then she joined her friends. But her request and the king's answer were not mentioned. She thought, let the king be a king, and in again referring to this subject let him speak thoughts that spontaneously arise in his mind without being reminded of previous utterances. And besides, she had too much sympathy and reverence for the leading missionaries to drop a word to show that her prayer before the throne had been more availing than theirs. A few days after, the king (Kamehameha II) and several of his chiefs called, and sat with the mission family at table. There, in presence of them all, he expressed his full approbation of their erecting their house. He likewise renewed his former permission to allow our company to remain in his kingdom to labor as missionaries. **ARTICLE 39** There was a clique of foreigners whose interest and influence it was to have the reign of darkness continue, and who opposed the missionaries with all their power. They would have induced the king to give a very different turn to affairs. They had a withering influence on his downward habits. But respecting the missionaries, the king thought with manly independence. He said, "*Those men will talk, and talk, and talk, but they know nothing of what they are talking about.*" They spread wide the report of the missionaries being spies, that their concealed aim was to take the Islands, and that the house and cellar was for storing firearms and ammunition. Multiplied were the stories put in circulation of seeing articles to that effect in the publications of the day, of vessels of war being on the way, when they would arrive, and etc. As one story failed, two more would be fabricated. Some discerning natives saw through the fallacy of it and inquired, "*If that is their object, why did they bring their wives and children?*" The missionaries leaving it to Hopu to disabuse the native mind, attended to their own business like as soldiers in the day of battle, whose part it is to load and fire, load and fire, without attending to the rattling of musketry on the side of their opponents. When company after company came to see the house, having much to say about guns and powder, Hopu facetiously warned them, "*Don't approach so near as to be injured should the magazine explode!*" **ARTICLE 40** Mr. [Elisha] and Mrs. [Maria] Loomis called to see an orphan babe. Its little body clothed as it were with disease, was reduced to a very skeleton. Its mother only lived to give it birth. Another woman after having charge of it four months—died also. Four weeks had since worn away. The child's only food from the first had been fish and poi (traditional Hawaiian food). The father, a white man, without exercising the least care for the child, had taken a new wife and gone to the opposite side of the island. The woman, with whom it lodged, said it would die. Mrs. Loomis offered to take it if she would give it up to her to keep as her own. She, with tears, immediately laid the afflicted, forsaken one in her arms. By the faithful care of Mrs. Loomis by night and by day, it recovered from its diseased state, and was beginning to thrive. But a more fatal disease fixed upon it—dropsy in the head. To hear the groans and cries of the little sufferer, to see it waving its little hands, no larger than those of a newborn infant, was very touching. In seven weeks from the time of its admission into the Mission Family, it followed its mother to the "land of silence." **ARTICLE 41** Again the king made us a call, dressed for once like a gentleman, with ruffled shirt, silk vest, pantaloons and coat. How he moved among his subjects with all the nobility of a king! He was in one of his very best moods. Everything we did was good in the superlative degree. He examined the house and cellar and was delighted. He wished the good people of America to send him a house, three stories high, one story in which to worship Jehovah, as by and by, in five years, he was going to pray. He wished to have the missionaries learn all the Hawaiian sounds, he would assist them, and then books and prayers in the native language could be printed. He criticized the pronunciation of some dozen words. He wished to know how far his favorite young men under Mr. Thurston had proceeded in their spelling books and Testaments. When he was shown, and had looked at their writing books, he three times expressed how very sorry he was that he had left off learning—felt vexed with himself for so doing. He was ashamed to begin a second time, and many people had told him that they should think he would be. In giving his aloha, his parting address was, "*Don't pray for rain today, because we are going to have a grand dance.*" **ARTICLE 42** (Asa Thurston to Lucy's father, Abner Goodale) *Honolulu, October 7, 1821. Sire*, when I take up my pen to address a far distant and honored friend, a thousand thoughts and feelings rise to give utterance. I think I hear you ask, with all the tenderness and affection of a father, "*Where now is Lucy—what new and trying scenes has she passed since I gave her the parting hand and the last look? Has the presence of Jesus sustained and comforted her in times of affliction and distress? Has she enjoyed the smiles of the covenant God? Yes, often have we had occasion to speak of divine goodness. Often have we bent the knee in united thanksgiving to that gracious Savior, to whose service we have sacredly devoted our lives, our all. But on the morning of the 28th of September, we had occasion to sing of special mercies. Through the interposition of the supporting delivering hand of our heavenly Father, Lucy was made the joyful mother of a fine little daughter. We wept, and prayed, and rejoiced together over this new accession to our comfort and care, and in view of that new relation which we how sustain as parents. Lucy is feeble. A slight cough has newly set in, which prevents her gaining strength. We hope it may be better in a few days. If it should not, our fears for her health will be aroused. We have no physician, for the doctor and his wife left this place three days after her confinement for America. Everything is done for her, which we know how to do. She is now taking those medicines which she used when in America under her father's roof. Our only hope is in the great Physician, who is ever with his servants and will preserve their* lives so long as he has anything for them to do, or during all the days of their appointed time. The Lord will do right. I beg you not to be distressed on her account." **ARTICLE 43** Again I am permitted to hold my pen, which I sometimes thought had been dropped forever. When in a very weak state, a very slight cough commenced and increased. I knew its features. It seemed to look me mockingly in the face and say, "*I have tracked you from your father's house, have waited and watched my opportunity, when I could best seize upon, and become your victor.*" My state became critical. There was no physician in the kingdom. But I was tenderly nursed. The ladies at the station were kind, but such were their circumstances that the principal care in the sick room devolved on Mr. Thurston. He was equal to it, even as a mother would have been. It is an important qualification in a missionary who goes to an unenlightened land, well to understand the beautiful lesson of girding himself with a towel, and being able with skill and tenderness to wash the disciple's feet. When I became convalescent, it was said to me, "*We thought we should lose you by a quick consumption.*" Yet I have again the promise of life, having a double being to consecrate to the Giver and Preserver. **ARTICLE 44** The wooden structure had been reared and finished, having board floors, glass windows, and two flights of stairs, leading the one up chamber, and the other down cellar.—The front door opened into the hall, which extended through the house. At the right, on entering, was the large common receiving room. On the left, my own private apartment.—The two back rooms on either side the hall, were for the accommodation of two other families. The table was spread in the basement, and the cookhouse was separated a little distance from the house. Our families had entered and made it our home. The royal party with a large retinue came to view a thing so unique. I was still in retirement, but they must see all that was to be seen. Of course, for a time, my room was pretty well packed with the grandees of the nation. It had its attractions. There was their white teacher under new circumstances. And there was her white infant, neatly dressed in white. A child dressed! Wonderful, most wonderful! To witness home scenes and the manner in which we cherished our children, seemed, in a childlike way, to draw forth their warmest affections. Then the room! It was lighted up with two glass windows. The floor and trimmings were painted. A friend gave us some paper to cover its walls, just such as he happened to have, delicate and gay—its color pink, its vines tinsel. How eloquent the natives were in referring to their own naked neglected children and their dark, dingy, thatched huts! The royal party, closely followed by their large retinue, left our house and premises. It was a satisfactory interview. What happy influences from it we hoped would light down upon our opening prospects! But behind the scenes lay a sequel. Motherhood had not reached the point of endurance, for before midnight Mr. Thurston and Mrs. Chamberlain were called to my bedside, to stay the tide of fever and delirium. It was also a memorable night to two personages of the royal party. It is a custom in the nation that women—and girls even, become leading parties in proposing marriage. Kaahumanu and Kaumualii, while walking to the mission house—touched, for the first time on a tender subject. Again they alluded to it while reclining beneath the shades of that wooden structure. While returning home over the Plain, they conferred upon it still more freely. That night Kaahumanu, associated with the king in the government of Hawaii, Maui, Oahu, and etc., and Kaumualii, tributary king of Kauai, reclined side by side on a low platform, eight feet square, consisting of between twenty and thirty beautiful mats of the finest texture. Then a black kapa (native cloth) was spread over them. The significance of it was, it pronounced the royal pair to be husband and wife. An important political union was likewise peaceably affected, connecting the windward and leeward islands, under one crown. [Thomas] Hopu was present and witnessed the simple ceremony so full of meaning. **ARTICLE 45** An alphabet of twelve letters was fixed upon which would give every sound in the pure Hawaiian dialect. In one year and nine months after the missionaries left the brig *Thaddeus*, a Hawaiian spelling book was issued from the press. The chiefs received it with deep interest, the scholars with enthusiasm. Writing letters in the native language was soon introduced. A door was now opened which allowed learning to become general. Governor Cox, of Maui, brother of Kaahumanu, dreamed that he saw the whole island on fire, and all the water in the surrounding sea could not quench the flames. He sought for safety, but in vain—he could find no shelter. Awaking in horror, his heart turned to the teachings of the missionaries, how they told of escaping destruction by a Savior. In the evening he sent a messenger for two missionaries to come to him. A goodly number of chiefs were there, many of whom were lying on the mat learning to spell or read, and some to write. Governor Cox communicated to the missionaries the cause of his inquietude, and sought instruction. They preached to him of Jesus, and fervently prayed for his salvation and that of his people. They were requested to come again in the morning at daylight, to conduct family worship. In the morning more than sixty natives of rank were there assembled, and all behaved with an effecting decorum, rarely seen at public services. Thus, evening and morning the missionaries continued to repair to his house, to teach and to assist him in establishing family worship, which he said he was determined should daily be performed under his roof. He said, "*Others might do as they pleased, but he should have all people taught to read and write, and to understand the Good Word.*" So he not only opened his own house for the worship of God, but for school instruction for himself and others. Governor Cox's example produced happy effects. A multitude flocked to attend public worship, headed by kings and chiefs, on whose movements under God hung suspended the interests of the nation. The principal characters, almost without exception, together with a throng of common people, united in the cry, "*Give us books. Give us teachers.*" This new impulse called into exercise all the energies of the mission. Scholars from the school already established at our house, afforded important aid in instructing the people. Three chiefs of magnificent stature and lofty bearing came to the mission house for a teacher. All were already employed, down to George, six years old, a native child that had been given to me. He possessed a good mind, was an English scholar, had been thoroughly instructed, and was perfect in his Hawaiian lessons. One of the chiefs placed the little fellow on his shoulder, and bore him away in triumph, saying, "*This is my teacher.*" He proved to be efficient, and manfully, with much pleasure, continued to repair twice to their place daily. The king sent for one hundred spelling books, to give to his friends and attendants who were destitute, and gave commandment to have his five wives learn both to read and write. In consequence of which, some of his servants came to us to borrow tables and chairs for the accommodation of those high ladies at their lessons in this new and wonderful art. **ARTICLE 46** We were on terms of social intercourse with our foreign neighbors. One afternoon, three of the most intelligent and influential were invited to sit with us at tea. One was an officer of the American Government [and] two were captains of merchant ships. They were all, with each other, congenial spirits. Hand joined in hand. After they were seated in the midst of our circle, conversation flowed readily. Captain D., who was the very life of society, never at a loss for a theme, even though it involved a boon companion, thus ventilated his ideas. "*I never acknowledge the claims of a Superior Power. I am my own, and have my liberty to do just as I please, and to seek my own happiness in my own way. It is proper for me to do so. But when I see a man at home, on sacramental occasions, carrying around a silver platter, then, in coming round here, I say, he has no right to live like us, poor sinners.*" He knew where the remark fitted, and so did Captain E. (at home called Deacon E.) who sat at his left hand. He had the grace to blush, and left the room to recover in the open air from his confusion. Sometime after Captain E., alias Deacon E., received a private letter of admonition from the body of missionaries. The purport of some part of it was this, "*If a standard bearer of a church plunge with his own hand the banner of his great Captain in the slimy mire of the streets, and thus trail it along, a dishonored and contemptible thing, his own church ought to know it.*" He felt something now beside blushes. The whole man was moved. He repaired to the mission house, with a comrade, entered unbidden, and forced his way through different apartments, to the private bedroom of a missionary. There, in the presence of his wife, he brandished his heavy cane like a madman, and with fury gave utterance to his own expressive language. "*Apologize for that letter, or I'll kill you. I have a family at home that I respect, and I am not a going to have information conveyed to the ears of my church.*" No apology was made, and no murder committed. It was simply a threatening, boisterous interview of two hours continuance. The feeble wife of the missionary, who was just rising from a critical illness, in which she had been three months confined to her couch, was completely prostrated. The little daughter of five summers, who saw it all, asked why it was that natives were so kind to her father, and white men so cruel. No obstruction was placed in the way of the captain, alias Deacon, from brushing up his professional coat in rounding Cape Horn, and returning to exercise his spiritual functions in his own church. He would be sustained by his adult son, his companion in travels and sojourn. For the son well knew that the father could turn upon him and say, "*Keep close, for I can make disclosures respecting you.*" **ARTICLE 47** An intelligent sea captain called on us, an old familiar acquaintance of ours. He spoke most decidedly on the subject that no permanent good could be affected among these islanders. I directed his attention to the change which had taken place in the South Sea Islands through missionary effort. He seemed to understand the nature of many of our severest trials, and said "*that the debasing influence of the many foreigners that touched here was an insuperable obstacle to the conversion of this people.*" I freely acknowledged how keenly trials were felt from that quarter, but told him that they had no tendency to cause the missionaries to give up. "*Oh, he had no objections to instructing the natives, thought, indeed, that it was very well, but men ought to do it, without subjecting ladies to the trials of this heathen land.*" Although he belonged to the same class as those to whom I alluded, I could not forbear saying that if the ladies had accomplished no other good, they had been the means of securing a footing for their husbands, as some of our American friends had agreed that they would drive every missionary from the Islands, were it not that they so much respected the feelings of the ladies. We both smiled, and were both willing to change the subject. **ARTICLE 48** Hopu, in visiting the back part of Maui with the king, was particularly attracted by one of the daughters of the land. When he returned to Honolulu, he brought to our cottage the girl of eighteen, wishing to commit her to me for special training. He said, "*As the Almighty has excited in my heart such strong yearnings for her, I think it is his will that I marry her.*" I therefore received her as the betrothed wife of our beloved Hopu. A little cottage for her accommodation was erected near our own, and for more than a year she became my pupil and close companion. As she developed, she exhibited a rare character among her fellows. Private domestic life was congenial to her native taste, in opposition to free, and open, publicity. Amiable, piously disposed, with a warm heart, ever open to receive instruction, she daily did much, very much, to promote my happiness. At length, Hopu felt that she had been sufficiently instructed to warrant his leading her to the hymeneal altar. Their marriage was publicly solemnized in the church. The king and principal chiefs were there. Hopu appeared as usual in his gentlemanly black suit. By his side stood Delia, dressed in a style that raised her to his standard. To her complete and fashionable dress in white, was added a trimmed straw bonnet. It was the first native woman's head that had been thus crowned. All seemed pleased, and after the services were over, shook the new-made pair most cordially by the hand, giving their aloha. **ARTICLE 49** *Honolulu, October 20, 1822. My Dear, Dear Husband,* your tender farewell note I have just received. My feelings prompt me to reply. Yes, the same Providence which, in a mysterious manner, connected and placed us in the missionary field, has now called us, for the first time, to separate. I truly rejoice in the prospect of your contemplated short excursion, viewing it as placing you in a situation to facilitate your gathering up, and becoming master of this unwritten language. Still this heart will keenly feel the absence of such a friend, of such a husband. I shall find an unspeakable happiness in often commending you to Him, who has promised to be with His devoted servants. The little concert at nine, I shall regard with peculiar interest. You assure me of your prayers. How comforting the reflection! I hope you will be unwearied in your daily efforts to become thoroughly acquainted with the language, and that you will not too long delay addressing the people, independently of an interpreter, though with a stammering tongue. I shall make my little room as pleasant as I can, and devote my attention to the needle, the pen, the language, the school, and our dear little one. She will be a great comfort to me, and help to cheer many a pensive hour. Oh, for wisdom to govern her aright! I shall think much of you, and the privations you are called to suffer in the cause of Him who had not where to lay His head. May He comfort you by His presence, and make you instrumental of bringing many to knowledge of that salvation which He died to purchase. Adieu. *Your loving wife.* **ARTICLE 50** I had a scholar about eight years of age. Her erect figure, clear smooth skin, regular features, slightly curling hair, and full black eye, with the long black fringes of its covering, made her a good specimen of the loveliness of childhood. But the beauty of that fine production of nature was marred by violence. The ball of her right eye had been scooped out entirely, so that the full orbed eye of death in its gentle sleep was far less revolting than that concave appearance. *"My child, how did you lose your eye?" "I ate a banana."* She could not have been more than five years old when the idols were destroyed. Had she been of mature years, her life would have been taken. The priests taught the people that breaking kapu would be visited by the gods with death. Yet they were very assiduous in keeping spies abroad in the land, to obtain knowledge of facts, that they themselves might bring vengeance on the unwary. **ARTICLE 51** (Welcome to Elizabeth Edwards Bishop) *Honolulu, April 27th, 1823.* It is possible that in the long expected Mrs. Bishop, I am to find my much-loved friend Elizabeth Edwards. I was overcome by the first intelligence. Welcome, doubly welcome to the warmest affections and sympathies of this heart, to the comfort and privileges of this establishment, to the pleasures, toils, and work of missionary life. How I long to embrace you, to receive precious intelligence from my dear friends and native country—you how gracious the Lord has been in two days ago bringing me to this bed of confinement and comfort, laying in my fond arms another precious treasure, another daughter. Much love to each individual of your dear female band. I shall anticipate an early interview with feelings more easily felt than expressed. *Very affectionately, Lucy G. Thurston.* **ARTICLE 52** Mrs. Loomis was one day walking on the wide path of the Plain near the Mission House at Honolulu. A village merchant, who had in a social manner been admitted to our social board, approached on horseback. That was his season of relaxation, and there was an opportunity of exciting healthy, pleasurable emotions. So he guided his high, mettled (spirited) steed toward the lady, to go just as near as possible without collision. He wanted to give her a start. Her bonnet and shawl, and high trade winds, and the merchant, and the merchant's horse, were too much for her. The first she knew she was prostrate on the ground, and her whole person was exposed to the tramp of heavy hoofs. There was no police, no courts of justice, no standard of public opinion. Everyone did what was right in his own eyes. Well, the lady had a start as was intended. She was, in fact, thoroughly frightened. Yet, in mercy to us all, her life was spared. She was confined for a season to her bed, to woo nature to the slow process of obliterating injuries, which violence was so quick to give. Her suffering husband and two infant children, long continued to see day open and close upon them, without the cheering activities of the wife and mother. As the merchant's recklessness proved to be something more than a joke, he expressed his sorrow and sympathy by presenting to the lady a shawl. A shawl! How many of the downtrodden women of the land were lured into sin for a like reward! And the wife of a man of holy calling was trifled with, and received a similar gift. **ARTICLE 53** In the latter part of the year 1823, we again embarked on board a native vessel, as we were designated by the mission to re-occupy the station at Kailua-Kona. Naihe and Kapiolani, principal chiefs, were on board and extended over us a paternal care. We were always invited, and usually partook with them at their meals. To be sure the style and manner, in their present circumstances, was not altogether such as would meet the most fastidious taste and appetite. When the faithful, half clad servant so kindly cleansed a bowl on the flap of his only garment, in which to prepare some tea, lading in the sugar with unsparing hand, and crumbing in the sea bread with his teeth, I could not do else than receive and drink it, saying nothing for conscience sake! We were accommodated in the cabin. It is impossible to tell how often the pipe came along, passed from hand to hand, from lip to lip, and the room became perfumed with all that is odorous in tobacco smoke, rising and issuing from their mouths as from a chimney. Then the containers for food were introduced, and the most nauseating messes of fish laid open. But when the group, sitting upon their heels, encircling the dish, sucked their besmeared fingers, and smacked their lips with so much apparent gusto, the result might perhaps prove that my senses of sight and smell were at fault. This I can state for certainty, the annoying cockroaches, which gathered in such swarms around every corner of my berth, now and then took such liberties as to make me start. During the night the natives kept dropping in till the cabin was crowded. With deadlights closed, so much heat and such confined air, it seemed almost suffocating. Disregarding quietude, even during the hours when nature calls for rest, their united songs and chitchat, went to form a prolonged clamor. Such were the circumstances in which we were called to resign ourselves to seasickness, such the state in which two little ones were demanding the care and sympathy by night and by day, yet had circumstances permitted, I should myself have been laid prostrate. I survived the voyage, nor with all my sufferings did I once dream it otherwise, save when in all the gloom of midnight, a tumult on deck would arouse us from short "disturbed repose," with apprehensions that the vessel was foundering. What the captain's knowledge and skill were, I knew not, but judging by external appearance, he was on a level with the lowest sailor before the mast. He was the only white man on board beside Mr. Thurston, but there was a deck completely covered with men, women, children, dogs and puppies, of whose aid in case of any emergency or real danger, I suppose there would not be much choice. After being out four dreadful nights from Honolulu, we reached Lahaina. It was as the haven of rest, for I was almost exhausted. Mrs. [Clarissa Lyman] Richards pronounced me as looking more ill than when on a bed of sickness. By the kind attentions of our friends I revived, and in the united families of Messieurs [Charles Samuel] Stewart and [William] Richards, we spent a week long to be remembered. But the sweets of friendship and Christian intercourse were again to be exchanged for the trials of the vessel. To reach it we were necessarily accommodated in a single canoe. Mr. Thurston took charge of the elder child, and the younger fell to me. On my first entering the canoe, my feet became completely drenched with water. A piece of wood that crossed the top I accepted as a seat, and thankful I was that my strength held out, thus to poise myself, and retain my grasp of the struggling babe, until reaching the far off vessel. There after a few hours spent in adjusting our things and getting out to sea, everything seemed as perfectly natural as though we had not seen Lahaina. The next afternoon we were safely anchored off Kailua-Kona. An English vessel had arrived a little before us, bringing the king [Kamehameha II]. The captain kindly offered a boat for our accommodation, and we reached the shore a few minutes after his majesty. He had advanced a short distance, and stood fixed a little way from his circled multitude of subjects, long reciprocating their loud and affectionate wailings (cries). The governor's attention being directed to the king, we were thrown on the kindness of Mr. [John] Young, who introduced us to a house belonging to the governor, and ordered coffee, fresh fish and potatoes to be set before us. Mr. Thurston's writing desk and dressing case were placed together upon the mat, making a neat little table. It was completely covered with dishes, and not a vacant plate or utensil save Mr. Thurston's ever present helper, which he drew from his side pocket. We sat in the enjoyment of this most comforting repast, on the mat, holding conversation with Mr. Young, who sat at a little distance, ever watchful to give commands to the waiting attendants. The king made us a call, and mentioned his early intention of visiting in person England and America. The evening closed upon us in peace. We spread our bed upon the mat—gave our aloha to the last lingering native—and once more enjoyed undisturbed solitude and repose. Early the next morning Mr. Thurston went on board the vessel, and spent most of the day in landing our effects, and placing them in a building assigned us by the governor. With my two babes and two boys I remained a spectacle for the rude throng which pressed around the door. That evening we were enabled to spread our own table beneath what we might transiently be allowed to call our own roof.

ARTICLE 54 (Trials of Life) In consequence of my distressing voyage to Kailua-Kona, and the subsequent trials of getting settled, pulmonary symptoms were again induced. Our dwelling was not privileged with a yard. Of course our doors and premises were thronged with natives from morning till night. Had I been thus situated without domestic duties to perform, I could have mingled with the multitude and acquired knowledge of their language and character. But I was reduced in health, with two babes, the elder fast picking up language, and receiving permanent impressions. Everyone experienced in the nursery knows how little it comports with the feelings and active spirit of the child to be abridged the pleasure of walking abroad, to be imprisoned within walls where no prospect is enjoyed, no cheering ray of light admitted, except from two doors at one end, almost continually half-darkened by natives, with whom it is not allowed to have intercourse. Many days were almost exclusively spent in directing our child's attention so as to shield it from danger. It was this, which, in feelings, caused the cottage to become the dungeon, and home the heathen world. At Honolulu, the key note had already been struck, *"children in childhood must be sent to America or be ruined."* My response was, *"Make better* *provision for them, or such will probably be the result."* And deep in my heart was engraved the motto, *"God helps those who help themselves."* In this season of great distress came the news of a death, which sank into my heart. I had no longer a father on earth to pray for me in my struggles. **ARTICLE 55** At noonday, a person at the bottom of a deep well, by looking up, will see stars. I felt as if at the bottom of a deep well, and in dark, sleepless, suffering midnight hours, I could obtain distinct and far-reaching views of what a pioneer missionary's home ought to be. It should consist of three distinct departments, so closely connected, that one lady could superintend them all. One department should be for children, one for household natives, and one for native company. Let each class know its own place, and the whole move on without collision. To a lady, such an arrangement would invite to efficient activities in health, and to repose in sickness. It would inspire and enable her to attempt great things, and to expect great things. **ARTICLE 56** (Funeral of Hopu's Father) Seldom do I see a native whose hair is silvered with age. How conspicuous then that mercy that preserved the life of Hopu's father fourscore years, till a son long absent should return from a foreign country, bringing the news of a Savior. The son, in teaching his aged father, was instant in season and out of season, faithful and persevering. The father, docile and humble as a little child, lovingly received Jesus into his heart, and longed for future blessedness. Hopu exhibited a bright example of filial piety. He caused a brother to bring his father from a distant part of the island, so as to reside near him. As a specimen of that care which he continually exercised in supplying both his temporal and spiritual wants during the period he was called to conduct family prayers at the governor's, together with maintaining them with his own household, he would still regularly go back to the little hut, to pray with, comfort and instruct his "poor old father." Nor did he cease till after kneeling in prayer by his sick and lowly couch, he looked, and beheld the spirit had fled. For four years he had been permitted to teach him in the school of Christ. All was now at an end. He wrapped the body in a white kapa and enclosed it in a decent black coffin made with his own hands. The bell tolled. As Mr. Thurston, and myself reached Hopu's cottage, two natives advanced bearing the coffin. Hopu and his wife appeared, habited in black. We all entered the church. With that curiosity which novelty inspires, a large concourse of people assembled. They appeared wild and fidgety as I never before saw them. Mr. Thurston addressed them from the words, "*Prepare to meet thy God.*" We then proceeded to the place of interment, in the yard back of the church. It was the first grave ever opened on the island of Hawaii to receive the remains of a fellow mortal, over whom Christian rites were performed. Never did a similar scene inspire me with sensations so awfully solemn. The sun was fast sinking beneath the horizon. The eager multitude of untaught natives closed in, and so encircled the spot as to leave no way of retreat. As we looked down into the grave, a human skull was seen, as if to remind us of the generations which had been swept away all in the darkness of nature. After a short address to the people by Hopu, and a short prayer by Mr. Thurston, those two sons, Hopu and his brother, with their own hands, let down the coffin containing all that was left of their aged father, and covered it deep in the bosom of Mother Earth. No one turned to retire till the mouth of the grave was closed. Hitherto it had been the practice of burying their dead in the night, to escape the ridicule of being hooted at, and asked whether they had a pig for sale, and such like raillery. **ARTICLE 57** During the first few years of missionary life, the ladies were limited to the free use of their own houses and yards. To go beyond domestic premises, like prisoners or like queens, they must have an escort and proceed with limited freedom. When a nation of drunkards became, as it were, one great temperance society, and a holy influence was distilled from on high, a king in his power and woman in her weakness, recognized a bodyguard lining all our streets, and wherever man was found. It was after a residence of four and a half years, that for the first time I walked alone through the village and thus soliloquized. Whence this freedom? Where am I? I can identify the scenery. The trees and the mountains are the same, but the people—how different! Soon my attention was arrested by a loud wail which burst forth from a hut on a little eminence. Like as a bird, loosed from its cage, goes flitting from brough to bough, so with all the freedom of thought and action I directed my steps thither. On reaching the house, I was told that a woman had just died within. Revolting as seemed to be that dark abode of death, without a window, with a solitary low door, requiring a half double stoop, I entered. A passage was at once made through the crowd, inviting me to proceed to the farther end of the hut. There lay a woman apparently lifeless, stretched across the laps of six women, three on each side. On examination, I found she still had a pulse. Assuming the tone of direction, so acceptable to common natives, I said, "*Hush, retire, admit the air—she will revive.*" The crowd immediately withdrew, and nothing more was heard but now and then a half stifled sob. In a few minutes the supposed dead one opened her eyes. On me, standing over her, swinging a fan, she fixed a placid look, joined noses with those in whose arms she lay, and remained silent, the tears trickling down her cheeks. I asked for something to give, to revive her, the house afforded nothing but a calabash of poi and a tobacco pipe. Her husband, seeing her in a fainting fit, and knowing that some comforts were wanted, had taken the calabash and hastened back to the mountain, a distance of two miles, for a draught of fresh water. I obtained a cordial from my own home. The sick woman received it with gratitude, and was soon able to sit up and converse. She had long been ill, but that morning had been suddenly laid prostrate. She had several times been to the church, built by the governor, where the new religion was taught, but she never got near enough to hear anything, the doors and windows were so crowded. I returned home joyful and with a glad heart. After a long night of privation and darkness, light and freedom had dawned upon my pathway. **ARTICLE 58** Hawaii is the largest island of the group, and Kailua-Kona, on its western coast was the most important spot for a missionary station. This village contained three thousand inhabitants, and along the coast within twenty miles was twenty thousand. It had been the favorite abode of the kings of Hawaii, and the governor of the island still lived here. On the mountain Hualalai, just back of Kailua-Kona, is a large crater. It is now extinct. But our old people tell us of the time in their childhood, when they were aroused from their midnight slumbers, to see red hot balls hurled into the air from out of the crater on this mountain. Torrents of molten lava flowed from crater to coast, extended the shore farther out into the sea, and encrusted the surface of the earth, besides leaving an abundance of large loose scoriae, tossed about in every direction. Along the coast for two miles back, it is sterile, but there is a belt that is very rich, about a mile wide at the foot of the mountain, which is dotted here and there with the kukui (candlenut), breadfruit and orange, all splendid trees, of smaller growth, pineapple, sugar cane, arrowroot, taro and potatoes. Above this fertile belt is quite a width of forest, after which the bare sides of the mountain rise to a peak. It stands towards the rising sun. These distant scenes of the mountain, and perpetual verdure of forest and vegetation, are ever to be enjoyed. On the west we have a most extensive and delightful prospect of the ocean, also a view of the whole village, in which is the church lately erected by a heathen ruler, encircled by a wall from a fallen temple, where so lately were offered human victims. All along the shore are a few kou (tree) and many coconut trees. Kailua-Kona is distinguished for clear sunny days, brilliant nights, and magnificent sunsets. The mountain most thoroughly shields it from trade winds, but the daily sea breeze—and that in the evening from the mountain, are very refreshing. The mercury seldom stands higher than 84° or lower than 60°. The climate is soft and delicious. Where it is sterile there is no humidity at night in the air. We always have to go two miles back to find a sparse supply of fresh water, and sometimes five miles. Such beauties (views) and desolations are the attractions and repulsions of Kailua-Kona. Back of the village on that arid slope, a third of a mile from the shore was an unoccupied, eligible site for a house and grounds. There we set about making such a home as circumstances would allow, and as the double responsibilities required, of molding heathen society, and of forming the characters of our children. Five acres were enclosed with a stone wall three feet wide and six feet high, with simply the front gate for entrance. A large thatched house was erected. Space was allowed for a yard twenty-five feet in breadth. Two close partition walls were built six feet high, running from the outer wall each side of the front gate, close up against the side of the house, each side of the front door. That first apartment, twenty-five feet square, is the reception room for the natives. They know precisely where to enter the yard and the house, and they have learned where to stop. No one is permitted to go beyond that room without permission or invitation. There is Mr. Thurston's study table and his study chair. Another room of equal size is our dining room. In that, and in a small thatched cookhouse beyond, are our facilities for living. There is the sphere of action for our household natives. I teach my schools in that dining room, and Mr. Thurston, his in his study. Another partition wall from the rear comes up close against the back of the house, forming a backyard, where our household natives have a thatched house and a home. Thus the large house and yards have distinct accommodations, for household natives, the work of the family, for native company, and schools. At the back side of the house is a hall which leads both from the dining room and study to a door, the only entrance into a retired yard of three acres. There stands another thatched house, built after the custom of the country. The frame is tied together with the very strong bark of a certain tree. Then from the ridge pole to the ground, the frame is entirely covered with long slender poles, tied within a few inches of each other, over which the long lauhala (hala palm) leaves are laid, leaving the two ends to hang down on the outside. That house is the home of our children. There is our family sitting room, eighteen feet square, and there are our sleeping apartments. And inasmuch as I often wish to invite my native friends to that sitting room, we enclosed the further bedroom in a yard sixty feet square, with a wall six feet high, coming up close to the house on both sides. There is no entrance to the [enclosed] yard through the wall, but a door into it from our bedroom. Then if I am entertaining company in the sitting room, the children can pass from thence into the bedroom, and so out into their own yard and place of recreation, having without interference, the enjoyment of freedom and action. I, left in the sitting room, devoted to the natives, am still porter to the only door that leads into the children's special enclosure, and have the satisfied feeling of them being safe, beyond the reach of native influence. In our kitchen yard, directly opposite and within a few feet of each other, are the two mouths of a large cave of volcanic formation. The larger opening gives us the novelty of a subterraneous walk one-fourth of a mile toward the sea, where we reach a pond of brackish water. Some of the rooms of this cave are quite spacious. The natives made it a place of concealment in times of war. The smaller mouth of the cave leads into a low cave which extends three miles up the mountain, where there is an opening, and when obliged to hide in the lower cave, the natives stole through the upper one to procure their food. The name of the cave is Laniakea, signifying the broad Heavens. As it is enclosed in our premises, the natives were quick to give the name to our establishment, so that it has become universally known as Laniakea. **ARTICLE 59** When public worship was there, first established, in a new native church, conducted by a missionary in their own language, the natives naturally showed a great lack of training. For instance, after the sermon, when the minister closed his eyes to commence the last prayer, the people would commence retiring from the house, so that when he opened his eyes at the end of that exercise, he would find it nearly empty. But they had gradually learned orderly habits, and had attended public Sabbath exercises for about a year. Then it was that we received, simply in manuscript, a translation of *Watt's Easy Catechism for Children*. It was a talent not to be buried in a napkin. Our associates were absent. I was in active life, but my health seriously suffered, exhibiting incipient symptoms of pulmonary disease. In my circumstances, I could only conceive the plan of a class coming to be taught after Sabbath service in our promised piazza. Until that is built, stay and meet them at the church. Mr. Thurston engaged to take charge of the children, and Honolii promised to secure a class of scholars. When the time arrived, Mr. Thurston descended from the pulpit, gave a hand to each of the little girls, two and four years of age, and retired. Thus released from maternal cares, I looked around, and to my utter amazement, the whole congregation had resumed their seats. Every chief (there were five of the first class present) every man, woman and child, all as one, wished to be taught the catechism. I saw at a glance that I had unintentionally stepped into the harness. But I resolved to go forward and begin at the beginning. Honolii was to me what Aaron was to Moses. With all the docility of children, they suffered themselves to be seated according to their rank, sex, and age. Honolii then took one side of the house, and I the other, and they all attended to this one question, "*Who made you?*"—"*The great God who made Heaven and earth.*"—This question was answered separately by every individual. Then, not to tax their patience, Honolii closed the school with a very short address, and a very short prayer. Such was the extreme weakness and simplicity with which that first Sabbath school sprung into being. But they dispersed, every one of them carrying away a grand idea, of which the great Kamehameha had no knowledge. This first movement necessarily led to duties which were laborious and exhausting. I selected eighteen of the best scholars, furnished each with a manuscript copy of the lesson for the next Sabbath, taught them separately, and taught them together, what they were to teach their future scholars. The institution of the Sabbath had been established in the land by government. The day of rest and of privileges again dawned upon that simple people, just waking into life. The public services of the Sabbath had been conducted by the missionary. The people were dismissed. The entire congregation remained as before, and filed off to their several places. Then came forward a band of teachers prepared to teach orally their assigned classes what they had been taught. They engaged in their new employment with interest and success. The school prospered and multiplied to be between four and five hundred scholars. A mighty impulse was given to the native mind, which so exceeded all the means used as to render it apparent that there was in operation a renovating influence, secret and divine. **ARTICLE 60** (Kapulikoliko) She was the daughter of Kamehameha I. In her father's court she sustained the honor of princess. When the common people passed her, they prostrated themselves on the ground.—But when her father's reign ceased, of the children of twenty-one wives, those only were grouped in the royal family whose mothers descended from kings.—Of course, Kapulikoliko, born on her mother's side of plebeian blood, lost position, yet she still had influence, and by the people was held in great reverence. She was married to a substantial man of common birth, and with great ease adapted herself to her thorough change of circumstances. She was about making a permanent removal, by leaving [the] Kailua-Kona [area] for a distant part of the island. Before going, she with her husband and attendants came and made a farewell call, by spending the day with us. Before taking leave, as her parting request, with great simplicity and assurance, she asked me to give her—yes, looked me full in the face, and on opening her mouth said, *"Give us your elder child"* (four years old) *"and let us take her with us to our new abode."* Without offending her ladyship, I refused her the precious boon, in a manner too decisive to leave her any encouragement of renewing her request. What was such a shock to my feelings is a common custom here. They dispose of their children without one idea of building up a family of brothers and sisters. Indeed, parents are tacked together very loosely. They come together and separate as convenience and inclination dictate. One man will have several wives, or one woman will have several husbands. Here is a mass of humanity in a chaotic state. Take half a dozen of them, and put them into some school in the United States and something can be done with them. But it requires a great influence to lift a nation. **ARTICLE 61** Mrs. [Elizabeth] Bishop and myself acted in concert. We conceived the idea of endeavoring to lift our female population, by meeting with them every Friday, PM. We were each to sustain the responsibility of the thing, by alternately presiding at the meetings. For many months they have been attended. At first, I think, there was not an individual who had learned to say "*Our Father.*" Now they can lead in prayer with great propriety, and think it a great privilege. In acquiring this gift, they exhibit the greatest simplicity and freedom, never neglecting to exercise one talent, because they have not ten. With great freedom, and seriousness too, they express their religious convictions. We read to them a portion of scripture. But Bible leaves (pages) in the Hawaiian language have been very scarce. Once I was driven to extremity, being obliged to take the first chapter of *Matthew*, the only portion remaining. That was the way they rehearsed the names of their own kings, and preserved them by simply retaining them in memory. Two women of cultivated tenacious memories, came up to our house after meeting, and wished me to read that chapter again. After I did so, they assisted each other, and began by repeating the line of names from Abram to David, to the captivity, to Jesus. They went through successfully, only asking aid in recalling two names. One more subject was brought up in these meetings. This people were in a state of nature. There was only one point where I ever saw them exhibit shame. Both men and women were disposed and allowed to move around in public in a state of perfect nudity. But if they appeared so without having one hand become a substitute for an apron of fig leaves, it would among themselves be severely condemned. Childhood was ever taught to press in and be present at the birth of children. In all social acts, they too were taught to be alike skilled with those of adult years. They divided and subdivided this knowledge, laid it up on their tongues, and then scattered it right and left to vaunt their own knowledge or promote their pastimes. Impurity of speech with both parents and children had become a giant in the land, stalking everywhere. We could not defy it in its native element. But we were moved to drive it from our retired sitting rooms, the homes of our children. Whoever wished the privilege of crossing the thresholds to those apartments, consecrated to purity, must be subject to criticism. Whatever was there uttered which we disapproved we penned, and read in the Friday meeting. Thus we tried to give them a standard of what was right and began by endeavoring to form a healthy moral atmosphere in two rooms, eighteen feet square, where natives were allowed to tread. I carried my little manuscript book and pencil in my pocket, and used them on the spur of the occasion, and thus prepared notes for a future meeting. I had a severe struggle with my own feelings in establishing these things, and passed painful, sleepless hours, lest I had offended. But it proved the reverse. For heavenly dews had prepared the soil to receive seed as into good and honest hearts. **ARTICLE 62** (Death of Elizabeth Edwards Bishop) Mrs. Bishop lived and moved among us, exhibiting by her activity, by the rosy hue and radiance of her countenance, a high state of health. She exerted herself in the day school, in the Sabbath school, and in the Female Friday Meeting. But the scene was changed. Her bloom and strength gave place to debility and internal sufferings. There was no physician in the kingdom to detect the disease. For more than half a year she quietly remained in her home, with great humility and patience struggling through just what was meted out to her. Then, in shipping season, she, with her husband and children, sailed for Honolulu, with the hope of meeting with a traveling physician. In this they were successful. The doctor pronounced her disease dyspepsia (indigestion). [Elizabeth Bishop's health issues were incorrectly diagnosed an inexperienced doctor.] But no professional skill diminished her great sufferings. After the lapse of several months, she returned to Kailua-Kona. As she entered the harbor, several women went off on board to meet her. She said to them, "*I shall soon die, and my unfaithfulness to you makes me afraid to meet God in judgment.*" Her expressing herself in that manner, proved very impressive to the natives. For they said, "*If after doing so much for us, she is afraid to meet God, how will it be with us?*" On coming ashore, they passed their own establishment, and entered our family. Mrs. Bishop was again with us. But she was a wreck of her former self. During her absence, disease had made great ravages. She had become very feeble, very much emaciated, and distressingly nervous. Her internal sufferings were excruciating. She sometimes compared them to fire. There was a singular and incessant palpitation at her stomach, and according to her own account, the reception of even a spoonful of chicken soup caused it to be too intense and agonizing to admit of sleep. Consequently her ordinary practice was, at early dawn to take one, two, or three spoonfuls of soup, and as she happened to feel, sometimes once or twice a similar pittance during the forenoon. The afternoon was spent in fasting, to have an empty stomach to go to bed upon at dark. Several times there were intervals of twenty-four hours without her swallowing the least thing. This course seemed to us a great error. But anything by way of persuasion was not only altogether unavailing, but an occasion of grief. She would weep and say, *"You don't know anything about the state of my stomach."* By the time she left us, she became one of the most emaciated forms my eyes ever beheld. From evening twilight till early dawn, her state required the most profound stillness through the thatched building, as the rooms, above the partitions, were all thrown together. So I transferred the nursery to the other cottage, packed three little girls into a wide children's crib, and had the disjointed accommodation of a sailor's hammock and the dining table for myself and babe, five months old. Mr. Thurston, with his consideration and self control, entered the house at the opposite end from the invalid—in the dark, with the stealth of a thief, and lay softly down on his bed. During the day we were all admitted into the common sitting room, where she reclined on the settee. At the expiration of one week, the native men of our village had completed their work of love. On an eligible site in our yard, beneath our care, but beyond the reach of household sounds, they had erected a commodious thatched building, twenty by twenty-four feet, more or less. It was for their suffering teacher, Mrs. Bishop. From the very first, and so long as the house stood, it received the name of "Bishop Retreat." Mr. and Mrs. Bishop immediately entered it. Her commodious couch was placed in the middle of the room, immediately before an ample door where she could have the full play of a delicious sea breeze. From that period to the end, two intelligent native women came successively and sat by her couch through the night. She spoke with much satisfaction of their improvement and the relief they afforded her. Mrs. Bishop's sufferings increased. Weeks of anguish, paroxysms of agony, and the frenzy of delirium were measured out to her. We traveled with and watched over her, by night and by day, to sustain her in the darkness, and in the storm. It was midnight, the tempest was high, the billows rolled near her. Suddenly there was a lull. "*Let me depart in peace*," she said calmly, and fell to sleep as peacefully as the infant in its mother's arms. Mrs. Bishop had left us—had left with us her two infant children under three years of age, and gone to her rest. Then with deep love and respect we neatly dressed and enclosed our precious dead in a coffin. The natives in their transition state were delighted with this new order of things. A large concourse of chiefs and people assembled at our house, all habited in black. With as much order and decency as I ever witnessed in my own country, the procession moved to the church—and from thence to the grave, where we committed the sacred deposit to the silent bosom of Mother Earth. And we taught them to restrain their boisterous expressions of natural affection under the bereavement, and to bow with submission and thanksgiving to Him who is the Resurrection and the Life. Mrs. Bishop's deep religious feelings, her Christian faithfulness, her severe sufferings, and her early death, powerfully enlisted the tender and close sympathies of the natives. It was at our expense that the soil was thus prepared for early planting a church at Kailua-Kona. (Eleven years after Mrs. Bishop's death, it was found necessary to remove her body. Our whole family and Dr. [Lorrin] Andrews were witnesses. When the box and the coffin were unearthed, they were found to be in a very decayed state. When the coffin was thrown open, the garments, flesh and small bones were seen all reduced to fine, dry dust. The long spinal column remained entire, and in the lower half of it was a very prominent curve. The first words spoken were by the doctor. "*Of what disease did she*

die?" I replied, "*A doctor pronounced it dyspepsia.*" He answered, "*The spinal column could not be thus distorted without great suffering.*" Two years after this, I was in America and saw Mrs. [Julia Brooks] Spaulding who formerly belonged to our Hawaiian Missionary band. Here she lost her health, and it was not until she was bedridden that her disease was found to be an affection of the spine. She is now in health. She very particularly inquired in regard to Mrs. Bishop's last illness. After learning the facts she remarked, "*As you describe her symptoms, I have not a doubt but her disease was* (of) *a spinal affection. I have been taught by experience to have a deep sympathy in many of her feelings.*")
ARTICLE 63 (Death of a Sister) Six weeks after Mrs. Bishop's death, a letter arrived announcing the heavy tidings that my own sister, Mrs. Persis G. Parkhurst, was gone. Thus the two sisters on whom I most relied, the one at the Islands, and the other in America, were removed from me as with a stroke. The fact that I drooped for years with fatal tendencies, while they bloomed with vigor, then that they both were removed, while I was sustained in active life, appeared marvelous. "*Even so, Father, for so it seemed good in thy sight.*" In the last precious letter which my sister Persis wrote me, she mentioned hearing Dr. [Edward] Payson preach from these words, "*What I do, thou knowest not now, but thou shalt know hereafter. I felt,*" she said, "*as if I could hang forever on his lips.*" Then, after giving an account, with all a mother's feelings, of being called to resign a little prattling son to the grave, she added, "*But God has done it, and I will not complain, for I know that he does all things well.*" **ARTICLE 64** (Extracts from Letters) My heart often turns toward the pen and toward you. Did you know my situation, and the active and responsible duties devolving upon me, there would be no need of an apology for neglect. Think of a hotel in the middle of your town, of a house thus public I am mistress. Think of children, cut off from the benefits of the sanctuary, of schools, of associates, of children thus exiled, I am the mother. Think of a heathen people who have just begun to ruminate upon the wonders of *Revelations*, their eyes and their hearts are turned towards the teachers who

brought these new doctrines and duties to their shores, and in the language of implicit confidence and affection they say, "*You are our father, you are our mother, tell us what to do.*" Among such a people I stand connected. Pray for me that I may serve my generation faithfully, and that as my day is, so my strength may be. *November 4th.* We have been at this station six years. During the greater part of the first year I felt what it was to live among heathen. I had acquired such knowledge of the language and character of the people, as to realize with what revolting characters I was surrounded. A few months previous to the decease of my ever to be lamented friend, Mrs. Bishop, a new impulse was given to their feelings. During the last year, reformation has been a silent and progressive work. Such was the propensity to flock to our house for religious instruction, that we found it necessary in order to the performance of other duties, to have restrictions. During the forenoon our house was under a kapu (forbidden), that is, the people were not allowed to visit it. Yet to this general rule, the chiefs and principal teachers must be made an exception. In the afternoon, our doors were open to any and to all, and our house has been thronged. The principal people take chairs, but the common people enter, and as their habit is, seat themselves on the mat at our feet, saying, "*We come to declare to you our thoughts, we are sinners, we are thieves, and liars, and adulterers, and murderers, we are afraid of sin, we are afraid of eternal death, we are afraid of the Son of God, we are in darkness, we are in the shades of death, teach us.*" Others again thus express themselves, "*We are great sinners, we repent of our sins, we forsake them, we rest our souls in Jesus Christ, He is our salvation, He is our sacrifice, we love Him, we rejoice in Him, we desire his righteousness, we wish to sit at his feet and learn of Him, and serve Him, we wish to be in His hand.*" Forty-three have been baptized and received into the church at this place. Probably fifty more give evidence of piety. The good people are active. What they have freely received, they freely give. Their little missionary excursions have been very interesting, they have been out to distant villages, searched out the aged, the blind, the sick, the infirm, and told them of Jesus and of Heaven, they have taught the ignorant, and excited all to attendance on public worship. About three weeks ago, a new and general excitement commenced. At the dawn of day they (villagers) tapped at our doors with the anxious inquiry, "*What shall I do.*" All regulations were prostrated, and from daybreak till ten o'clock at night, one company succeeded another in rapid succession. Mr. Thurston has only been able to command time for his meals. From morning till night he has been in his study chair, with an individual or a cluster at his feet, sometimes a company of fifty or sixty, which entirely filled the room. Some days we have received calls from several hundreds. I devote as much time to the instruction of the women as I can redeem from my family. My labors are more particularly directed to the members of the Friday Female Meeting. Two years ago their names were enrolled and a discipline introduced. A moral standard was raised. Whoever wished to join the Society must forsake all their former vile practices, and pay an external regard to the Word and Worship of God. They must uniformly have a full covering (clothing) for their persons, both at home and abroad, and follow whatever is lovely and of good report. Such has since been the change in public opinion—that scenes which were then familiar to the eye would now be scouted out of the village as shameful indecencies. This Society has prospered, for in two years, from seventy it has increased to fifteen hundred. The names of five hundred have been enrolled within the last three weeks. These are all divided into classes, and each class has a particular teacher to whom to look for instruction. The number of female teachers has risen to twenty, all hopefully pious. This is my class. I teach them what I wish them to teach others. The men's society is conducted on the same plan. Two large thatched houses have been erected for the accommodation of these societies. I will introduce you to one of the many [individuals] in whom I feel most interested, named Pulukai. Not that he is the most important character among us, yet in works of love, none surpass him, I know not where he acquired his politeness, but probably abroad, as he has visited foreign ports. He is here nearly every day, yet he never comes into our presence but he bows, presents his hand to his face, and all so heartily, and with so much reverence (as if some great personage stood before him for the first time) that it always makes me smile. His presence never fails to give me pleasure. The other day he spoke with tears of his former state and feelings. He said, "I returned home from the northwest coast, and found my former friends were all dead. One day I went back into a solitary place, and there I remained, and walked, and wept. It was not for my soul—I neither knew, nor thought about that—but I wept for my body, for if I should die, I had no friend that would bury it, it would lie and decay on the face of the earth, and when any person passed along and asked, 'Who is that?'—the reply would be, 'It is Pulukai.' But now I have many friends. They give me food and clothes. They are kind to me while I am living, and they will take care of my body when I am dead. It is because the love of God is in their hearts." During the sickness of Mrs. Bishop, his anxieties were employed about that part which is of more importance than his poor body. I shall ever remember, that one day as I went to the door to smooth the couch for her emaciated form, and stood seeing her borne away, reflecting that the manele (chair) must soon be exchanged for the bier, that Pulukai, who had been watching his opportunity for a word of instruction, came up to me, saying, he had passed three sleepless nights thinking about his sins, and his exposure to eternal death. It was a short time after—that the love of Jesus became his theme and his life and conversation have since given abundant evidence that he was taught of God. Humility and love were the characteristics of Pulukai, and they shed a luster over the tawny features of our humble friend. **ARTICLE 65** (To Reverend William Goodell, Missionary at Malta) *Kailua-Kona, October, 16, 1829. My Dear Cousin and Brother*, you going to western Asia seems to have made you our neighbor, and caused me to think of you with peculiar nearness. Notwithstanding the convulsive nature of things, that region has appeared to me one of the most interesting fields into which the American Board is casting imperishable seed. Your conflicts there have caused you all to become tried characters, and I rejoice that grace has been given you to be found faithful. I am now going to introduce to you Mr. Thurston, for never since I knew him have I witnessed in him such application to his studies, such devotedness to the natives. He speaks the Hawaiian language with greater ease and fluency than the English, preaches without notes, ever devoting the last hour or two before entering the pulpit to his sermon, and with as much solemnity as if the veil was withdrawn which conceals futurity from his view. When translating the Scriptures from their original language, he sits at the study table overspread with books. From that same chair he does more by way of preaching repentance toward God and faith in our Lord Jesus Christ, than from the consecrated desk. The afternoon is almost wholly thus devoted, talking individually with the natives. The shades of night change his employment, for then the people who come to converse give way for the "fa, so, la" company, as it is here called. What is to become of our children has been a question agitated throughout our mission families, and a subject which has pressed heavily upon parental feelings. The general sentiment has been, *Send them to America for education.*" A joint letter was written to the American Board, expressive of such desires. An answer has been received, but they can grant no facilities, and advise that they remain with their parents in this land. However, of the few families from the brig *Thaddeus* who still remain in the field, ours is the only one but what has already, by gratuitous passages, sent home the precious gift of a child to personal friends. To send away children at an age so early, while I am sustained in active life, is what every feeling of my heart revolts against. But when the period arrives that they must pass from under the ever watchful eye of a parent, when an employment, trade or profession for future life is chosen—the Sandwich Islands is no longer a place for them. I have not felt like some of our, mothers, that children must be sent away or be ruined. I harp upon another string, and say, make better provision for them, or that will likely be the result. And in the first place, houses and dooryards must be laid out to meet the character of the people, and the exigencies of the times. Ours is planned for comfort and usefulness on heathen ground. Missionaries are public characters, and their houses must be public houses. I am sure ours is, at present, from morning till bedtime and often so thronged, that we cannot, without difficulty, pass from room to room. But if children are suitable appendages to a mission family, they must be taken care of, and I know not on whom this duty more appropriately devolves than on a mother. And in order to take care of them, there must be a child's department. Sooner ask me to furnish a dinner without a table, to sit down without a chair, or spread my couch without a bedstead, than to rear such a stately edifice as the moral and intellectual character of a child without some facilities. The first rule to be attended to with regard to children is that they must not speak the native language. It is an easy thing to make such a law, but it is a mother's duty to guard it from being violated, and to form in her children fixed habits of doing as they are required. It of course, follows, that they are never left to the care of natives after reaching the age of prattling. No intercourse whatever should exist between children and heathen. On this point I am very particular. Establish a loose system here, and I would say with everyone else, "*Send children to America, no matter how soon.*" Of all the trials incident to missionary life, the responsibility of training up children, and of making provision for their virtue and usefulness when they pass from under the watchful eye of parents, is, comparatively speaking, the only one worthy of being named. When my thoughts turn to their future prospects in life, a darkness visible seems to brood over their path. But hush my anxious heart. It is mine to perform present duties, and cast my cares on Him who is Almighty. *Affectionately, your cousin, Lucy G. Thurston.* **ARTICLE 66** *October 30, 1830.* Mr. Thurston is entirely devoted to works of a public nature. My duties are of a more private character. I am the housekeeper, the mother, and the domestic teacher. What time I can redeem from family cares, I give to our native females. Twenty-six hundred have been gathered into our Friday meetings. This society is in a very flourishing state. As I cannot see them all at our house, I teach them by proxy, selecting from the most intelligent ones a class of teachers to come under my instructions. When night closes upon me, and there is a suspension of maternal and domestic duties, I take my chosen season to meet the natives. I pass from a hushed nursery to the long dining room, where a table is extended for the accommodation of twenty-five. It is lighted up and the women are in their seats. Our governor's wife attends. It is on the whole a social interview. But one theme is before us in everyone's hand. We turn over together the pages of Holy Writ, as it is issued from the press. The Word of God is powerful. I have lived to see both sides of the picture. I saw this neglected portion of our race, groping along in all the darkness of nature, listening to messages from Heaven with indifference and contempt—and for a long time hearing as though they heard not. Man can speak only to the ear. I looked again, and a secret energy was transforming their moral characters. Those very beings who were once bowing down to stocks of wood and stone, worshiping sharks and volcanoes, and slaves to all the sins which degrade human nature, are now sitting at the feet of Jesus, learning and doing his will. Two years ago last February, when our dear Mrs. Bishop bade them farewell, till she should meet them at the bar of God, no native at Kailua-Kona had been baptized. Since that time sixty five have been admitted to the Holy Communion, and a much larger number give evidence of having experienced the renovating influence of the Spirit. Yesterday one of our native neighbors called on us for the first time, a man perhaps forty years old—one who had been notoriously wicked. His wife by her frequent calls was quite familiar with us. She accompanied, and introduced him to us a stranger. "*I came,*" he said, "*to tell you my thoughts. I have been very wicked.*" In addition to other crimes, he mentioned some particulars of a crime he had committed. "*But,*" he said, "*I have now got my works straight on the outside. But I look into my heart, and the law of God is there broken. It is so this day, and that day, and every day. In my heart it is sin, sin. I do not* love it, but I cannot get rid of it. I break God's law and repent, and break God's law and repent. My heart is made sore on account of it, and my thought is from day to day, that the end of it will be eternal death." Here he paused to wipe away his tears. His wife then remarked, "*Thus it is when he asks a blessing before eating, his tears often flow.*" He then said, "*Great love to God is the cause. When I retire for prayer, I often weep, so that for a time I cannot utter a word. My mind does not turn upon anything that is made, but rises and fixes upon God and feels so much love, that I weep and pray together. I have stayed at home and kept my feelings to myself—have not conversed with my neighbors, but my wife has urged me out, to come and converse with the teachers. I have come. You know my thoughts. Tell me what they mean? I am greatly afraid of the sins of my heart.*" Such are the feelings which knowledge of God's Word produces in the minds of those heathen around us in very many instances. The box of books you sent were safely received in six months from the date of your letter, and were very acceptable. All that is printed at these Islands is in the Hawaiian language, for the exclusive benefit of the natives. But many ships touch at these Islands in need of instruction, in need of Bibles, in need of tracts. Our own countrymen, too, who have left a sailor's life for a residence on these Islands, are in perishing need of some friendly messengers to turn their feet from their downward course. I have distributed some of those you sent among them, and I was not a little astonished, a few weeks ago, to find they had united in one little body, about a dozen of them in all, and purchased a suitable house for their own use, to be dedicated to the worship of God, and are now fitting it up in a very neat and suitable manner. Time only will show in what this beginning will end, but it is beyond a question that they have many serious thoughts. Eternity is a dreadful word to them, as they feel that without holiness no man can see God. **ARTICLE 67** (To Mary Goodale, Marlborough, Massachusetts) *Kailua-Kona, September, 1831. Dear Sister*, last June the General Meeting of the Mission was held at Honolulu. It became an interesting question, shall I make one of the party, or in such solitary circumstances, remain behind? Friends at Honolulu had interested themselves in my prospects, by sending a vessel for our accommodation, with invitations for us to come down. The way was opened, and duty seemed to require that I place myself within the reach of medical skill. We sailed on board the brig *Waverly* with our whole family. Messieurs [Artemas] Bishop and [Samuel] Ruggles likewise accompanied us. We were accommodated on deck at first, both night and day. I congratulated myself in being placed (allowed) in circumstances of safety. But during the darkness of the third night, we entered the channel between Hawaii and Maui. The wind was high, the sea boisterous, the vessel rolled, seasickness increased, the water dashed over the deck, and to escape being drenched, we were obliged, for the first time, to retire to the cabin. After reaching my couch below, I alluded to the Black Hole of Calcutta, as ever standing associated in my mind with the cabin of a native vessel. At length we passed the tumultuous channel. Our seasickness subsided. We slept. My sleep was somehow interrupted. It is because my couch is so in heaps. I arose and smoothed it, again slumbered, again arose and smoothed my couch. This I several times repeated. At length truth at once flashed upon my mind. What does all this mean? My first thought was, there is no chance for safety, but by being restored to pure air, the bilge water was so very offensive. I hastened to the deck, clambered over the companion way, the door being kept closed and fastened, and availed myself of the best accommodations of the place, the body of a tree, on and around which a multitude of natives were reclining. I begged Mr. Thurston to return to the seasick children, while I remained alone. I looked off upon the dark black water, and thought of the precious names of home, physician, sister. The tears rushed into my eyes, but thinking them unseasonable when everything depended on my own exertions, I checked the impulse, and returned them to their sockets. Yet in bringing my mind to my circumstances there was a struggle. I called to mind the duty and the privilege of laying myself with childlike simplicity and submission, into the hands of my heavenly Father and awaiting his will. Tried to do so, and there was peace. I spent a short time only on deck, before I awoke one of our natives, to signify to Mr. Thurston that I wished to return, and bid him awake, Mr. Bishop. After we had all reached the cabin, I said to them, "*I am called upon in this place to ask the aid of you all.*" Mr. Bishop proposed taking opium until reaching Lahaina. I answered, "*No, it is too late, and if my apprehensions are just, no time is to be lost.*" The first embarrassment that we felt was that we were in utter darkness, for during the forepart of the night we had trimmed, replenished and lighted the only lamp we could find on board. Being so often called to repeat this care, we left off in despair. Now one more effort was made, and our flickering lamp appeared as if invigorated by sleep. Again, the handbasket which contained the keys of trunks had been misplaced. A whole half hour had been spent the day before in unavailing search. Means were soon found to burst the lock of a single trunk, which would supply all the wants of the emergency. In the meantime Mr. Ruggles repaired with the children to the deck. Mr. Thurston and Mr. Bishop alone remained. Everything was in due order. In one half hour from the time a general movement was made, infant cries from the cabin apprised those on deck of what was passing below. Scarce was I informed of the danger that the child's breath might be stopped on the very threshold of life, when the light expired and its cries ceased altogether.—"*Silence and Darkness solemn sisters!*"—The lamp was passed upon deck, through an avenue overhead, "*A light, a light.*" It was renewed, returned, and a spark still more precious again lighted up. The child was safe. But the mother's life was, ere long, felt to be in danger. Never before had I so much reason to feel that I had reached the isthmus which lies between this and the invisible world. My medical volume I had put into the trunk. It was taken therefrom, and the two divines sat on the stairs of the companion way, to study out their medical lesson. After the lapse of eight hours, the feelings of danger were exchanged for those of unmixed gratitude. All was safe. In the fullness of my heart I repeated the beautiful words of a poet, "*There is mercy in every *place, and mercy, encouraging thought, gives even affliction new grace, and reconciles man to his lot."* We were now near Lahaina. Messieurs Bishop and Ruggles wrote notes to Mr. Richards, stating our situation, and requesting a double canoe. When intelligence reached the shore, Miss Ogden wept, and Mrs. Richards sobbed aloud. Messieurs [Lorrin] Andrews and [Samuel] Whitney came off in a double canoe. Meantime husband and I were busy in the cabin. Before leaving my berth, I erected my arm from the elbow to the tip of the fingers, thinking in length it equaled the height of the opening to my couch. But it fell short by several inches. The other side, head and foot, top and bottom were all alike closely boarded. According to my early educated eye, it seemed like a cupboard. Mr. Thurston first smoothed down Mrs. Thurston, and laid her aside on the top of a row of barrels, standing on their ends, near the companion way. There she lay in her traveling dress, ready for onward travel, looking just as she did when she left her home. Above and below we were all in readiness to depart. Mr. Thurston took me in his arms like a child and carried me on deck. Mr. Bishop then assisted him in swinging me over the side of the vessel, where was a mattress supported by Messieurs Andrews and Whitney, and by them let down onto the elevated arms which connected the double canoe. On reaching the shore, we were met by Mr. Richards, Mrs. Andrews and Miss Ogden. I was borne on the mattress by natives to Mr. Richard's house. On entering the gate, the mattress was necessarily brought up together, and in so doing, I became as completely enclosed as if lying in a coffin. No farther consciousness remained, but that of pressing through doors, turning corners, and ascending stairs. At length, I was let down, and beheld myself lying on a board floor, in the middle of a room, with plastered walls and glass windows. To me, who had spent eight years in cottages thatched with leaves, with mats for floors, and doors for windows, it seemed a novel scene, and powerfully reminded me of the days of other years. Here I found Mrs. [Clarissa Lyman] Richards. Both she and her husband received us with a freedom and hospitality that made me feel like reaching a father's house. As I lay there, with all my friends gathered round me in a circle, Mrs. Richards said to me, "*Now you may have your choice whom to have to dress you for bed.*" I replied, "*I choose Mr. Thurston.*" At the expiration of a week after reaching Lahaina, Mr. Thurston went on to Honolulu, to the "General Meeting" of the Mission. He was accompanied by every brother on the island. I was still confined to my bed, but I had a medical book laid beneath my pillow, dishes brought into the chamber for the use of the three children, and our native man, under the general direction of Mrs. Richards, prepared and brought up refreshments. Thus I guided my family and took care of my babe, having for neighbors Mrs. Richards below, and Mrs. Andrews in the next house. Mrs. Andrews came in every morning, and washed and dressed the babe. Had the strength of the station been called out at this time, there would have been found three feeble females, and ten children all under eleven years of age. After a three weeks's absence, our company returned, and I was able to go below, and join them in surrounding the social board, and the domestic altar. The next day we went on board the vessel. Three more days and nights of oppressive heat and seasickness, with three children and the infant, all involved in the common calamity, all prostrate on the floor, by the side of their mother, when we reached Kailua-Kona, and our own home. There we reared an altar to the God of all comfort, who had been mindful of us in our low estate—who had graciously prospered our way, and brought us in peace to our own habitation. *Your loving sister, Lucy G. Thurston.* **ARTICLE 68** (To the Second Mrs. Parkhurst, Marcia Harriman) *Kailua-Kona, November 14th, 1832. My Dear Sister*, there is no distant friend on earth toward whom my heart turns more frequently, and more affectionately, than to the successor of my departed sister Persis. Of her orphan children I can say, "*Like Reuben and Simeon, they are mine,*" and all that care and love which they are made to experience, excites in my heart the same gratitude as if done for my own children. For twelve years past I have been in the heart of a nation, who have just washed their hands from the guilt of infanticide, yet their standard falls infinitely short of those who have been rocked in the cradle of piety and intelligence, so that an enlightened, pious, devoted mother, seems to me one of the finest specimens of female piety which this world exhibits. And when that link that nature gives, is wanting, to bind one to those self-denying duties, it must be a service lovely in the eyes of angels, well pleasing to God. As you express a wish to know what articles I seldom get, and most want, I will tell you what one of my missionary sisters said to me. "Mrs. Thurston, I think you had better get some new bonnets for your daughters." My reply was, "These are very good, they are in no wise shabby." She continued, "It would be an expense, but bonnets with more plainness and less luster would be a better example. We must look at example." I replied, "It is a good example to give durability to articles." "It is, and I approve of it in you, still I think your daughters had better have some new bonnets." I replied, "I have neither time nor means. If other people think so, they must furnish them." The fact is, seven years ago a kind missionary sister of Honolulu made and sent my two oldest daughters some light silk hats, decorated with artificial flowers. For dress these have ever since been used up to the present time. A northern constitution cannot labor here as in America. One of our missionaries of much observation and wisdom remarked, "Had the ladies shrank from those active labors which are performed in the New England States, before trial had been made, I should have imputed it to indolence. But now, by experience, we know the consequences, and it makes me angry to see any one attempt it." We all employ female cooks, yet we have to make them out of raw materials, and withal submit to lesser evils in order to avoid greater. It afforded me some amusement to hear one of the newly arrived ladies expatiate on native neatness. While at Honolulu, happening to step into the cookhouse, she saw a negligent fellow peeling potatoes for the table with his fingers! She said, "I would tell them to make use of a knife and fork." Yes, and as soon as the white person turns her back, finding himself in the predicament of David with his armor, he throws down the awkward irons, for without any lessons, and without knowing that such utensils had been invented, he could ever from his childhood, with those facilities which nature furnishes, peel potatoes with great dexterity. Your husband, in his letter, remarked that he did not see why our children should not learn the native language, and be taught in connection with the natives, etc. Just so we felt, just so we conducted our operations for more than two years. Mr. Chamberlain's children were taught in the same school, and ranged in the same classes with our interesting scholars gathered from among the heathen. Mr. [William] Ellis, on a visit from the Society Islands, was the first one to open our eyes to the evils of such a course. Now, natives themselves are our monitors. No one is more particular than Kapiolani, and if in her intercourse among the families of the Mission, she observes native language on the lips of the children, or even if their eyes speak looks of interest and familiarity with the natives, she notes it with feelings of the deepest pity. Even Kaahumanu sighed for the privilege of having her little adopted son David, of royal birth, her future heir, taken into one of our families, and prohibited the use of his own native language. I had the offer of a trust so responsible. Yet who would dare undertake thus to educate a prince, cutting him off from all intercourse with his noble relatives and interested countrymen, and still in their very midst? He is a little boy of noble mien, intelligent and interesting, and it fills our souls with sadness to listen to the impurities which are intermixed with his infantile prattle. He obtains language, not from the printed works of missionaries, where the precious is separated from the evil, but as it floats in society around him, and aside from the pollution of heathenism, native converts to Christianity fail of being suitable models for a child's imitation. They may be clothed—they may be Christianized, yet from want of early culture, from being children of nature, there is an utter destitution of those feelings of delicacy which in refined society seem inseparable from virtuous tastes and principles. Now, in estimating the character of Sandwich Islanders, we pass over what cannot be corrected, it is a tarnish (failure) which reminds us of the pit from whence they were digged. Not so with the children of American extract. Our patrons expect, the world expect, the heathen themselves expect that they will rise up and reflect honor upon an enlightened origin. Well might St. Paul add, in enumerating his trials and labors, the care of the churches. We looked at the vine planted in this heathen soil, that it should bring forth grapes, and behold wild grapes! Well, might we expect defection, for here the flames of persecution have never been lighted, and to become a member of a church gave to a common person the influence of an inferior chief. They acquire the language of Canaan, too, with so much dexterity, that the defect cannot be detected in pronouncing the word shibboleth (tradition). Of one hundred and eight who have been received to the church at this place eleven have been suspended from its privileges, and what is an aggravating circumstance, they were all, with one exception, leading characters in schools and in meetings. The crime is adultery. All profess repentance. One of the number, who lay smarting under the salutary castigations of her infidel husband's wrath for nearly a year, has exhibited a spirit which has called back, not only the affections and confidences of the church, but of her husband also, who now treats her with every possible kindness. In the midst of these troubles I have had in my hand a complete copy of the New Testament, printed in the Hawaiian language. It has been as an anchor to my soul. For here a door is open to communicate blessings to unborn multitudes, which no man can shut. *Your affectionate sister, Lucy G. Thurston.* **ARTICLE 69** *Kailua-Kona, September 3, 1833.* Of all the scenes of my life, none seem so precious and vivid at this distant period, as those of our paternal home. I often think of you, and frequently do it by way of contrast. On Sabbath mornings, while we are at breakfast, you are in church. In the winter, when you are sitting by a warm fire, we open the doors to admit the refreshing breeze. You ride in a carriage or on horseback—we sail in vessels and canoes. You see nature stripped of its foliage, and covered with snow, we have before our eyes a verdant (green) landscape. In your intercourse with your neighbors, you speak English, we Hawaiian. You send your children to school, we keep ours at home. Yours can ramble unattended, from field to field, and from house to house, ours are cooped up in their own enclosure, and beyond the limits of that they never are permitted to go unattended by a parent. Every week or day yours are conversant with society, with the exception of Mr. Bishop's family, all the friends with whom ours exchange thoughts, are scattered over the [Hawaiian] Islands at different distances, from sixteen to two hundred miles. Yours go to the sanctuary for instruction, ours, when they repair thither, listen to language which we do not wish them to learn, and which is to them unintelligible. It is as much my regular work to select suitable and interesting pieces for them to read while there, as it is for their father to prepare a sermon for the people. I often think of the delight which my own daughters would experience could they associate in labors of love with kindred helpers. But their situation is isolated. Last week they took leave of the only remaining daughter of the mission of corresponding age, who removes with her parents to their native land. They felt the separation very deeply. So did their mother. Yet they are happy in remaining in this land. They know not a better. They love their homes, their books, their friends, the climate, and they love to have their parents teach the natives. We lately received a visit from a very intelligent sea captain. He remarked, "*I am a great friend to missionaries, and their cause, but I do not think it right to have families here. I told my mate that I would assist men in coming out, but I never would give ladies a passage on my ship. I would do everything in my power to assist them back again, and to remove children, I would give up my own berth and sleep on deck. It seems to me Mr. Thurston that you should be relieved, after having been here so many years, and your children so large, by going home and staying a few years. It would be of great importance to them.*" I smiled at his freedom, and loved him for his sympathy. Mr. Thurston answered him by saying, that in such circumstances, a missionary needed a family in order to support his character, and that women were as willing to come as men were. "*I know,*" he said, "*they are willing to come, but children are the sufferers.*" After he retired one remarked, "*If he thinks the way is for men only to come out, he had better go himself and commence a new station and then he will know what it is to live alone in such circumstances.*" He felt for the children of missionaries, and well he might, for there is not a class of children upon the face of our earth, who are the offspring of Christian parents, for whom my sympathies have been so much moved. When all the host of God's elect comes up as one man to the great work of evangelizing the natives, and they become enlightened and ready to sustain measures, which the American Board, from their superior knowledge, would probably even now approve, then will a greater latitude be allowed to those who go forth to fight the Lord's battles in the camp of the enemies than was ever thought of in former years. We received letters from our missionaries at the Marquesas the other day. Their situation there is quite unlike what ours is now at the Sandwich Islands. But it reminds me of other years. Mrs. Armstrong writes that she would as soon trust herself in the mouth of a lion, as out of the house alone. We, who have seen society in its heathen state, can better form an idea of the import of that expression, and better realize the dangers with which she is surrounded. Let all remember those thus situated in the dark places of the earth. **ARTICLE 70** (To Reverend Goodell and Mrs. Goodell, Constantinople, Turkey) *Kailua-Kona, October 24, 1834. Dear Cousins, William and Abigail [Perkins Davis Goodell]*, last June when we went down to Oahu to the General Meeting of the Missionaries, we repaired immediately to Mr. Bingham's. His family was soon collected in the parlor, and it was at once suggested to our minds that the presence of Mr. and Mrs. Whitney was alone—wanting to make out all that remained of the pioneers of our mission. Being in a neighboring house, they were soon called in. There were no children by their side. They, four in number, were far separated from their parents and from each other. Mr. and Mrs. Bingham appeared with two little children. Two had been sent home, and two they had laid in their graves. Ourselves—with our four children—alone appeared an unbroken family. Mr. Whitney remarked that his heart never came so near breaking as when he sent away his last child. But he said, "*If I had not sent away my children, 1835 would not find me at the Sandwich Islands.*" It was after learning distressing intelligence from abroad that Mr. Thurston said to me, "*You must take our children and go home with them.*" I answered, "*It is recorded in the minutes of the General Meeting that twenty years is as long a service in this climate as can be expected of any one missionary. Such a term would carry our two oldest daughters up to the age of sixteen and eighteen, and our son to twelve. In our situation, with our regulations, I am willing to sustain maternal responsibilities in this land so long, but no longer. Let us perform our measure of service within that period, and then all go home together.*" This was entering upon a new subject never before alluded to during the struggles of fourteen years. But, thought I, how will such sounds fall on the ears of our associates, destitute as we are of any such passports as the dyspepsia, liver complaint, etc. However, I suggested the plan to Mr. Bishop, our associate, and was a little surprised, a few days after, to hear him say it was a measure which he cordially approved. As opportunity occurred I conversed with Mrs. Richards on the subject. She thought that retaining a child in this land for a period of eighteen years was incurring too great a risk. Yet, she said, "*Our young missionaries are not prepared to listen to your suggestion, you had better not name it to them.*" Several months after, coming in contact with one of our young members, I was interrogated respecting the future prospects of our children, with an interest and sympathy, which will ever endear her to my heart. To the inquiry, "*Can you see your way through?*" I replied, "*I have dared to say, that if the God of nature upholds me during a period of six more years, I shall then hold myself in readiness to quit the country, yet it does not depend on us, but upon our associates and patrons.*" The answer was, "*No one on either side of the ocean can object to such a measure.*" There the subject rests, and my heart is at rest. For the present, I only wish to stand in my lot, and do my appointed work. At our last General Meeting, no less than forty-seven children of our mission were brought together. The missionaries daily assembled in a retired schoolhouse, near the Mission Houses, so that the children were allowed at any hour to repair thither. I often attended, and was sometimes amused to see the scene which was spread out before us. One father with a child on his knee—another with one slumbering at his feet, a third walking to and fro at the vacant end of the house—leading a little one by the hand. Here a boy by his father's side, making dogs and horses not to be distinguished there a group formed, trying their skill in drawing geometrical diagrams, or perhaps braiding rushes, while at a little distance others would be engaged with a book, or plying their needles. In this way I have seen twenty children dispersed through the house, while their fathers were engaged in their sage discussions. Mrs. Judson assigns as a reason why a missionary should have a wife, because she "*presumes Mrs. Marshman does more good in her school, than one half the ministers in America.*" I do not know as to that, but in our situation, I approve the motto, that "*The missionary best serves his generation who serves the public—and his wife best serves her generation who serves her family.*" Until about two years ago, I uniformly attended church every Sabbath when my health permitted, always taking all the children with me, even down to babyhood. But as they were in the same predicament as the poor unlettered hearers of Jesuits, whose devotions were performed in Latin, they took their English books with them. So, while the minister preached, they read. However, as our oldest daughter increased in years, the practice of walking half a mile beneath a tropical sun, and then being seated in a crowded assembly, for the sake of being within sounds, which she could neither understand, nor was allowed to utter, became exceedingly irksome, and many a time has she returned home in tears, saying, "*Mama, what do I go to church for?*" To require her statedly to thus attend, when likely to imprint on her mind indelible impressions of pain, connected with the day of God, and the house of prayer, appeared to me the greatest trial attending a continued residence in this land of exile. I proposed an alternative, that of staying at home and having the hour dedicated to religious instruction in our own language. The children acquiesced readily in this. So did their father. I explained the matter to the natives at a Friday Female Meeting. The purport of my remarks was as follows, "*You see how it is at Keauhou and at Kekaha Kai. They have no teacher. Every Sabbath Mr. Thurston or Mr. Bishop goes and teaches them. We think it right for them to leave their places in the church so that they may go and instruct the destitute. There are others in Kailua-Kona who are destitute, who shall instruct them? They are the children of your teacher. Their young friends and relatives in America write and tell them of their meetings and of their schools. On the Sabbath they are blessed with privileges. Mr. Bingham's oldest daughter, and Mr. Ruggles's oldest daughter, and Mr. Whitney's three oldest children have all been sent away to enjoy the advantages of that good land. Our children remain in an isolated state. They go to the church, but there is no instruction for them in that place. They return home and weep, for though they see their own father in the sanctuary—he speaks not to them—his voice never reaches their hearts. For your sakes it is, that he labors, for your sakes it is, that his children are alone, cut off from kindred and country. Yet they love to have it so. They love to dwell among you, and to have their parents teach you. One thing only they ask and they ask it with tears. Let the return of the Sabbath bring privileges to us—let us attend on instruction in our own language. In consideration of these feelings, and of their destitute and exiled state, I have thought fit, while their father is devoted to you, to be myself devoted to then. The same bell which calls you to the church—assembles them at their own home, to be taught the worship and will of their Maker. And you, mothers, when you see me feel the importance of making such provisions for my children, if you follow my example, you will every Sabbath lead yours to your place of worship and instruction. In this respect, as you know what I do, 'go and do likewise.'* " When I thus presented the subject to their minds, they wept, and with much good sense and good feeling said, "*Yes, it is right. You take care of your children, but we do not take care of ours.*" Now, I do not believe that the people of Kailua-Kona any more feel that they may stay at home because I stay to teach the children, than that they may stay at home because Mr. Thurston's place is empty when he goes to teach the people at Keauhou. Nor do I believe, in my situation, that to go and sit in the church, as the people of God sit, is a service any more acceptable to the Good Shepherd, than to stay away and "feed his lambs." I however have my appointed season for meeting a Bible class, and an arithmetical school, at which times Mr. Thurston not only stands sentinel, but improves the opportunity by teaching the children sacred music. He walked in one day after dinner, with his singing book under his arm, and from that time to this, has been both persevering and successful in his instructions. We style him, too, our "Professor in the Latin Language," and have it regularly served up at the conclusion of every meal. This forms one of our most pleasant exercises, as with the exception of the baby, our whole family circle is included. I joined in for the sake of relieving their father as much as possible, and besides that, I could be companionable, and in this manner attach the children to their home, to their studies, to their parents—turning it all to the formation of their characters. Their other studies are under my direction, such as grammar, geography, history, arithmetic, philosophy, etc. I have adopted many methods of management by way of conducting our family school, but in nothing have I succeeded so well as with the clock and bell. At eight in the morning the bell rings, which brings us all to our assigned seats.—The first half hour in silence and application, when the bell gives a signal for release.—We then all engage in active employments, performing the various duties which go to promote the comfort and happiness of the family. The bell rings at nine. All learn punctuality by repairing at once to their seats, and to their studies. Half past nine, the tinkling of the bell is heard, and whoever wishes may be released. Thus we pass most of the day by regular half hour diversions. It saves from indolence and yawning beneath a tropic sun, gives an impulse in circumstances where there is nothing to stimulate, and to system adds interest and industry. In this way, too, they are so under the direction of the clock, that in case of my absence, lessons are not interrupted. Were our oldest children sons, I would by no means retain them here till they were far advanced in their teens, no longer, indeed, than would be suitable to place them under the same regulations as daughters, within a mother's province. Our associates tell me, "*It is because your children are girls that you can keep them within prescribed limits. You will never be able to do so with a boy.*" My reply is, "*On no other conditions will I retain one in this land.*" Our son, as yet, though possessed of all the feelings of the boy, and a share of his grandfather's energy, is happy within his mother's realm. I do not, however, with uplifted hands exclaim, "*What! A devoted missionary furnish amusements for his children!*" Our home affords no recreation at once so happy and so healthful as that of bathing in the waters of the ocean, with a high sea, and a spring tide. In order to the enjoyment of this, the children and I form a party, and repair half a mile to the seashore, having a couple of natives in the rear to carry accommodations, such as a tent, changes of raiment, etc. Mr. Thurston compares us to a caravan on the plains of Shinar (Babylonia). A wooden house, sent out to Mr. Charles Samuel Stewart by his friends—which reached here (Hawaii) after he had returned to the United States—was by the mission sent to Mr. Thurston. It is placed in our large retired yard of three acres, and is especially devoted to the accommodation of our children. It has been to me like a "great rock in a weary land." *Your affectionate cousin, Lucy G. Thurston.* **ARTICLE 71** (To Mrs. Coan, Hilo, Hawaii) *Kailua-Kona, August 6, 1835.* Dear Mrs. [Fidelia Church] Coan, we remained at Honolulu just one fortnight after your departure, and then bade them an affectionate adieu. We passed by Lahaina, where we spent two days, visited the grave of that dear child, Mary Clarke, bade a last farewell to Dr. [Alonzo] and Mrs. [Mary Ann Tenney] Chapin, received into our arms the newborn babe of Mrs. [Rebecca Howard] Hitchcock, ushered into life a few hours after our arrival. Such is life, and such its passing scenes. Six days from Oahu brought us in peace to our own habitation. O, home, sweet home! None of the children were propounded to become members of the Mission Church before leaving Honolulu. It seemed not to meet the feelings of Mr. Richards, so far as his were concerned, nor of Mr. Thurston, so far as his were concerned. They thought that should they prove promising candidates for church membership, they could be both propounded and received at the next General Meeting. When my heart is too cold to feel the emotions of gratitude for common mercies, I can thank my heavenly Father for giving us friends, who with so much interest and condescension take our children by the hand, and help to give such an impress to their characters, as will fit them for both worlds. The Savior rewards every such effort a thousand fold. *Yours affectionately, Lucy G. Thurston.*

ARTICLE 72 (To Mrs. Isabella Homes, Boston, Massachusetts) *Kailua-Kona, October 28, 1835. Dear Mrs. Homes,* sixteen eventful years have run their round since that interesting period, in which we threw a die, which can be equaled only by that which is thrown for eternity. Oft as the mind reverts to those scenes, your home and its hospitalities ever come up with vivid interest before the mind. Since that period new relations have arisen in our family, father and mother, son and daughter, brother and sister. We behold ourselves multiplied to six, a number still unbroken, either by death or separation. A gentleman, who visited us from Boston, told me that a lady from that place wished him to ascertain whether the missionaries kept servants in their families. She had heard so by way of a young lady who had visited the Islands, but "could hardly believe it." In our own house we have the various classes of master and mistress, of children, and of household natives. There is a native family attached to our establishment, whose home is a distinct house in our common yard. They give us their services. One man simply cultivates taro, two miles up the country, and weekly brings down a supply of the staff of life for ourselves and our dependants. Another man every week goes up the mountain to do our washing. Frequently he finds water within two miles. Often he is obliged to go five, sometimes ten miles. He likewise brings fresh water for the daily use of our family, from like distances—brings it (over the rugged way, overspread with lava) in large gourd shells suspended at the two ends of a strong stick, the heavy weight resting upon his shoulder. In like manner a third man brings brackish (unsanitary) water from a distance of half a mile, to be used in household purposes. He, too, is master of the cookhouse, a thatched roof, with the bare ground for the feet, with simple stones laid up in the middle for a fire place. No chimney, no oven, no cooking stove. But there are the facilities of a baking kettle, a frying pan, a pot, and a saucepan. He, who under the old dispensation, officiated as priest to one of their gods, now, under a new dispensation with commendable humility, officiates as cook to a priest and his family. Then, aid in the care of the house, of sewing, and of babyhood, devolves on female hands. We commenced mission life with other ideas. Native youth resided in our families, and so far as was consistent, we granted them all the privileges of companions and of children. Not many years rolled on, and our eyes were opened to behold the moral pollution which, unchecked, had here been accumulated for ages. I saw, but it was parental responsibilities which made me so emphatically feel the horrors of a heathen land. I had it ever in my heart the shafts of sin flying from every direction are liable to pierce the vitals of my children. It was in these circumstances that I met with an account of the celebrated Mrs. Fry's first visiting the wretched inhabitants of a prison. The jailer—after vainly endeavoring to dissuade her from a step so perilous said, "*At least leave your watch behind.*" Mrs. Fry left for a few hours her well ordered home. But had she taken her children with her, and there patiently set down to the formation of their characters, beneath the influence of prison inmates, she might have found in her path some such trials as fall to a mother's lot in the early years of a mission. In looking at my own situation, no comparison seemed to my mind as just and vivid, as the necessity of walking unhurt, in the midst of red-hot plough-shares. Here it was that I found myself soiled with the filth of the slough of despond. I reviewed the ground on which I stood. The heathen world was to be converted. But by what means? Are missionaries with their eyes open to the dangers of their situation, to sit conscientiously down to the labor of bringing back a revolted race to the service of

Jehovah, and in so doing practically give over their own children to Satan? If children must be sacrificed, better a thousand times leave ignorant mortals to do it, than for us who know our Lord's will. In investigating this subject in the heart of a heathen land, I could see no alternative but that a mother go to work, and here form a moral atmosphere in which her children can live and move without inhaling the infection of moral death. As Jews can educate children to be Jews among Gentiles, and Roman Catholics can educate children to be Roman Catholics among Protestants, so let Christian parents educate children to be Christians among the Heathen. Some decisive steps must be taken or the appalling vices of the heathen will become inwrought in the very texture of our children's characters. The first important measure was to prohibit them altogether the use of the Hawaiian language, thus cutting off all intercourse between them and the heathen. This, of course, led to the family regulation, that no child might speak to a native, and no native might speak to a child, babyhood excepted. This led to another arrangement, that of having separate rooms and yards for children, and separate rooms and yards for natives. The reason of this separation, and this non-intercourse was distinctly stated to household natives, and to native visitors. We are willing to come and live among you, that you may be taught the good way, but it would break our hearts to see our children rise up and be like the children of Hawaii, and they will be no better if exposed to the same influences. The heathen could see that it was such evidence of parental faithfulness and love, as was not known among them, and looked on with interest and amazement to see how it was that children could be trained to habits of obedience, a thing they never heard of. But if I wished to make trial, they would not be in the way. Indeed, they would like to see the experiment tried. I have often seen them shed tears while contrasting our children with their own degenerate offspring. When in the dining room and kitchen, attended by my children, nothing was uttered in the Hawaiian language but by way of giving or receiving directions in the most concise terms. When the hour for instruction came, and

I left my children behind me, I could sit down with the same circle and the restraint was removed. Thus they learned that in the presence of my children I was the mother, and that when alone in their own presence, I was the companion and the teacher. Thus they were situated, attached to our household, but excluded the privileges of children. To me, it appeared no more in the light of affecting ease and style, than does the conduct of Elijah, fleeing from the anger of Ahab, to be fed twice a day by unclean birds. I had experienced the debilitating effects of this long summer, commenced in 1820. I had felt disease so invade my frame as for years to render domestic aid essential to my very existence. During this season of adversity, far away from the comforts and aid of civilized man, far from that medical skill which visits the couch of suffering humanity to alleviate distress, and to raise from debility, my reliance was my husband. The responsible office of the physician, the tender duties of the nurse, and the menial services of the kitchen, have all been his. But how can an individual give efficiency to public labors, when from hour to hour, from day to day, from week to week, and from year to year, his attention is divided between the cookroom and the nursery. In these helpless circumstances I have been thankful for the imperfect services of natives, even though their entrance into our family caused apprehensions and mental sufferings, which have often excited reflections like this. Crucifixion is the torture of days.—These maternal anxieties which hourly prey upon the heart and produce so many sleepless nights is the anguish of years.—But why do I dwell on conflicts, when I am allowed to sing of victory. Our two oldest children opened their eyes when thick darkness was still brooding over this polluted land. Without being left to stumble on the dark mountains, they have been borne along the tide of life, till at the age of twelve and thirteen years, they came to the same fountain for cleansing as is opened for the poor natives to wash in. So well-established are their Christian habits and principles, that we have, of late, allowed them free access to all our Hawaiian [language] books, and to listen to preaching, besides to each, a class of little girls, whom they every day meet for instruction under school regulations. But the restriction of non-intercourse among the natives is not removed as yet. Dear Mrs. Bishop, who was laid in her grave six weeks before the arrival of the reinforcement, longed exceedingly to see and give them a charge from her sick couch. The purport of it was this, "*Do not be devoted to domestic duties. Trust to natives, however imperfect their services, and preserve your constitutions.*" I needed no such warning, for I had learned the lesson by my own sad experience, and when, after years of prostration, I was again permitted to enjoy comfortable health, I availed myself of the aid of natives for the accomplishment of such domestic services as they were capable of rendering. I found that the duties of the housekeeper, of the mother, of the teacher of our children, of day schools and weekly meetings, among the natives, often drew me down to the couch. For as one of our physicians told me, "*You may as well talk of perpetual motion, as to think of performing as much labor here as you could have done by remaining in America.*" I have spoken simply of our own domestic arrangement, but all our mission families are regulated much on the same plan, and were our patrons, or our husbands, now to say, "*Look to New England for examples, there ladies of intelligence and refinement, holding superior stations in life, often sustain, unaided, the labors of their own families—go thou and do likewise*"—it would be one of the most effectual means that could be taken to send the sisters of this mission, either down to their graves, or home to America. As to the effects produced upon natives thus employed in our families, they have more intelligence, more of the good things of this life, more influence among their fellows than they could otherwise possess, and numbers of them, I doubt not, will be added to that great company, which no man can number, redeemed out of every kindred, and tongue, and people, and nation. This letter far exceeds the limits I prescribed (assigned) to myself when taking the pen. But knowing that heavy oars are plied on that side of the waters for the benefit of those who are here your servants for Christ's sake, I thought good to spread before you our situation and principles of action. *Yours affectionately, Lucy G. Thurston.* **ARTICLE 73** (To Mrs. Judd) *Kailua-Kona, December 25, 1835. Dear Mrs. [Laura Fish] Judd,* the scenes of last General Meeting have caused many pleasant associations to stand connected in my mind with you and the young plants rising up beneath your care. The intelligence that twins had been added to your family, awakened new interest. It touched a chord in my heart which vibrated with emotion. For thus it was that I commenced my being, thus it was that I was cradled in my mother's arms. Eight summer suns beheld us twin sisters closely walking hand in hand the pathway of life. How sweet those early memories! Then together we descended to the very verge of the grave. There we separated. Lydia's character had become perfected for another state of existence, and Lucy was raised for a then unthought-of destiny. **ARTICLE 74** (To Mrs. Judd) *Kailua-Kona, November 14, 1836. Dear Mrs. Judd,* I guessed that you understood what poor human nature was, and that you thought that by this time I might be in want of what Solomon says, is as good as a medicine. Be that as it may, the reception of your letter, which found us in a temperate region, caused an immediate rise of ten degrees in the elasticity of our spirits. As to picking up a pen when the governor's schooner was bound straight to Hilo—had I done so it would not have been to have written the name of Judd, for I did not think you would have been there. But on that day, after attending to my family school and nursery, after acting as superintendent to a native school of one hundred and eighty, making out two notes on business, and putting up oranges for five stations, I was satisfied with paying my respects to such only as presented themselves before me in person, and this I had the opportunity of doing by the arrival of Mr. [Cochran] Forbes and [his] family. This apology has opened a loophole through which you can peep and obtain one glimpse of us, situated alone on these shores of Hawaii. We have, since General Meeting, had none other than favorable gales (strong winds), and we are now under full sail, going at the rate of ten knots an hour, but I know not how soon we shall find ourselves in the Gulf Stream. Baby thrives, and is quite an important personage among us, being the substitute of the Reverend Bishop and family, who have removed to Ewa. *Affectionately yours, Lucy G. Thurston.* **ARTICLE 75** (To Miss Elizabeth Goodale) *Kailua-Kona, November 15, 1836. My Dear Niece*, tell your dear mother that I was better pleased with the intelligence of her being a member of a Sabbath school than of anything I have heard respecting her since leaving America. Tell her, too, that I learn a Bible lesson every week to recite in English. My own children are my classmates. By giving Mr. [Asa] Thurston the class book, we contrive to form one united family circle. Thus we are engaged every Sabbath night at sunset, the usual time for evening family worship. When Saturday comes round I attend to another Sabbath school lesson in Hawaiian. Instead of being there a scholar to recite with scholars, I am a teacher to instruct teachers—some thirty of them, who are employed in our Sabbath school. We have now no associate at our station, Mr. [Artemas] and Mrs. [Delia Stone] Bishop having removed to Ewa, on Oahu, in consequence of Mrs. Bishop's impaired health. The arrangement will probably be permanent. We have a neighbor on one side of us, Mr. Forbes, by water distant sixteen miles, and on the other side, Mr. [Lorenzo] Lyons, within thirty miles. At the last General Meeting the ladies of the Mission formed themselves into a Maternal Association. Their meetings became frequent and very interesting. At the various stations the ladies have formed similar associations among the natives, reports from which are to be brought in at every yearly meeting. Situated in such solitary circumstances, I find much comfort and aid from our two oldest children. The older of these is now fifteen, and their scholars about their own ages, yet they look up to their young teachers with as much deference as they do to me. The future destiny of our children I know not. We have never yet seen the time, when we could thrust them from those guardians which are theirs by nature. We are daily expecting a letter from Dr. Anderson which I hope will throw some light on our path. I always hold it up before the children that in three years, that is, when the oldest is eighteen, they must go to the land of their fathers. I find it necessary to do this as a stimulus to effort beneath this tropic sun, where there is so much that is indolent and uncivilized to meet the eye. Nine children of the mission will probably be sent away in a few weeks. With the exception of our own family, no daughter in the mission will be left upward of seven years of age. When we sailed for Honolulu to attend the last General Meeting, and were not yet out of sight of our own shores, we looked back and saw the flames ascending to the Heavens. We had little doubt but one of our dwelling houses was laid in ashes, but in two or three weeks after, we learned that it was our church—the work of an incendiary not yet discovered. It was said by a white man then on the spot, that there had never been such mourning among the people since the death of Kamehameha. It however, only hastened the work of starting a permanent stone building, which is now nearly completed. The belfry, spire and vane, give quite an American look to our village. *Your affectionate aunt, Lucy G. Thurston.* **ARTICLE 76** (Epistle of the Thurstons to the Honoluluans) *April, 1837.* Lucy with Tatina (Asa Thurston) her husband, and all the children that are with us, to all that be, in Honolulu called to be saints. As we trust shortly to be given you through your prayers, even at the approaching convocation, we thought good to write unto you in order, that withal ye prepare us also a lodging place. And as it was made a statute and an ordinance for Israel, that as his part was, that went down to the battle, so should his part be that tarried by the stuff, they should share alike, even so we pray, that the end of a campaign, performed single-handed, may introduce us to the full communion and fellowship of those who remain by the stuff, to the full enjoyment of social privileges, to be comforted together with you, with those consolations, with which you also abound. Salute Rebecca and her household. They of Hawaii salute you. Grace be with you all, Amen. Written to the Honoluluans from Kailua-Kona, and sent by Kuakini, servant of the church. **ARTICLE 77** (To Mrs. Coan, Hilo) *Kailua-Kona, September 25, 1837. Dear Mrs.* [Fidelia] *Coan,* Dr. [Lorrin] Andrews has just sent up a note, saying, that an opportunity offers of sending to Hilo by the way of

Waimea (Big Island), and as I have a caution to press upon you, I immediately turn to my pen. It is this, take care of your health. I hear the same story this year that I did the last, that your duties through the day made you too weary to rest at night. That is enough of itself for one who has been in the post of observation for seventeen years, to raise the warning voice. There are emergencies when people are called upon to show their devotion to the cause which they have espoused, by adventuring with life in their hands. Not so in prosperous circumstances, performing the daily routine of common duties—I do most fully believe that it is the will of our Lord that we take care of flesh and blood, of bones and sinews, these forming the grand, the only instrument with which we are to serve our generation. If it is an instrument with which we are to serve, then let it be a servant. But let us give it such rest as will best secure prolonged and energetic action. Tell our young missionary ladies, that to live a holy life is one thing, and to sap one's constitution in the ardor of youthful feelings is quite another. I watch over these young plants with something of maternal feelings. *Yours affectionately, Lucy G. Thurston.* **ARTICLE 78** (To Mrs. Mary Parkhurst, Massachusetts) *Kailua-Kona, February, 1839. Dear Niece*, Dr. Andrews and wife, myself and children have all just returned from spending a week at Kealakekua, in the family of Mr. Forbes, sixteen miles from this. Mr. Thurston conducted us thither and returned. I had not before, since my illness, been beyond the precincts of our village, notwithstanding it had been so strongly recommended. The doctor was rising from sickness, having twice had the run of a fever. We went and returned in a double canoe. We all spent one day and night with Kapiolani, whose residence was two miles from Mr. [Cochran] Forbes, back in the country. I was delighted with the air of civilized and cultivated life, which pervaded her dwelling. She had a stone house, consisting of three lower, and three upper rooms. Several of the rooms were carpeted with very fine mats, and curtained. Three high post bedsteads were hung with valances (drapery) and mosquito curtains. Three Chinese settees (couch or sofa), handsomely trimmed, were placed one in each of the lower rooms. The house was furnished with a writing desk, tables, chairs, looking glasses, and etc. A table was spread, covered with a white damask table cloth. Tea was served up with a waiter.—China cups and saucers, and silver tea spoons.—Then she had soup served out with a silver ladle on soup plates, and boiled fowls, baked pig, with various kinds of vegetables, as squash, potatoes, kalo (taro), breadfruit, and radishes, on dining plates. Then there was the domestic altar, the Holy Book, the sacred hymns and reverential (adoration) prayer. Thus were we entertained at the house of a Sandwich Islander. *Lucy G. Thurston.* **ARTICLE 79** (To the General Meeting of the Sandwich Island Mission) *Kailua-Kona, April 6, 1839. Brethren*, it was when maternal cares first pressed upon my heart, that I was made sensible of the dangers of that sea on which I had embarked. The cable that confined my bark was cut, and no idea existed in my mind of again reaching my native land. Thus launched, sustaining such responsibilities, I beheld my situation upon the very verge of the outer circles of a maelstrom. But firmly believing that God helps those who help themselves, I learned, as it were, while with one hand I wrought, with the other to stem the tide. Thus was I sustained day by day, during the first fourteen years of missionary life, without any star of future promise to guide me to the port of safety. Then new and appalling intelligence from abroad moved Mr. Thurston to say to me, "*You must take our children and go home with them.*" I answered, "*It is recorded in the minutes of our General Meeting that twenty years is as long a service in this climate as can be expected of any one missionary. In our situation, with our regulations, I am willing to sustain maternal responsibilities in this land so long, but no longer. Let us perform our measure of service within that period, and then all go home together.*" For nearly five years this is as the subject has existed in our minds. Mr. Thurston has harped upon the string of sending home mother and children, while I have been buoyed up with the hope that he would accompany us. But the nineteenth year of missionary life seemed to call upon me to look at my prospects and prepare for changes. But what was duty? Abram, in leaving his country, and offering up his son Isaac, had a plain command by which to walk. But from *Genesis* to *Revelations* I found no one to meet my case, On first opening the Bible, we read that a man shall leave his father and his mother, but we look in vain to the only sure guide of faith and practice, to find, either by precept or example, that he is forever to leave his own offspring. This sentiment of modern days seems to be introduced to meet the wants of our world, probably destined to flourish only while the science of Missions is in its infancy. When Moses became a public character in the land of Egypt, we find that his wife was left behind in the land of Midian with his children. Hannah, the only example of the kind in Holy Writ, either in the Old Testament or New left her son Samuel at the tabernacle under the care of the High Priest, and returned fifteen miles to her own home. The three great Jewish feasts, required husband to visit the spot three times a year. Moreover his mother made him a little coat and brought it to him from year to year, when she came up with her husband to offer the yearly sacrifice, where, with her own eyes she could behold her own son ministering before the Lord, girded with a linen ephod. The command, *"Go ye into all the world and preach the gospel to every creature,"* is drawn from the same source as the prediction, *"Many shall run to and fro, and knowledge shall be greatly increased."* In turning to view the human family in the 19th century, among the heterogeneous mass which went to people our earth, I behold three distinct classes of children, laboring under a system of measures which tend to deprive them of both their natural guardians. I allude to the traffic of African blood, the burning of Hindu widows—and the exile of missionaries from their country for life. To be myself drawn into such circumstances, to be instrumental in giving birth to immortal natures, and then myself exercise an agency to thrust them from me, perhaps to be crushed, perhaps from their unprotected state to be led into temptations and sin, was more trying to my feelings, than sustaining maternal duties in the very heart of a heathen land, when gross darkness was upon the people—a darkness that could be felt. When at the inexperienced age of twenty-four, I was called to decide upon the important question of quitting my native country for a heathen land, my father and all my friends referred the matter entirely to myself. Without advice, without influence, I alone sustained the responsibility. At the more experienced age of forty-three another question of equal moment came up before me. But independence of action was no longer mine. A long array of "powers that be," rose up before me. Husband—associates—the Prudential Committee [with] the American Board—and the Christian Public. In such circumstances, not communicating my trials to mortal ear, not aware of my danger, and not taking heed to my steps, I found myself in the Slough of Despond. By efforts too much for human nature, I extricated myself, and reached the side opposite my own house. It was on the 27th of August, 1838, that I made the surrender of laying my children on the altar. Then I resolved to take my proper place, to remember that I was a daughter of Eve, a wife of a minister of Jesus Christ, of a missionary to the heathen. I resolved to be led and guided like a little child, by those who managed the affairs of Christ's kingdom, even though I alone was called to wander to a far off land, there to be deprived of those in whom my strength lieth, and to return with the weakness of a Samson shorn of his locks. The result was such as might be expected. Like a poor Christian, I lost my burden. But what excited my astonishment was I could no longer say I am weary. The distress of my mind and the pains of my body had taken flight together. For three days there was an unnatural degree of rest, repose and languor, when I experienced an attack of paralysis on the right side, so very slight, at first, as not to interrupt my usual routine of duties. It continued to increase daily, and precisely one fortnight from the night that I formed my purpose of action, I was extended on my bed, encircled by friends, commending, for the first time, my children in their coming orphanage to the guardianship of Mrs. [Mary Wilson] Andrews. During the following week, my life was despaired of from one day to another, and at periods, from one hour to another. My head was so disordered that eight weeks passed away before I was once removed from that sick bed on which I had been laid, during which time I was fed with a teaspoon like an infant. But although cast down, I was not destroyed. He, who knoweth our frame, and remembereth that we are but dust, said to the destroying angel, "*It is enough.*" That I live, again to act my part in the theatre of life, possessing the use of my limbs and mental faculties, is the Lord's doings and marvelous in our eyes, But I am not in the possession of equal powers, either of body or mind as formerly. Besides a sense of weight, on my right side from head to foot, hourly reminds me of what I have been, of what I may again be. But although deep has called unto deep, and all God's waves and billows have rolled over me, it has only fixed the steadfast purpose of my soul, to let others lead, and while I follow, accepting of trials and sacrifices as my portion, not counting even my life dear unto myself. And now, after a campaign of twenty years, it is our desire to have the privilege of providing for our own house also. By the Prudential Committee we are referred for direction to this Body. Now our waiting eyes are turned to you. Were I allowed to speak my feelings, my petition and my request is, if it please this Mission, and we have found favor in their sight, and if the thing seem right in their eyes, that they permit me to conduct my children across the ocean to the land which is theirs by birthright, to a land of industry, of civilization, and of Christian institutions. If it is made a question whether the husband and the father accompany us or not, you and he, will, of course, decide according as the finger of Divine Providence seems to your own minds to direct. *Lucy G. Thurston.*

ARTICLE 80 (To Mrs. P. P. Andrews, Hilo) *Kailua-Kona, July 25, 1839. Dear Mrs. Andrews*, last night, as the sun was sinking beneath the horizon, we set foot on the shores of Kailua-Kona, on our return from the General Meeting at Honolulu. But it was not necessary to come to these scenes, to be reminded often and tenderly of you. Short as has been the time since I saw you, I have seen some of the varieties of human life. Yesterday, in solitary circumstances on the schooner, we were accommodated upon the naked deck, eating from the poi dish with our fingers. But the other day, while at Kaneohe, we were seated at the table with twenty, where luxury and etiquette seemed to preside. At one time I had the apprehension of fleeing for life before the face of enemies. Yet another, watching, day and night, over the sick couch of my elder boy, while no tongue but gave utterance to the deep feelings of the heart, "*Is Asa a-going to die?*" Then we again found ourselves buffeting the rude surges of the ocean, in the same schooner which touched upon the rocks on the way down, and in which I extinguished fire in coming up, having no appendage of boat or canoe on board for any emergency. Then even the voyage had variety. The first part was exceedingly rough, the little children asking with tears, "*Will the vessel tip over?*" However, our native mariners had no such fears, and even if it did, they knew how to right it by cutting away the masts. The last part of the voyage was as calm as a summer's day, and served to remind me of the end of the voyage of life, after the conflicts and trials of the way. *Affectionately, Lucy G. Thurston.**

*What Lucy Thurston is referring to is known as the Laplace Affair (named after Captain Cyrille Laplace) or the French Incident. It seems protestant missionaries of which Thurston was a part of attempted to bar Catholics from establishing a foothold in the Hawaiian Islands. Under threat of war, Kamehameha III agreed to France's demands that Catholics be treated the same as protestant missionaries and pay reparations for the initial slight.

ARTICLE 81 (To Mrs. Coan, Hilo) *Kailua-Kona, January 9, 1840. Dear Sister Coan*, I rejoice once more in being able to address you. This I have ever intended to do before leaving the Islands, even if I could not take my pen before being on the way for Oahu. But since our excursion round the Island, my cares have been like wave behind wave, requiring head, and heart, and hands to buffet them. Our stay here has been unexpectedly prolonged. But I thank Him without whose cognizance not a sparrow falleth to the ground that we are still dwelling in the quietude of our own home. To make preparations for a voyage of twenty-four weeks, for a family of seven members, under the equator and around Cape Horn, in sickness and health, in touching perhaps at foreign ports, and in landing on our native shores, is not all. In ploughing the ocean's deceitful waves, I wish to feel that whatever betide—all will be well with me and mine. Jesus, too, is passing in our midst. What time so opportune to ask Him to lay his hands upon all my children, and to bless them. You were kind to speak a word in behalf of a child of unformed character, about to be sundered forever from both natural guardians. Under what influence is the scale to turn, which will fix that child's destiny in both worlds. Without calculating on probabilities, I am called to lay my children all as blanks into my heavenly Father's hands, to let him write upon them as seemeth good in his sight, and to hold myself in readiness, either to be used—or dashed as a potter's vessel. O, for that humility, for that submission, for that gratitude which becomes a dependent being. I beg you to tender my parting salutations of love to each of your kind associates. Peace, that peace which the world neither gives nor takes away, be with them and you. Brethren and sisters, pray for us. Farewell. *Affectionately yours, Lucy G. Thurston.* **ARTICLE 82** (To Mr. Armstrong, Honolulu) *Dear Brother [Richard],* since you have the kindness to allow me to spread before you my feelings, permit me to state, that the danger of the return of my former disease, the paralysis, may be rationally apprehended during my voyage to the United States. That in case of another attack, no other prospect would seem to be before me, than either a speedy dissolution, or being left to drag out existence, a wreck both in body and mind.—That the liability of its occurrence will depend much upon the quiet state of my own mind.—That there are two subjects which lie with oppressive weight upon my feeling, my children who go with me, and my husband who is left behind. That the sorrow and anxiety which I shall feel in view of leaving Mr. Thurston in such desolate circumstances, will be greatly augmented or lessened, in the consideration of whom he has for associates. His retiring habits, his dereliction of self, and a slight cough from which he has not been free for the past nine months, all lead me to wish to commend him to the watchful care and sympathy of known and tried friends. Therefore, my petition and my request is—if I have found favor and the thing seem right—let Dr. [Lorrin] and Mrs. [Mary Wilson] Andrews remain at Kailua-Kona. My prayer is now before you. Nothing remains for me, but to lay my hand upon my mouth, and prepare myself to say, whatever may be the result of the deep surge which is now passing over our family, Amen and Amen. *Yours in the kingdom and patience of Jesus Christ, Lucy G. Thurston.* **ARTICLE 83** (Our Children) The natives knew I had a systematic school for them in the sitting room in the house, situated in the retired yard, and they learned to obtain permission quietly to drop in and silently witness the novel scene. They could at once behold order and application, and though ignorant of the English language, they shrewdly judged that our children were prodigies of obedience compared with their own degenerate offspring. With them, could be seen at the end of their dwelling house a little urchin with a stone in his hand at open defiance against his father, crying out, *"You don't need to dodge, father, I am not a-going to throw yet."* While the natives have been observing my school, I have often and often seen the tears trickle down their cheeks. They were grieving that they had destroyed their own children on the threshold of life, and parental desires were awakened of having themselves sons and daughters thus molded. Whenever I walked abroad, or entered the church, every eye was turned upon them, bespeaking looks of astonishment and admiration. So that notwithstanding they had no intercourse with the people, they were emphatically public examples in a nation that had never before seen the effects of a Christian and civilized education. When our eldest daughters were twelve and fourteen years of age, their habits were so formed, and their principles so established, that we gave them permission to learn the native language from pure sources. They were instructed in it by their parents, allowed access to Hawaiian books, attended on their father's [Asa Thurston] ministry, became teachers in the Sabbath school, also in the day school, and each had a chamber in which she gathered her own Sabbath school class around her for religious exercises. They were allowed to come in contact with natives as teachers, under school regulations, but not as associates. They were very much revered, and exerted a powerful influence over the native mind. Thus it was that they cheerfully and devotedly labored for five years before they left the [Hawaiian] Islands. We stood alone in thus making the experiment of retaining children on heathen ground. At this time when the mission is in its twentieth year, more than forty missionary children have been conveyed away by parents that have retired from this field of labor. Eighteen have been scattered about in the fatherland [United States] without parents.

☐☐☐☐☐☐☐☐☐☐

Part Second—1841-1869. **ARTICLE 1** (Safe Arrival in New York and Death of a Daughter) *February 20, 1841.* Accompanied by four children, I sailed from the Islands on the 3rd of last August, passed a fortnight at the Society Islands on our way, and arrived at New York six months from the time of our embarkation. At the Sandwich Islands I parted from him (Asa Thurston) who has been my stay and staff during my pilgrimage from my father's house. He stayed to feed the flock over whom he had been made overseer. I left to make provision for the education of our children. In crossing the ocean, and in my reception in this country, I have cause for the most unbounded gratitude to Him who has caused my pathway to be strewn with comforts. We have spent two weeks in the benevolent family of Mr. Benson, and are now entertained in the family of Mr. [Abijah Preston] Cummings, an editor of the *New York Observer.* I intended to leave next week for Boston and Marlborough, but my plans are frustrated by sickness. Lucy is confined to her bed with inflammation of the lungs, and is an object of care and solicitude. We have every attention and care which our situation demands. We are afflicted but not cast down. While God chastens with one hand, he supports with the other. *February 25.* In one week from the time Lucy felt the chill of a fever, she felt the chill of death. Day before yesterday I traveled with her down to the dark valley—no, not dark—all was light. Many precious words fell from her lips, and her feelings were characterized by sweet submission to the Divine will, and an unshaken reliance on the Savior. For many hours I reclined by her side upon her dying bed, till all was hushed and calm in death. Now I can say more than I ever could before. Four children on earth and one in Heaven! Mr. Ely, an elder in Dr. Spring's church, kindly permitted the remains of our loved one to be laid in his own family vault. On Monday, Lucy was pronounced out of danger, and I was strengthened with the hope of her living, until Wednesday morning, when it was announced that she would die. It was a very great shock to me, both in body and mind. All strength left me, and I felt like Belshazzar when his knees smote together. I retired and was alone with God. A simple thought passed through my mind. *"I will try to bear whatever is laid upon me."* The change in my feelings was as if I had received the touch of an angel. I was strong in body, strong in mind, equal to meet the emergency. I returned to my friends with composure and fortitude, which never for a moment forsook me in all the varied trying scenes through which I was called to pass. I was sustained, I was comforted. *March 9*. Since Lucy's funeral all the children have been prostrate. The remedies employed have been bleeding, cupping, leeching, blistering, purging, etc. One child has been so low with a complication of diseases, that every hope of life seemed cut off. Now, all are gaining health and activity. God has in a wonderful manner raised up friends. Mr. Cummings, wife and sister, have been most solicitous to promote our comfort and happiness, Indeed, the manner in which they, strangers, sought us out, and conducted us to their home, seems to me a distinguished Providence. **ARTICLE 2** (Advice to a Daughter) *New York, March 1, 1842. My Dear Daughter Persis*, in pursuing your education, next to taking care of your heart, take care of your constitution. On this subject I feel great anxiety. The better scholar you are the greater will be the danger of your taxing your powers too heavily. If your health allows, secure to yourself a thorough course without being diverted from your object. Pursue your studies without anxiety as respects pecuniary means. You know that, as long as your mother inhabits the same globe with you, in order to have this object accomplished, she will share with you the last dollar at her command. Ever keep me informed of your situation, feelings, prospects, progress, etc. After spending three or four years at the Seminary, a year devoted to teaching would be very improving to you. I cannot now advise you respecting your future course in life. You know my general views. Throw yourself unreservedly upon the guidance of your Heavenly Father, and watch the developments of his providence. In that far off land of your childhood and youth, you have still a father's home (Hawaiian Islands) and parents ever ready to welcome your return. After granting you that training and those privileges which will fit you for any desirable situation, in any part of the world, my work respecting you will be done, and I shall leave you free as air to choose your pathway in life. I know you will wish to serve your generation, to serve your Savior. I will not disguise it—life is replete with anxieties, perplexities, cares, toils, sufferings, and sorrows. Well, let them come. It is a state of probation and of discipline—and all things are so arranged by infinite wisdom—and benevolence that even we may become in a high degree possessors of the rich stores of quiet self-denial of holy fortitude, of cheerful resignation, and of Heaven-born benevolence. We will then travel on in the vale of mortality, in the depths of nothingness, if such be the will of our Lord, until from exalted heights we hear a seraphic voice saying, "*Come home to your rest.*" What your father said to me, let me repeat to you. "*Never let one murmuring thought arise in your mind as though your lot were a hard one.*" Thank God that he gave you birth in this 19th century of our Christian era, that you were early saved from unholy influences, and instructed in the principles of our holy religion, that you and your parents have a name among God's people—thank him that your sister is now before the throne, that yourself and brother are permitted to enjoy the rich literary and religious privileges of our American institutions—that the young members of your family are allowed the prospect of still enjoying privileges, and giving life and interest to the parental abode. O, thank Him for those light afflictions, which are but for a moment and which may work out for you a far more exceeding and eternal weight of glory. My own daughter, endeared to me by every consideration that can affect a mother's heart, in now bidding you farewell, my mind reverts to the hour when you were first laid in my bosom, when your father kneeled by the bedside, and with many tears consecrated you to the Savior. Since that memorable day, twenty years have run their round, always finding mother and daughter side by side. And can I give up my daughter, my firstborn, my might, and the beginning of my strength? None but He who knoweth the unutterable feelings of tenderness and love which I have felt for my child, knows the corresponding agony which the prospect of a separation has produced. And yet, when I three years ago lay upon an isthmus between time and eternity, balancing between two worlds—redemption, the great work of the soul's redemption, was opened to my mind with amazing vividness. Then I thought of the manner in which Mary of old expressed her love to the Savior with a box of costly ointment. I had an offering still more precious, such as would honor the deepest feelings of a mother's devotion. I could rejoice to express my love and gratitude to the Redeemer of the world by laying upon the altar in any manner most acceptable to Him, my two youthful daughters—my most precious treasures. Our own Lucy has since been called for in an unexpected way. But I know to whom I have consecrated her, and have found it one of the sweetest acts of my life to give her up to the gracious hands of Him, from whom I received her seventeen years before. May a sanctifying influence rest upon her memory—and life-giving breezes waft over her tomb. The revolution of one year has again brought us to the spot where Lucy took her upward flight—where two other children and my own country are about to recede from my view. While others are giving 25, 50 and 100 percent in addition to what they have before done, wine are offerings not to be estimated by dollars and cents. God loveth a cheerful giver. I thank my Savior that he first gave you to me, affording me the opportunity of giving you back to him. I give you to him to live, and toil, and suffer on earth, or to go and behold his glory in

Heaven. I give you to him who has all resources at his control, and whose wisdom and benevolence are infinite. But if he loves you with a wise love, and sees that you need purifying in order to reflect his own image, he will inflict discipline. He will cause thorns to spring up in your pathway. But do not stop to weep over the trials of this life. It is yours to accept them in such a way as will cause them to become your richest blessings. Lay then one hand upon your mouth, the other upon the head of the "sin offering" of our world, and, with humility, with holy love and joy and activity, pass through this wilderness world to your Father's home on high. There, beyond the conflicts of sin, I shall again behold what I am here called to resign. *O, gracious hour, O, blest abode, we shall be near and like our God, and flesh and sense no more control the rising pleasures of the soul.* My own daughter—child of my heart—[I bid] adieu. **ARTICLE 3** (A Letter to Two Cherished Children Presently in America) *Kailua-Kona, November 30, 1842. My Dear Son and Daughter*, we reached Kailua-Kona [on] October 24th, in safety, where we found your father alive—well—in prosperity—and in the possession of his accustomed (usual) cheerfulness. He was alone at the station, and had been so for three months. During these two years of solitude and trial, he has found solace in his labors. When we left him, his church consisted of six hundred members. When I returned, [it is] of eighteen hundred. He is much gratified with the situations and prospects of both his children in America. Now act well your part, and thus strengthen the hearts of your parents, and of your numerous friends here, who inquire after you with great interest. For two days and nights after my return to Kailua-Kona, I neither slept nor wept. I was raised above the conflicts of mortality. My being, seemed ethereal. I had reached the port of peace. I had reached my husband and my home. Natives crowd to see me by the hundred. They must all shake hands. My quiet schoolroom is now the public room for natives. We all sleep upstairs. When your father's study is completed, and things are adjusted, I will tell you how we are situated. This letter must go tonight, and I must stop, though I have sheets of intelligence to communicate. I pen this on my knees by my bedside, a position favorable to dispatch. So you must not wonder if it does not look like me. Good night. The same Eye that now sees me sees you, which affords consolation to the heart of your ever affectionate and sympathizing mother. **ARTICLE 4** (To a Missionary Sister) *Kailua-Kona, November, 1842.* Is it so that I am again at home, or am I dreaming? Letters from yourself and others, a visit from friends, the shaking hands with hundreds of natives, my own home and husband, would seem evidence enough to convince me of the reality—and yet I cannot realize it. Is it so that I am no longer upon the lap of the world, either meeting friends from whom I have been separated twenty years, or taking final leave of them, or experiencing first the unpleasantness of meeting strangers, and the pain of separating from them as friends? And the rattling and jolting, the puffing and screeching, the dashing and wetting, the whistling and howling, the running and shouting, the rocking and creaking, and groaning of stage car, steamboat and ship, of winds, waves, and mariners, are they exchanged for the purest pleasures that have survived the fall, the peace and tranquility of domestic life? Here I sit in my corner of the room, in my rocking chair, at my writing table, as I used to sit. The three other corners are vacant. But they speak silent volumes to me of those who once filled those seats, and sat at those tables. Yet in viewing these vacancies, no feeling of desolation or sorrow has given me shade of sadness. I rejoice that I have, in so high a degree, tasted the felicities of maternal love. I rejoice in the assurance that he has accepted the offering at my hands. You, too, know what it is to receive a gift, and to restore the same to the Giver.—A lamb of the first year without blemish.—What a precious offering! Thank the blessed Savior for the rich experience which such scenes of unutterable tenderness and sublimity bring with them. **ARTICLE 5** (To Mrs. M. M. Cummings, New York City) *Kailua-Kona, December 10, 1842.* I have written you once since I left America, but as there is a vessel lying at Honolulu, bound directly to New York, I cannot refrain from dropping you a line, dictated from my own home. It was on the 24th of October that I found rest in the house of a husband that my children found a father's hand and a father's home, added to a mother's care. The natives were overjoyed at my return. Those who had lived in our family knelt around me, and wept aloud, bathing my hands with their tears. For several weeks there was a continued series of calls, the kindhearted natives coming by schools and by districts to welcome my return. Of these, some burst out into a wail, but the more enlightened only wept. Some spoke of their joy, and some of God's long-suffering in permitting us to meet. Some spoke of the manner in which they had prayed for us in the social circle and in secret places, and some of their love to their teacher who left his family to dwell alone with them. Some spoke of the great turning of the natives to the Lord during my absence, and some named the scholars of my children, most of whom were now sisters in the church. Some spoke of the sad fate, and others of the blessedness of the departed Lucy. Some sympathized with our children left in America, bereaved, separated, and made orphans in that far off land of strangers. Those children, they said with tears, are our children. They were born and reared in our land. Great is our love for them. Now that I am once more established in my own home, I increasingly feel my obligations to make it an asylum for the invalid and the stranger. A voice from yonder distant shores seems to follow me, saying, *"Freely ye have received, freely give."* My three eldest children are all far, far away. But I have given them all to a God of infinite wisdom and benevolence. In so doing each contributes to the happiness of every waking hour of my life. There is Lucy's corner, her window, her table, her chair. There she sat, and studied, and wrote. Now, mortal has exchanged for immortality. In strains gentle and joyous she speaks from Heaven. What do I say? How shall I sufficiently praise God on earth, for connecting with our family, by natural bonds, an heir of glory? I gaze at her upward flight. It is, as it were, a golden chain, mooring our family within sight of the celestial city. O, for a heart to praise the Lord with every breath, and with childlike simplicity and confidence trust Him with all my concerns, serving and glorifying Him, just in the way he is pleased to direct. *Yours most* affectionately, Lucy G. Thurston. **ARTICLE 6** (A Meeting of Thanksgiving) *Kailua-Kona, November 9, 1845. My Dear Daughter Persis*, at the last General Meeting a fast was observed, quite at the commencement of the meeting. At the first exercise your father presided. Read the third chapter of first *John*—and you will see what he took for the foundations of his remarks. He trimmed as closely as ever you heard him trim anybody, and concluded by saying that he had been twenty-three years a member of this mission, during which time they must have heard of and seen him do many things contrary to this feeling of love. He made confession of his deficiencies and sins, and asked their forgiveness. Before the day was through, six other missionaries, each in turn were seen presenting themselves individually before the house making confession and asking forgiveness. A meeting thus commenced was concluded with thanksgiving. The brethren expressed themselves as I never before heard them, respecting that spirit of love, of tenderness, and of forbearance, which had been exhibited throughout the meeting. Your father was called upon to conclude the meeting. He commenced in strains of thanksgiving, was overcome by emotion, paused—only adding, with a faltering voice, "*In union may we be one, in heart and action one, then we shall be one with Thee in Heaven.*" **ARTICLE 7** (Strychnine Poisoning) *Kailua-Kona, April 3, 1850.* For a fortnight I had experienced multiplied ills. I had overcome all. Debility alone remained. A tonic, of all things, was what I most wanted. O, for some quinine! The doctor had pointed out a particular vial of it to your father for his own use. He had frequently spoken of it, but it was not prepared, and he said he knew not how to put it into a liquid state. After consulting a medical book, I sent for the doctor and asked your father for the vial of quinine. It was brought. The label is French, I thought. The name, what is it?—Strychnine. The last syllable is like quinine in English. I am alike ignorant of the French and of the medicine. But Mr. Thurston and Dr. [Lorrin] Andrews know.—Now for mixing it.—This shall be done by my recipe, 19 grains of quinine dissolved in one hundred teaspoons of diluted alcohol, with three drops of sulfuric acid, ten teaspoons would then contain a grain, 3⅓ teaspoons ⅓ of a grain. This last shall be a potion. I first tried it by taking one teaspoonful. It did not affect me much anyway. So the next morning, before breakfast, I took one-third of a grain. Having already exercised to the extent of my strength, I lay down on my bed, facing the north. Singular sensations suddenly came over me. I turned halfway over, in order the better to be heard from the schoolroom, saying, "*Mary, come here, do, I feel so strangely, I don't like to be alone.*" This was no sooner uttered, than I became transfixed in the very position in which I had turned to speak to her. "*Where is Thomas? Let him go for your father. Let him come first and see how I am. Don't alarm him. Tell him it is from taking quinine.*" Ever and anon, a wedge seemed driven through me, the tension becoming higher and higher, and still another and another wedge to very extremity. To touch me was renewed agony. To hold my hands and feet with a firm grasp seemed to stay me from being sundered in twain. Every window and every door was thrown open from the first. Your father at length said, "*I feel very faint.*" He let go my hand, halted a little, and reeled to the door. After taking water he revived, asked to see the medicine, and expressed his doubts of its being quinine. One hour had now elapsed. My first stage of suffering was ended. But it was succeeded by another still more severe. I was as immovable as ever, while convulsions took possession of my frame (body). Every minute or two a strong spasm passed over me. What was more—it required the stillness of death to prevent these spasms from being constant upon me. To touch me—to touch the bed, to step on the floor, to swing the fan—caused my whole frame to be shaken with intense suffering. A teaspoonful of water, put into my mouth and swallowed, produced convulsions of double strength. "*Leave me in the room alone. Stay on that side the threshold.*" Yet there was I myself. My very teeth closed so into the gums as to produce spasms. To open them a little produced spasms. To move my tongue or speak, produced spasms. I was hard-pressed to hold onto life without breathing. In my thoughts, I hushed myself as if dealing with infancy. "*Be quiet, be quiet—be* quiet. Hush—hush—hush." I said to myself, "*I am cut off from human aid, shut up in the hand of the Almighty. Jesus was immovably suspended on the cross. He knows how to be touched with the feelings of our infirmities. In such pitiable distress and helplessness, I cling to such a Savior, I yield myself to Him for suffering, or ease, or action, for life or death. Only purify me from sin, even as silver is purified in the furnace.*" I repeated many times to myself the hymn, commencing, "*Jesus, Savior of my soul.*" Thus shut up to utter helplessness, to solitude and thought, it proved one of the most interesting seasons of my existence. From seven to eleven I was in one position on my bed, as if in bands of brass. At one, your father assisted me to recline on pillows in the armed chair in the schoolroom. Convulsions ceased altogether by two. The children sat by the center table, industriously employed in tumbling over the leaves of half a dozen volumes. Now and then sentences were read aloud for general edification. Strychnine was the chosen subject, and their investigations showed the drug to be a most deadly poison. Four o'clock in the PM, found me, with my cane, just able to set one foot before the other, abroad in the balmy air. I accommodated myself to feebleness by sitting down by my little nursling tree, and removing its tiny twigs. The lamps were lighted, the supper bell rang, and four cheerful faces were grouped at that evening meal. Then reading as usual—Carlyle's *Cromwell*.—His last sickness and death.—Cromwell! How I have wronged him by ranking him among hypocrites. Now I count him among earth's worthies. But I forget that I am simply giving you a peep at our house on the 25th of March. Fare ye well. [After taking the strychnine, three months elapsed before I reached the state in which I was before my nearly fatal mistake. Then the improvement still went on, and the heaviness that I had experienced on my right side ever since my attack of paralysis, and also the frequent feelings as if another attack was impending, left me entirely and forever.] **ARTICLE 8** (Note Before a Voyage) *Kailua-Kona, September 15, 1850*. I address a line to the companion of my youth, my protector, my counselor, the father of my children, my husband. For thirty years we have traveled life's pathway together. Now I go to be repaired like a worn shoe, that in active life I may hold on by your side. But I am borne up by your sanction, advice, and wishes, and by the approval of our fathers, great and good men. I go, and in so doing, strip your home of its remaining olive plants. I leave you in a house so solitary, that in midnight silence you will hear no other sound than the ticking of the clock. As Lucy on her deathbed, said, "*Alone, all alone.*" Thus desolate, should sickness prostrate, and death do its work, farewell.—The life to come. *The life to come.*—For myself, I give up rest and the quiet pleasures of domestic life in the house of an affectionate indulgent husband. Without a shield, with woman's weakness and woman's infirmities, I go to take my chance, and become a wanderer on ocean and on land. A shipwrecked vessel, fire at sea, famine in a boat, a desolate island, and lawless pirates—these are some of the dangers that lie in ambush on the highway of oceans. Nor do I forget, that though I plant my feet in safety on the shores of the Pilgrim fathers, fell disease is there. Open vaults are there. Let us stand in our lot, girding ourselves anew, having on the whole armor. Let us be of good courage, play the man for our people, our children, ourselves, and the Lord do what seemeth him good. You have, with unsurpassed kindness, opened our way before us. Now, day by day, lift up your heart on high, that faithfulness and wisdom, that humility and grace be given us liberally. Often write to me across the continent. Tell me of your welfare, and how you prosper. Remind me of my duty. Thus I shall be ever made to feel your left hand beneath my head, and your right hand embracing me. Like the mysterious influence of the North Pole over the magnet, so you will be to me, to restrain, to beckon, and to bring back to a state of rest. At home and abroad, in life and death, I am your affectionate *wife*. **ARTICLE 9** (To a Daughter left in a Seminary in the United States) *My Dear Daughter Mary*, thirty two years ago, at the age of twenty-four, I first passed this way. Then, by my side, I had my only earthly stay, my new-found husband, a strong support, firm in principle, fixed in purpose, refined in feeling, indulgent, and faithful in love. Now at the age of fifty-six, I am again here on my fifth voyage around Cape Horn. But it is the first time in my pilgrimage from my father's house that moons wax and wane, while I am called to thread alone the rugged pathway of life.—Now, alone, yet not a widow.—Alone, yet not childless. No, not alone. My multiplied precious ones cluster continually around my heart. Alone?—No, I see them. I feel their mighty influence. Husband, sons, daughters, granddaughters, all are mine—mine to give warmth, and richness—and depth—and fullness to a fountain within, ever fresh, ever flowing, ever widening. I go to rejoin the husband of my youth, the father of my children. They have now all left the parental roof, to obtain privileges found only in the fatherland. Father and mother will still be there, if it be the Master's will, serving in the enjoyment of a green old age. We stop not to inquire, what will become of us in sickness—what in the decline of life—what in case of bereavement? But what is present duty? What are we able to accomplish? What endure? My daughter, my nurse, housekeeper and shield, my companion, pupil, and counselor, three times my fellow passenger around Cape Horn, now our pathway diverges. I go away and leave you—leave you all alone. Yet it is self-denying parental affection, it is trust in God, that bids us say, "*Go avail yourself of the advantages of enlightened America and thus become to your friends and society as a 'cornerstone, polished after the similitude of a palace.'*" Yet can I go through all this without having my heart probed to the very bottom? In my lone room my tears often flow. But I thank the Author of my nature that he has enlarged my being by endowing me with these affections, and by giving me such an object on whom to place them. Now that I can do nothing more, it soothes and sustains me to commit you, unreservedly to the wisdom and love, the care and guidance of the blessed Savior. With uplifted heart, I wait for the winds to bear me intelligence of the opened pages of providence respecting you. May both mother and daughter cultivate a spirit of willingness to go where he bids us, to live where he places us, to bear what he lays upon us, and to die when he calls us. That you have been allowed to remain within the family sanctuary till your ideas, tastes, habits, and principles have been formed, till your young affections for your own parents, brothers and sisters have been ripened and matured, I count among my greatest earthly blessings. Now you go forth on a pilgrimage, but you go cherished and sustained by some of the strongest feelings that cluster within the human heart. You know and can confide in the care and love of your father and mother, your sister and brothers. Those two little buds, too, will learn to lisp and love their aunt. And Lucy, our sainted one! In the midnight hour I often think her near my pillow. On my breath is the whisper, "*Go, be to Mary a guardian angel.*" Your parents have been blessed with a heritage of toil and self denial, urged on by love, trust, and hope. Treasures, our all, have multiplied beneath our hands. One-fifth part of these priceless possessions is vested in you. Occupy for the great Master's use, neither wasting by imprudence, nor burying in a napkin. Prepare yourself for useful service in earning day by day your daily bread. Still think of your father's home as yours, and yourself as ours. At the same time think of yourself as at your own disposal. You will first obtain knowledge of books, of life, and of human nature, then according to your own tastes and judgment, select your future pathway in life. In whatever circumstances you are placed, in heart and action, cherish a spirit which will sympathize with the Savior in his work of benevolence to our revolted race. I wish to point you to the temptations and trials of earth. You are treading a pathway strewed with magic thorns and flowers. If you go forward and tread resolutely upon the thorns they will become flowers. If you turn from the path of duty to gather the flowers, they will become thorns. The softening, elevating influence of a virtuous sister's love, in forming a brother's character is immense. Think of this, and take for your motto, "*She hath done what she could.*"—When an inmate in the families of those who welcome you to their fireside, strive to render yourself useful.—In doing so, and learning their method, the greater benefit will be your own. Housekeeping is woman's profession. I wish you to give special attention to this subject. To be able to sustain the responsibility to regulate and to perform every part of household good in the most accomplished manner is woman's glory. It is a subject of untold importance that you attend to your health. A good constitution is one of the cornerstones to a useful and happy life. Study and obey nature's laws. Let understanding and prudence be your counselors, leading you to take good care of the delicate machinery of your own system. A dozen years ago, ours was an unbroken family, together surrounding one family board. New, without looking at the wanderer on this great and wide ocean, we are scattered on two islands, in two countries, and in two worlds. Still we are all bound together in love. That this love may become sanctified and perpetuated on earth and in Heaven, is the heart's desire and daily prayer of, your affectionate *Mother*. **ARTICLE 10** (Surgical Operation for Breast Cancer) *My Dear Daughter Mary*, I have hitherto forborne to write respecting the surgical operation I experienced in September, from an expectation that you would be with us so soon. That is now given up, so I proceed to give a circumstantial account of those days of peculiar discipline. At the end of the General Meeting in June your father returned to Kailua-Kona, leaving me at Honolulu, in Mr. [Townsend Elijah] Taylor's family, under Dr. Ford's care. Dr. [William] Hillebrand was called in counsel. During the latter part of August they decided on the use of the knife. Mr. Thurston was sent for to come down according to agreement should such be the result. I requested him to bring certain things which I wished, in case I no more returned to Kailua-Kona. Tremendous gales of wind were now experienced. One vessel was wrecked within sight of Kailua Kona. Another on her way there, nearly foundered, and returned only to be condemned. In vain we looked for another conveyance. Meantime, the tumor was rapidly altering. It had nearly approached the surface, exhibiting a dark spot. Should it become an open ulcer, the whole system would become vitiated with its malignity. Asa said he should take no responsibility of waiting the arrival of his father. Persis felt the same. Saturday PM, the doctors met in consultation, and advised an immediate operation. The next Tuesday (12th of September), ten o'clock

AM, was the hour fixed upon. In classifying, the doctor placed this among "capital operations." Both doctors advised not to take chloroform because of my having had the paralysis. I was glad they allowed me the use of my senses. Persis offered me her parlor, and Asa his own new bridal room for the occasion. But I preferred the retirement and quietude of the grass-thatched cottage. Thomas, with all his effects moved out of it into a room a few steps off. The house was thoroughly cleaned and prettily fitted up. One lady said it seemed as though it had been got up by magic. Monday, just at night, Dr. Ford called to see that all was in readiness. There were two lounges trimmed, one with white—the other with rose-colored mosquito netting. There was a reclining Chinese chair, a table for the instruments, a wash stand with wash bowls, sponges, and pails of water. There was a frame with two dozen towels, and a table of choice stimulants and restoratives. One more table with the Bible and hymn book. That night I spent in the house alone for the first time. The family had all retired for the night. In the still hour of darkness, I long walked back and forth in the capacious dooryard. Depraved, diseased, helpless, I yielded myself up entirely to the will, the wisdom, and the strength of the Holy One. At peace with myself, with earth, and with Heaven, I calmly laid my head upon my pillow and slept refreshingly. A bright day opened upon us. My feelings were natural, cheerful, elevated. I took the Lord at his own word, "*As the day is, so shall thy strength be.*" There with an unwavering heart, I leaned for strength and support. Before dressing for the occasion, I took care to call on Ellen, who had then an infant a week old by her side. It was a cheerful call, made in a common manner, she not being acquainted with the movements of the day. I then prepared myself for the call. Dr. [Gerrit P.] Judd was early on the ground. I went with him to Asa's room, where with Asa and Sarah [Andrews Thurston] we sat and conversed till other medical men rode up. Dr. Judd rose to go out. I did the same. Asa said, "*You had better not go, you are not wanted yet.*" I replied, "*I wish to be among the first on the ground, to prevent its coming butt end first.*" On reaching my room, Dr. Ford was [already] there. He introduced me to Dr. Hoffman of Honolulu and to Dr. Brayton of an American Naval ship, then in port. The instruments were then laid out upon the table. Strings were prepared for tying arteries. Needles threaded for sewing up the wound. Adhesive plasters were cut into strips, bandages produced, and the Chinese chair placed by them in the front double door. Everything was now in readiness, save the arrival of one physician. All stood around the house or in the piazza. Dr. Ford, on whom devolved the responsibility, paced the dooryard. I stood in the house with others, making remarks on passing occurrences. At length I was invited to sit. I replied, "*As I shall be called to lie a good while, I had rather now stand.*" Dr. Brayton, as he afterwards said, to his utter astonishment found that the lady to be operated on was standing in their midst. Dr. Hillebrand arrived. It was a signal for action. Persis and I stepped behind a curtain. I threw off my cap and dressing gown, and appeared with a white flowing skirt, with the white bordered shawl purchased in 1818, thrown over my shoulders. I took my seat in the chair. Persis and Asa stood at my right side, Persis to hand me restoratives, Asa to use his strength, if self-control were wanting. Dr. Judd stood at my left elbow for the same reason—my shawl was thrown off—exhibiting my left arm, breast and side, perfectly bare. Dr. Ford showed me how I must hold back my left arm to the greatest possible extent, with my hand taking a firm hold of the arm of my chair, with my right hand, I took hold of the right arm, with my feet I pressed against the foot of the chair. Thus instructed, and everything in readiness, Dr. Ford looked me full in the face, and with great firmness asked, "*Have you made up your mind to have it cut out?*" "Yes sir." "*Are you ready now?*" "Yes sir, but let me know when you begin, that I may be able to bear it." "*Have you your knife in that hand now?*" He opened his hand that I might see it, saying, "*I am going to begin now.*" Then came a gash long and deep, first on one side of my breast, then on the other. Deep sickness seized (overcame) me, and deprived me of my breakfast. This was followed by extreme faintness. My sufferings were no longer local. There was a general feeling of agony

throughout the whole system. I felt, every inch of me, as though flesh was failing. During the whole operation, I was enabled to have entire self-control over my person, and over my voice. Persis and Asa were devotedly employed in sustaining me with the use of cordials, ammonia, bathing my temples, and etc. I myself fully intended to have seen the thing done. But on recollection, every glimpse I happened to have, was the doctor's right hand completely covered with blood, up to the very wrist. He afterwards told me, that at one time the blood from an artery flew into his eyes, so that he could not see. It was nearly an hour and a half that I was beneath his hand, in cutting out the entire breast, in cutting out the glands beneath the arm, in tying the arteries, in absorbing the blood, in sewing up the wound, in putting on the adhesive plasters, and in applying the bandage. The views and feelings of that hour are now vivid to my recollection. It was during the cutting process that I began to talk. The feeling that I had reached a different point from those by whom I was surrounded, inspired me with freedom. It was thus that I expressed myself. "*It has been a great trial to my feelings that Mr. Thurston is not here. But it is not necessary.—So many friends, and Jesus Christ besides.—His left hand is underneath my head, his right hand sustains and embraces me. I am willing to suffer. I am willing to die. I am not afraid of death. I am not afraid of hell. I anticipate a blessed immortality. Tell Mr. Thurston my peace flows like a river.*" Upward I lift mine eyes. From God is all my aid. The God that built the skies, and earth and nature made, God is the tower to which I fly. His grace is nigh in every hour. God disciplines me, but he does it with a gentle hand. At one time I said, "*I know you will bear with me.*" Asa replied, "*I think it is you that have to bear from us.*" The doctor, after removing the entire breast, said to me, "*I want to cut yet more, round under your arm.*" I replied, "*Do just what you want to do, only tell me when, so that I can bear it.*" One said the wound had the appearance of being more than a foot long. Eleven arteries were taken up. After a beginning had been made in sewing it up, Persis said, "*Mother, the doctor makes as nice a seam as you ever made in your life.*" "*Tell me, Persis, when he is going to put in the needle, so that I can bear it."—"Now, now, now," and etc.—"Yes, tell me. That is a good girl." Ten stitches were taken, two punctures at every stitch, one on either side. When the whole work was done, Dr. Ford and Asa removed my chair to the back side of the room, and laid me on the lounge. Dr. Brayton came to my side, and taking me by the hand said, "*There is not one in a thousand who would have borne it as you have done.*" Up to this time, everything is fresh to my recollection. Of that afternoon and night, I only remember that the pain in the wound was intense and unremitting, and that I felt willing to be just in the circumstances in which I was placed. I am told that Dr. Ford visited me once in the afternoon, and once in the night, that Persis and Asa took care of me, that it seemed as if I suffered nearly as much as during the operation, and that my wound was constantly wet with cold water. I have since told Persis that "*I thought they kept me well-drugged with paregoric* (morphine)." He replied, "*We did not give you a drop.*" "*Why then do I not remember what took place?*" "*Because you had so little life about you.*" By morning light the pain had ceased. Surgeons would understand the expression, that the wound healed by a "union of the first intention." The morning again brought to my mind a recollection of events. I was lying on my lounge, feeble and helpless. I opened my eyes and saw the light of day. Asa was crossing the room bearing a Bible before him. He sat down near my couch, read a portion, and then prayed. For several days, I had long sinking turns of several hours. Thursday night, the third of suffering, Thomas rode nearly two miles to the village for the doctor, once in the forepart of the evening, again at eleven. At both times he came. At two o'clock he (the doctor) unexpectedly made his third call that night. It was at his second call that he said to Persis, "*In the morning make your mother some chicken soup. She has starved long enough.*" [They were afraid of the fever spreading.] Persis immediately aroused Thomas, had a chicken caught, a fire made, and a soup under way that same midnight hour. The next day, Friday, I was somewhat revived by the use of wine and soup. In the afternoon, your father arrived. It was the first time since the operation that I felt as if I had life enough to endure the emotion of seeing him. He left Kailua-Kona the same day the operation was performed. A vessel was passing in sight of Kailua-Kona. He rowed out in a canoe and was received on board. Hitherto, Persis, Asa and Thomas, had been my only nurses both by day and by night. The doctor gave direction that no one enter the room, but those that took care of me. For weeks my debility was so great, that I was fed with a teaspoon, like an infant. Many dangers were apprehended. During one day, I saw a duplicate of every person and everything that my eye beheld. Thus it was [like] sixteen years before, when I had the paralysis. Three weeks after the operation your father for the first time, very slowly raised me to the angle of 45 degrees. It seemed as if it would have taken away my sense. It was about this time that I perceptibly improved from day to day, so much so, that in four weeks from my confinement, I was lifted into a carriage. Then I rode with your father almost every day. As he was away from his field of labor, and without any family responsibilities, he was entirely devoted to me. It was of great importance to me, that he was at liberty and in readiness ever to read simple interesting matter to me, to enliven and to cheer, so that time never passed heavily. After remaining with me six weeks, he returned to Kailua-Kona, leaving me with the physician and with our children. In a few weeks, Mother (Lucy Thurston), Mr. (husband of Persis) Taylor, Persis, Thomas, Lucy (daughter of Persis), Mary (daughter of Persis), and George bade farewell to Asa and Sarah, and to little Robert (son of Asa), their black-eyed baby boy. Together we passed over the rough channels up to the old homestead. Then, your father instead of eating his solitary meals had his family board enlarged for the accommodation of three generations. And here is again your mother, engaged in life's duties, and life's warfare. Fare thee well. Be one with us in knowledge, sympathy, and love, though we see thee not, and when sickness prostrates, we feel not thy hand upon our brow. *Your loving Mother.* **ARTICLE 11** (Death of Eldest Son) Asa G. Thurston, our oldest son, leaving his wife and children on Hawaii, went to Honolulu, accompanied by his mother, to consult a physician in regard to a tumor on his breast which had caused excruciating pain for many months. He lived only a few days, dying suddenly of what the physician pronounced to be aneurism of the great aorta. *Honolulu, December 20, 1859. My Dear Husband and Daughter*, my mission here is accomplished and I am ready to return to my lonely husband. My trunks are in the basement, packed ready for starting. In a pleasant bedroom stand Asa's trunk and saddlebags. His boots, his hat, his all, all are laid aside. His earthly house too, is taken down, and treasured in a sacred spot. Mortality has been swallowed up of life. Together we walked a peaceful pathway, leading to an open grave. But it lay through green pastures, and beside still waters. For a week and a half before he left us, his soul entered into rest respecting his wife and children. With full confidence he could trust them, as he had long been able to trust himself, to a covenant-keeping God. After that I saw no more tears. At the funeral service, Reverend Mr. Eli Corwin, a former classmate, returned thanks for the example of one who had come into this community to teach us how to die. Men of the world said they would give all they possessed could they thus attain the serenity of soul with which Asa lived in hourly expectation of sudden death. *Renewedly yours, Lucy G. Thursto*n. [Letter addressed by Asa to his parents, written at intervals, in great weakness, from the 6th to the 12th of December. He died on the 17th.] *My Dear Father and Mother*, standing as I am on the borders of the eternal world, still an inhabitant of earth, yet in daily, yes, hourly expectation of the summons that will call me hence, I would commend to your parental care and kindness the wife and babes I leave behind, still to toil on in this world of care and suffering. Father! Mother! They are your children, the loved ones of your son. Let them fill in your affections the place I have filled, and share in the benefactions as I should share. If want and distress should overtake them, may I not ask a home for them beneath your roof tree? It is pleasant to me to think of my sons growing up under the same home influences, amid the same scenes, and under the same holy teaching as those in which my own infant years were passed, and through the force of which, after long years of wandering, I was at last brought back, as the returning prodigal, to acknowledge for my God, my Savior, Him to whom, beneath that roof, my infant lips had learned to lift the voice of prayer and praise. Cherish them, dear parents, as you have ever cherished their father. Let my Sarah ever be to you as a daughter beloved. Through six years of wedded life, in sickness and in health, in adversity and in the full tide of prosperity, she has to me fully realized the anticipations and wishes, the hopes and desires of our joyous and happy courtship. She is eminently worthy of your love, none even of your own well-loved daughters more so. A virtuous woman, her value is "far above rubies." I am satisfied to leave them all in the hands of a prayer-hearing God. The assurance that they will be provided for, robs death of its sting, and leaves me joyfully to meet the summons that is to call me hence. And now, dear parents, farewell for a brief season, until we meet again in those mansions of bliss, where pain and sorrow are unknown, where with the innumerable company of angels and justified spirits, we shall ever dwell in the presence of Him with whom is fullness of joy amid those holy pleasures which shall be forever more. *Your dying son, Asa.* **ARTICLE 12** (Death of Two Grandchildren) My daughter Mary, a widow, had just returned from Illinois to Honolulu, with her three little children, to find a home in her father's house, and to minister to her parents in their declining years. Our son Thomas, having finished his theological course in New York, returned with her. *Honolulu, May 29, 1866. My Dear Children in California,* I take up my pen to speak to you of the departed, and will first mention Edwin (son of Mary Thurston Haydon Benfield). He reached us on the Sabbath. Thursday eve he had an attack of croup (respiratory infection). When the doctor came Saturday morning, he immediately and freely gave his views. There was no hope of his life. It would terminate in a few hours. The mother uninterruptedly ministered to her dying child, *"You are going up into the sky, to the Happy Land, where papa is and where God is."* By repeatedly shaking his head, he expressed strong aversion, and said, *"Wait till Mother* *goes."* His mother told him decidedly that she could not go now. She could not go till God called her.—The 23rd *Psalm* was read. Your father prayed. Then his son. Save the soul of the child. Give us submission.—We felt that both petitions were answered. A holy calm pervaded the room. Ed looked up to his mother and asked, *"Is Ed going up into the sky?"* She replied, *"Yes,"* and inquired, *"Do you want to go?"* With a pleased countenance, he repeatedly nodded assent so sweetly, so fully, afterwards he uttered with difficulty, *"Come and get Ed."* With a satisfied air he then turned over, laying his little hand beneath his cheek. In fifteen minutes he had ceased to breathe. We had approached very near to the Savior—we had, as it were, laid our precious child lovingly and trustingly into his own blessed arms, to be borne away from our sight. He showed his acceptance of the gift, by giving us light and love, consolation and strength. In the forenoon a friend rode up to the door and inquired, *"Are you all well here?" "All are well. Yet death has entered our doors." "Ah! Has the old gentleman gone?" "Walk into the parlor and see what has befallen us. Not the aged with gray hairs has been selected, but the child of five years."* The funeral was attended the next day, Sabbath, just one week from the day of their arrival. The first line of the piece sung was, *"There is a reaper whose name is Death."* Little Mary (sister of Edwin) went with us to the cemetery. She enjoyed the ride, and was interested in the scene at the grave. That evening, our son Thomas, lately arrived from New York, preached in Fort Street Church. His first hymn, *"And let this feeble body fail."* Connected with the events of the day, and the manner in which it was read, it was very impressive. His text, *"And Jesus himself began to be about thirty years of age."* In three hours from the time that we stood by the first opened grave of a grandchild, we were listening for the first time to the preaching of a son, for whom we had been laboring thirty years. A son!—Qualified for the gospel ministry.—It is enough. A grandchild! Gone to be where Jesus is, that he may behold his glory. Amen. Little Mary, at the interesting age of first prattling infancy—lived and moved among us five weeks. How happy she was in independently ranging the yard in the open air! How delighted in visiting the young brood of yellow chickens! How unsuccessful in trying to turn round and sit down on a moving tortoise! How satisfied and calm in planting herself by the side of her brother, on the lap of mother earth! She was attacked with a hoarse, hard breathing, which in four days resulted in death. When we unmistakably read the call—*"Mary, come up hither"*—in the fullness of our hearts we responded, *"Go, Mary, to thy Savior."* Edwin was the only one in the land of spirits that she knew on earth. In one short month, as we count time, I think he was matured, and commissioned to become a ministering spirit to his little sister, struggling in the swellings of Jordan. Such is the love of a good shepherd to a tender lamb—such the consolation given to our stricken hearts under bereavement. Mary's hands and feet were cold as death. She was leaning against her mother, sitting in an erect position. *"Cold,"* she many times repeated, and nestled still nearer to her mother. Suddenly her languid eyes became animated and lustrous. She looked attentively as toward some object. Her mother asked, *"What is she looking at?"* and turned around her head to see. Little Mary spoke, *"Oh! Ed! Ed! Ed!"* till the sound of her voice died away with her failing breath. [Unknown to Lucy Thurston and her daughter at the time, it appears her late grandson returned to comfort his dying sister.] The funeral was at four the next afternoon. Previously little Mary rode with us in the carriage to the grave. She still rode with us, but in her coffin. How much more soothing than to place a loved one alone upon the black hearse! In the midst of our crushed hopes, I do not forget the great mercy which saved them from the dangers of their long journey. I am thankful that we were permitted to see the faces of our grandchildren, and to hold communion with them for a little season. How kind the arrangement, that they were permitted to die in the bosom of our own family, and find a peaceful rest in our own sepulcher. I rejoice that in the counsels of Heaven, our own child was chosen to give being, and to watch over the earth life of two immortal beings, lent treasures, to be transplanted, at the Master's will, to a higher life. Bless the Lord, O my soul, and all that is within me, bless his holy name. *Your loving mother, Lucy G. Thurston.* **ARTICLE 13** (Last Days of Asa Thurston) *Honolulu, December 8th, 1867. My Dear Daughter Persis*, many times of late we have thought your father's days were about to be numbered.—First by an attack of paralysis (his third attack) affecting speech and intellect.—This was followed from day to day with spasms of pain at the heart, sudden, short, severe. He had hardly rallied, when a gash from an axe on his right foot, cutting off three toes, kept him on his back more than three months. I now know that I have been preserved to be his nurse in old age. I never forget that he may be cut off any day, but he may be continued for years.—The grass to us looks green, the flowers beautiful.—They speak of a better land ever blooming. *January 25th, 1868*. Three weeks ago today, your father first complained of headache, so very unusual a symptom, that it seemed to us very threatening.—The second week, in addition to pain, he saw shining, glimmering appearances lowered from the upper ceiling, and drawn up again.—The third week he suddenly became utterly unable to find the way aright from one room to another. Neither can he at any time tell what room he is in. The appearances he witnesses in space seem sometimes to overwhelm him. He sees crowds of men. He points and exclaims, "*Ke aupuni, Ke aupuni,*" the Kingdom, the Kingdom. He is completely enveloped in a cloud of bewilderment. Of his whole family affairs, explained to him, he says decisively, "*I don't know anything about them.*" *March 23, 1868. My Dear Children and Grandchildren*, I write to tell you that your father Thurston, your grandfather Thurston has entered into rest. He died March 11th, aged eighty years and five months. We had lived together forty-eight years and five months. His reason was at times dethroned during his illness of nine weeks. He forgot almost everything [possibly the effects from Alzheimer's disease—then unknown to science in the 1860s] even his own wife and children. But in the midst of all, with unvarying constancy, he ever showed his love for prayer. The last two days of his life he did not speak. Tuesday was a day of extreme restlessness. It was almost as much as one could do to adjust his bed clothes, so weak that he was quite unable to turn himself. At evening he lay composed. Two o'clock came. He never moved after. His laborious breathing, his convulsive movements, his clammy sweat, told me that the last sands of his life were falling. That whole night I lay on the back side of the bed, unable to sit up from extreme prostration. Once he turned his head, fixed his eyes fully upon me, but could not utter a syllable. The morning dawned. A sudden change took place. Its language was, "*Behold the Bridegroom cometh.*" All our household came at once around the bed to watch the ebbing away of life. I took hold of his arm with one hand, and placed the other upon his forehead. His serene eyes were fixed upon mine. I repeated the most appropriate hymns I know of in our language.—"*Rock of Ages, cleft for me,*" and "*Jesus, Savior of my soul.*"—His convulsions had ceased. His hard respirations had gradually ended. His breathings were shorter and shorter, softer and softer, till they became gentle as those of infancy. Then he calmly closed his eyes, and gave up the ghost. It was eight o'clock. The strongest tie that bound me down to earth was then severed. Standing by his cold remains, how vividly were brought to mind his words, spoken beneath a father's roof, "*You shall have my care and love, till these—hands and this heart are cold!*" Now I am written a widow, having the promise that God will be my husband. I adore that power and love which formed and watched over our companionship for more than forty-eight years, and for the great privilege allowed me of smoothing his rough pathway through life, even down to the river's brink.—May his fallen mantle rest on me, on our children, on our children's children, on every individual of our posterity, down to the latest generation.—*From your bereaved mother, Lucy G. Thurston.* **ARTICLE 14** (From the *American Church Missionary Register*, New York, October, 1868. *A Cypress Bough* by Reverend F. S. Rising) On the 11th day of March, 1868, in the city of Honolulu, the Reverend Asa Thurston fell asleep. He closed his eyes upon the bright sunlight of his dear Hawaii nei, and the celestial glory burst upon his sight. He laid aside the staff of his old age and grasped the unfading crown and the palm of victory. He ceased from his life of unintermitted missionary labor, and went hence to serve his Lord day and night in the heavenly temple. Near his earthly home the ever-surging Pacific, emblem of eternity, beat upon the shifting sands. Now he listens to the dash of the endless ages at the feet of the Ancient of Days. He walks no longer under the fierce heat of the tropical sun, but in the genial warmth and blessed light of the Sun of Righteousness. As he is parted from our gaze, we would, with hearty affection, write this memorial of him as one who glorified his divine Savior, and in whom the grace of God was magnified. He sailed out of Boston harbor in the brig *Thaddeus* in October, 1819. His face was set toward the Sandwich Islands. The *Duff* had carried the Gospel light to the Society Group in the South Pacific, but in the north, deep darkness brooded. Out of it rose the death cry of Captain James Cook. Imagination easily sketched the horrors of a land where a savage club laid low the English navigator. A Hawaiian lad [Henry Obookiah], brought by a sea captain to New Haven, told the idolatry of his countrymen, and besought some to hasten thither with the good news of God. Hiram Bingham, Asa Thurston, and five laymen, with their wives, heard this boy's touching appeal, and in answer girded themselves for their grand venture of faith. Foreign missions were not then popular. The chilly October day, when the sails of the *Thaddeus* were unfurled, typified the coldness of the Christian heart toward the heathen world. But these pioneers were born heroes. Thurston, by his physical strength and courage, had won, years before, at Yale College, the much prized staff of "bully." With a moral courage and strength more sublime, he and his companions kissed their brides, and led them from the hymeneal altar to dwell in mid-ocean amid savage islanders. Our hearts beat quick as we recall the heroism of those young men and women putting America behind them to win a nation for Christ. The American Board of Commissioners for Foreign Missions sent them out. For the results of their work the Lord be praised! It was Thurston's lot to labor at Kailua-Kona, on the island of Hawaii. What a parish for a novice to handle! It was a filthy village of thatched huts, built upon beds of indurated lava, on which the fervent sun poured his furnace heat every day in every year. It nestled amid a grove of coconut trees, and reached down to the shore, whither came rolling in the white-crested billows. Behind it rose the lofty volcanic peak of Hualalai. Standing at its base one could trace the perennial green of the forests reaching nigh unto the summit, deeply scored with hideous black tracks of lava reaching unto the sea. The luxuriant foliage hid from distant view gaping fissures, thirty-nine extinct craters, the grim ruins of the temple of Umi, and other tokens of wild desolation. Further down the coast rose the loftier peaks of Mauna Loa and Mauna Kea, 13,000 feet high, snow-capped, fierce fires raging within, and now and then breaking out with quakings, roarings, mighty rushings, and terrific hissings, as the lava threw itself red-hot into the sea. Very solemn to dwell in such a land with these volcanoes ever in sight! Then Kailua-Kona was, at the time of Thurston's landing, the residence of the king. He was a profligate, and the royal city was the fountain of the kingdom's pollution. Here the tabu had been broken and the idols destroyed, that there might be no check to iniquity. The ruins of heathen temples were everywhere about, heart-sickening to behold, and heathen vices were enthroned in every hut and stalked abroad in every village. Men, women and children were like the volcanoes. Raging fires of wickedness within broke out ever in desolating flows. In a thatched hut in the midst of this physical desolateness and moral degradation, Thurston and his wife found their earliest Hawaiian home. Amid such scenes their firstborn came to them. Here the Gospel was first preached for the regeneration of Hawaii nei and the salvation of many thousand souls. When nearly half a century had passed, partial paralysis compelled the heroic Thurston to rest from his toil. He was no longer young. His locks were gray, and grandchildren made more, happy his home. During this long period he did not once leave the Islands. Others came and went, but he remained the tireless evangelist. Tropical heat did not abate his vigor. Long journeys on foot over lava tracts did not exhaust his strength. The hardness and wickedness of the heathen heart did not discourage him. Preaching in season and out of season did not weary him. The love of Christ constrained him, and he did not pause in his labor until his body cried out, "It is enough." During these fifty years he bore an active part in all the remarkable changes which God wrought among the Hawaiians. The king and the common people alike felt his influence. His huge church-building within a stone's throw of the royal residence attested this. When the capital was removed to Honolulu, he did not follow the king, but the common people still heard him gladly. We can imagine the grateful joy of his soul as, year by year, he saw the heathen people become Christian and the absolute despotism changed into a constitutional monarchy. It was our privilege to spend a few days under his hospitable roof after paralysis had disabled him. We cannot soon forget his venerable form, crowned with flowing silver locks, his gentle, modest spirit, his earnestness of soul, his simple faith, his calm expectation of the future. The king might well bow before him and the young do him reverence, as one of the fathers of the kingdom. When he landed, Kamehameha II was a half-clad savage, dwelling in a filthy hut, rioting in degradation. When he went hence, Kamehameha V resided in a stone palace (located in downtown Honolulu) within sound of the church going bell, with every appliance of modern civilization and Christianity about him. Let unbelieving and half-hearted men sneer at Foreign Missions, if they will. One life like that of Asa Thurston, so sublime, so self sacrificing, so successful, far outshines any diamond that they can bring from their mines. After paralysis came upon him, he went to California in quest of health. There, though nearly eighty years of age, he first saw a railroad and telegraph. The world had been busy with its inventions while he was absorbed in his chosen work. When he returned to Honolulu, to await the Lord's summons, he must have mused upon the superior facility for missionary work which the Lord gives in our day. Young men, ponder the life of Asa Thurston. Emulate his faith and zeal. Unnumbered millions call to you for the bread of life. The Gospel is in your hands as a power. Go forth and wield it in the midst of the nations. We may be pardoned one word of reference to Asa Thurston's widow. She shared his trials, went with him in his long missionary tours on foot, and equaled him in heroism. She taught the Hawaiian men to love their wives and their Savior, the Hawaiian women to fear God and honor their husbands, the Hawaiian children to obey the Lord and their parents. So she carried into the huts of that dark land those blessed words—Love, Virtue, Home, Jesus, [and] Heaven. Many a Hawaiian household today blesses God for the gifts sent by her. She now awaits her Lord's call, and we may have ventured upon her retirement that we may appeal to mothers, wives and sisters to show forth such missionary spirit as hers. Christian women, do not keep back your husbands, brothers and sons. Do not stay at home yourselves. Make speed to fill the world with the glory of Emmanuel.

ARTICLE 15 (Funeral Address, Delivered March 12th, 1868, by Reverend Eli Corwin, on the Occasion on the Death of Reverend Asa Thurston, one of the American Pioneer Missionaries to the Hawaiian Islands.) No ordinary event is that which calls us together in solemn assembly today. Two races unite to pay a grateful tribute of respect to the departed patriarch of a mission which has been the best gift of the one race to the other. Forty eight years ago this very month, on the 31st of March, 1820, the deceased reached the shores of Hawaii with the pioneer missionaries sent out by the American Board to evangelize these then benighted and barbarous islands. This day of his burial is just one month less than forty-eight years from the day when he and the still surviving companion of his earthly pilgrimage (who has cared for him during the closing years of his life) were stationed at Kailua-Kona, the ancient residence of the Hawaiian kings. And there, for more than forty years, he continued to reside and to labor as the honored pastor of a large and very important parish. The instructor, for a time, of both Kamehameha II and Kamehameha III, his influence upon the conduct and disposition, especially of the latter, must have been very great, at a period in Hawaiian history when it was most important to secure the good will of those highest in authority and when the word of the king was law and his will was absolute. But, as is ever the case with the faithful minister, his influence was greatest and his usefulness most apparent among the masses of the common people. Never once leaving the Islands for forty years, he was honored of natives and foreigners alike as a faithful, patient, persistent worker, steadfast, and abiding in one stay far beyond the ordinary duration of missionary life. Indeed I know not that in the entire history of missions a like instance is recorded of one remaining so long upon the field and at a single post, during the lifetime of a whole generation, without revisiting the home of his childhood or visiting any other land. Only when advancing age and repeated strokes of paralysis had rendered him incapable of service, only when his strong hand lost its cunning and his tongue had begun to give a doubtful utterance, did he consent to resign his pastorate at Kailua-Kona that he might spend the closing years of his life in this city. Here, how beautiful the evening time of his life. What a privilege to us and to our children to have before us that venerable form and that benignant countenance, a perfect picture of the patriarchs and prophets of olden times not soon effaced from the memory! Infancy with its budding beauty and its fragrance of a new life is lovely in its gentleness and innocence. Youth with its vigor of ripening ambitions and maturing powers is interesting indeed, but no sight on earth is more impressive than a beautiful old age. In his case the outward appearance was but the truthful expression of the inward life, a calm and undisturbed repose of faith, a rest in Jesus which knew no solicitude, a sublime quietude of soul which felt no fear. The hoary head is indeed a crown of glory, if it be found in the way of righteousness. But he died not of old age. With marvelous physical powers, perhaps unsurpassed in his day by those of any other resident upon these Islands, whether native or foreigner, he might but for the attacks of disease, have survived a century. The brain and nervous system were first to give way, before his hearing was impaired, his eye became dim, or his natural force abated. That well-proportioned frame seemed too strong to be torn down even when the mind had ceased to maintain a logical succession of thoughts, and his conversation, a strange mixture of Hawaiian, English and Latin had for the most part ceased to be coherent. Those of us who were permitted to visit him near the close of life cannot soon forget those more lucid intervals when for a little the soul reasserted its power over the tongue, and with indescribable pathos and earnestness he exclaimed, "*My love for Jesus is very great.*" Nor can I soon forget that responsive smile with which he gave assent to what was said of the preciousness of Christ to the believer's soul, when his tongue could no longer give utterance to his thoughts, and his eyes were already glassy with the film of death. Governed by principles, and not by impulse, in his habits of devotion, he persisted in leading at family prayers as a priest in his own household, till he could no longer frame sentences correctly, and after that to the last day of his life, nothing made him more restless and uneasy than the omission of the regular family devotions at the appointed hour, nor did anything soothe and comfort him so much as prayer. Though remarkably taciturn all through life, yet he was hardly less remarkable for a quiet humor which was kept in subjection to his Christian dignity, while it did much to make him agreeable in social life, and to make him buoyant in spirit under all the trials of missionary labor. And this cheerful temper and Christian mirthfulness characterized him to the last. No pleasantry was lost upon him even when his memory of the past became a blank, and he could not recognize his family or his friends. His peculiarly rich and well trained voice, even when age had somewhat shattered it, gave forth at times such tones as made it a feast of melody to my ear to have him seated for years close at my right hand in the sanctuary. Neither the choir nor the congregation were ever disturbed by his singing out of time or out of tune, while the general effect of congregational singing was greatly improved by that remarkable voice of manly power, yet of womanly sweetness, to which we shall listen, in the service of song, nevermore. Alas, one more praying voice is silenced, one more loving heart is cold—one more tongue so eloquent in praise is still. But though the organs of utterance fail to communicate his thoughts and feelings to mortal ears, who can tell the higher blessedness of that intimate communion he holds with Him who planted the ear and who knows our thoughts before we utter them? That powerful frame, that manly form, is shut up within the narrow house of Death, but his freed spirit is not beholden of his dominion. The weary body rests, but the soul has entered upon a career of higher and holier activity. That hoary head shall soon be a buried crown, but how far are its beauty and excellence transcended by that crown of glory which he wears who already reigns with Christ, consecrated a king and a priest unto God. And there are stars in that crown. How many already garnered in glory, while ascribing all the honor to Christ, the sin atoning Lamb, have occasion to welcome him with peculiar joy as, under Christ, the faithful shepherd and bishop of their souls. What a debt of gratitude does the vast congregation worshiping in this sanctuary owe to the God of all grace for the services of the departed! Their beloved pastor, whose absence today is so much regretted, could speak eloquently to his people of his personal indebtedness to him whom he greatly honored and tenderly loved as a spiritual father. For it was to the blessing of God upon a sermon preached by Father Thurston that he ascribed that personal interest in religion which resulted in his conversion. So in the life of the deceased reproduced not only in the missionary life of his own son laboring upon another island of this group, nor yet alone in the lives of many natives still living who mourn for him as for a father, but with redoubled power and energy is it reproduced in the ministry of him who now occupies a central position of influence as pastor of the great congregation accustomed to worship here. The materials are wanting for a complete record of the life of the deceased, but his record is on high. And what a life as it is recorded there, and as God and angels contemplate it! What a life of honor and usefulness as even we are permitted to see it! What an encouragement to the pioneers of Christian missions who go forth to the waste places of the earth to plant the standard of the cross among the barbarous tribes, the thought that they too may be permitted to witness the fruit of their toil in a renovated nation, in a converted people, in a heathen tribe lifted up by the power of the gospel! What a life devoted to the temporal and eternal well-being of thousands upon thousands who have lived and died under his honored ministry. What a life, compassing in its span the entire history of Christian civilization in these islands of the sea! Yet what is this to that unending life of glory and blessedness upon which he has entered? The days of the years of his pilgrimage have been four score years, but that heavenly life is measured by larger cycles, and its successive periods shall be made more and more illustrious by yet higher joys and more distinguished services. Heaven is not mere reception of knowledge and absorption of bliss, it is holiness in action. There is fullness of joy, because perfection of love. There are pleasures forevermore, because spiritual employments in which the soul can never grow weary. With renewed zeal and untiring patience let us labor, that we too may see the fruit of our toil, and win at least the welcome plaudit (praise), "*Well done good and faithful servant, enter thou into the joy of thy Lord.*" **ARTICLE 16** (Letter to Reverend Arthur Dart Bissell, Pastor of Fort Street Church, and to the members of Fort Street Church.) *Honolulu, September 29th, 1869.* In 1819 a church of seventeen members was formed in Park Street Church, Boston, prominently by Reverend Dr. [Samuel] Worcester, first secretary to the American Board of Commissioners for Foreign Missions. That church was organized to be transplanted to the then far off, unlettered, and heathen islands of "Owhyhee." I was one of the members of that church. Mr. Thurston was one of its pastors. Thus it was that he became my pastor. I dwelt beneath his shadow—lived in his strength, experienced his watch and care and priestly offices, during a pilgrimage of forty-eight years. Then, from my heart went up the wail, "*My father, my father, the chariot of Israel, and the horsemen thereof.*" The last original pastor of that transplanted church, known by the name of the "Old Mission Church" had now passed away. After that event, at the first celebration of the Lord's Supper in this church, I awoke to the consciousness that I stood alone. To me there was now no head, no nucleus—no enclosure. For months my heart has yearned to be in the bosom of a church of Christ, and to renew covenant relation with his people. All unworthy as I am, will you receive me into this fold—that I may thereby gain consolation and strength, the intimacy of fellowship and love, and be found, even unto the end, walking in all the commandments and ordinances of the Lord blameless. *Lucy G. Thurston.*

☐☐☐☐☐☐☐☐☐☐☐

Part Third—1870. **ARTICLE 1** I have been writing reminiscences of life fifty years ago. A vote of the Hawaiian Board last year invited the pioneers to the work. So far as I was concerned, I heard of it, with perfect indifference. Mr. [Hiram] Bingham, who had been several years in America, was invited, and expected to come out, and would be all sufficient, but he died. Here was Mrs. [Mercy Partridge] Whitney and myself. She was suffering and very weak. One of the leaders of the Mission came to me. "*Can you write a little without injury to yourself? Describe the day you came on shore.*" "*That was too barren of incident to be interesting. There should be a wider view taken.*" "*Well, just as you please, do it your own way.*" I took my pen reluctantly. It was hard work to make a beginning. When I did begin, it was to describe events two years after being here. Gradually I came into the work, with my whole heart, of reviewing and describing those early days. I then wrote to the Members of the Hawaiian Board. *Fathers*, I speak as unto wise men, judge ye what I say. I have taken for my motto, "*She hath done what she could.*" By spending months oblivious of 1870, by deep and long silence, solitude, and contemplation, together with the aid of old journals, I have written two documents. The first embraces Hawaiian and New England scenes, as taking place simultaneously, the position and prospects of the Missionaries during a voyage of more than five months, the first appearance of a heathen nation, their incipient approaches to better things, and the comforts and struggles of pioneer missionary life. The second contains anecdotes, sketches or tales, illustrative of social life, of native and foreign character, as exhibited some fifty years ago and thereabouts. Over this review of past scenes in my deep seclusion, many tears have been shed by eyes that have been trained not to weep. Then I have exercised entire self-control while I read my sketches for criticism. In passing I would say, I have no manuscript to put into the hands of the future secretary at the meeting of the Evangelical Society, to be read by him, and then pass into its archives. Forgive me, but these two documents are twin sisters, children of my old age, and I consider them exclusively my own. Yet I am ready to say, "*He that hath ears to hear, let him hear.*" Will not that suffice? After being shut up to my own aspirations, a knowledge that they met the favors of my sons and daughters, did my whole being good, even though nothing should come of it. In order to action, I await your approval in the language of the one who induced me to write these reminiscences, "*Just as you please. Do it your own way.*" Respectfully, submitted to the consideration of the Hawaiian Board. *Lucy G. Thurston*. [Hitherto it had not been encouraged to have woman's voice heard in meetings. But when the Hawaiian Board was asked permission for me to give a public reading, every liberty was respectfully granted. A part of these manuscripts written in 1870, were not publicly read. Some that were read, I have arranged in their historical order in another part of the book.] **ARTICLE 2** Having been sustained and blessed in this the land of her adoption for fifty years, and being still allowed to measure off days and nights, fringed with light and peace, *Mrs. Thurston*, as a Tribute of Thanksgiving, proposes to give a Public Reading of Reminiscences of Fifty Years ago and thereabouts. All, who dwell on the soil and breathe the air of Hawaii, understanding the English language, are embraced in her sympathies, and are affectionately invited to come within the sound of her voice, on this the occasion of our Nation's Jubilee. **ARTICLE 3** *Preamble.* Our eyes were turned on Mr. Bingham, who, in 1820, was one of the pioneer missionaries to this nation. He was invited to come cut from the eastern States, and would have become a pioneer mouthpiece at this semicentennial meeting. But the Master said, "*Come up hither.*" The fact then stood before me, there is no man here to remember, and repeat the A-B-C of the mission. Yielding to official advice so tenderly urged, I most reluctantly addressed myself to the work of sketching scenes of the past to spread before the present generation. With the aid of old journals I was enabled to look through the long vista of fifty years. I went back, back—back to olden times, and there alone long tarried. When I returned, it was with the strong desire of speaking to my familiar and sympathizing friends, to those who dwell on the same soil upon which I labored with those, who in troublous times, laid the foundations of generations. I have not here many brothers and sisters. All below fifty-five, I consider my children. I come, then, in the character of a mother, addressing my children, speaking to them of bygone days. **ARTICLE 4** The morning after the death of Kamehameha I, their usual national mourning, for the death of a great chief, commenced. They went upon the idea that their grief was so great, that they knew not what they did. They were let thoroughly loose, without law or restraint, and so gave themselves up to every evil, that they acted more like demons incarnate, than like human beings. Without any shield, rank and sex were upon a level with the meanest and most outrageous of the populace. Their grass-thatched cottages were left empty, their last vestige of clothing thrown aside, and such scenes of wholesale and frantic excesses exhibited in the open face of day, as would make darkness pale. A tornado swept over the nation, making it drunk with abominations. These then dark outskirts of creation were left, in that one particular, to work out and reach the highest heights, and the deepest depths of heathenism that earth has ever seen. It was among their more decent and innocent extravagances, that they burned their faces with fire, in large, permanent, semi-circular figures, and with stones knocked out their front teeth. There was at that time, a foreign resident, who had dwelt some thirty years at the Islands. He had a family of children, all of them in the bloom of youth. One of them incidentally remarked that, as a thing of course, they should attend that public mourning for Kamehameha. The father immediately replied, *"If my children do attend, they will never again cross the threshold of my house."* So he nailed up every avenue to his dwelling, and sat with his native wife and five children, without the light of the sun during those days of riot. He had all along been a rare example in that degenerate age, of building a hedge about his family, and standing in the gap thereof. When occasion offered, he spoke with energy and decision, giving a certain sound well-understood by his children and by strangers. By marriage, by deeds and by counsel, he had justly risen to the eminence of becoming a peer with the first chiefs of the nation. Saxon blood flowed in his veins. He was Mr. [John] Young, the noble grandfather of our most noble Queen Emma. **ARTICLE 5** Sometime near the year 1800, an infant daughter was born into the Hawaiian nation. It had no sooner crossed the threshold of life, than its own mother adopted the heathen practice which filled the land, of hastening to lay it in a pithole and concealing it from the light of day. After passing through the scenes of birth and burial, the heathen mother sat down to rest. Soon a friend came along, who deeply regretted that the child had been buried, as she would have become its nurse, and she hastened to ascertain the true state of things. In uncovering the loosely made deposit, she came to a large piece of lava so suspended at both ends as to prevent its coming down with crushing weight on the body. Quickly removing it, the little thing appeared on its knees and arms. And the babe wept. Her arms gave a welcome to the forlorn stranger. She took it to her home, and reared it with love to a mature childhood, then returned it to its mother. In the meantime, the child had learned the history of its dawning life. So when her mother requested her to do a thing she had a quick reply, *"At my birth you had no love for me, I will not obey you."* She lived to become an idolater, and to feel the iron laws of kapu—a woman cold and cruel as the grave. She lived to see the idols all swept away, and woman, in a good degree, restored to social privileges. She lived to see a new era dawn upon the nation, by having the revelation of God to man reach them, to whom it was alike addressed with the rest of our races, She lived to become a member of an organized Church of Christ, to become an helpmate for a deacon, who for more than forty years has been a presiding officer, and one of the most substantial pillars of the Hawaiian Church. She lived to show that she possessed talents, which with culture, would have adorned any society in any nation. She died, making a great vacancy on earth, that she might fill a higher place in Heaven. **ARTICLE 6** There was a family of five daughters, between the ages of twelve and twenty, who early became members of the Mission School. Saxon blood flowed into their veins. By becoming instructed, they became more intelligent, more attractive and more sought after by the cultivated and refined. In their generation they were the leading characters of the day. Rising into life within in a new era, and thoroughly instructed in a new system of morals, they put forth the tender leaves of hope. Alas, alas, for vines that have no hedges! The boar out of the wood doth waste them, and the wild beast of the field doth devour them! Paternal authority, secured by wealthy influences, was as the east wind in the day of the strong wind, to sweep away all that was sacred. I could tell facts respecting their young lives that would cause the ears to tingle. But I pass over those never-to-be-forgotten memories, briefly alluding to the eldest sister, who in age, had attained independent action. She was more mature and meditative. She said that before the missionaries came, when she looked abroad, the inquiry came into her mind, "*What great man made this world?*" Her mind seemed to be instinctively prepared to receive instruction. She was our joy, and the crown of our school. We even dared to hope that she loved the truth, but the test came. Official power, accomplishments and wealth combined, turned the scale. Yet her conscience was so ill at ease, that she packed her wardrobe and was on the very point of retiring from the position, which she had accepted, when her plans were frustrated. Although living in the same village, she was no longer under the influence of the missionaries. One day a teacher met her. She was as cordial and communicative and in relation to the choice she had made, said, "*I cry every day.*" These girls were all my own scholars. I loved them. Through all the scenes that I have passed from that time to this, I have, without record, remembered their names, even as I have remembered the names of the children of my own brothers and sisters. And here, let me mention one of the keenest trials that a pioneer missionary is called to experience. He plants a vineyard. When he looks that it should bring forth grapes, it brings forth wild grapes. "*O that my head were waters, and mine eyes a fountain of tears, that I might weep day and night for the slain of the daughters of my people.*"

ARTICLE 7 The London Missionary Society sent out a deputation of two gentlemen, Reverend Daniel Tyerman and George Bennet, Esquire, to visit their Missions in the South Seas. While there, two converted Tahitians and their wives of high standing in the church were set apart as missionaries to the three destitute islands of the Marquesas, Mr. William Ellis, their pastor, and the deputation wished to accompany and see them established in their new field. A very obliging sea captain, bound to the Sandwich Islands, engaged to take and set them down at the Marquesas, but the wind proving unpropitious, he deferred going there until his return voyage. Thus it was that they became the welcome guests of the Mission House, at Honolulu. The Tahitian missionaries, with their simple piety, were received with no less interest. And although they were not accommodated at the Mission House, our terms of intercourse were intimate, affectionate and confiding. The captain of the party, too, was introduced to us as a man of high moral principles, who had been to them a brother. He was young, amiable, and cultivated. Nothing was more natural, while he lay in port, than that he made himself familiar at the Mission House. Sometimes he sat with us at the family board, oftener made social calls. During the day, our numerous family branched off as duty or inclination led. When evening hushed the cares of life, some dozen of us assembled in the sitting, room to enjoy the high privilege of social intercourse. On a certain evening, the day was being thus delightfully crowned, though eliciting thought with an ease and freedom which English courtesy exhibited and encouraged—when we were startled by a knock at the door. One of the Tahitian missionaries had come with the astounding intelligence that their own captain, with a band of his sailors, had just been to their house, and from before his eyes, had borne away his wife to his ship. To the panic-stricken husband, there was no redress. The thing must take its course. Law had not then raised its powerful arm in the nation. Everyone did what was right in his own eyes, and looked his neighbor straight in the face. On that dark and black night, standing aghast at the revelation of such fearful villainy, within our own trusted circle, I turned to my husband and asked, "*What protection have I against being carried off in like manner?*" He replied, "*You have none.*" Then I remembered with dismay, that only two days before, that same captain leisurely spent hours in the afternoon at the Mission House, and as a natural thing invited me to walk on the Plain. It was one of the daily duties of us ladies to walk for health, but never without an escort. We had perfect confidence in him, and yet I declined, I hardly know why. The next morning Mr. Ellis visited the ship, and when he asked the woman to go ashore, she replied, "*The captain will not let me.*" There were two hackneyed expressions in those years, which have become obsolete. The one was, that "*These islands lay at the end of the earth.*" The other, that "*Men who visited them left their consciences at Cape Horn.*" After a season, the Tahitian missionary's wife was graciously permitted to return to her husband. The pastor, alive to her interests, said to me, "*She is bent on spending the days abroad in the fields. She seems to be somewhat partially demented. Do go and speak to her words of comfort.*" I found her on the Plains, with a square covering drawn tightly around the whole length of her person, and her chin resting low on her chest. She was roaming about, she knew not, and she cared not whither. She neither wished to see, nor speak to anyone. Desolation and despair had taken fast hold of her soul. A blight had fallen upon her whole being. Instead of an early opportunity of returning, our English and Tahitian friends were unexpectedly detained more than four months. Then that captain and that vessel were ready for sea. Our friends, as travelers, did the best they could, embraced the only opportunity that offered for a return, entered the same vessel, under the same captain, that brought them here. The ill assorted inmates were shut up to themselves, and sailed away together. The sole object for which those three English gentlemen projected the voyage, was quashed. A visit to the Marquesas, and there establishing a Mission, was necessarily given up. No thanks to transgressors that other benevolent plans employed their activities. On the passage back, a woman died. Under the auspices of the captain, the remains were sewed up in a strong canvas, weighted with two eighteen pound balls, and committed to the deep, with Christian rites. It was the corpse of the crushed wife of the Tahitian missionary. She was born in idolatry, and hers was a checkered life. Her pastor was with her in her last hours, and hoped she sought and found mercy. The bereaved husband returned to his old home, a three-fold mourner, the loss of his wife, the defection of her character, and his total failure in the mission to which he had been appointed. In a public journal, a volume of 500 pages, in progress at that period, and given to the world in 1831, cognizance was taken of this affair. The wife of the Tahitian missionary was called by name. She was compared to the woman who was a sinner. She was spoken of as having brought disgrace on herself, and occasioned much grief to her Christian relatives and friends. The captain passed on with an unsullied reputation. And, in consequence of his attentions to his passengers to and from the Sandwich Islands, he was presented with six large hogs, a great number of coconuts, some breadfruits, and other presents of native growth and manufacture. Thus, the reputation of those two individuals, are even now sailing down the stream of time (history). And this is a specimen of the manner in which the scale was poised between civilized man and olive-complexioned woman in these Pacific Seas (Ocean), in the former part of the 19th century. Wise men did it, who knew the times and saw the phase of public opinion, and who sat the first in the kingdom as journalists and editors. **ARTICLE 8** I now approach a subject compared with which all personal missionary trials sink into insignificance. It was forming the characters of children on missionary ground in pioneer life. Captain [Daniel] Chamberlain brought out with us five promising children, between the age of one and twelve. No one of us had conceived the idea that children with unformed characters must be separated from the people to whom we were sent. Those children were in full connection with the native children of our family boarding school, in their studies, in their amusements, and in their employments. When our English missionary friends came, they saw at a glance that we had begun upon a wrong track with our own children. They spread before us the developments and experiences of missionary life for thirty years at the Society Islands. Some items of intelligence were most startling in their character. The earth seemed to be receding from beneath our feet, with no firm foundation remaining on which to stand. Then it was that the pioneer missionaries renounced their republican principles, and, with one stride, became autocrats of the first water. The next influence exerted by the English deputation respecting our children, was, in giving to their young American brethren a piece of advice. It was this, *"Let Mr. and Mrs. Chamberlain take their six children, go home and train them up for God. They never can do it here. As society now is, for unformed characters to come in contact with natives as foreigners, is moral death."* Those most interested exhibited their true characters, by silently laying the case before the brethren to await their decision. They unanimously said, *"Go."* Thus we younger ones lost our parents. With two infant sons and five infant daughters lying on our arms, we were left to stand in our lot, and breast the sweeping tide as best we might. From the lips of one of Zion's watchmen at that time, fell the following startling words, which became engraved on my brain, as with a red-hot iron. *"The nation must be converted, or our own children will go down with them into the same pit."* We were going forth weeping, bearing precious seed. Our own families and this nation were both in the house of bondage. **ARTICLE 9** Kuakini, or Governor Adams as he was called by foreigners, was the governor of Hawaii, and made his permanent residence at Kailua-Kona. He belonged to the first class of chiefs, was a noble looking man, and rose higher in civilized habits than any other chief of his time, he used coffee and tea daily on his table, dressed uniformly in American costume, and was distinguished for knowledge of the English language. In the third year of the mission, when he was at his place alone, without the presence of a missionary, he built a church for the white man's God. When we were stationed there, he established family worship, and induced Mr. Thurston to go daily and officiate at his house. During the second year of our residence at Kailua-Kona, the church became too small for the increasing numbers who would fain (gladly) attend. Governor Adams then erected another, larger and more commodious, one hundred and eighty feet by sixty. It was superior to any house of native workmanship upon the Islands. When this was burned by an incendiary, the Governor erected a large stone house of worship, with galleries and pulpit. The latter cost five hundred dollars. The Governor himself occupied, for awhile, a very pretty framed house with green window shades. It was brought from America, and was placed in a capacious yard surrounded by a wall ten feet in height, and about the same in width. It made quite a distinguished appearance at the head of the village. He afterwards changed his residence towards the center of the village, where he erected another dwelling house in more costly style. His influence was altogether on the side of civilization, order, and improvement. He gave good laws, patronized schools, and for a time had both a reading and a writing school in his own yard, under his own instruction. He read through his English Bible with care, and assisted in translating the Scriptures, asked a blessing at table, and attended public worship regularly. For awhile, though he exhibited so many good traits, he was not decidedly pious. He was the first person at Kailua-Kona who solicited baptism, and it was a very trying thing to him that he could not be among the first led to the baptismal font. But his religious character rested in the clouds. Another company presented themselves for baptism, while he held a retired seat. He then dispatched a letter to Oahu in the form of a complaint saying, if he were not baptized that year, he never would be. His threats were as unavailing as his solicitations. There was a meeting of the members of the church. He thought he would meet with them, but the door was closed against him, even by his own sister Kaahumanu, who was of still higher standing in authority than himself. So he sat down on the threshold of the door, and indulged in his own agitated reflections. He returned home, sat up and read his Bible during the whole night. Thus he struggled—until he felt himself to be a "lost man"—was willing to accept of salvation on the humiliating terms of the gospel, and enter the kingdom, not as a chief, but as a little child. The usual congregation at that time numbered about five thousand. The day the Governor was baptized, it was computed there were about eight thousand in and around the church. Governor Adams, in calling on his teachers, was most entertained in visiting the room where domestic operations were performed. He continued to observe the process of making butter, till he felt himself master of the art. I think he was the first native in the nation who undertook its manufacture forty years ago. He commenced thus, after separating the cream from the milk, he threw the cream away, and put the skimmed milk into the prepared container. Application and perseverance presided over that churn. But the labor was all in vain. He hastened to compare his notes respecting the process of making butter with those of his teachers. He thus discovered his mistake, and learned by deep experience that the churning of cream brought forth butter. Again he was in perplexity. The teacher's butter was all one color—yellow. His was not so. Various hues of the rainbow were detected in it—red, green, and etc. Some parts of his butter were fully salted, other parts not at all. Between these two points, salt was worked in, in different degrees. And time gave different hues to the various strata. But with the docility of a child, he took, as it were, for his motto, "*Try, try, try again,*" so that not many moons waxed and waned before, in the art of making butter, he was, from the shoulders and upwards, taller than any of his fellows. When we first reached the Islands, not one woman in the nation, and but one man, appeared with a covering on her head. The first native woman who was seen with a bonnet in church, was the bride of Thomas Hopu, at the time they were married. From that period, the custom gradually extended, led off by the nobility. After the mission had been established many years, Governor Adams made a law that no woman should enter his yard without a bonnet. If the law was broken, the penalty was to have the hair cut off close to the head. After that, he made another law, that no woman should enter the church without a bonnet. The natives were quite ingenious in manufacturing hats and bonnets out of the palm leaf which is indigenous to these Islands. **ARTICLE 10** Naihe was a principal chief, and the husband of Kapiolani. He was of commanding stature, and distinguished for refinement and polish of mind and manners. Such was his fluency and eloquence in speech that he was styled the national orator. When Governor Adams was absent at Oahu for two years, Naihe was appointed to attend to his official duties on Hawaii. As a magistrate he was as firm as he was affectionate, and in passing sentence upon offenders, the tears were often seen chasing each other in quick succession down his cheeks. We enjoyed frequent intercourse with him, and less than a fortnight before his death, saw him at his own place. He walked out with us to our conveyance and there, for the last time, pressed my hand between both his own with all the exhibition of a father's feelings. He had then been feeble for a few days, but several times we received encouraging intelligence of his health. How then was I amazed at the expiration of a week, to hear that he had been suddenly seized and lay senseless. Mr. Thurston went and saw the termination of the fatal apoplexy. A few days previous to this event, he called into his presence two of his confidential men, to whom he thus spoke, "There is something in me which tells me that I must die." After giving charge respecting his power and possessions, now to be transferred, he added, "*Take care of the missionaries. Do for them as I have done.*" As a Christian, Naihe was decided and devout. Well, I remember one Sabbath, when the Lord's Supper was celebrated. Naihe was present, from his residence a distance of sixteen miles, a circumstance of frequent occurrence. He sat there with his accustomed dignity, such as begets in mortals respect and esteem. I looked at him and looked again. Something more deep, more reverential than I had before observed, seemed to sit upon his countenance. He appeared as if in the presence chamber of his Maker. It proved to be the last time that we worshipped together in earthly courts. **ARTICLE 11** I have seen a woman of portly dimensions go dripping from her bathing place in the ocean to make a call on the missionaries. In the presence of them and their wives, she entered their sitting room. With the ease and self possession of royalty, she took a seat on the settee, and carried on conversation with freedom. Did I say she came from the bathing place? She came as it were from Eden, in the dress of innocence. Ten years after the work of molding her character and of her molding the character of the nation, ceased. For fifty years she had lived in heathenism. Then she entered upon a new life. A brighter example of the power and grace of God never passed from Hawaii to Heaven. It was Kaahumanu, the highest chief in the nation, possessed of royal authority. As a heathen, she was the haughty, majestic sovereign of Hawaii. As a Christian, she was energetic and decided, but the humble Queen and Mother of her subjects, from nobility down to peasantry. All the missionaries, she adopted as her own children, and instead of doing as she had done, giving them her little finger with arrogant and imperial airs, she gave them her heart with maternal tears. **ARTICLE 12** What I am now about to relate, fell under my own observation, or was received from the lips of him, of whose eventful life I speak. Far, far back in the prosperous reign of Kamehameha I, a vessel visited these Islands. She had on board a blacksmith. Kamehameha was every inch a king. All these Islands were made for him, and so he thought was that foreign blacksmith [Samuel Rice]. Power and skill so interlaced providences, that when the vessel sailed, the blacksmith was detained on shore. Stung to very frenzy by being left in those revolting circumstances, to drown thought, he turned to the bottle. When his spree was over, he worked for his royal master but with the full purpose of embracing the first opportunity to leave the Islands. Kamehameha had never been introduced to the code of Christian morals. Another vessel came and went, and the pioneer blacksmith was still detained. The frightful idea of a long and hopeless captivity now burst upon him. He drank more deeply, to assuage by oblivious sleep, his burning madness. But for him there were no soothing influences, no gentle whispers. His further experiences were simply recurrences of the bitter past. When power slipped from the hand of the great Conqueror, a vigilant eye was no longer necessary. The man had been crushed. He no longer desired to return to his native country. His highest ambition was his bottle. He knew, by deep experiences, the horrors of *delirium tremens*. He knew the agony of mind which precedes suicide. He had made all preparation. The hand containing the fatal poison was on the way to his mouth. An impulse suddenly arrested him, and influenced him to hurl that death potion to the winds. Such was his sad state when the American Missionaries reached these Islands in 1820. Other foreigners came and took us by the hand. For four years he never approached us. His first call was one never to be forgotten. His embarrassment was overwhelming. We were then living in a mud-walled hut made for a cookhouse—simply having such surroundings as enabled us to live. His confusion of mind was simply from coming into the presence of one of his own country women. It would naturally give a fresh view of better days, and a more realizing sense of the deep pit into which he had fallen. He was more at ease before he left us, something of a kindly feeling must have kindled within him, for he ever after made us calls. His house was the rendezvous for the gang who kept their blue Saturdays. When this line of life ceased with him, and he had footed the last bill, he estimated that he had spent seven thousand dollars for himself and others in liquor. He had been roused to attend public worship. By placing himself beneath gentle and renovating influences, he at length stood up a temperance man, and a humble Christian. With the feelings of a conqueror he then looked to achieve one more victory. He had an only child, a daughter, approaching womanhood. Her type of character was similar to the young in those years, under very little control, [no] more than the wild goats of the mountain. In two respects she differed. She was smarter and proportionately more mischievous. He went into his own shop and made an iron ring in which to incase her ankle. He then chained her to the post standing in the middle of his thatched house, reaching from the ground to the ridge pole. After being thus confined for three weeks, her ankle became chafed and swollen. She promised fair. He pitied and released her. She immediately left his premises, went straight to a neighboring outhouse, and secreted herself in a barrel. He sought and found her, and, with an unwavering purpose, secured her as before. With a persistence allied to that of Grant (Ulysses S. Grant) on a broader scale, he now kept her chained to that post three additional months. The battle was won. The daughter had learned to fear, to obey, and to love her father. She then came under his guidance, the instruction and influence of the missionaries, as had never been thought of before. She married, became a faithful wife, a devoted mother, and a humble Christian. The name of her father has been obliterated among men, but his female descendants have honorably received the names of five foreigners. He died and was entombed in his own yard. But he still lives on these Hawaiian Islands, lives in his posterity of three generations. His conjugal vicissitudes, all with the sable daughters of the land, were not tragic like those of Henry VIII, for at the time of his death, there were three ex-wives, and still another living with him. His fourth wife was a crown of glory to her husband. In manner she was at once humble and dignified. She belonged to nature's nobility. In being introduced as mistress of that wrecked house, she reigned as queen of hearts. Her husband was fully sensible that through her influence he had become elevated to a higher plane, and grieved that so few years remained in which to enjoy a happiness he had never before tasted. Number four entered that family with her eyes open. She knew that number two was still a member of that household, as it were to grind at the mill. She heeded it not but gathered up her strength to be to the desolate white man a helpmate and a solace. Thus years were measured off to him beneath a serene setting sun. Then he was cut down with a stroke. I saw him enclosed in a coffin, which was sustained at an elevation of common chairs. By the head sat in repose, two female forms, habited in black. The weeping eyes of both were fixed upon one countenance. They were number four and number two. No envy, or jealousy, or suspicion, ever seemed to mar the kindly feeling of the ill-assorted inmates of that home. They were borne along the quiet stream of life in peace and simplicity. Honor be to the memory of the humble old patriarch. I knew him well. He had my most profound sympathy in his deep degradation, in his mighty conflicts, and, in his great conquests. **ARTICLE 13** When Mr. Thurston first commenced his Hawaiian labors at Kailua-Kona, the new native church was every Sabbath filled to overflowing, with doors and windows crowded. There was a company of natives, common men, who, for a time, went and stood on the outside of the church, by an open window. Their object was to scoff. They pointed the finger of ridicule and said, "*The priest shuts up his eyes to pray.*" Then uttering expressions of contempt, they went away laughing, when prayers were half through. After a while, they felt differently, and attended seriously. These new feelings grew upon them, till they too, wished to worship God. But they did not know how. They had only learned his name that was all. Everything else was dark. Yet their feelings inclined them to meet for social worship. They had learned from the teacher's family the manner of kneeling. They had learned through the open windows of the church that they must first shut their eyes and then speak to Jehovah. In praying to their idols, they always kept their eyes open. What they had learned, they wished at once to put in practice. They therefore appointed a prayer meeting the next Sabbath evening in a large house, made for storing canoes. They met accordingly, and in sitting down, formed a straight line across the middle of the house, from end to end. Then, all kneeling, the first man at one end of the row, carefully closed his eyes, and repeated this prayer, "*O, Jehovah, we pray to thee.*" They could say no more. They knew no more. Everyone there, in the same manner in course, repeated that same prayer "*O, Jehovah, we pray to thee.*" The meeting was then ended. But before they dispersed, they appointed another prayer meeting. Again, the next Sabbath evening, they met. Again they ranked and prayed, in course and manner as before, and were able to add to their prayer, thus, "*O, Jehovah, we pray to thee. Take care of us this night.*" In this way they proceeded, step by step, and continued to prolong their prayers from meeting to meeting. They likewise introduced a new exercise by way of variety. They sent one out to stand alone in a spot where all was silence and darkness to obtain a thought. When he returned, he was asked, "*Have you obtained a thought?*" "*Yes.*" Without inquiring what it was another was sent out after the same manner, and so on. If one returned quickly, though he professed to have obtained a thought, it was not acceptable to those within, but he must go again, go out farther into the dark, stay longer, and thus obtain a better thought. They expected that by waiting on God under such circumstances, he would reveal himself to every heart. Such were their first unaided efforts in feeling after God. One of these men belonged to our household during a quarter of a century. It was in after years that he told me the manner in which he learned the ABC of prayer. Then he was able to pray with the fervency and wide scope of a minister, and was often called on to officiate at funerals. In connection with this account, the importance is impressively shown of putting out a talent to usury. **ARTICLE 14** Kaenaku was a distinguished native woman. She was tempted, and lured into sin. Her husband was an unbeliever in the new religion. There were no newspapers in those days, to give intelligence. He availed himself of the usages of the times. In the early hush of evening, with a loud voice, he proclaimed through all the length and breadth of the village, that a church member had been guilty of adultery. Then he went home to comfort the culprit. His dingy, thatched hut had but one opening. It was in the middle, through which they entered half doubled. He placed his wife in one of its close darkened corners and forbade her leaving it. When church members came to see her, he would stand between them and her, to say, that there was no use in their coming there to speak to her words of encouragement. She could no more do right than a stone could roll up hill. When he ate his meals, if he so willed, he rolled her a potato, and she ate it. Otherwise she had opportunity of fasting. Yet he had grace to allow her one privilege. When the bell rung for a religious exercise, if conducted entirely by a missionary, she might attend by going directly there and coming directly back. When moral darkness brooded over the land, a darkness that could be felt, Kaenaku arose like a bright morning star, harbinger of coming day. Then how fallen! She was denied freedom, denied social intercourse, discarded utterly and forever by her husband, doomed to live continually beneath his frowning brow, his cruel government, and made a target to be daily pierced with his sharp arrows. One day he went abroad. She embraced the opportunity, slipped out, and went a mile to see her female teacher. She frankly told her story, acknowledged that in walking with a large company, in an unprotected state, across the wide waste of the island, she had fallen into sin, and was very sorry for it. But the unfeeling manner in which her husband was crushing her for a vice so common, highly exasperated her. The teacher said to her, "*You have been guilty of a great sin against your husband. Unless he requires you to do wrong, accept with meekness and obedience, whatever he is pleased to measure out to you.*" In the depths of her distress, to be thus received by her teacher, whom she loved and trusted, was to her a blank disappointment. She had fled to her for consolation, but she had only painfully probed her, and ordered the most self-denying remedies. A long conversation followed. At length she arose and stood face to face with her teacher. Eye met eye, hers without a blink, and without a movement in a single muscle of her face. Stern resolve was written on every line of her countenance. Just in that attitude, a long, long silence was measured off. Then she opened her mouth and said, "*I'll do it*" tenderly gave her hand and her aloha, and returned to her wretched home to begin anew. *And she did it*. The next time she called upon her teacher, she was a free woman. She carried in her hand a manuscript of some fifteen or twenty pages [in length]. In her seclusion, and under her serious but salutary discipline, she poured forth her views, and the feelings of her heart upon paper. It is worthy of note that not a word was dropped alluding to the abuse and severity of her husband. She had found her proper place of self-abasement. The fifty-first *Psalm* was a transcript of her heartbroken for sin. She said, long as she lived on earth, she should make it her study to do God's will. When she died, he might dispose of her just as he pleased. The recreant manner in which she had treated Christ and his cause, made her feel that she merited crucifixion with her head downward. Occasionally she would sit, as if lost in deep thought, and then sigh, as if from the very bottom of her heart. Possessing talents of the very first order, and cunning with her needle, she was an appendage of nobility. She had white embroidered dresses, and silk ones of brilliant colors.—All these she laid aside, feeling that they were not suitable for her who had sinned so deeply, thus to adorn her person.—She aimed only at respectability. A black silk dress, a black mantle, a plaited palm leaf bonnet trimmed with black, formed her usual Sabbath habit. With her jet black hair and jet black eyes, it was a very becoming costume. By her meekness and wisdom she soothed the fierce anger of her husband, and completely won back his affections. He fully reinstated her in her former position. She was again gladly received as a Sabbath schoolteacher, where she was a model of faithfulness. The church welcomed her return to its bosom, with tearful rejoicing, and with increased affection and confidence. She again approached the Lord's Table with the deepest penitence and humility. Much had been forgiven her, and she loved much. On the eve of thus being most happily restored to all her former privileges, her teachers sailed to attend the General Meeting of the Mission. When they returned, Kaenaku was in her grave. Even then the sad story of her defection was being told in Gath, and published in Ashkelon, causing the enemies of the church to triumph, and her own children to be made sad—but her teachers knew, and that infant church knew, and the angels knew, that from polluted Hawaii, from the ashes of idolatry, her soul had struggled up, to swell the notes of redeeming love. **ARTICLE 15** During the first twelve years of missionary life, we dwelt ten years in eight successive thatched cottages, all without a floor. Five of them had no other window than that of cutting away the thatch, leaving the bare poles. After reaching the Islands, two of these cottages had been successively the abode of royalty. Two thatched ones made under our own direction, were divided into rooms by thatched partitions, having also glass windows, few and far between. Those thatched buildings made comparatively comfortable summer houses. But during bleak, rainy seasons, to those with any constitutional disease or weakness, it involved both health and life. It was in these circumstances that pulmonary complaints took fast hold of my frame. I looked around for means to resist this invasion. Horseback rides seemed desirable. **ARTICLE 16** It was in 1825. Horses were very scarce in those days, owned only by the first class of chiefs. I asked Governor Adams (Kiiapalaoku Kuakini) if he had one of established habits for sobriety. He assured me that he had, and that I should make trial of it. It was brought. It had a kind of cloth pad, a foot and a half square, on its back, confined with ropes, and a rope for its bridle. Necessarily leaving the two children under the care of their father, I went out and mounted. But by ordinary means, there seemed to be no such a thing as getting a single step out of the animal. At length, by having one native go before and pull, and another go in the rear and drive, locomotion slowly commenced. Seated on a curve, without any facilities for preserving my equilibrium, urgency compelled my free hands to grasp the mane. We had just surmounted all obstacles, and I was becoming mistress of that new state of things, when suddenly we came to a dead stand, by reason of a substantial stone wall, which crossed our pathway. It could not of course be turned aside like a gate, but the expected medical aid was not to be given up. As there was no alternative to success, the two natives went to work cheerfully in laying stone by stone aside. After some delay, we proceeded on as before, and entered the village. All left their houses to come and gaze. Evidently there was a novelty beyond that of getting on the stupid beast. It was this—a woman was riding with both limbs accommodated on one side of the horse—a thing never seen before, although the Governor and head woman had given them examples of female horsemanship. After becoming the observed of all observers, and having received a reflection of their happy faces, we turned back, put up the gap in the wall, and reached home with merry hearts, having enjoyed in the ride all that was ludicrous. I then remembered that when at Honolulu, a newly arrived sea captain called on the missionaries and informed them that he had brought out for them some notions (items), such as high post bedsteads and side saddles. The English Deputation of the London Missionary Society were then inmates of our family. They never forgot, and they never allowed *us* to forget, our American notions, high post bedsteads and side saddles. I sent and obtained one of those saddles. We had a wicket gate, hung with leather hinges from a worn out shoe, introduced into the stone wall. Governor Adams kindly allowed me his own fleet saddle horse. Thus I was accommodated for sanitary rides. **ARTICLE 17** My youthful years opened upon life with a great degree of physical health and vigor. A little more than a year before I first left my country, my mother from active life was suddenly laid upon a bed of fever and great helplessness. A sister [Elizabeth Edwards Bishop] or myself were constantly by her side both by day and by night. In one short week the disease proved fatal. A few hours before she breathed her last, in the chamber of death, I expectorated blood from the lungs. For six weeks it was the cause of much debility. Then a very slight cough commenced, and it constantly increased till it was very harassing. The scales were vacillating. Powerful remedies brought it to a severe crisis. It was life, recovery. Again I engaged in active scenes, and for several months sustained the responsibilities of the schoolroom. It was never alluded to by anyone, in deciding about engaging in the enterprise of a foreign mission. Three years after those sufferings, I became a mother. Two days after that event, a slight cough commenced. It increased and kept me in a prostrate, perilous position. But I at length rallied, and apparently stood again on firm ground. Three years more run their rounds in health. Then the hard struggles of pioneer life, its efforts and its privations again prostrated me with pulmonary complaints. Nature triumphed, and I was again free. Scarcely a year had elapsed, when we were visited by storms of fierce winds and deluging rains, uncommonly long and severe. No ray of light was admitted into our dwelling but through an open door. Our house was thatched with lauhala (hala) leaves, and these were loosely put on by unfaithful hands. The only spot I could call home was damp, cold, and bleak. When the evening mountain breeze came down in its strength, I enveloped myself in flannel and found refuge beneath the double curtains of a bed. Thus, all had been well had not heavy dampness acted upon me as a blight. Disease took fast hold of my frame, and became obstinate. The very breath I drew daily fastened on my mind the impression that I should soon die of consumption. Four years passed away before I was restored to my former vigor. But as it appeared in after life, victory over disease was then most complete. The penalty for accidental overexertion in my mother's short, fatal sickness was entirely paid in ten years. Afterwards, for more than thirty years spent at Kailua-Kona, not even sweeping influenzas seemed to touch me, nor was I affected with common colds. I shared both in common with others, after passing from that to other climates.

ARTICLE 18 We were taught that unprovoked, the natives of these islands conspired the death of the great navigator, Captain [James] Cook, cut off vessels, murdered crews, and chewed the flesh of their enemies as the sweetest tidbit of revenge. Conversing with the captain of our vessel, a few weeks before reaching these islands, in 1820, he remarked that he must get his guns out, for it was not safe to approach these islands without being in a state of defense. "*What,*" I replied, "*leave us, a feeble company, in a defenseless state, among a people you cannot approach without firearms?*" "*Ah,*" said he, shaking his head, "*it is* *not my wish to leave you in such circumstances."* We were dropped down on their shores, and left in their sole power. From personal acquaintance and a thorough knowledge of their character, we found them, as a nation, ignorant, debased, polluted, wedded to their sins, but all was done in a good-natured way. Alcoholic drinks had the same effect on them as upon the civilized world, it turned men into brutes. But to be implacably cruel and revengeful toward their enemies formed no part of their character. They were peculiarly simple, and childlike, affectionate and confiding. There is no figure of speech in saying that when Queen Kamamalu, who afterwards died in England, found a daughter of America, a stranger in a strange land, under peculiar trials—she, being possessed of ample dimensions, cradled the afflicted one in her arms, pillowed her head upon her bosom, and wept over her tears of sympathy. And now after a lapse of fifty years, a review of those friendships, formed with those children of nature, in those early days, stirs within me the deepest emotions of my soul. O Kamamalu, Kamamalu, thou, too, didst become a stranger in a strange land, and when there so early called to plunge into the dark, cold stream, didst thou reach a better land? The [British and American] missionaries by accommodating themselves to new circumstances, both with firmness and with elasticity, by quietly dropping the seed of the Kingdom as opportunity offered, passed along five years beside the still waters. It was when the seed sprung up, and brought forth fruit, that they were called to put on the whole armor, that they had prepared, in which to face a savage nation. Their heaviest missionary trials came by inversion, came from the other side of the globe, from the representatives of the proud Christian nations of England and America. Ten natives stood propounded (suggested) for admission into the church. Among them were Kaahumanu, the energetic and decided ruler of the Kingdom, Kalanimoku, her powerful Executive, the two dowager queens that sailed with us on board the *Thaddeus*, the ex-queen of Kauai, a son of King Kaumualii and Kapiolani, a high chiefess, second to no one in noble aspirations and acts. As yet no native church had been organized in the land. There was simply that transplanted church from Boston, to which had been added reinforcement. Under such circumstances, an English ship touched at these islands, bringing some strange animals. They were white-skinned bipeds, of the genus called *Homo*. They appeared to have a fellowship one with another, for, after leaping ashore, they seemed to cling to each other in a body, in number about forty. They bore along with them what in the hands of soldiers would have been called weapons of death. They had, too, the gift of speech, for, from their lips, in English accents, proceeded sounds like these, "*If the missionary will teach the people that they are absolved from obeying the Ten Commandments, it will be well with him. Otherwise, we will take his life, and burn down his house.*" The wife of the missionary was then isolated, looking alone to her husband for protection. She was a refined lady, then in a most delicate state of health. But she was equal to the emergency, and both she and her husband rose to the heroism and sublimity of the spirit of martyrdom. Then it was that the people, known through our world as barbarians and savages, formed a garrison around their teachers, and stood day and night with pointed bayonet. Then it was [Ulumaheihei] Hoapili, of the first-class of chiefs, stood up in his power and strength, and portly bearing, and said, "*If they shoot my teacher, the ball shall pass through me first.*" He had become the husband of the dowager queen of the white dress. They were helpmates for each other, and long lived to be a nursing father and a nursing mother to the church of Lahaina. Thus, when the Bible was brought to these islands, it made great confusion. It was invading the strongholds of an opposite power, which had maintained undisturbed sway for ages. Its foreign emissaries were active and bold. They entered a territory belonging to a Sovereign Power. They cast their eyes upon a vineyard where the first gush of joys had been experienced by the missionaries and natives, mingling prayers and tears and labors together. The intruders said, "*We will slay the people here with physical and moral death. We will beat down their vineyard, destroy its hedge, and sow it with salt. We will lay the whole village in ashes.*" That was the purport of their sworn purpose. Their weapons of warfare were stones, clubs, knives and cannonballs. The great war between good and evil, between right and wrong was then instituted. Passing by vessels of an inferior class, a naval ship of the United States became an antagonist. The Captain's demands were well defined, and his great boast was, that whoever opposed him, would find his vessel to be like fire. So while his men smashed in the windows of private houses, and imminently imperiled life, he rode, roughshod, over the heads of the rulers of the land, and with the bold front of Apollyon (destroyer), asserted his right and his power to inoculate the people with physical and moral death, and so far succeeded, that the acclamations of triumph rent the air, and where heard in the distance. In this great crisis of the nation, missionaries were wanted that counted not their lives dear unto themselves. The nation saw that there was a wide, impassable gulf between the spirit of the two parties. There were those, on the one hand, who hissed (hated) the idea of having Christianity engrafted on this wild stock, whose aim was to crush Christianity in the bud, who would blast with the breath of their nostrils everyone that opposed their measures, and who claimed ignorance and sin to be the only natural inheritance of these islanders, leaving disease and death to follow in the train, unthought of, and uncared for. On the other hand, there were those who opened up to them happiness, both here and hereafter, by leading them to virtue, to intelligence, to duty, and to God, standing firmly at their posts, ready to seal their teachings with their blood. This was a heathen nation, just waking into life, and seeing men as trees walking. Not the tongues of forty missionaries, if they possessed a perfect knowledge of the Hawaiian language, and the eloquence of angels, could, in words, have so vividly portrayed the contrast between the spirit of the world and the spirit of the church, between selfishness and benevolence, as did those hostilities. God made the wrath of man to praise Him, and the remainder thereof he restrained. The missionaries, in planting churches in a land deluged with the iniquity and scum of ages, made no compromise with Evil. The government of the churches required them to be wiped from impurity and intemperance, even as a dish is wiped, wiping it, and turning it upside down. The state, Christian in its front and bearing, noble in its general aspect, has, nevertheless, compromised with Evil. By receiving money into the public treasury for means of impurity, and of intemperance in drugs and alcoholic drinks, vultures have been allowed to prey upon the very vitals of society, and a fearful blot to mar the beauty of the escutcheon of the nation. May the afflatus of the Almighty lead the Legislative Assembly, on this the year of the nation's jubilee, to present Hawaii, the firstborn of this vast Pacific, a distinguished spectacle to the nations, revealing a youthful form, in symmetry, in beauty, and in glory, clear as the sun, fair as the moon, and as terrible to all opposition as an army with banners. **ARTICLE 19** Three days after landing, the queen, Kamamalu gave the sisters a promising boy twelve years of age as a pledge on her part that their friendship should be permanent. He loved to learn, and acquired the knowledge of language very readily. When at any time he saw a tear, with much tenderness he ever inquired the cause by asking, "*Is it love to your father?*" He often sat down on the mat by my side, and said, "*Mrs. Thurston, talk about Jehovah, talk about [Henry] Obookiah.*" Every new thing that he learned respecting God and his laws, of Jesus and of Heaven, he imparted to others in the village. A poor blind man (Bartimeus Lalana Puaaiki) listened, and at once believed and loved. Without further instruction, he began to pray and exhort. Some listened, others laughed, and others mocked. The King had him before him to see what the gabbler had to say, when he heard so good a confession that he was sent away from the royal presence with liberal approval. He discontinued eating dog's flesh, live vermin, and other loathsome garbage, of which the natives are ravenously fond of. A man who lived under the same roof with him, feeling this abstinence as a tacit reproach on his own more filthy feeding, became indignant, and complained to the King, that his blind neighbor, under the influence of his strange religion, refused to taste the national dainties alluded to above, and begged that he might be punished, to compel him to do as other people did. "*The man is right,*" replied Liholiho. "*I will not suffer him to be harmed. I intend myself soon to learn the new system, and to leave off these bad ways. Then you must all do the same.*" After the blind man lovingly received his first ideas of the new religion from juvenile lips, which was in the early part of 1821, he exhibited one uniform character. He would be seen early Sabbath morning, without hat or shoes, without pants or shirt, with his girdle and a slight kapa (fabric) thrown around his person, with a staff, a long beard, sightless eyes, and diminutive bending form, wending his way to the missionaries house. There planting himself by the gate or outer door, he would sit long in meditation, waiting for a passing salutation. I have known the foreigner, with crowned head and shod feet, with all the paraphernalia of dress in the last most approved fashion, in feelings wither into insignificance before his love and devotion, his pathos and humility. Here is a tame specimen of what he often expressed in grimaces, in gestures, and in words, all combined. "*Let me feel your hand. Let me cling to it. Let me weep over it. Let me express the feelings that swell my heart. The glory of this great salvation I owe first to God, and then to you.*" He was the first marked Christian convert, and became the [famous] blind preacher of Maui, so distinguished for ability, fervor, and eloquence. **ARTICLE 20** Under God, the people of these Islands are indebted to Kamehameha I, for bringing them all under one Government. To [Henry] Obookiah, for first touching chords, the vibrations of which, with ever increasing force have caused Jehovah to become Hawaii's God.—To Kamehameha II, (Liholiho) for abolishing idolatry—and receiving a Protestant Mission.—To Kamehameha III, for allowing his subjects (citizens) to hold land in fee simple, for a written Constitution of Laws, for limiting his own power, and enlarging that of his subjects, by giving them the elective franchise, thereby, through their own representatives, having a voice in the councils of the nation (Hawaii).—To the American Board of Commissioners for Foreign Missions, for reducing a verbal dialect to a written language, and for [alphabet] letters and Christianity.—To the American Bible and Tract Societies, for fertilizing streams (minds) through the land.—To England, France, Belgium, and the United States, for receiving them as a sister nation in the constitution of nations that encircle the globe.—To Admiral [Richard Darton] Thomas, for the continued independence of this nation.—And to Individual Enterprise, for political advice, for educational aid, for the learned professions, for commerce, the arts, and agriculture. **ARTICLE 21** (Extract from a Honolulu Newspaper) On Monday evening the same church was again filled with a large audience to listen to Mrs. Thurston's Reminiscences of early missionary life. The fact that she was one of the pioneer band, which the brig *Thaddeus* brought out in 1820, that she was teacher of the old chiefs and that she was to read her own narrative, created much curiosity to hear her. Although nearly seventy-five years of age, she executed her task, which occupied one hour and a half, without faltering, and in a clear voice, which could be heard in every part of the house. The narrative commenced with the touching story of [Henry] Obookiah, the young Hawaiian who went to America to learn of true Christianity that he might return and teach his countrymen. He and three or four other Hawaiians were taught in the mission school in Cornwall, Connecticut. It was their arrival and appeal to Christians in America that led those who embarked in the brig *Thaddeus* to devote themselves to missions, against the remonstrance of their relatives. So eager were some of the pioneer band to leave, that one or two of them broke off in the midst of their college course at Yale that they might join in the novel expedition. Mrs. Thurston narrated some incidents about the young King Liholiho, Kaahumanu and other chiefs, which were new and interesting. She and her husband, the late Asa Thurston, having been the teachers of these noted chiefs, she had opportunities which few of the missionaries enjoyed to collect facts about them. Her narrative was made up of short anecdotes, so minute in detail and so touching in pathos, that they awakened the deepest interest in her hearers. Among them was the story of blind Bartimeus [Lalana Puaaiki]—the conversion of John Ii—a royal feast in 1820, when the young king [Liholiho] brought a luaued dog into the missionary's house, sat down and asked them to join in. The story of the venerable John Young and Isaac Davis, the counselors of the great Kamehameha, under whose advice and assistance he had conquered, the group was very touching, as was that of Keopuolani, the wife and mother of kings. In connection with the remarks relating to this heroic chiefess, Mrs. Thurston exhibited a silk shawl presented to her by Kaahumanu forty-four years ago—a beautiful memento of a noble Hawaiian, whose memory will always be dear to those who knew her. Not the least interesting was the story of the erection of the first framed house on Hawaii, which the Board of Missions had sent out. The erection of framed houses had been tabooed, but woman's influence prevailed with the king, and he allowed the tabu to be set aside and the house to be built. The closing remarks, in which she described the fierce opposition encountered by the early missionaries from base foreigners, whom she termed "*bipeds of the genus homo*" was one of the most withering and deserved rebukes ever uttered by woman's lips. The exercises occupied one hour and three-quarters, and the interest of the audience seemed unabated at its close. Before adjourning, His Excellency the Minister of Foreign Affairs rose and suggested that a collection be taken up for the two remaining pioneer missionaries—Mrs. Thurston and Mrs. [Mercy Partridge] Whitney—to which call the congregation generously responded by contributing the sum of $350. Two verses of the missionary hymn closed one of the most interesting meetings ever held in Honolulu. **ARTICLE 22** How can I write reminiscences of fifty years ago, without turning to a father's home? It was in a rural spot, twenty-five miles west of Boston. His house was red, its heavy color enlivened by deep trimmings of white. Two chimneys, at a due distance from each other, issued from the roof beside the ridgepole. It was two stories high, the two tiers of windows exhibiting the taste of modern architecture. Enter the massive front door, of ample width, turn to the left, and you will find two front rooms with their chambers. In those rooms, cast your eyes aloft, not very high, and you will see well-seasoned beams that speak of perpetuity. Look on the floor by its walls and you will see that the beams whereon the house rests, project sufficiently to accommodate childhood to seats. Speak reverently of those ancient well-seasoned beams. They were laid in the earlier part of the eighteenth century, when Queen Anne reigned over the Colonies, and they remain to this day. The sixth generation, in a direct line, is there now being trained for earth and for Heaven. It is an entire family of five orphaned children of Hawaiian birth. The strong framework of those four rooms formed a nucleus to a large farmhouse, whose doors in my childhood years, used to be counted up as fifty-one. That antique western chamber, with two windows, through which to view the splendor of the setting sun, with a chimney, and a closet filled with wood, to give warmth to solitude beneath the reign of a long, bleak winter, was my *sanctum sanctorum*. Our large family was made eligible for life's work, by having its thrift depend on the activities of every individual. We were a world by ourselves, under the reign of one united head, whose natures and whose titles were "All Power" and "All Love," the father and the mother. The daughters were linked with an active, discreet mother, to give with their own hands comfort and happiness to all the departments of domestic life. They were made familiar with wielding every implement of the kitchen, and introduced into the mysteries of preparing, both the substantial and the elegant comforts of a farmer's table, the limited places from which to select materials, being the cellar, the garret, the pantry, the dairy, the garden and the orchard. They plied the needle, having in that line of labor to accommodate themselves to the warmth of summer, and the rigors of winter. "*They sought wool and flax, and worked willingly with their hands.*" The comparison of "*days being swifter than a weaver's shuttle,*" was to them very impressive, because so well understood. "*They were not afraid of snow for their house, for all were clothed*" with woolen of home manufacture. There were several of the family whose business it was to work, and whose pastime it was to study. And industry enabled them to do a day's work at each. An efficient father led forth his sons to the toils of the day. In the summer, at six o'clock in the morning, the family breakfast was taken with dispatch, as if to go forth to meet the king of day. Yet he, who officiated as priest of that house, under most pressing employments never thought of omitting the customary reading of a chapter in course from the large family Bible, placed on the small stand before him, within the family circle. Then they all arose and stood, while he laid incense upon the family altar, always with a full volume of voice. Commencing business thus early and laboring late in the decline of day, five seasons of refreshments were called for, but the meal of meals, for variety, and for social intercourse, was at noon-tide leisure. At a given signal the laborers from abroad hastened to exchange meridian rays for the shades of home. There from every point was a reunion of the whole family band. At the announcement of "Dinner is ready," the united head stood side by side, at the upper end of the large oval dining table, the children promptly followed into line, the sons standing at the right hand of the father, according to their ages, the youngest son and the youngest daughter completing the oval circle, standing at the foot of the table. Then the father spread forth his hands and led in an exercise of devotion called "asking a blessing," thus, "*Almighty Father, command thy blessing upon this food. Give it strength to strengthen us. Give us grace to enable us to live suitably under all our enjoyments, temporal and spiritual, for the Redeemer's sake.*" "Order is Heaven's first law," could not be found written on the walls. But at a glimpse, the spirit was seen. At that table, the mother was mistress of the carving knife and of ceremonies, receiving aid from her elder children.—The father, at liberty, led off in conversation, by remark, by recital, or by instruction as the case might be.—Although he was puritanical in his religion, after the straightest sect, yet neither that, nor the heaviest toils of life, prevented him from being prone, at this noontide season, to pass into the lighter regions of anecdote and hilarity. His family followed hard after him. But they were very careful not to raise sails, till he had first raised a wind. With delighted feelings, eye met eye, and heart met heart. And that allowed, chastened exuberance of mirthfulness was not without its use in causing the bones to become moistened with marrow. An air of gravity assumed by the father was, as in a mirror, reflected from every face. After a moment's pause, they simultaneously arose, and stood with precision and reverence. The father's voice was again heard, reading in a second exercise of devotion, called "returning thanks," thus, "*Source of all being and happiness, we thank Thee for life with its surrounding blessings. We thank Thee for this social repast. We thank Thee for the day and means of grace, and the hopes of immortal life beyond the grave.—Through Jesus Christ.*" Thus the young beings of that family, in animal, in social, and in spiritual wants, were so fed from their father's storehouse that they gradually returned to the renewed duties of the afternoon, with feelings prepared to say to the children of dissipation, "*You may go and dance at balls, but we'll enjoy our friends at home.*" In that region in those days it was the public opinion dividing a father's property, where sex alone was the guide—that it took two daughters to poise against one son. At the same time it was a matter of consideration and forethought, that the son be trained to an employment that would secure to him the comforts and happiness of life. No such provision was made for a daughter. His time, when he came to be of age, was of value, and turned into dollars. When the daughter came of age, the line of freedom was not observed, but she, like a child at home, lived on and labored without remuneration. No calculation whatever was made for her, but that, according to the constitution of things, some one of the sterner sex would take her by the hand, and lead her forth into the mazes of human life. Under such influences, a character was manufactured not very far from my father's dwelling. She belonged to a family of substance and position. The market was supplied, and she was left, without forming any new ties of life for herself, which would draw forth her activities and affections, and engage her in the commerce of life with her fellows. Her parents, too, died, and she was left alone to lay her hands upon their cold gravestones. Without any aim in life, without any self-reliance, she was thrown back upon herself, to sustain the full responsibility of her own existence. The fierce ordeal caused the juices of social life to be dried up. She avoided society, even public worship. As a natural result when she was seen her manner and dress appeared odd. One chamber, her paternal inheritance, left her in her father's will, till the day of her marriage—which never came—that one chamber was her refuge. When she ceased to breathe, came her funeral, and mother earth received her child of vacant life to her silent bosom. There was another maiden lady near my father's house in another direction. She was independent, enterprising, and self-reliant. The tendrils of her nature clasped humanity. The afflicted knew where to go for sympathy, and the perplexed for counsel. She laid her soft hand upon the heads of childhood, her still softer voice of love fell upon their hearts as they rose up and called her blessed. She was eminently a lady of mark. Every lip pronounced her name with respect and deference, as being one whom they delighted to honor. In the year 1822, soon after the printing of the first sheets of the spelling book in the Hawaiian language, a missionary was sitting at a table in his own house, with a chief, teaching him the rudiments of his own language. The chief grasped at an idea he wished to communicate. So turning to his attendants, seated on the mat, he said, "*The consonant is a man, the vowel is a woman, put them together, they make something, apart they are nothing at all.*" We, who are more thoroughly instructed, know that a *vowel* makes a perfect syllable by itself. It is a consonant only that makes nothing at all, standing alone. At the distance of half a mile from my father's house, by an unfrequented pathway, there was a district school of forty or fifty pupils, gathered from a section of agriculturalists. In morals and intelligence it was number one. There respect to superiors was diligently inculcated. Boys bowed, and girls courtesied. In the morning, as the teacher was seen to approach the schoolhouse, the scholars were at their seats, rank and file, standing ready to receive their teacher with an obeisance, as they would have done to a king. He returned the salutation. This was the greeting of a new day. During all its hours, no scholar retired from, or returned to his presence, without a similar act of courtesy. Did a scholar come before the school to read a composition, or speak a piece?—He knew as by instinct what was the Alpha and what the Omega. And the beautiful result of that school of nurtured virtue was seen along the streets by children and youth always respectfully recognizing their friends and superiors.—An accomplished teacher, (of blessed memory), taught his pupils, in that school, to love learning for its own sake, and when school was closed to the higher classes for nine months, until another winter revolved upon them, he bade them, at their own homes, search for knowledge as for hidden treasure, and to pursue a daily course of study, even without a teacher's aide. And I know that under his influence, some of his scholars thus spent all the time they could command. The first class of girls had passed through the higher rules of [Daniel Adams] *Adams's Arithmetic*. At the examination, the tall, educated minister stood up, and made an address according to custom, to the reverently-standing scholars. During the exercise, a blush was seen to pass over the cheeks of the girls of the arithmetic class. The words dropped were simply these, "*There is no use in girls going so far in arithmetic, other than setting themselves up as candidates for the wives of merchants.*" There was one there who had higher aspirations than to make education a matrimonial ticket. She had been taught by the schoolmaster mentioned above, that daughters had been endowed with minds capable of culture, and that intellectual attainments raised them in the scale of being. But, in female education, would her father, the Deacon, go ahead of his minister? It was not to be expected. She wished to go forty miles away. And nothing would satisfy her short of hearing a negative come from the lips of her decided father. So, choosing a calm hour, replete with home enjoyment, she stood behind his chair of repose, so as to elude the penetrating eye of a bluff refusal. She then summed up all her resolution, and said, "*Father, I have a strong desire to attend Bradford Academy. May I?*" A response came, not anticipated. He was pleased—was moved—granted every indulgence asked—and from that moment the love of a father for a daughter expanded into the bright hues of deep respect. He allowed influences to be exerted over him, and his mellowed character to be molded in a manner very touching. At the age of twenty-four, the most important proposition of the daughter's life was laid before her. By a written communication she learned that her father felt that "*he had consecrated her to God, and though such a separation would be most trying to nature, yet the thing proceeded from the Lord, his will be done.*" She inquired, "*Do you advise me to go for life to a foreign heathen land?*" He, whose casting vote had always decided the important questions of her life, for the first time was silent. "*Lucy,*" he said, "*you must choose your own pathway in life. It is for yourself to walk in, apart from your father.*" Then she stood on the mount of independence, with full liberty to dispose of herself. Contiguous to this eminence lay the deep, dark vale of crushing responsibility and agonizing thought. It was a salutary lesson to her, that, unaided, she there tarried and counted the cost. Alone with the Savior, she made a decision, where he led, however dark the pathway, she would follow, to stand or to fall. The burden was removed from her mind. With an elevation of soul, with cheerful, unmoved feelings, she coupled, by contrast, the friends and country of home, and the privations and dangers of a pilgrim's life. The day she left her father's house, he had eight married children, and eight sons and daughters-in-law. Of that sixteen in the home circle, she, who took her life in her hand, and went to the heathen, is now the sole survivor. To have her early friends restored to her, in all the vigor of immortal youth, one more beautiful change in her alone is wanting—going to sleep on earth, and waking up in Heaven. **ARTICLE 23** I have thus long veiled this experience within my own family. When I am gone, withholding names, let it come in as part of my life's history. During the last fifty years, I have taken five voyages, each of eighteen thousand miles in length more or less. In looking back over them all, one stands out very prominently. It proved to be a rare school. Deeply expensive—almost revoltingly so.—But the acquirements were worth all their cost. The branches pursued were, *poverty of spirit, forgiveness of injuries, self-control in bearing one's share of the ills of life, forming the hearts of childhood to piety, and ultimately rejoicing in tribulation*. As a straw, thrown into a stream will show the course of the current, so, now and then, through a loophole, I give a partial glimpse of the manner in which lessons were impressed on the mind. As there was neither name nor book to its belongings, I designate it from what it was to me. **SECTION I** (From New York to Valparaiso with Two Youngest Children.) *My Dear Daughter Persis*—I learned more of human nature on my voyage than I ever learned before, since I had existence. You know how the 27th *Psalm* became endeared to us as being the last we read at family prayers. Before the voyage was ended, I read it again and again, feeling as if every verse had been prophetic.—"*The Lord is my light and my salvation, whom shall I fear?*"—etc. And did the captain report that he had incurred more risk in defending and upholding me than ever before? What chivalry! For a time that was true. May blessings descend a hundredfold on his head, and on those most dear to him, for every effort thus made. Two months from seven may thus happily be deducted. Engrave it in marble, and whisper it in the ear of the Most High. But now we are approaching inclement weather, and furious winds. Sociality is suspended. Sympathy is withheld. Aid is withdrawn. What of that? From persons in such situations, must I require continued evidence of their continued friendship to be at ease? Far be it from me. And so I counted off the days and nights, and dreamed that tomorrow would be as yesterday. True, I encountered well-aimed arrows dipped in poison. But I was sustained by an inward consciousness of striving to do what was right, and while they diminished my happiness, they failed to pierce my heart. Yet that, too, was to come, and from a source so unexpected and aggravating, that it seemed to wither my very being. I was not in the state of David and his men at Ziklag, who wept till they had no more power to weep. I wept till I had no power to refrain from weeping. Oh, could I have forgotten memories the most precious and tender. After being out some two months, for several weeks we had most tempestuous weather. For three days a gale continued with unabated fury. At one time our situation was such as I never before then witnessed. As the sailors express it, the ship was wallowing in the trough of the sea, and as the poets express it, the waves were running mountain high. Behold one of them, not in the distance, not ahead, but in looking up at the very side of the vessel, which in her tremendous rolls, would, on the leeward side, dip the water into the ship from over her very bulwarks. A depth of it tumultuously crossed and recrossed the skylight, as I never before beheld. What can they be doing on deck? I do not hear the waves thrown over and yet the water rushes to and fro, as if the very ocean was let loose upon us. The door of the companion way was closed and fastened, but as the cover happened to be drawn off sufficiently to admit my head, I went up the stairs to take a peep, and at once beheld the situation of the ship, and the sublimity of the ocean. The liability of a wave soon rendered it necessary to close the companion way entirely, and I reluctantly withdrew from a view of the ocean in all its strength and majesty, to my dark abode below. The captain, too, was about wearing the ship—in a gale of wind—one of the most dangerous maneuvers there is performed. However, nothing was experienced from it of a nature more serious, than that of a pitcher of water, which was standing in its assigned place ever since being aboard, discharged its whole contents onto our books, and our largest chest, standing within cleats, jumped out of its fastenings, turned a somersault, had its top torn off, and lay on its side at the foot of the stairs. Thus the day dawned upon us. The captain remarked at the breakfast table, that if he had not tacked the ship before that time, its decks would have been entirely swept. Then there was a day of disasters. In going from the companion way to the house on deck, there was quite a little space to pass, where there was nothing to lay hold of, to enable one to maintain a perpendicular position, when very rolling, wet and slippery. There the strong arm of the practical sailor was appreciated. Not thus accommodated, the result was, I fell and was sent down to the leeward side of the ship with a velocity and force, of which I had not before conceived. I struck upon my chest against the stairs which led to the upper deck. At first it affected me very much. I enveloped myself in flannel, and kept in my berth, but by night I found it difficult to bring a long breath, or make an effort to help myself. The next day I was, about appearing as usual. In going up to the same meal, in just the same place, a strong active man, a passenger, fell, and was considerably injured by being sent across the deck. He, too, lodged against the stairs. Then he was laid up in his berth. Since the gale his wife and children had kept their room. Now she was called to make efforts. But before the day was out, she fell with great force, her eye coming in contact with one corner of a chest. The eye became very much inflamed, and the parts around looked frightfully bruised, but she made the best of it, bound it up, and spent most of the night in wakefulness and effort, to prevent her children being thrown from the berth.—Said the captain to a passenger, *"You look ten years older than you have done. The howling of the wind, the groaning, and creaking, and rolling of the vessel, the clashing of the waves, and our running, and hallooing, and pulling ropes, has frightened you. Be of good courage. It is time enough for you to be discouraged when you see that I am."*—It was in that extremity that I was singled out and disciplined by finding myself silently imprisoned under lock and key. No anger or indignation crossed my mind to bear me up, but I felt—I felt crushed. I knocked, and knocked, and vainly knocked, to obtain release. There were two doors between me and my children, who, with others belonging to the second table, were at their evening meal. They all thought the thumping was outside on the upper deck. And others happened to be in various parts of the ship. After a lapse of time, the steward returned to his pantry, which was on the same aisle opposite my prison. I called him and he released me. I soon returned with the children through the darkness and howling of the storm, and closed the door in my little room below. But such a sense of utter desolation I had never felt before. I sat down and wept like a child. The children said, "*Mother, what makes you cry so? Mother, what does make you cry so.*" I presume before two hours had elapsed, every soul on board that vessel had learned the humiliating position in which I had been placed. I passed the thing in silence, but an irrepressible curiosity sprung up among the passengers, as to "*Who did it?*" When away from me, my children were incessantly plied on the subject, charged with having done it, and found no end in being questioned and cross-questioned respecting it. Nothing short of sifting things to the very bottom could silence their persevering inquiries. Thus a week passed away, feelings within, and elements without, seeming to be in strange sympathy, all antagonistic to repose. Then the secret came out. The author of the deed, to pacify feelings, assumed its responsibility. The captain himself said to me with his own lips, "*It was I that fastened you in last week. I did it because you visited the place before the second table was served.*" **SECTION II** (At the Port of Valparaiso Where Our Vessel Stopped a Few Weeks) On reaching port, both body and mind became refreshed, and I again experienced a return of my wonted firmness and elasticity of spirits. Cold, desolation, and those long dreary nights of darkness, the contending elements, lashed to very fury, we had left far in the distance. We again came in contact with a busy world. We partook of its refreshments. We saw happy countenances. We felt the renovating influence of light and warmth. In my inmost soul I longed for the return of peace and harmony, of kind looks and kind words. If any advances, if any concessions, if any forgiveness was wanted on my part, I would most cheerfully make them. In this spirit I wrote the captain a letter. He made no reply to it, but it led to a long conversation. The best apology that he made for himself was, "*That a continued dropping would wear away a stone.*" O, it was unfortunate for me, most unfortunate for him, that he chose for his companion and most intimate friend one who most unaccountably became my avowed enemy. He held the position of Haman, I of Mordecai. He had already reached the height of seriously meditating driving me from the cabin. His real name I spare, and distinguish him by the fictitious appellation of Haman. But we were not through with our conversation. During it, we were standing alone on the farther end of the upper deck, looking out upon the green waters. His criticisms were ever grateful to my private ear. (At the public table, I only endured them.) I now elicited them, so as to know wherein I had offended. I give you one of his most aggravated specimens. I was told before sailing that we should have a stove. Provision was made for it. The other three vessels that sailed about the same time, all had their warm stoves. In one there was even a second stove, one in the forecastle. The stove in our ship was not brought forward. In the cold region of Cape Horn, on the Sabbath, public, services were held in the upper cabin. It was of much lower temperature up there than between decks. I put on my silk quilted bonnet, made for the voyage, to go up. As I felt the cold, and as it was favorable, too, toward concealing the tears that sometimes trickled down my cheeks in spite of all my efforts, I retained it on my head. I did not consider, I did not even know, that it would be construed into disrespect, and that the "*wearing of a bonnet was proper only for a meeting held in a bar room, or in a barn.*" Thus endeth the second lesson. Soon after reaching Valparaiso, the captain called on a distinguished family from my native state, pious, wealthy, and living in good style. The lady, through him, extended an invitation to me, to come with my children and spend the time in her family, during the weeks the ship lay in port. She apologized for not inviting a second family, on the ground—that she had but one spare bedroom. The captain excused me for that reason, saying it would be inconvenient for me to come with my children, and only have one room for our accommodation. There was nothing for me to say. But it was natural enough for me to compare in my own mind, one bedroom in that capacious house, with the manner in which we were then stowed away, confined to one stateroom, with two close berths, the one above the other. There was another objection, he said, to my becoming domesticated in her family—the bold declivity that surrounded their premises. There would be danger of the children's rolling down it. In the fullness of my heart, I now, for the first time, ventured to speak, by asking, "*Have not they themselves children, a dooryard, and roads?*" "*Yes, but they are accustomed to their situation. Children were heedless, and did not always keep within proper bounds.*" To get the cargo ashore was the business of the ship. To accomplish this, two hatchways to go down into the lower hold of the ship must needs be thrown open and kept so. One of them was within a few feet of the door of my stateroom, and hard by the stairs which led to the deck. We will go on deck and get away from these dangerous places. But on deck stands a machine to raise the cargo aloft from the hold of the ship. "*Mind that machine! By its powerful whirl, an iron appendage is liable to be thrown. One stroke might break a limb or prove fatal. Mother—take care of your children.*" In the forepart of the voyage, the captain said, that on reaching port, I should, of course attend a church there. I remembered what he had formerly said to me. Every Sabbath morning I laid out every article necessary for me and for my children in going to church. The first Sabbath, the captain went. Not a word was said to me on the subject. The second Sabbath at the breakfast table, he thus expressed himself, "*I am going to church today, who else is going?*" The captain said not another word. After rising from the table, he went directly down to a passenger's room, to see what was the matter, "*It was as plain,*" said he, "*that you were offended at table, as that you have a nose on your face.*" She said to him, "*You have always treated me well, but I do sympathize with Mrs. Thurston, who feels deeply on the subject of being criticized so much at the public table. She does not come and tell me her feelings, but I see tears fall as she passes our door to go to her room.*" They reconciled matters. She thought he went to my room to do the same, but no. The captain mentioned to a passenger whether it could be possible that Mrs. Thurston's mind had lost its balance, because she vindicated (justified) eating meat three times a day. What I said was that, since I had eaten more, I had had far better health in several respects, and far less headaches. We had, had fresh provisions, vegetables, and meat after having been destitute of both. Was it the benevolent sympathy of his anxious heart that led him the same day at tea to put ten slices of salt-dried beef on my plate? They were about the size as if cut from the middle part of a beef creature's tongue. In as respectful a manner as I could, I begged a part to be returned. He took away five pieces. I ate one piece, as much as I was accustomed to use at that hour, when I ate any. The four remaining pieces I left in a circle on the rim of my plate. When the passenger told me the captain's remark, my reply was, "*If my mind has lost its balance, I should not have one doubt respecting the cause of it.*" It was before reaching port, that every few weeks I was prostrated for a day or two with pain in my head. Then I turned to tea for comfort and refreshment. It came, as usual, once in twenty-four hours. I was satisfied with that. But the captain must, needs say at the public table, that he had no more sympathy for Mrs. Thurston, when she had a headache, than he had for a drunk.—Notwithstanding, at his recommendation, I had for months discontinued the use of fat meat and gravy.—After reaching port, my health so rapidly improved as to have it remarked by all. The captain mentioned it one day at the table, and asked the cause. "*It is, sir, because since coming into port I have eaten more.*" I several times, as above, aimed to have my remarks form a check upon the captain. He was afterward far more guarded at table. The only lashes I attempted to give him were to hold up virtues in which he was alarmingly deficient. The passengers thought I had given him a tremendous rap on the knuckles. He did not leave the dining table ignorant of the manner in which it was received. But what surprised me was, that after I had taken this new position, he took occasion on deck to express his satisfaction in my increased efforts to please him, and even thanked me, I was glad to dismiss this kind of warfare from my mind, and even regretted that I had ever attempted it, for, "*It is enough for me to cultivate humility and self-control. Then from this school of adversity, I shall carry with me lessons that will be of use in the most trying scenes of life.*" **SECTION III** (From the Port of Valparaiso to the End of the Voyage) I had several lady fellow passengers. Not an action, not a word, not a look proceeded from either of them, of a personal nature, through the whole voyage, that ever cost me an unpleasant feeling. I could say the same of one gentleman passenger. Haman wrote me a note of two pages. The character of it is well-defined in Bible language—"*False witnesses are risen up against me, and such as breathe out cruelty.*"—I sent a reply to him by the steward. He would not receive it, but bid him return it to the writer. An extract of my reply reads, "*Dear Sir, I received and read your note last evening with placid feelings. You wish that all intercourse should stop here. For reasons of which I am utterly ignorant, yours has ceased with the mother some time since. My children are now included. It is enough. As it respects social intercourse with you, to promote your happiness, I shall follow where you lead. To promote my own I shall cherish for you the kindest feelings. As intelligent and accomplished I respect you, as a youthful traveler passing to another country through the wild wastes of this, I pity you, as erroneous in any respects toward me or mine, I freely forgive you.*" Matters now fast ripened, and soon reached their climax. I was "*put under axes of iron, and harrows of iron, and made to pass through the brick-kiln.*" The captain was one of the most active in these scenes. And after being an actor in such a drama, how could he say that, in those last days of peculiar trial, the "wisest course was pursued?" And again, as an eyewitness report, that in that season of my extremity my "feelings suffered depression!" It was not so. I do not remember shedding a single tear. They proceeded much too far to reach their own aims. I was not thus to be crushed. Through suffering I had become strong for trials. I was lifted up. With calm, undaunted feelings, and an equal eye, I could look on all the powers of earth and hell. **SECTION IV** (Sequel) In the eighth month of the voyage I reached Honolulu. Before anchoring, a boat had arrived. I was in readiness to depart. I had reached my friends. I had reached an atmosphere of love, of kindness, and of sympathy. I had been taught their value. My lips were sealed to everything of an opposite nature. By skillfully evading direct questions, I was enabled to pursue that course. [Unnamed

Captain] had just received a letter from my husband, commending me to his care. After reading it, he said, "*Father Thurston is fast ripening for Heaven.*" What he said in relation to his wife was soothing to her lacerated feelings. "*Many daughters had done virtuously.*" When I went ashore there was a domestic vessel lying in port with her flag flying from the top of her mast. It was bound to the place of my home, and waited for me till the next day. I then sailed with my children, leaving before the ship, so late my abode, entered the harbor. The note which I had formerly written, I now sent to him, adding an additional note, containing the following lines, "*As we shall probably meet no more on earth, perhaps you will now be willing to read what I penned for you on board. You have a mother in America, I have a son. I know how to sympathize with mothers, and I know how to sympathize with sons. Farewell.*" I could give many other curious specimens of human nature. I add in the language of one of our passengers that "*that ship was the queerest world that I ever jumped into.*"

□□□□□□□□□□

Part Fourth 1871-1876—Conclusion. **ARTICLE 1** (To Persis Thurston Taylor) *Honolulu, December 23. My Dear Daughter Persis*, from different pens I have a full view of your thanksgiving dinner. Now I will give you a description of mine. Opposite where I sat, your father's accustomed place, there was a quart glass tumbler that was filled with flowers for him. On the right there were three common-sized tumblers of flowers, each one for a child.—On the left—four little tumblers with opening lilies—each one for a grandchild.—These, all surrounded with evergreens, were for my family that had passed to the summer land. Those, still in the flesh, were represented by piles of the old blue China plates, family by family, placed across the upper end of the table, the numbers of plates in each pile corresponding with the number of members in the family it represented, making in all nineteen plates. A native boy sat at the other end of the table. There were no dishes of food along the middle, but my plate and his, with two large circles of small plates, were replenished with baked beef, sweet and Irish potatoes, bread, biscuit, milk, cucumbers, apples, bananas, and guava preserves, to which were added from Oakland, dried apples stewed, and preserved cherries. I enjoyed my Thanksgiving dinner. In my youth, I separated myself from my native home and friends there, and with a beautiful staff, passed over to this then heathen land. Now I have large investments in two countries and in two worlds. What though for a point of time I am detached from what are still mine, there is a glowing future, when I shall, in a higher sense than I have ever yet experienced, enjoy my acquisitions. *Your loving Mother.* **ARTICLE 2** (From the *Friend* (newspaper) of Honolulu) The rare privilege was afforded us on the 28th of August (1872) of being present at a gathering of grandmothers in honor of Mrs. Betsy H. Judd, who completed on that day her ninetieth year. One of her granddaughters, Mrs. Laura Dickson, wishing to honor the occasion, devised the highly appropriate plan of inviting all the foreign grandmothers in Honolulu to a tea party at her residence. The weather was most propitious, and the occasion such as enlisted the gathering of such an assembly as would reflect the highest honor upon any Christian community in the most favored part of the world. Most fortunately we entered when between thirty and forty ladies, a little past middle age, with a few verging onward to the period of the "sere and yellow leaf," were seated at the tables sumptuously spread with the good things of this life. These ladies were served by a company of their daughters and others, in the fresh season of young womanhood. When all were thus gathered, the venerable Mrs. Thurston invoked the Divine blessing in the following touching language, "*Our Father, who art in Heaven, we thank Thee that Thou dost satisfy us with long life. Enable us to yield fruit in old age.—May our last days be emphatically our best days.—Bless this social interview. Bless to our use this food. Make it a feast of love. While we tarry till Thou come, may we day by day be preparing, so as to be unclothed, that mortality may be swallowed up of life. For Jesus sake. Amen.*" While the ladies were seated, Mrs. Thurston arose and read the following address, "*I remember the time when at this metropolis of our little world, the highest* perfection of the female picture of a family would be a mother standing with an infant in her arms, and a toddling child by her side, hanging on to her skirts. Now I open my eyes to behold a venerable company of forty grandmothers, including four great grandmothers. This leads me to invite your attention for a few minutes to the origin and increase of foreign female society on Hawaii." In 1820 the first foreign ladies reached these shores that were ever seen by the eyes of natives. They were seven in number, including one mother with five children. That company had only liberty to come on shore and stay one year. What circumspection, what power of endurance they were called upon to exercise! The ladies were a rare curiosity to the nation, the children more so. To turn from scenes of pressing their own children beneath the sod with their own heels, or, if allowed to live, to go entirely naked—then to behold our children dressed with shirts, pants and coats, with dresses and neck attire, with stockings and shoes, with hats and bonnets, they were delighted—they were fascinated with them, as much as our children would be with a fresh importation of London dolls. Kalanimoku, a great warrior, who put down the rebellion in favor of idols, who sustained the position of prime minister of the nation, and was called the Iron Cable, passed by educated men and chose little Daniel Chamberlain, five years old, to be his teacher in learning the English alphabet. When Mrs. Chamberlain started to go to church with her family, by the time she got there, she was as destitute of children as young married ladies. One queen would secure a child, and so on. We had ten queens in those days. A deputation from the London Missionary Society was providentially brought to us. They were thirty years ahead of us in knowledge of the experience of missionary labors. They awoke us from a dream of security. Their advice, after being months in our family, was gratuitous and full. "Let Mr. Chamberlain take his six children, go home with them, and train them up for God. He never can do it here. As society now is, to come in contact with natives or foreigners would be moral death." Our own missionaries too said, "Go." Thus they did their missionary work up quick, and returned to their native land. But the winning influence they exerted over the minds of natives in causing the Mission so quickly to become the acknowledged teachers of the nation, will never be appreciated in this life. During successive years, several other families, parents and children retired, and their places were filled with new recruits. Some nine or a dozen children in early childhood were torn from the arms of their parents, and sent across the waters for education. A returned missionary lady from the East said to me, "*A child left in the streets in America would have a better education than in the best family in a heathen land.*" One divine among us who had a regard to the sacredness of the family institution, thought that these human clippings went to make a family look like a coconut tree. Another, fourteen years after the commencement of the Mission, with all the ardency of his nature hoped, that no daughter would ever remain in this land up to the age of her fifteenth year. But the good hand of our God was upon us. Punahou School rose up to bless our land. It worked together for good that some of our children were there educated, that some were sent to America, and some trained in private families. The Cousins Society is a monument of glory to the American missionaries. The instructions given to the nation had its natural result. A standard was raised of what was right. Vice fled from the open face of day to dens and secret places. When a white man died in former times, a line in his yard was drawn around his dwelling. Everything within that line went to the king, even down to a pewter spoon. The natural heirs were stripped of everything. So all the land belonged to the king, and could not become alienated from him. He could at an hour's warning dispossess any subject of his home. Thus, we lived for twenty-seven years. Kamehameha III, who was emphatically the Father of his country, gave to his people salutary written laws. He put land, too, into the hands of his subjects, to become theirs, their heirs and assigns forever. Then it was that grandmothers migrated to this land from abroad, and mothers here became so by generation. Then it was that our sons and daughters were retained by the side of their parents. It was good to bring woman here when gross darkness was upon the people. It was good to bring grandmothers here when the light began to shine. It was very good to plant children on Hawaiian soil—sons to become the sinews of the land and daughters to become corner stones, polished after, the similitude of a palace. This first conspicuous "grandmothers" tea party is to congratulate her, who in our whole little realm stands preeminent in age. With physical and mental powers in good preservation, she this day completes the count of ninety years. She is able to look down and see her house sustained by grandchildren, seven pillars all in the prime of life, and around their tables olive plants are clustered, like lilies by the water brooks. *"Peace be to grandmothers, who have children and grandchildren to lead them down the slope of life, over green fields, and beside the still waters. Peace be to grandmothers, whose lines are fallen to them, in pleasant places, having a goodly heritage, a heritage enlightened by the beams of the sun of righteousness and blessed with a knowledge of his salvation."* Respecting this gathering of grandmothers, the following statistics may prove interesting to our readers. At the tables were seated 27 grandmothers and three great-grandmothers, representing 155 children, 221 grandchildren, and 20 great-grandchildren. Twelve grandmothers residing in Honolulu were not present. It is a noteworthy fact that among these grandmothers, there were 21 widows, indicating that long life is the portion of the female, rather than of the male sex, at the Sandwich Islands. **ARTICLE 3** (Life Alone in Old Age) I have been reflecting in regard to those going forth to the fierce battlefields of life. To me the most noble and sublime spectacle ever witnessed in our world is a person standing up in righteousness and triumphing over accumulated sharp and heavy trials. I constantly pray for such with my firmest faith that as their day is, so their strength may be. I depend on a native to prepare my food and wait on me. I commune with the secrets and mysteries of solitude. Every Saturday night, I pay off all services rendered through the week. I expect death to creep over me in just such circumstances as it happens. I have written a letter to the undertaker, anticipating directions. I am not prepared for sickness. It would be very inconvenient. It is said to be a sin. I try to avoid it. Other houses are visited, and there is such a commotion—doctors in counsel, nurses, watches, and all Honolulu awake and active in expressions or acts of sympathy. The storm is tempered to that of a shorn lamb. **ARTICLE 4** (To Mrs. Persis Thurston Taylor) *Honolulu, January 11, 1874. My Dear Daughter Persis*, you have accomplished your mission. Go, return to your husband and your children. Give my love and gratitude to each one of them for encouraging and aiding you to cross the ocean to visit your lone mother. I was blessed in having you come. I am blessed in seeing you return to the center of a circle, bound to you by the strongest ties of nature. You have reached the period when a clustered family begins to scatter. You are in the noontide of life, subject to its struggles. Your aged mother has reached the calm and quiet of even tide. It is not dark. The western sky is lighted up with golden hues. I wait the summons to pass to higher scenes. It is easy to linger. It will be easy to go. In all God's universe, I occupy, now and ever, just the niche that he assigns me. I have been vividly reminded of your childhood years. Could I then have divined what you would be to me in 1873? May your children be to you what you have so lovingly been to your affectionate and grateful, *Mother*. **ARTICLE 5** (Death of a Grandson—Robert Thurston—Aged 19 Years) *Honolulu, April 28th, 1874. My Dear Children and Grandchildren*, I address you all as one. But let me write your names. Let me count my treasures. [Family relations to Lucy Thurston were added in parentheses to indentify names of relatives mentioned.] Persis (daughter).—Mr. Taylor (son-in-law).—Lucy, Mary, Henry, James and Eddie (grandchildren).—Sarah (daughter-in-law).—Lorrin and Helen (grandchildren). Mary (daughter)—Marcus (son-in-law).—Asa, Lily, and Clara (grandchildren). Thomas (son) and Alice (granddaughter).—Of my own loved ones, still mine, but who have passed beyond the veil, there is your honored father, Asa (husband).—Lucy (daughter).—Edwin (son-in-law)—and Frank (unknown).—Ed, Mary, and Eric, George and Robert (grandchildren). In what I have written, the tale is told, for Robert has passed to higher scenes. *April 4th, Saturday.* The ball of his right foot became exceedingly painful. It was considered a stone bruise, the result of fishing in the water barefoot. For a whole week his sufferings were intense. He was scarcely able to eat or sleep. *April 8th, Wednesday.* The doctor was sent for. He entered into the same ideas that had been entertained, of it being a stone bruise, and continued poultices, ordering them to be made of flax seed, and changed once in two hours. He lanced it Wednesday and Friday without relief. *April 11th, Saturday.* Doctor visited him five times. *April 12th, Sunday.* Doctor was up before breakfast. Again at noon.—Again in the afternoon bringing another doctor with him as counsel.—He called Robert's attention, if possible, to trace back his steps to the point where his foot received a hurt. Thus quickened, his recollection reached the time, when going into the water, he stepped on a piece of coral, but it was a thing too insignificant to receive attention. The counsel at once gave an expressive look to the family physician. It was the first moment that the idea of poison had dawned upon the mind. He had once lost a patient when poison had been communicated in the same manner. One whole week had now elapsed since his sufferings commenced. It is now supposed that he was poisoned by a small shellfish, a species of annelids, which attaches itself to coral rocks when in the sea. Natives are frequently wounded in this way, and unless prompt remedies are applied, it often proves fatal. They usually burn the wound with a coal of fire, or apply the leaves of a weed—but physicians generally cauterize it with nitrate of silver. This is the first instance of a foreigner having been poisoned in this way that we have known. Toward night, a friend rode up to my door to say that the doctors thought Robert would not live. That night I did not close my eyes in sleep, till after three in the morning. Every relative tie (connection), every inferior consideration, was absorbed in his securing eternal life. It was a night to be remembered. Deep solitude, and silence, and darkness reigned. With my dying son, I approached very near to the Savior. I laid him with entire trust, fully into his compassionate arms, with one request, only one, in that I would not be denied. Make him a pure spirit, to glorify God and enjoy him forever. *April 13th, Monday.* The doctor remarked that in a hundred chances, he had but one of living. At evening twilight, his aunt gently revealed to him that he would likely soon leave them. The idea seemed to enter his very soul. He quivered all over. Then closed his eyes and lay for a time. After which, he conversed with his aunt. He said he "*longed to be a Christian but he didn't know how.*" He asked her to pray with him. She felt that God was there, and sought for spiritual blessings with great fervor. When she ended, he said, "*Amen.*" He inquired if he should be likely to live a week, and received for answer, that he would probably die before morning. When the doctor came in the evening, he was quickly informed by an outsider that Robert had been told of his danger. The doctor was greatly annoyed. He said in his very weak state, it was enough to snap the thread of life, and to ninety-nine cases out of one hundred patients, it would be an injury. On entering the sickroom, Robert said to him, "*I want to know how I am. Tell me the truth. I am not afraid to die.*" The doctor told him not to worry, to be calm in his mind, and spoke to him words of encouragement. When he returned to the parlor, he told the family that Robert's pulse was in an improved state. *April 14th and 15th—Tuesday and Wednesday.* Doctor said that Robert had one chance in seventy-five for life. His pulse was better, one hundred and twenty in a minute. It had been one hundred and fifty, and on so fast that they could not be counted. He had, had considerable fever, was very weak, and felt "so tired." He said to his watcher, "*They told me night before last that I might die before morning, and I prepared for it.*" He asked a friend, "*How am I?*" He replied, "*You are very sick.*" He folded his hands, closed his eyes, and for sometime appeared to be in prayer. *April 16th and 17th, Thursday and Friday.* His breathing, every breath was a gasp, was somewhat relieved, the swelling in his chest, abdomen, and leg, somewhat diminished. He ate more, slept more, and was stronger. It was sweetly sad to see how he longed for the presence of his mother [Sarah Andrews Thurston], absent on another island. Although the schooner to bring her was not expected till Saturday, he often asked if she had come, and often sent his brother [Lorrin Thurston] to see whether the schooner was in sight. The feelings he expressed respecting his spiritual state, were, "*that he longed to be a Christian, but Christ seemed a great way off. He was afraid he did not believe in him. He did not know how. He could not get the hang of it.*" Intelligent, discriminating Christians thought his will was subdued, and that his safety did not depend upon the comfort he received. With me it required neither his testimony nor theirs to enable me to lay trustingly into the hands of the Savior my heart's treasure. My consolation through the sacred page came directly from Him. Once Robert said, "*Dear aunt, I know what suffering is.*" Yet, inexperienced as he had hitherto been in that school, not a single repining word ever dropped from his lips. But he often said, "*I am so tired.*" Under this severe discipline, a softening touch had been given to his character. All along he was humble, docile, patient, loving, and so unceasingly attentive, in the midst of sufferings, to preface his requests with please, and close kind acts with thank you, and in his seasons of delirium so perfectly pure in every sentence, and in every word, that the spirit he breathed on that sickbed was very beautiful. Having spent Friday there, with the setting sun I returned to my own home. In the edge of the evening, a friend called to say, "*We think he is going.*" Through the darkness of the night, we silently pressed our way to the chamber of death. On entering, there lay our own Robert, speechless and unobservant. Even in such circumstances, the beauty and the aspect of the youth, ripening into manhood were ill-concealed. It was previous to this, within about two hours of his release, he said, "*Dear aunt, help me to hold my breath.*" Some time had elapsed after that, when he shouted, as if answering to a call, "*I'm coming, I'm coming.*" They were his last words. [Robert, like his cousin in April 1866, seems to be seeing a dead relative (possibly his father or grandfather who had already passed) right before his own demise.] The dying one now experienced one, then another short but severe paroxysm of pain. It was the shattering of the

body to allow the soul to walk forth in its immortality. Then life quietly ebbed away. No sound broke upon the stillness of that hour, save the repetition of select stanzas from precious hymns. Robert was no longer there. In the midnight hour I returned to my home, I entered the dark solitary abode, where I had five nights kept vigils for Robert, while he lay between life and death. My prayers for him were now entirely ended. Then, instead of allowing grief and sadness to be my guests, I invited thanksgiving to abide with me. I had only to express my gratitude, ere the channel became deeper and deeper, broader and broader. I was so borne along over the space of nineteen years, to the time when the spark of life was first lighted up, and so borne upward that it formed one of the green spots in my life, where memory will ever love to linger. Under this visitation, among friends and the community, there was one pulsation of sympathy and aid. Was Jesus, in his infinite power, wisdom, and love, less kind, even though he called three widows to lay their son and grandson, their hope and strength, on the altar, an offering without blemish? What I do, thou knowest not now, but thou shalt know hereafter. *Your loving mother and grandmother, Lucy G. Thurston.*
ARTICLE 6 (Marriage of a Granddaughter in California) *Honolulu, June, 1874. My Dear Granddaughter Mary*, I revert to the time when I was first introduced to a little toddling girl in her second year. During these succeeding years she has been growing into womanhood, I have been domesticated with her for months and months together in various places. And now, on the eve of her wedding, she comes with her cozy letter, and spreads before her distant grandmother, her very self, her surroundings, her prospects, and her aspirations, just as if she indeed belonged to me. How your freedom, affection, and confidence warms and melts a heart encrusted with age and solitude! With ease and simplicity you introduce "Charlie" [Charles Henry Kluegel] as your new-found husband, and my new-found grandson. I accept and place him with Mary in my heart of hearts. God Almighty, bless you both, and may you together walk before him in truth and love. I thank you ever so much for your photographs. I put them

into a large frame, wholly devoted to our family. It was very interesting receiving samples of your dresses. I pronounce your trousseau to be quite modest and economic. But the best of all is that you have learned self-support. I yesterday read an impressive piece respecting a daughter of affluence. She was above doing or learning anything belonging to the labors of life. Her youth, and prime, and wealth had all passed away. Incapable of effort, crushed with the responsibility of sustaining herself, she fell, with eyes weakened by weeping, from the high eminence to which riches raised her, to the lowest strata of honest society, the poor and shiftless, while the daughters of her poor and despised neighbor, the washerwoman, were made wise under the teachings of stern necessity, qualified themselves for earth's duties and rose to posts of usefulness and emolument. *Your loving grandmother, Lucy G. Thurston.* **ARTICLE 7** (A Letter to Martha Chamberlain, Corresponding Secretary of Mission Children's Society) *Honolulu, September 2nd, 1874.* From your own hand I received the twenty-second annual report of the Hawaiian Mission Children's Society. There I learn officially that they have admitted by a single vote, as honorary members, all the surviving fathers and mothers of this Mission, and likewise placed upon this list the names of those who have departed this life. Such a loving act touches the heart. I thank them for myself. I thank them for the living. I thank them for the dead. In contemplating this society, my mind runs back to other years, when the eldest children of this Mission were grouped beneath parental guidance, shut in by a dark horizon.—Without schools, without a future sphere, without a parental foothold in the (Hawaii) nation.—The Alpha and the Omega of their promised privileges lay in the homes of their unassisted and overtasked parents. Thus peculiarly situated, the ladies of the Mission formed a Maternal Association. At the yearly gathering of the General Meeting, it continued to hold its sessions. In a marvelous manner, light, liberty, and privileges became the inheritance of our children. In 1852 the Mission Children's Society was organized. It may be that one organization was the upshot of the other. Be that as it may, a power for good changed hands. A rapid stride was made in the right direction. Children increased in number, age, strength, and action. Their circle was extended by alliances of marriage and of friendship. In a less, but somewhat similar ratio, parents have declined. And now with them, in the day when the keepers of the house tremble, and the grinders cease because they are few, and those that look out of the windows be darkened—or the silver cord has been loosed, and the golden bowl broken—now it is that loving hearts and strong hands, in the full tide of prosperity, have beckoned the living to soft green seats in their own enclosure, and so registered the names of all, all, as to have them held in honored remembrance. I only add, that by this reverential and hallowed act, the Society encircle their own brow with a halo of glory. *Lucy G. Thurston.*

ARTICLE 8 (To a Granddaughter in California) *Honolulu, October 12th, 1874. My Dear Lucy*, and have you, my inexperienced granddaughter, launched forth on the sea of matrimony? And in so doing, waved your hand to your grandmother to send you a chart that will guide you happily over the unknown waves of life? Now in the vicinity of eighty years, with all its prolonged experience and broad observation, could I begin anew to measure off human existence, it seems to me I should reach forth to a far nobler life than I now look back upon. But I can only measurably give this off to another. A new generation begins life anew, fresh and empty, and their impress of character is largely derived from their own observation and experience. Of all the institutions of earth, marriage stands preeminent, inasmuch as it was founded by God himself. The happiness flowing from it, in comparison with all human organizations, is as precious stones to granite. I rejoice that my oldest grandchild, who of the fourth generation bears the name of Lucy, has found the one in whom her heart can trust. God Almighty, before whom your ancestors walked—bless you, bless your husband (Jacob Pearse Winne)—and make you blessings to each other. It is very beautiful to have two lives mingle and flow into one, producing a union of hearts. The delight of conjugal love consists in this, that the will of one is that of the other. When I was twenty-four years of age, I became a wife. God chose for me. I received my husband as from His hand. United, through untried and varied scenes (events), we traveled life's pathway together for forty-eight years. On entering this relation, I sought from the Bible to know its duties. To me they were clearly defined by the Author of our being, and the Author of this great institution. Wives, love, submit to, obey, and reverence your husbands. I never felt it a servile lot. I was lifted up into a higher sphere of grace and dignity. But these duties of the wife are to be placed in conjunction with those of the husband. Such is the dictate of a God of Order, of Wisdom, of Beneficence. Husbands—love your wives, even as Christ loved the church, and gave himself for it. What wife but would feel it her delight and glory to throw herself with docility and confidence on a love so tender, beautiful, wonderful, and unchanging? Not angels, but human pairs are brought together. As they are possessed with the frailties of our nature, they should begin life's pathway with this motto, "Bear and Forbear," I once knew a man and his wife. They were professors of religion, and admitted into the upper circles of society. Their house—table—and wardrobe all bespoke in a high degree the cultivation and enjoyment of order and good taste. Their bearing toward each other in public was charming. No lack of attentions. Such was the general appearance to the outside world, to their neighbors even. Yet in one thing between that pair, will was pitted against will. Each individual thought, "*I am all right, but the other is all wrong.*" Neither would yield. In the bosom of each was a caldron, always heated, sometimes boiling over. There was a skeleton in their house which remained until the first funeral came off. Some married people speak of the defects and the faults of their partners to a third person. Others there are who keep their tongues pure from such utterances. That is well. If there is a burden, let it be given to the Savior. How many, even of the pious and cultivated, carelessly mar their dearest interests! How many seem not to realize that conjugal love is a plant, liable to be dwarfed by rude touches, but tenderly cherished, increases in growth, beauty, and fragrance. Take for instance, it was a little thing. How little? The husband, wife, and several children were grouped around a table, all listening to every utterance. The wife, addressing me, said, "*My husband's instincts are more prominently developed for his children, than for his wife.*" Then she looked him full in the face and broadly smiled, as if she thought a good joke had slipped off her tongue, and wondered how he would take it. He, like a wise man, answered not. By this I would illustrate, how I reprobate, in the highest degree, little touches of that nature. A gentleman who rose to eminence in his profession, alluding to his wife, said, "*In talk, I have it by the pailful how to do right, but I had rather see it exhibited in the life.*" A wife should never try to be a second conscience to her husband, reminding him continually of his shortcomings. The tendency is to drift him away from her, from his home, and from duty. I once knew one, who brought home a new mother to his orphan children. She was a lady of culture and principle. How her husband cherished her! How she revered him! How devoted she was to his children, as if they were her very own! May you, in being introduced to a new name, to new friends, and to a new field of action, become the light of your husband's house, the center of home, that sacred spot of love and harmony, of comfort, quiet, and ease, that wealth alone cannot give, nor poverty take away. *Your loving grandmother, Lucy G. Thurston.* **ARTICLE 9** (To Mary Thurston Benfield in North Carolina) *Honolulu, November 12th. My Dear Daughter Mary,* I have received your letters giving accounts of a birth and death in your little family. And you have lived through it all. How you have been called alone in the darkness, and in the storm, to walk a thorny pathway! And how the departed one must have suffered! But it is a blessed path that leads to a blessed death.—And the little girl, my seventeenth grandchild.—You incidentally gave me a peep of her, cheering the suffering one with her "tiny smiles." I am glad that in my mind she is so pleasantly photographed. At present I have the aid of a schoolboy, two hours in the morning and two hours in the afternoon. I am quite alone at night. My heart yearns for loving companionship. As I was once your mother, so I now wish you to become mine. I wish to set my house in order, and to die in my own family. On your entering my home, I wish the responsibilities of the table and house to fall into your hands absolutely, I retaining my bedroom and study as ever. Then I will trust to you, as you once trusted to me. Let the children be to the house what flowers are to the garden. While I remain, I live in you and in them, and you all live in me. When I pass away you will be my memorial. In 1823 we separated from the Mission Family at Honolulu, and branched out to form a station at Kailua-Kona. With two babes of two years and two months old, we were closely packed five days and nights in a crowded native vessel. After reaching Kailua-Kona, I often said with the utmost sincerity, "*Never ask me again to go upon the ocean. Let me live and die here.*"—So much for the value of sentimental feelings, after having suffered to extremity.—Since that time, in visiting America, I have been around Cape Horn, as many times over the way between this and California, and more than a hundred on these seas that separate our group of Islands. I have just received a large photograph of your father. I have put it in a frame and encircled it in the same frame with small photographs of his family who are with him in the world of spirits. Including the whole circle, there were four cut off in the prime of life, sustaining parental responsibilities, three in the bloom and vigor of youth between sixteen and nineteen, and—three children between sixteen months and five years of age. My Savior, how can I give expression to my gratitude that my dear departed ones have found rest in thee? All, all, I trust, have attained to that better land. How pleasant, how rich the memories of having such a family in Heaven! In another large frame, your mother's large photograph is in the center, surrounded by the living members of our family. **ARTICLE 10** (Death of a Grandchild) *Honolulu, December 29th, 1874. My Dear Daughter Mary*, and so little Ida was born, a daughter of earth, thus early to take her flight to happier climes (climates). I, too, had learned to love her, and everywhere she follows me with an expressive smile. Beloved child! She will be reared by redeemed ones advanced in knowledge, with more than a mother's love. As her faculties develop, she will learn of them her birthplace, who her mother is, and with what brothers and sisters her earth life was grouped. I think of her as becoming a bright ministering spirit, often commissioned to be your guardian angel, to help you to bear the burdens of life, and to lead you to that heavenly rest to which she has attained. Blessed mother! I congratulate you in having such an angel child as little Ida. What a precious offering to make to God! It may have ten thousand instructors in Heaven, but you will be its parents. To have a child in Heaven is worth all the sickness, sorrow, and toil it has cost you. *Your sympathizing Mother*.

ARTICLE 11 [After an absence of more than two years, Mrs. Mary Benfield and three children returned to her mother's home in Honolulu, having laid her husband and infant daughter to rest beneath the pine trees of their retreat in North Carolina. The [twice] widowed daughter again became the stay and support of her aged mother.] *Honolulu, August, 1875.* The two years and a half in which, in my family, I have been like a coconut tree, stripped of every leaf, is past. By the union of the remnants of three generations, the solitary one is again set in a family. The pattering of small feet, and the music of little voices is again heard. A faithful staff is placed by my side on which to lean, and I linger on the border land toward the setting sun. During this past season of discipline, I accepted my lot, and my feelings assimilated to my circumstances. Fear became a stranger to my bosom. In the long black night, I enjoyed the music of nature, and felt the sublimity of deep solitude. I am blest. I have entered my eighty-first year. I have food, raiment (clothing) and home convenient for me, and my latter days are those of peace. *Lucy G. Thurston*. **ARTICLE 12** [Epilogue] In the spring of 1876, Mrs. Thurston was suddenly attacked with a heart disease, which in a few weeks confined her to the house.—Though in daily expectation of a fatal termination (death), her life was prolonged with frequent recurring spasms of pain and extreme distress (gasping) for breath, till six weary months were fulfilled.—During all this time she was compelled to sit upright in her chair by day and by night. Defended by a cap, veil, and gloves, or a lace canopy from the annoyance of mosquitoes, she patiently lingered through her protracted sufferings sometimes compelled by extremity of weariness to cry, "O, Lord, how long?" Faithful friends cheered her painful pathway to the grave. Amid these distresses, she completed her selection of papers to be published after her death. Her sudden release was thus announced in a letter from her daughter, Mrs. Benfield, dated Honolulu, October 14, 1876. *"What a joyful reunion that must have been, when yesterday afternoon at 4 o'clock, our suffering mother rejoined the husband of her youth in the 'Happy Land.' Without a word of farewell, she suddenly left her chair of suffering, and the loving watches at her side, and obeyed the Voice that called, 'It is enough. Come up higher.' She has been laid to rest in the same grave with our father."* "Her children rise up and call her blessed." Statement from Persis G. Thurston Taylor, Nordhoff, California, March, 1880. **ARTICLE 13** THE LIFE AND LAST DAYS OF LUCY G. THURSTON—LAST OF THE PIONEER MISSIONARIES—A MEMORIAL PREACHED BY REVEREND WALTER FREAR ON OCTOBER 22, 1876. I have selected these words in memoriam of Mrs. Lucy Goodale Thurston, because they were much in her mind in the last weeks of her life, and because she realized that they had been remarkably fulfilled to her. The varied experiences, in view of which she appropriated to herself these words of her Savior, were vivid in her memory. Her thoughts went back over the past a good deal. She thought of the old home in Marlborough, Massachusetts, where she was born on the 29th of this month, 1795. She thought of the large circle of friends, of the father, and of the eight or nine brothers and sisters, and of the numerous respectable and godly uncles and aunts and cousins that she had left, and of all the pleasant associations that she had forsaken, and then her thoughts would dwell on the portion that she had received on these far-off islands (Hawaii), and the grateful feeling would arise that it had been far better for her that she had left all. For some months, and I might say years, she had been living quite largely in her reminiscences. Her pen had been busy with them. The scenes of earlier times were before her mind daily. She lived over again the experiences through which she had passed to an unusual degree, so that it was with more than an ordinary significance that she with clear remembrance, and in direct reference to all that she had lost and gained, suffered and enjoyed, opened her Bible a few weeks ago, and pointing with her finger to this passage, said to me, "*This has all been true in my case.*" Let us see how true it has been. It was in a literal sense that she left houses and friends and country for Christ's sake. She, at the time, had no thought of the mild healthful breezes of Hawaii that now invite so many from the colder climate of the States. She had no thought of the grand mountains and volcanoes that now attract the tourist, and are counted among the wonders of the earth. There was no anticipation of the delightful homes and genial society that in late years have given to these islands a charm. She left a land and home to which she was greatly endeared, to go by long and dangerous voyage, to one of the most remote and least known parts of the earth, to a people in the greatest of heathenish darkness, a people among whom life was cheap, and that offered human sacrifices, and had fearful regulations of tabu, and were naked savages. She and all on board the brig *Thaddeus*, as Dr. Anderson says, "*Expected a protracted and perilous conflict with pagan rites, human sacrifices and bloody altars, for no intimation had been received that the idols and altars of superstition had been overthrown.*" We can also readily imagine with what a grave appreciation and consciousness of the magnitude of the sacred mission, she gave herself to be a missionary. I doubt if ever a missionary surrendered home and friends, to take up so great and critical a work for Christ, with a deeper sense of what we might call the ideal proprieties of so high a calling. It was in a spirit far from all levity, and in which human loves had but a second place while Christ had the first, that she was not disobedient unto the heavenly call. It was in a seriousness and heroism that takes one's life in his hands that she left the comforts of a pleasant home, expecting a rude hut to be her habitation, and that what had been necessaries of life were henceforth to be to her luxuries. In place of the refinements of society, she was to come in contact with gross ignorance, disgusting vices, brutish drunkenness and all unnamable immoralities. Thus she forsook all. Among other things in leaving all for Christ and the Gospel's sake, she at that time gave up the thought of a long life. Her stronger brothers and sister were around her. She was thought to be the frailest of them all. She had already had premonition of early disease in the lungs, with attacks of hemorrhage. Her doubt was, whether she could endure the tropical heats and exposures to which she expected to be subjected. It was thought that amid the hardships and privations there she would find an early grave. When speaking of this passage of scripture and its fulfillment to her, she said to me, "*all at home thought that Lucy would be the first to die.*" She herself thought so. They all had no other thought, than that in that heathen land her life would go first. They bade her farewell, as one whom they never expected to see again on earth. She would be in Heaven long before the rest of them. "*But,*" said she, "*here I am still, spared the longest of them all. All those brothers and sisters are gone before me. Not one of them is left.*" Thus she gave her life to Christ, expecting that the giving of it would shorten it, and he has given her more years than would have been hers if she had kept her life. She found the words of Christ true, that "*he that loseth his life for my sake shall find it.*" She thought of this lengthening of her days as one of the ways in which the hundredfold had been given to her. She felt confident that long ago she would have been in her grave had she stayed in the old New England home. But as it is, she has been spared to outlive by a day the 57th anniversary of her marriage, and to almost complete her 81st year. And instead of never looking upon the faces of the home friends, in the ordering of Providence she has been permitted twice to visit the land of her birth. She has doubled Cape Horn five times, has traveled over 90,000 miles by sea, has been through perils and sicknesses, and prevailing diseases, and yet God has suffered her to be the last to die on these islands, of all that worthy pioneer band who sailed in the brig *Thaddeus* on the 23rd of October, 1819, and landed in the following April at Kailua-Kona. Again, among the things that she forsook for Christ and the Gospel's sake, was any cherished ambition that she might have had, any thought of being known, esteemed and honored among her acquaintances, or of having a name and a place in the world. Those were first days in the missionary work. Honor had not come upon those who had gone to carry the lamp of life into the regions of darkness. The missionary cross had not yet been garlanded in the popular esteem. The work had not yet taken to itself other aspects than that of self-sacrifice for the sake of those perishing in ignorance and sin. To come at that time to these dark islands was the conscious giving up of personal culture, and of place in society, and of influence in the progressive development of one's own country. It was going out to unknown ends of the earth, to spend one's days in humblest work of teaching a gross and degraded people, to have one's faith and patience tried, and to lay one's body at last among heathen bones, instead of in the old village churchyard.—But how true it is that God has given her more than all that she gave up in this respect.—Her name is a familiar name to a large part of the best people in America. She is known and held in honor over a large part of the Christian world. She has a place in the hearts of thousands who probably would never have heard her name had she not left society and kindred for Christ's sake. She has received more than a hundredfold in friends. Her influence has been far more widely extended. She has a noble place in the grand history of missions. She has a high niche in missionary fame. And is there any fame better, or more to be desired on earth, than that which now belongs to such heroes of the cross? Does not a true missionary receive a wider regard and a higher place in the thoughts and love of the Christian world than would have been his if he had stayed in his native land? There may be still some who think it a pity that anyone of culture and of promise should throw himself away, by abandoning prospective positions of influence at home, to be a humble missionary in out-of-the-way pagan lands. But God gives, in honor and esteem, to his faithful ones, manifold more than all they surrender. Mrs. Thurston thought not of this at the time, nor did she speak of it in connection with the passage of scripture but we may speak of it for her. She did, however, think and speak of the many friends, the Christian brothers and sisters, that God had given her in missionary life. She thought gratefully of the interest that had been taken in her, of the favors that had been done to her, of the kindnesses and assistance that had been generously given, and of all that God had put into the heart of others to do for her. She felt that she had not been left friendless, but that the promise in this respect had been fulfilled, that the hundredfold had been given, that more hands had ministered to her in her last sickness than, she could have expected had she never left all for heathen shores. But in a yet higher respect has it been better for Mrs. Thurston that she left home and friends for Christ. I mean in her usefulness. God can give us few great blessings that will add more happiness to life than to put it in our power to be really useful. That which adds to our usefulness adds to the good of our life. Much has been added to Mrs. Thurston in this respect. In the days of her strength she was a faithful worker, and the good that she has been permitted to do have doubtless been a hundredfold more than she would have done in New England. Among her first pupils were Kings and Queens, whose influence soon led the people generally to desire gospel instruction. She was the educator of some of the first minds in the nation. Judge Ii, who became such an honor to his race, was early selected by the King to be instructed by Mr. and Mrs. Thurston, and he was long their diligent scholar, receiving much of his solid worth and finish from them. She endured hardiness as a good soldier in that earnest fight to secure a hold for the gospel on Hawaii. She stood firm while others failed. She suffered, passed through exceeding great trials, persevered and was brave, as some others were not. She had a full share in those trials, and burdens, and hardships, and dangers through which the mission was brought to a success, and a heathen people Christianized. How much greater is the work that she has been permitted to do, than if she had stayed in her native land! How many more inquiring souls has she directed to Christ, how much more has she done in preparing the way for the coming of Christ's kingdom! It has been granted to her to fulfill a great and useful ministry, and will there not be more stars in her crown of rejoicing, than if she had not left all for Christ's sake? Has not even her present life been more full of the satisfactions that come from a noble Christian usefulness? It may be said of her also that in giving up all for Christ, she has at no time wished to take back any part of the gift. She has never turned her look regretfully back to her first consecration to the missionary life. And by this I do not mean simply that she did not leave the field through disappointment, or as thinking it too hard, or that she has never been sorry that she became a missionary, but I mean that she has never taken back the original surrender in which she gave up the world to be a missionary of the cross. She has not departed from the missionary spirit with which she left home. Having left houses and lands for Christ's sake, the desire for these has never come back into her. The fashions and riches of this world have not reoccupied her thoughts. She did not again come to measure men and things by the standards of the world nor to seek that which is coveted by the world. She thought of herself as a missionary unto the end. She never aspired to wear any other character, or to appear before the world in any other light. Naturally she had strong desires. She enjoyed life. She was hopeful. She had a strong mind, and a strong self-will. As she said to me the day before her death, she had a great deal of human nature. She had those traits and qualities that would have enabled her to take hold of the world and be prominent in it. But she never again turned toward the world to covet it. To be as a missionary, and to do that which was becoming in a missionary, to suffer, if need be, and be true to her calling, was her thought to the last. Among the mercies also in which she saw God's gracious dealings with her, was his sparing her to do last things. By degrees during the last six years there has been growing in her the inclination and the feeling of duty encouraged by others, to leave behind her some reminiscences of earlier missionary days, a view of the work as seen from the inside, and that by the mothers, instead of the fathers. A mass of material was in hand for such a work. Her pen had ever been a good deal in her hand and she had from the first carefully treasured her letters and sketches, all of them written in her quaint and pleasing style, bearing the impress of originality, and showing her own individuality in every sentence. When her last sickness fell upon her so suddenly, she felt that it was her last. Her strong desire was that she might survive until she could collate and arrange this material. And so hourly, day after day, and sometimes by night, as she sat in her chair, now writing and dictating, she busied herself as she had strength, with this her last work. She cared to be spared for nothing else. God gave her, her desire, enabling her to leave her material so that it could be readily finished in satisfactory shape for the press. At length she came to the time about three months ago when she felt that her work was done, and that she was ready to be taken. In her former sicknesses she had clung to life. She had seemed to baffle the power of diseases by the sheer force of her will to live. She had held to life feeling that there were responsibilities and work that she could not yet lay down. She had braved the surgeon's knife, and had risen up out of prostrations, beneath which most persons would probably have succumbed. But in her last sickness, she felt that she had finished her course, and that she was ready to be offered. She waited day and night in great physical discomfort, and wondered that she was still kept in life, and almost feared that months more of suffering were appointed to her. A few hours and even minutes before her death, the end seemed no nearer to her than it did a month or two before. But God at last took her quickly out of her distresses, into the rest for which she was longing. In the last few weeks of her life she also came to feel that God was sparing yet a little for a purpose, especially that she might learn more of the fullness of Christ, and come more into the peace that passes understanding, and have wrought in her more of the gentler graces. Months ago, and in fact for years, the experiences beyond this life, what it is to die, and just what will be immediately after death, and just what the resurrection is, were themes that interested her and occupied her thoughts a good deal. She thought and reasoned and loved to talk about them. She has often in years as well as months past opened up conversation in regard to them. But in the last few weeks she has wanted to know more about the present indwelling of Christ, and how much his promise of peace included. She became, we might almost say, an anxious inquirer in this direction. The week before her death, as she asked question after question about the peace of Christ in the soul, she told me that she felt that she had yet very much to learn. The most earnest conversation I ever had with her was the day before her death. I had hardly taken my seat at her side before she began with an inquiry that came right from her heart. Repeating Christ's words—"*Behold I stand at the door and knock, if any man hear my voice, and open the door, I will come in to him and sup (drink) with him, and he with me."*—she asked, with a manifest interest, and a childlike spirit of inquiry, what it was to open the door, and how she could do it more fully, that Jesus might come in more, and sup (drink) with her. She sought for direction in receiving the Savior in greater fullness to her heart. Her faith had been strong and firm in Christ. Her hope had all along been anchored within the veil. She had trusted fully in the God of her salvation. She had not doubted his love or care of the crown of life that he had for her. She not only had a mind of unusual strength but also the courage of faith to an unusual degree. She had been strong to do, to bear, to suffer for Christ. The elements of strength had always been prominent in her character. She did not like foibles. She was naturally commanding in her qualities, and perhaps somewhat in her temperament, and so long as she could work, these strong traits had their easy and joyful play in her life. But now when all her work was done, and she could only sit and be patient, it was as a change of life to her. It was as it were, a trial of faith in a new direction. New lessons seemed to be coming to her to be learned. She realized more deeply the importance of receiving from Christ, as well as doing for him. She had been patient under responsibility, and now with some chafing (irritation) of spirit it may be, she was seeking to learn to be patient without any responsibility pressing on her. She would sit at Jesus's feet and learn of him. The sanctifying love of Christ pervading her nature is what she thought upon and desired. The gentleness and childlike submissiveness of the Christian spirit seemed to her graces more difficult to exercise and be filled with, than the hardier and braver virtues. But these also she was learning as last lessons, deeply and blessedly, in the very hours when her Savior came and received her to himself. Her life surely impresses upon us all the great truth, that Christ will deal well by those who make sacrifices for Him, and that His promise of the hundredfold in this life to those who leave all for him, is a sure promise. It is a promise on which no one need fear to go out in service to Christ. The life of Mrs. Thurston leaves to her children and to her grandchildren and to us all, the confirmation of this promise, as a rich legacy.

Lucy Thurston compiled material from her journals and letters kept from the 1820s until the mid 1870s in a handwritten memoir that was probably edited by her daughter Persis Thurston Taylor before its 1882 publication. The original handwritten copy of the manuscript for this book is located at the Mission Houses Museum in Honolulu. It should be noted that there are sections throughout this memoir where specific years are skipped over in the published version—alluding to possible additional writings from existing journals covering the missing years not included in the original edition—but it is unclear as of this publication if material still exists from possible lost journals.

Linda Arvidson

**When the Movies Were Young
An Autobiography**

☐☐☐☐☐☐☐☐☐☐

Just off Union Square, New York City, there is a stately old brownstone house on which future generations someday may place a tablet to commemorate the place where David W. Griffith and Mary Pickford were first associated with moving pictures. Here has dwelt romance of many colors. A bird of brilliant plumage, so the story goes, first lived in this broad-spreading five-story old brownstone that still stands on Fourteenth Street between Fifth Avenue and Broadway, vibrant with life and the ambitions and endeavors of its present occupants. Although brownstone Manhattan had seen the end of peaceful Dutch ways and the beginning of the present scrambling in the great school of human activity, the first resident of 11 East Fourteenth Street paid no heed—went his independent way. No short-waisted, long and narrow-skirted black frock coat for him, but a bright blue affair, gold braided and gold buttoned. He was said to be the last man in old Manhattan to put powder in his hair. As he grew older, they say his style of dressing became more fantastic, further and further back he went in fashion's page, until in his last days, knickerbockers with fancy buckles adorned his shrinking limbs, and the powdered hair became a periwig. He became known as the "Last Leaf." A bachelor, he could indulge in what hobbies he liked. He got much out of life. He had a cool cellar built for the claret, and a sun room for the Madeira. In his impressive reception room he gathered his cronies, opened up his claret and Madeira, the while he matched his game cocks, and the bets were high. Even when the master became very old and ill, and was alone in his mansion with his faithful old servant, Scipio, there were still the rooster fights. But now they were held upstairs in the master's bedroom. Scipio was allowed to bet a quarter against the old man's twenty-dollar note, and no matter how high the stakes piled, or who won, the pot in these last days always went to Scipio. And so the "Last Leaf" lived and died.

Then in due time the old brownstone became the home of another picturesque character, Colonel Rush C. Hawkins, of the Hawkins Zouaves of the Civil War.—Dignified days, when the family learned the world's news from *Frank Leslie's Illustrated Paper* and the *New York Tribune*—and had Peter Goelet and Moses Taylor for millionaire neighbors.—For their entertainment they went to Laura Keene's New Theatre, saw Joe Jefferson, and Lotta [Crabtree], went to the Academy of Music, heard [Adelina] Patti and Clara Louise Kellogg, heard Emma Abbott in concert, and rode on horseback up Fifth Avenue to the Park. Of an evening, in the spacious ballroom whose doors have since opened to Mary Pickford, D. W. Griffith, and Mack Sennett, the youths, maidens and young matrons in the soft, flickering light of the astral lamp and snowy candle, danced the modest cotillion and stately quadrille, while the elders played whist.—Bounteous supper, champagne, perhaps gin and tansy.—But keenly attuned ears, when they paused to listen, could already hear off in the distance the first faint roll of the drums in the march of progress.—"Little Old New York" was growing up and getting to be a big city.—And so the Knickerbockers and other aristocracy must leave their brownstone dwellings for quieter districts further uptown. Business was slowly encroaching on their life's peaceful way.—Another day and another generation. Gone the green lawns, enclosed by iron fences where modest cows and showy peacocks mingled, friendly. Gone the harpsichord, the candle, the lamp, to give way to the piano and the gas lamp.—Close up against each other the buildings now nestle round Union Square and on into Fourteenth Street. The horse-drawn street car rattles back and forth where, number 11 stands with some remaining dignity of the old days. On the large glass window—for number 11's original charming exterior has already yielded to the changes necessitated by trade—is to be read "Steck Piano Company."

In the lovely old ballroom where valiant gentlemen and languishing ladies once danced to soft and lilting strains of music, under the candles glow, and where the "Last Leaf" entertained his stalwart cronies with cock fighting, the Steck Piano Company now gives concerts and recitals. The old house has "tenants."

And as tenants come and go, the Steck Piano Company tarries but a while, and then moves on. A lease for the piano company's quarters in number 11 is drawn up for another firm for $5,000 per year. In place of the Steck Piano Company on the large window is to be read—"American Mutoscope and Biograph Company." However, the name of the new tenant signified nothing whatever to the real estate firm adjacent to number 11 that had made the new lease. It was understood that Mutoscope pictures to be shown in Penny Arcades were being made, and there was no particular interest in the matter. The "Biograph" part of the name had little significance, if any, until in the passage of time a young actor from Louisville, called Griffith, came to labor where labor had been little known and to wonder about the queer new job he had somewhat reluctantly fallen heir to.

The gentlemen of the real estate firm did some wondering too. Up to this time, the peace of their quarters had been disturbed only by the occasional lady-like afternoon concert of the Steck Piano Company. The few preceding directors of the American Mutoscope and Biograph Company had done their work quietly and unemotionally. Now, whatever was going on in what was once the "Last Leaf's" gay and elegant drawing room, and why did such shocking language drift through to disturb the conservative transactions in real estate! "*Say, what's the matter with you, you're dying you know, you've been shot and you're dying! Well, that's better, something like it! You, here, you've done the shooting, you're the murderer, naturally you're a bit perturbed, you've got lots to think about, yourself for one thing! You're not surrendering at the nearest police station, no, you're beating it, beating it, you understand. Now we'll try it again—that's better, something like it! Now we'll take it. All right, everybody! Shoot!*" The neighborhood certainly was changing. The language! The people! Where once distinguished callers in ones and twos had come once and twice a week—now in mobs they were crossing the once sacred threshold every day. It was in the spring of 1908 that David W. Griffith came to preside at 11 East Fourteenth.

Here it was he took up the daily grind, struggled, dreamed, saw old ambitions die, suffered humiliation, achieved, and in four short years was well-started on the road to become world famous as the greatest director of the motion picture. For movies, yes, movies were being made where once the "Last Leaf" had entertained in the grand old manner. That was what the inscription, "American Mutoscope and Biograph Company," had meant. But movies did not desecrate the dignity of 11 East Fourteenth Street. The dignity of achievement had begun.

The old beauty of the place was fast disappearing. The magnificent old chandelier had given place to banks of mercury vapor tubes. There were no soft carpets for tired feet.

The ex-drawing room and ex-concert hall were overflowing with actors, and life's little comedies and tragedies were being acted where once they had been lived. Fourteenth Street, New York, has been called "the nursery of genius." Many artists struggled there in cheap little studios, began to feel their wings, could not stand success, moved to studio apartments uptown, and met defeat. But 11 East Fourteenth Street still harbors the artist, the building is full of them.—Evelyn Longman who was there when "old Biograph" was, (and) is still there.—On other doors are other names—Ruotolo, Oberhardt, John [Johannes] S. Gelert, sculptor, Lester, studio, the Waller Studios. Ye Studio of Frederic Ehrlich. In the old projection room are now stacked books and plays of the Edgar S. Werner Company, and in the dear old studio, which is just the same today as the day we left it, except that the mercury tubes have been taken out, and a north window cut, presides a sculptor by the name of [Alexander] Stirling Calder, who has painted the old door blue and hung a huge brass knocker on it. Now, when I made up my mind to write this record of those early days of the movies, I knew that I must go down once again to see the old workshop, where for four years David W. Griffith wielded the scepter, until swelled with success and new-gained wealth the Biograph Company pulled up stakes and flitted to its new large modern and expensive studio up in the Bronx at East 175th Street. So down I went to beg Mr. Calder to let me look over the old place and take a picture of it. My heart was going "pit-a-pat" out there in the old hallway while I awaited an answer to my knock. "*Please,*" I pleaded, "*I want so much to take a photograph of the Studio just as it is. I'm writing a little book about our pioneering days here, it won't take a minute. May I, please?*" Emotion was quite overwhelming me as the memories of the years crowded on me, memories of young and happy days untouched with the sadness that years must inevitably bring even though they bring what is considered "success." Twelve years had gone their way since I had passed through those studio doors and here I was again, all a-flutter with anticipation and choky with the half-dreamy memories of events long past. But don't be tempted to announce your arrival if you have ever been connected with a moving picture, for Mr. Calder has scarcely heard of them and when I insisted he must have, he said, with much condescension, "*Oh, yes, I remember, Mr. Griffith did a Chinese picture, it was rather good but too sentimental.*" And he refused to let me take a picture of the studio for he "*could not afford to lend his work and his studio to problematical publicity of which he had not the slightest proof.*" I felt sorry Mr. Calder had come to reside in our movie nursery at 11 East Fourteenth Street, for we were such good fellows, happy and interested in our work, cordial and pleasant to one another. The change made me sad.

□□□□□□□□□□

But now to go back to the beginning. It was a night in the summer of 1904 in my dear and fascinating old San Francisco, before the life we all knew and loved had been broken in two, never to be mended, by the disaster of the great fire and earthquake. At the old Alcazar Theatre, the now historic stock company was producing Mr. Hall Caine's drama *The Christian*.

In the first act the fisher-maidens made merry in the village square. Unknown to family or friends, and with little pride in my humble beginning, I mingled as one of the Fisher Girls.

Three dollars and fifty cents a week was the salary Fred Belasco (David's brother) paid me for my bit of Hall Caine interpretation, so I, for one, had no need to be horrified some four years later when I was paid three dollars a day for playing the same fisher maiden in support of Mary Pickford, who, under Mr. Griffith's direction, was making "Glory Quayle" into a screen heroine. Here at the old Alcazar were wonderful people I could worship. There was Oza Waldrop, John Craig, Mary Young, Eleanor Gordon, Frances Starr, and Frank Bacon. Kindly, sweet Frank Bacon whose big success years later, as "Lightning Bill Jones" in his own play *Lightning* made not the slightest change in his simple, unpretentious soul. Mr. Bacon had written a play called *In the Hills of California*. It was to be produced for a week's run at Ye Liberty Theatre, Oakland, California, and I was to play the ingenue. One little experience added to another little experience fortified me with sufficient courage to call on managers of visiting Eastern road companies who traveled short of "maids," "special guests at the ball," and "spectators at the races." New York was already beckoning, and without funds for a railroad ticket, the only way to get there was to join a company traveling that way. A summing up of previous experiences showed a recital at Sherman and Clay Hall and two weeks on tour in Richard Walton Tully's University of California's Junior farce

James Wobberts, Freshman. In the company were Mr. Tully and his then-wife, Eleanor Gates, the author, Emil Kreuske, for some years now "Will Nigh," the motion picture director, Milton Schwartz, who took to law and now practices in Hollywood, Dick Tully and his wife Olive Vail. Elmer Harris of the original college company did not go. Elmer is now partner to Frank E. Woods along with Thompson Buchanan in Mr. Wood's new producing company. The recital at Sherman and Clay Hall on Sutter Street was a most ambitious effort. My job-hunting pal, Harriet Quimby, a girl I had met prowling about the theaters, concluded we were getting nowhere and time was fleeting. So we hit on a plan to give a recital in San Francisco's Carnegie Hall, and invite the dramatic critics hoping they would come and give us good notices. The Homer Henley Quartette which we engaged would charge twenty dollars. The rent of the hall was twenty. We should have had in hand forty dollars, and between us we didn't own forty cents. Harriet Quimby knew Arnold Genthe, and, appreciating her rare beauty, Mr. Genthe said he would make her photos for window display for nothing. Oscar Mauer did the same for me, gratis. Rugs and furniture we borrowed, and the costumes by advertising in the program, we rented cheaply. We understood only this much of politics, Jimmy Phelan, our Mayor (afterwards Senator James H. Phelan) was a very wealthy man, charitably disposed, and one day we summoned up sufficient courage to tell him our trouble. Most attentively and respectfully he heard us, and without a moment's hesitation gave us the twenty. So we gave the recital. We sold enough tickets to pay the Homer Henleys, but not enough to pay the debt to Mr. Phelan. He's never been paid these many years though I've thought of doing it often, and will do it someday. However, the critics came and they gave us good notices, but the recital didn't seem to put much of a dent in our careers. Harriet Quimby soon achieved New York via the *Sunset* magazine. In New York she "caught on," and became dramatic critic on *Leslie's Weekly*. The honor of being the first woman in America to receive an aviator's license became hers, as also that of being the first woman to pilot a monoplane across the

English Channel. That was in the spring of 1912, a few months before her death while flying over Boston Harbor.

Mission Street, near Third, was in that unique section called South-of-the-Slot. The character of the community was such, that to reside there, or even to admit of knowing residents there meant complete loss of [important] social prestige.

Mission Street, which was once the old road that led over blue and yellow lupin-covered hills out to the Mission Dolores of the Spanish Fathers, and was later the place where the elegantly costumed descendants of the forty-niners who had struck pay dirt (and kept it) strolled, held, at the time of which I speak, no reminder of its departed glory except the great romantic old Grand Opera House, which, amid second-hand stores, pawn shops, cheap restaurants, and saloons, languished in lonely grandeur. Once in my young life Richard Mansfield played there, Henry Irving and Ellen Terry gave a week of Shakespearean repertoire, Weber and Fields came from New York for the first time and gave their show, but failed. San Franciscans thought that Kolb and Dill, Barney Bernard, and Georgia O'Ramey, who held forth nightly at Fischer's Music Hall, were just as good.

At the time of the earthquake a grand opera company headed by Caruso was singing there. Between traveling luminaries, lesser lights glimmered on the historic old stage. And for a long time, when the theater was called Morosco's Grand Opera House, ten, twenty, and thirty blood-and-thunder melodrama held the boards. At this stage in its career, and hardly one year before the great disaster, a young actor who called himself Lawrence Griffith was heading toward the Coast in a show called *Miss Petticoats*. Kathryn Osterman was the star. The company stranded in San Francisco. Melbourne MacDowell, in the last remnants of the faded glory cast upon him by Fanny Davenport, was about to tread the sacred stage of the old Grand Opera House, putting on a repertoire of the Sudermann and Sardou dramas. Frank Bacon, always my kind adviser, suggested I should try my luck with this aggregation. So I trotted merrily down, wandered through dark alleyways, terribly thrilled, for

Henry Irving had come this same way and I was walking where once he had walked. I was to appear as a boy servant in *Fedora*. I remember only one scene. It was in a sort of courtroom with a civil officer sitting high and mighty and calm and unperturbed on a high stool behind a high desk. I entered the room and timidly approached the desk. A deep stern voice that seemed to rise from some dark depths shouted at me, "*At what hour did your master leave Blu Bla?*" I shivered and shook and finally stammered out the answer, and was mighty glad when the scene was over. Heavens! Who was this person, anyhow? His name, I soon learned, was Griffith—Lawrence Griffith—I never could abide that "Lawrence!" Though, as it turned out afterward, our married life might have been dull without that Christian name as a perpetual resource for argument. Afterward, to my great joy, Mr. Griffith confided to me that he had taken the name "Lawrence" only for the stage. His real name was "David," "David Wark," but he was going to keep that name dark until he was a big success in the world, and famous. And as yet he didn't know, although he seemed very lackadaisical about it, I thought, whether he'd be great as an actor, stage director, grand opera star, poet, playwright, or novelist. I wasn't the only one who thought he might have become a great singer. Once a New York critic reviewing a premiere of one of David Griffith's motion pictures, said, "*The most interesting feature of Mr. Griffith's openings is to hear his wonderful voice.*" "Lawrence" condescended to a little conversation now and then. He was quite encouraging at times. Said I had wonderful eyes for the stage and if I ever went to New York and got in right, I'd get jobs "on my eyes." Sounded very funny—getting a job "on one's eyes." [He] advised me never to get married if I expected to stay on the stage. Told me about the big New York actors, Leslie Carter, who had just been doing *DuBarry*, and David Belasco, and what a wonderful producer he was, and dainty Maude Adams, and brilliant Mrs. Fiske, and Charles Frohman, and Richard Mansfield in *Monsieur Beaucaire* and Broadway, and Mrs. Fernandez's wonderful agency, and how John Drew got his first wonderful job through her agency at one hundred and twenty-five dollars a week! I was eager to learn more of the big theatrical world three thousand miles away.

I invited Mr. Griffith out home to lunch one day. A new world soon opened up for me—the South. The first Southerner I'd ever met was Mr. Griffith. I had known of the South only from my school history, but the one I had studied didn't tell of Colonel Jacob Wark Griffith, David's father, who fought under Stonewall Jackson in the Civil War, and was called "Thunder Jake" because of his roaring voice. He owned lots of Negroes, gambled, and loved Shakespeare. There was big "Sister Mattie" who taught her little brother his lessons and who, out on the little front stoop, just before bedtime, did her best to answer all the questions the inquisitive boy would ask about the stars and other wonders. This was all very different from being daughter to a Norseman who had settled out on San Francisco's seven hills in the winds and fogs. The South began to loom up as a land of romance.

□□□□□□□□□□□

When the Melbourne MacDowell repertory season (temporarily) closed, the stranded actors of the *Miss Petticoats* Company were again on the loose. While San Francisco supported two good stock companies, the Alcazar presenting high-class drama and the Central given over to melodrama, their rosters had been completed for the season and they offered rather lean pickings. But Lawrence Griffith worked them both to the best of his persuasive powers. Early fall came with workless weeks, and finally, to conserve his shrinking treasury, our young actor who had been domiciled in the old Windsor Hotel, a most moderately priced place on Market and Fourth Streets, had to bunk in with Carlton, the stage carpenter of the MacDowell show, in a single-bedded single room. Mr. Carlton was on a social and mental plane with the actor, but his financial status was decidedly superior. The doubling-up arrangement soon grew rather irksome. What with idle days, a flattened purse, and isolation from theatrical activities, gloom and discouragement enveloped young Griffith, although he never seemed to worry. He had a trunk full of manuscripts, one-act plays, long plays, and short stories and poems! To my unsophisticated soul it was all very wonderful. What a cruel, unappreciative world, to permit works of genius to languish lonely amid stage wardrobe and wigs and greasy makeup! On pleasant days when the winds were quiet and the fogs hung no nearer than [Mount] Tamalpais [State Park] across the Gate, we would hie (go quickly) ourselves to the Ocean Beach, where, fortified with notebook and pencil the actor-poet would dictate new poems and stories. One day young Lawrence brought along a one-act play called *In Washington's Time*. The act had been headlined over the Keith Circuit. It had never played in San Francisco. He wondered if he could do anything with it. It was approaching the hop-picking season. The stranded young actor's funds were reaching bottom. Something must be done.

In California, in those days, quite nice people picked hops. Mother and father, young folks, and the children, went. Being the dry season, they'd live in the open, pick hops by day, and at night dance and sing. Lawrence Griffith decided it would be a healthful, a colorful, and a more remunerative experience than picking up theatrical odd jobs, to join the hop pickers up Ukiah way.

So, for a few weeks he picked hops and mingled with thrifty, plain people and operatic Italians who drank "dago red" and sang the sextette from *Lucia* while they picked their portion. Here he saved money and got atmosphere for a play. Sent me a box of sweet-smelling hops from the fields, too! A brief engagement as leading ingenue with Florence Roberts had cheered me in the interval, even though Fred Belasco made me feel utterly unworthy of my thirty-five dollar salary.

"*My God*," said he when I presented my first week's voucher, "*they don't give a damn what they do with my money.*" However, Mr. Griffith soon returned to San Francisco. He hoped to do something with his playlet. Martin Beck, the vaudeville magnate, who was then manager of the Orpheum Theatre and booked acts over the Orpheum Circuit, said to let him see a rehearsal. Such excitement! I was to play a little Colonial girl and appear at our own Orpheum Theatre in an act that had played

New York, Boston, Philadelphia, Chicago, and other awesome cities. Mr. Beck booked for the week and gave us a good salary, but could not offer enough consecutive bookings to make a road tour pay, so that was that. In the meantime Oliver Morosco had opened his beautiful Majestic Theatre in upper Market Street, with *In the Palace of the King*. The New York Company lacking a blind "Inez," I got the part, and the dramatic critic, Ashton Stevens, gave me a great notice. In the next week's bill, *Captain Barrington*, I played a scene which brought me a paragraph from Mr. Stevens captioned "An Actress with more than Looks."

On the strength of this notice Mr. Morosco sent me to play ingenues at his Burbank Theatre in Los Angeles, at twenty five dollars per week. Barney Bernard was stepping out just now. He wanted to see what he could do away from the musical skits of Kolb and Dill. So he found a play called *The Financier*. "Lawrence" Griffith had a little job in it. The hardest part of the job was to smoke a cigar in a scene—it nearly made him ill. But he had a good season, six weeks with salary paid. That over, came a call to Los Angeles to portray the Indian, "Alessandro," in a dramatization of Helen Hunt Jackson's famous novel *Ramona*. It was pleasant for us to see each other. We went out to San Gabriel Mission together. Mr. Griffith afterwards used the Mission as the setting for a short story—a romantic satire which he called *From Morning Until Night*. His brief engagement over, "Lawrence" went back to San Francisco, and my Morosco season ending shortly afterward, I followed suit. In San Francisco, Nance O'Neil was being billed. She was returning from her Australian triumphs in Ibsen, Sardou, and Sudermann. The company, with [Arthur] McKee Rankin as manager and leading man, included John Glendinning, father of Ernest, Clara T. Bracy, sister of Lydia Thompson of British Blonde Burlesque and Black Crook fame, Paul Scardon from the Australian Varieties and now husband of a famous cinema star, Betty Blythe, and Jane Marbury. Mr. Griffith, hoping for a chance to return East with the company, applied for a job and was offered "bits" which he accepted. Then one day, Mr. Rankin being ill, Lawrence Griffith stepped into the part of the Father in *Magda*. Miss O'Neil thought so well of his performance and the notices he received that she offered him leading parts for the balance of the season. When in the early spring of 1906, the company departed from San Francisco, it left me with my interest in life decidedly diminished—but Lawrence Griffith had promised to return, and when he came back things would be different. So, while the O'Neil Company was working close to Minneapolis, I was "resting." I "rested" until eighteen minutes to five on the morning of April 18th, when something happened. *"Earthquake?" "I don't know, but I think we had better get up,"* suggested my sister. I sent Lawrence a long telegram about what had happened to us, but he received it by post. And then about a week later I received a letter from Milwaukee telling me that Miss O'Neil and the company were giving a benefit for desolate San Francisco and that I had better come on and meet him in Boston where the company was booked for a six weeks engagement. So, to Fillmore Street I went to beg for a railroad ticket to Boston, gratis. There was a long line of people waiting. I took my place at the end of the line. In time I reached the man at the desk. *"Where to?" "Boston." "What is your occupation?" "Actress."* I thought it unwise to confide my matrimonial objective. No further questions, however. I was given a yard of ticket and on May 9th I boarded a refugee train at the Oakland mole, all dressed up in Red Cross clothes that fitted me nowhere. But I had a lovely lunch, put up by neighbors, some fried chicken, and two small bottles of California claret. In another box, their stems stuck in raw potatoes, some orange blossoms off a tree that stood close to our tent. Ah, dear old town, goodbye! Every night I cried myself to sleep. Thus I went to meet my bridegroom. Boston! Everything a bustle! People, and people, and people! Laughing, happy, chattering people who didn't seem to know and apparently didn't care what had happened to us out there by the bleak Pacific. I was so annoyed at them. Their life was still normal. Though I knew they had helped bounteously, I was annoyed. But here "he" comes! And we jumped into a cab—with a license, but no ring. In the unusual excitement that had been forgotten, so we had to turn back in the narrow street and find a jeweler. Then we drove to Old North Church, where Paul Revere had hung out his lantern on his famous ride (which Mr. Griffith has since filmed in *America*) and our names were soon written in the register. The end of June and New York!—Just blowing for a thunderstorm.—I had never heard thunder, nor seen lightning, nor been wet by a summer rain. What horrible weather! The wind blew a gale, driving papers and dust in thick swirling clouds.

Of all the miserable introductions to the city of my dreams and ambitions, New York City could hardly have offered me a more miserable one! We lived in style for a few days at the Hotel Navarre on Seventh Avenue and Thirty-Ninth Street, and then looked for a "sublet" for the summer. I'd never heard of a "sublet" before. We ferreted around and found a ducky little place, so cheap—twenty-five dollars a month—on West Fifty-Sixth Street, overlooking the athletic grounds of the YMCA, where I was tremendously amused watching the fat men all wrapped up in sweaters doing their ten times around without stopping—for reducing purposes. But we had little time to waste in such observations. A job must be had for the fall. In a few weeks we signed with the Reverend Thomas Dixon, (fresh from his successful *Clansman*) my husband as leading man and I as general understudy, in *The One Woman*. Rehearsals were to be called in about two months.—To honeymoon, or not to honeymoon, to work, or not to work.—Work it was, and David started on a play. And he worked. He walked the floor while dictating and I took it down on the second-hand typewriter I had purchased somewhere on Amsterdam Avenue for twenty dollars. The only other investment of the summer had been at Filene's in Boston where I left my Red Cross sartorial contributions and emerged in clothes that had a more personal relation to me. They were happy days.

The burdens were shared equally. My husband was a splendid cook, modestly said, so was I. He loved to cook, singing Negro songs the while, and whatever he did, whether cooking or writing or washing the dishes, he did it with the same earnestness and cheerfulness. Felt his responsibilities too, and had a sort of mournful envy of those who had established themselves. Harriet Quimby was now writing a weekly article for *Leslie's*, and summering gratis at the old Oriental Hotel at Manhattan Beach as payment for publicizing the social activities of the place. Beach-bound one day, she called at our modest menage, beautifully dressed, with wealthy guests in their expensive car. As the car drove off, Mr. Griffith gazing sadly below from our window five flights up, as sadly said "She's a success."

The play came along fine, owing much to our experiences in California. One act was located in the hop fields, and there were Mexican songs that Mr. Griffith had first heard rendered by native Mexicans who sang in *Ramona*. Another act was in a famous old cafe in San Francisco, the Poodle Dog.

It was christened *A Fool and a Girl*. The fool was an innocent youth from Kentucky, but the girl, being from San Francisco, was more piquant. We'd been signed for the fall, and we felt we'd done pretty well by the first summer.

I'd learned to relish the funny little black raspberries and not to be afraid of thunderstorms—they were not so uncertain as earthquakes. And now rehearsals are called for Mr. Dixon's *The One Woman*. They lasted some weeks before we took to the road and opened in Norfolk, Virginia—where we drew our first salaries—seventy-five for him and thirty-five for her.

Nice, it was, and we hoped it would be a long season.

□□□□□□□□□□□

But it wasn't. After two months on the road we received our two weeks's notice. For half Mr. Griffith's salary, Mr. Dixon had engaged another leading man, who, he felt, would adequately serve the cause. So, sad at heart and not so wealthy, we returned to the merry little whirl of life in the theatrical metropolis of the USA. We had one asset—the play. Good thing we had not frivoled away those precious summer weeks in seeking cooling breezes by Coney's coral strand! Late that fall my husband played a small part in a production of *Salome* at the Astor Theatre under Edward Elsner's direction. Mr. Elsner was looking for a play for Pauline Frederick. Mr. Griffith suggested his play and Mr. Elsner was sufficiently interested to arrange for a reading for Miss Frederick and her mother. They liked it, so did Mr. Elsner, and so the play was sent on to Mr. James K. Hackett, Miss Frederick's manager at that time. It was Christmas Eve—our first. Three thousand miles from home, lonesome, broke.

In the busy marts of dramatic commerce poor little "D" was dashing hither and yon with his firstborn. Even on this day before Christmas he was on the job. The festive holiday meal I had prepared was quite ready. There were some things to be grateful for, each other, the comfortable two rooms, and the typewriter. The hamburger steak was all set, the gravy made, and the potatoes with their jackets on, a la California camp style, were a-steaming. The little five-cent baker's pie was warming in the oven and the pint bottle of beer was cooling in the snow on the window ledge. And someone all mine was coming.

We sat down to dinner. Couldn't put the plates on the table right side up these days, it seemed.—Had no recollection of having turned my plate over.—Turned it right side up again. I wished people wouldn't be silly. I supposed this was a verse about Christmas. But why the mystery?—Wonderingly, I opened the folded slip of paper.—Funny looking poetry. Funny look on D's face.—What was this anyhow? Looked like an old-fashioned rent receipt. But it didn't say "Received from." It said "Pay to. Pay to the order of David W. Griffith seven hundred dollars," and it was signed "James K. Hackett." "*Oh no, you haven't sold the play!*" Yes, it was sold, the check represented a little advance royalty. And were the play a success we would receive a stipulated percentage of the weekly gross, (I've forgotten the scale.) Oh, kind and generous Mr. Hackett! Isn't it funny how calm one can be in the big moments of life? But I couldn't grasp it, Christmas Eve and all.—An honest-to-God check on an honest-to-God bank for seven hundred whole dollars.—Was there that much money in the whole world? Now came wonderful days—no financial worry and no job hunting. True, we realized the seven hundred would not last indefinitely. But to accept a job and not be in New York when rehearsals for the play were called was an idea not to be entertained. So, to feel right about the interim of inactivity, David wrote yards of poetry and several short stories. And John A. Sleicher of *Leslie's Weekly* paid the princely sum of six dollars for a poem called *The Wild Duck*. A bunch of stuff was sent off to *McClure's*, which Mr. McClure said appealed to him very much, though not enough for publication. He'd like to see more of Mr. Griffith's work. And the *Cosmopolitan*, then under Perriton Maxwell's editorship, bought *From Morning Until Night* for seventy-five dollars. Things were looking up. In Norfolk, Virginia, a Centennial was to be held in celebration of the landing on Southern soil of the first of the First Families of Virginia, and a play commemorating the event had been written around Captain John Smith and Pocahontas. Mr. Griffith accepted a part in it.

The six weeks engagement would help out until the rehearsals of his own play were called. But the financial aid of *Pocahontas* must have been somewhat stingy according to the letter my husband wrote me in New York. We had felt we couldn't afford my railroad fare to Norfolk and my maintenance there. It was our first separation. And this, the letter, "*Dear Linda, I am sending you a little $3 for carfare. I would send more but I couldn't get anything advanced, so I only send you this much. I'll get my salary, or part of it, rather, Monday, so I'll send you more then and also tell you what I think we should do. I would like to go to Miss — if we could get it for $6 a week, or $25 a month but I don't like to pay $7.50, that's too strong if we can do cheaper. Of course, if we can't we can't and that's all there is to it. Let me know as soon as you get this money as I am only sending it wrapped up as I don't want you to have to cash so small a check as $3, so that's why I am sending it this way. I bet you I get some good things out of this world for her yet, just watch me and see. Her husband, David.*"

Pocahontas flivvered (flickered) out in three weeks. But as Shakespeare says, "*Sweet are the uses of adversity.*" While Mr. Griffith was away, I found time to make myself a new dress.

In a reckless moment I had paid a dollar deposit on some green silk dress material at Macy's, which at a later and wealthier moment I had redeemed. So now I rented a sewing machine and sewed like mad to get the dress done, for I could afford only one dollar-and-a-half weekly rental on the old Wheeler and Wilson. By the time *A Fool and a Girl* was to open in Washington DC there was just enough cold cash left for railroad fare there. Klaw and Erlanger produced the play under Mr. Duane's direction, and Mr. Hackett came on to rehearsals in Washington. Fannie Ward and Jack Deane played the leading parts. Here they met and their romance began, and according to latest accounts it is still thriving. Alison Skipworth of the *Torch Bearers* and other successes was a member of the cast. The notices were not the best nor the worst. They are interesting today, for they show how time has ambled apace since October, 1907. Said Hector Fuller, the critic, "*It may be said that the dramatist wanted to show where his hero's feet strayed, and where he found the girl he was afterwards to make his wife, but if one wants to tell the old, old and beautiful story of redemption of either man or woman through love, it is not necessary to portray the gutters from which they are redeemed.*" One week in Washington and one in Baltimore saw on its jolly way to the storehouse the wicked Bull Pup Cafe and the hop fields, etc.—And so back to New York.—In the Sixth Avenue "L" with our little suitcases we sat, a picture of woe and misery.

In the Sixth Avenue "L," for not even a dollar was to be wasted on a taxi. But when the door to our own two rooms was closed, and, alone together, we faced our wrecked hopes, it wasn't so awful. Familiar objects seemed to try and comfort us. After all, it was a little home, and better than a park bench, and the *Century Dictionary*—of which someday we would be complete owners, maybe—and the Underwood, all our own—spoke to us reassuringly. I do not recall that any job materialized that winter, but something must have happened to sustain us. Perhaps the belated receipt of those few hundred dollars of mine that were on deposit at the German Savings Bank at the time of the "Disaster" in San Francisco. To offset what might have been an unproductive winter, Mr. Griffith wrote *War*, a pretentious affair of the American Revolution, which Henry Miller would have produced had it been less expensive. *War* had meant a lot of work. For weeks previous to the writing, we had repaired daily to the Astor Library where we copied soldiers's diaries and letters and read histories of the period until sufficiently imbued with the spirit of 1776. *War* is still in the manuscript stage with the exception of the Valley Forge bits which came to life in Mr. Griffith's film *America* for Mr. Griffith turned to the spectacle very early in his career, though he little dreamed then of the medium in which he was to record the great drama of the American Revolution. We met Perriton Maxwell again. Extended and accepted dinner invitations. Our dinner was a near tragedy.

Before the banquet had advanced to the salad stage, I had to take my little gold bracelet to a neighboring "Uncle." The antique furniture necessitated placards which my husband posted conspicuously. For instance, on the sofa—"*Do not sit here, the springs are weak*." On a decrepit gate-legged table—"*Don't lean, the legs are loose*." At the Maxwells's dinner our host gathered several young literati who he thought might become interested in Mr. Griffith and his literary efforts. Vivian M. Moses, then editor of *Good Housekeeping* and now Publicity Manager for Fox Films, was one, as was Jules E. Goodman, the playwright. But a "litry" career for Mr. Griffith seemed foredoomed. A poem now and then, and an occasional story sold, was too fragile sustenance for permanency. Some sort of steady job would have to be found, and the "litry" come in as a sideline. David Griffith was ready for any line of activity that would bring in money, so that he could write plays. He always had some idea in his inventive mind, such as non-puncturable tires, or harnessing the ocean waves.

In the mornings, on waking, he would lie in bed and work out plots for dramas, scene bits, or even mechanical ideas. After an hour of apparent semi-consciousness, his head motionless on the pillow, he would greet the day with "*I hate to see her die in the third act*," or, "*I wonder if that meat dish could be canned!*" meaning, could a dish he had invented and cooked—a triumph of culinary art—be made a commercial proposition as a tinned food like Armour or Van Camp's beans and corned beef.

Pretty good field of activity, canned meats, and might have made David W. Griffith more money than canned drama.

□□□□□□□□□□

Winter passed. Spring came. On the Rialto's hard pavements, day in and day out, Mr. Griffith, his ear to the ground, was wearing out good shoe leather. But nothing like a job materialized, until, meeting up with an old acquaintance, Max Davidson, he heard about moving pictures. Since youthful days in a Louisville stock company these two had not met. And the simple confidences they exchanged this day brought results that were most significant, not only to David Griffith, but to millions of unsuspecting people the world over. Mr. Davidson had been going down to a place on 11 East Fourteenth Street and doing some kind of weird acting before a camera—little plays, he explained, of which a camera took pictures. "*You've heard of moving pictures, haven't you?*" "Why, I don't know, suppose I have, but I've never seen one. Why?" "I work in them during the summer, make five dollars some days when I play a leading part, but usually it's three. Keeps you going, and you get time to call on managers too. Now you could write the little stories for the pictures. They pay fifteen dollars sometimes for good ones. Don't feel offended at the suggestion. It's not half bad, really. We spend lots of days working out in the country. Lately we've been doing pictures where they use horses, and it's just like getting paid for enjoying a nice horseback ride. Anybody can ride well enough for the pictures. Just manage to stay on the horse, that's all." "Ye gods," said the tempted one, "some of my friends might see me. Then I would be done for. Where do they show these pictures? I'll go see one first." "Oh, nobody will ever see you—don't worry about that." "Well, that does make it different. I'll think it over. Where's the place, you said?" "Eleven East Fourteenth Street." "Thanks awfully. I'll look in—so long."

The elder Mr. [Wallace] McCutcheon was the director when David applied for a job at the American Mutoscope and Biograph Company and got it. There were no preliminaries. He was told to go "below" and put on a little makeup. So, he went "below"—to the dressing room, but he didn't put on a "little makeup." He took a great deal of trouble with it although it was largely experimental, being very different from the conventional stage makeup. The only instruction he was given was to leave off the "red" which would photograph black, thus putting hollows in his cheeks. And he didn't need hollows in his cheeks. When he came up to the studio floor, his dressing and makeup finished, the director and the actors especially, looked at him as though he were not quite in his right mind. "*Poor boob,*" they thought, to take such trouble with a "makeup" for a moving picture, a moving picture that no one who counted for anything would ever see. After a short rehearsal, an explanation of "foreground" and instructions about keeping "inside the lines" and "outside the lines," the camera opened up, ground away for about twenty feet, and the ordeal was over. When work was finished for the day, Mr. McCutcheon paid his new actor five dollars and told him to call on the morrow. So, the next morning there was an early start to the studio. They were to work outside, and there were to be horses! I shall never forget the sadly amused expression my husband brought home with him, the evening of that second day. Nor his comments, "*It's not so bad, you know, five dollars for simply riding a horse in the wilds of Fort Lee on a cool spring day. I think it wouldn't be a bad idea for you to go down and see what you can do. Don't tell them who you are—I mean, don't tell them you're my wife. I think it is better business not to.*" So, a few days later, I dolled up for a visit to the studio. After I had waited an hour or so, Mr. McCutcheon turned to me and said, "*All right, just put a little makeup on, this isn't very important.*" There was no coaching for the acting, only one thing mattered, and that was, not to appear as though hunting frantically for the lines on the floor that marked your stage, while the scenes were being taken.

Mr. Griffith and I "listened in" on all the stories and experiences the actors at the studio had to tell. We would have all the information we could get on the subject of moving pictures, those tawdry and cheap moving pictures, the existence of which we had hitherto been aware of only through the lurid posters in front of the motion picture places—those terrible moving picture places where we wouldn't be caught dead. But we could find use for as many of those little "fives" as might come our way.

Humiliating as the work was, no one took the interest in it that David Griffith did, or worked as hard. This Mr. McCutcheon must have divined right off, for he used him quite regularly and bought whatever stories he wrote. Only a few days were needed to get a line on the place. It was a conglomerate mess of people that hung about the studio. Among the flotsam and jetsam appeared occasionally a few real actors and actresses.

They would work a few days and disappear. They had found a job on the stage again. The better they were, the quicker they got out. A motion picture surely was something not to be taken seriously. Those running the place were not a bit annoyed by this attitude. The thing to do was to drop in at about nine in the morning, hang around a while, see if there was anything for you, and if not, to beat it uptown quick, to the agents. If you were engaged for a part in a picture and had to see a theatrical agent at eleven and told Mr. McCutcheon so, he would genially say, *"That's OK. I'll fix it so you can get off."* You were much more desirable if you made such requests. It meant theatrical agents were seeking you for the legitimate drama, so you must be *good*. Would it be better to affiliate with only one studio or take them all in? There was Edison, way out in the Bronx, Vitagraph in the wilds of Flatbush, Kalem, like Biograph, was conveniently in town, Lubin was in Philadelphia, and Essanay in Chicago. Melies was out West. It would be much nicer, of course, if one could get in "right" at the Biograph. Some of the actors did the rounds.

Ambitious Florence Auer did and so became identified with a different line of parts at each studio. At Biograph, character comedy, at Vitagraph, Shakespeare—for *King Lear* and *Richard the Third* with Thomas H. Ince in attendance, were screened as long ago as this, at Edison, religious drama. There she rode the biblical jackass. The Kalem studio was in the loft of a building on West Twenty-Third Street. You took the elevator to where it didn't run any further and then you climbed a ladder up to a place where furniture and household goods were stored. Bob [Robert] Vignola could be seen here dusting off a clear place for the camera and another place where the actors could be seated the while they waited until Sidney Olcott, the director, got on the day's job. Sidney Olcott was an experienced man in the movies even in those early days, for had he not played a star part in the old Biograph in the spring of 1904? As the *Village Cut-Up* in the movie of the same name we read this about him in the old Biograph bulletin, "*Every country cross-corners has its "Cut-up," the real devilish young man who has been to the "city" at some stage of his career, and having spent thirty cents looking at the Mutoscope, or a dollar on the Bowery at Coney, thinks he is the real thing. The most common evidence of his mental unbalance is the playing of practical jokes, which are usually very disagreeable to the Victim.*" In a few years Mr. Olcott had evolved from the "village cut-up" at Biograph to director at Kalem. Here he engaged Miss Auer for society parts and adventuresses.—Stopped her on the Rialto one day.—"*I know you are an actress,*" said Mr. Olcott, "*and that beautiful gray silk dress you have on would photograph so wonderfully, I'll give you ten dollars if you'll wear it in a scene—it's a society part.*" For a dress that was *gray and silk* too was a most valuable property and a rare specimen of wardrobe in the movies in those days. It came as pleasant news that a tabloid version of *When Knighthood was in Flower* to be called *When Knights Were Bold* was to be screened at Biograph. There were four, or perhaps five, persons in the cast of this premiere *Knighthood* picture. My husband was one—so was I. The picture commemorates our only joint movie appearance. I recall only one scene in this movie, a backdrop picturing landscape, with a prop tree, a wooden bench, and a few mangy grass mats, but there was one other set representing an inn.—I never saw the picture and couldn't tell much about it from the few scenes in which I played. A one-reeler of course—nine hundred and five feet.—Now, whether the cost of Biograph pictures was then being figured at a dollar a foot, I do not know. But that was the dizzy average a very short time later. Anyhow, our flowering *Knighthood* was cheap enough compared with what Mr. Hearst spent thirteen years later on his *Cosmopolitan* production, and was completed in the remarkably short time of one hundred sixty working days. Mr. Hearst's *Knighthood* had a remarkable cast of eighteen principal characters representing the biggest names in the theatrical and motion picture world, and the supporting company counted three thousand extra persons and thirty-three horses. Miss Marion Davies as Princess Mary Tudor was assisted by Lyn Harding, the English actor-manager, Pedro de Cordoba, Arthur Forrest (the original Petronius of *Quo Vadis*), Theresa Maxwell Conover, Ernest Glendinning, (of *Little Old New York*), Ruth Shepley (star of *Adam and Eva*), Johnny Dooley, (celebrated eccentric dancer), George Nash, Gustav von Seyffertitz (for years director and star of the old Irving Place Theatre), Macey Harlam, Arthur Donaldson, Mortimer Snow, William Morris (of *Maytime* fame). A few other names of world-famous people must be mentioned in connection with this picture, for Joseph Urban was the man of the "sets," Gidding and Company made the gowns, Sir Joseph Duveen and P. W. French and Company supplied Gothic draperies, and Cartier, antique jewelry. There were only two old movie pioneers connected with the production, Flora Finch, who back in old Vitagraph days co-starred with John Bunny and after his death held her place alone as an eccentric comedienne, and the director, Robert G. Vignola, who back in the days of our *Knighthood* was the young chap who dusted off the benches and furniture in the old Kalem loft. But Robert Vignola, who came of humble Italian parentage, had a brain in his young head, and was ambitious. Realizing the limitations of Albany, his hometown, he had set out for New York and landed a job in a motion picture studio. Young Vignola represented at the Kalem organization, in the early days, what Bobby [Robert] Harron did at Biograph.

But the Biograph, from ranking the last in quality of picture production, grew to occupy first place, while Kalem continued on a rather more even way. But Bob Vignola didn't, as the years have shown. Indeed, many big names have appeared in movies called *When Knighthood was in Flower*, but David Griffith's is not the biggest, nor was it the first, for before the end of the year 1902, in Marienbad, Germany, a film thirty-one feet long was produced and given the title *When Knighthood was in Flower*.

The descriptive line in the Biograph catalogue of 1902 (for it was a Biograph production) reads, "*Emperor Wilhelm of Germany and noblemen of the Order of St. John. The Emperor is the last in the procession.*" So, you see the Ex-Kaiser beat them all to it, even D. W. Griffith and William Randolph Hearst, though I'll say that Mr. Hearst's is the best of the "flowering" *Knighthoods* to date, and will probably continue so. The story has now been done often enough to be allowed a rest. But it was Mr. Griffith's big dream, very early in his movie career, along in 1911, to screen someday a great and wonderful movie of the Charles Major play that launched Julia Marlowe on her brilliant [acting] career.

And in this play which he had decided could be produced nowhere but in England, no less a person than [Edward Hugh] Sothern was to appear as Charles Brandon, and she who is writing this was to be Mary Tudor. Dreams and dreams we had long ago but this was one of the best dreams that did not come true.

□□□□□□□□□□□

We called him "Old Man McCutcheon," the genial, generous person who at this time directed the movies at the American Mutoscope and Biograph Company. Why "Old Man" I do not know, unless it was because he was slightly portly and the father of about eight children, the oldest being Wallace—"Wally" to his intimates. Wally was quite "some pumpkins" around the studio—father's right-hand man—and then, too, he was a Broadway actor. It was then the general idea of movie directors to use their families in the pictures. As money was the only thing to be had out of the movies those days, why not get as much as possible while the getting was good? The McCutcheon kids had just finished working in a Christmas picture, receiving, besides paychecks, the tree and the toys when the picture was finished.

So, the first bit of gossip wafted about was that the McCutcheons had a pretty good thing of it altogether.

In February, 1908, Wallace McCutcheon was closing an engagement in Augustus Thomas's play, *The Ranger*. Appearing in *The Ranger* with young Mr. McCutcheon, were Robert Vignola, John Adolfi, Eddie [Edward] Dillon, and Florence Auer. A school picture called *The Snowman* was to be made which called for eight children—another job for the little McCutcheons. Grownup Wally and [his] mother were to work too, mother to see that the youngsters were properly dressed and made up. A tall, slight young woman was needed for the schoolmistress and Eddie Dillon, whom Wally had inveigled to the studio, suggested Florence Auer. The story takes place outside the schoolhouse and a "furious blizzard" is raging, although I would say there was nothing prophetic of the blizzard that raged in D. W. Griffith's famous movie *Way Down East*, even though events were so shaping themselves that had Mr. McCutcheon held off a few weeks with his snow story, Mr. Griffith would have arrived in time to offer suggestions. And he would have had something to say, had he been so privileged, for the snowman's raging "blizzard" was made up of generous quantities of *sawdust*. The legs, arms, torso, and head of the snowman were fashioned of fluffy, white cotton, each a separate part, and were hidden under the drifts of sawdust, to be found later by the children who came to romp in the snow and make a snowman. The places where the snowman's fragments were buried were marked so that the children could easily find them. One youngster pretends to mold of sawdust an imaginary leg, but in reality is hunting the buried finished one, on locating which, she surreptitiously pulls it from beneath the sawdust. In this way, finally, all the parts of the Snowman are dug out of the sawdust snow, and put together, revealing a beautiful snowman. Then the Good Fairy of the Snows who all this time has been dreaming in the silver crescent of the moon, looking for all the world like the charming lady of the *Cascarets* ads, is given a tip that the children have finished their snowman. So, it is time for her to wake up and come out of the moon. From her stellar heights, by means of a clumsy iron apparatus, she is lowered to earth. Sadly crude it all was, but it thrilled the fans of the day nevertheless. With her magic wand the Good Fairy touches the snowman and he comes to life. Predatory Pete now comes along, sees Mr. Snowman, and feeling rather jolly from the consumption of bottled goods, he puts his pipe in the snowman's mouth, and when he sees the snowman calmly puff it, in great fright he rushes off the scene, dropping his bottle, the contents of which the snowman drains. In the resultant intoxication the snowman finds his way into the schoolhouse. Finding the schoolhouse too warm, he throws the stove out of the window. Then he throws himself out of the window and lies down in the snow to "sleep it off." When the children return the following morning, the snowman—who is still sleeping—frightens them almost into convulsions. Then the picture really got started—the "chase" began. Sufficiently primitive it was, to have been the first "chase" but it wasn't—for almost at the movie's inception the chase was a part of them. This snowman chase takes place in front of a stationary backdrop that pictures a snowdrift. The actors standing offstage ready for the excitement, come on through the sawdust snow, kicking it up in clouds, eating it, choking on it, hair, eyes, and throat getting full of it. Back and forth against this one "drop," the actors chase. On one run across, a prop tree would be set up. Then as the actors were supposed to have run some hundred yards at least, on the next time across, the prop tree would be taken away and a big *papier mache* rock put in its place. That scene being photographed, the rock would give way to a telegraph pole, and so on until half a dozen chases had been staged before the one "drop." Thus far advanced, artistically and otherwise, was the motion picture this spring of 1908 when "Lawrence" Griffith found himself astride a horse, taking the air in the wide stretches of Coytesville, New Jersey, and getting five dollars to boot. Also found himself so exhilarated, mentally and otherwise, that in the evening he turned author, not of poorly paid poems, but of the more profitable movies.—Wrote a number which he sold for fifteen dollars each, a very decent price considering that this sort of authorship meant a spot-cash transaction. The first little cinema drama of which he was the author—and which was immediately put into the works was *Old Isaacs, the Pawnbroker*.—Very bitter in feeling against the Amalgamated Association of Charities was this story of a kindhearted Hebraic money-lender. On May 6th, with "Lawrence" Griffith the star, was released *The Music Master*, but not David Belasco's. Then came *Ostler Joe* of Mrs. James Brown Potter fame, scenarioized by Mr. Griffith. He [David Wark] also played the part of the priest in the scene where the child dies.

In early July came *At the Crossroads of Life* and *The Stage Rustler*. Biograph's sole advertising campaign at this time consisted of illustrated bulletins—single sheets six to ten inches, carrying a two by three inch "cut" from the film and descriptive matter averaging about three hundred and fifty words. They were gotten up in florid style by a doughty Irishman by the name of Lee Dougherty who was the "man in the front office." He was what is now known as "advertising manager," but the publicity part of his job not taking all his time, he also gave scripts the "once over" and still had moments for a friendly chat with the waiting actor. Although every day was not a busy day at the Biograph for David Griffith, he felt the best policy would be to keep in close touch with whatever was going on there. So he did that, but he also looked in at other studios during any lull in activities. Looked in up at Edison and was engaged for a leading part in quite a thriller, *Rescued from an Eagle's Nest*. Lovely studio, the Edison, but not so much chance to get in right, David felt—it was too well-organized. Looked in at Kalem too, but Frank J. Marion, who was the presiding chief there could not be bothered.—Entirely too many of these down-on-their-luck actors taking up his time.—There were whispers about that Lubin in Philadelphia needed a director. So David wrote them a letter telling of all his varied experiences, which brought an answer with an offer of sixty dollars a week for directing and a request that he run over to Philadelphia for an interview. Now, one had to look like something when on that sort of errand bent. I had to get our little man all dressed up. Could afford only a new shirt and tie. This, with polished boots and suit freshly pressed, would have to do. But, even so, he looked quite radiant as he set forth for the Pennsylvania Station to catch his "every-hour-on-the-hour." But nothing came of it. Lubin decided not to put on another director or make a change—whichever it was. The husband [William Carr] of Mrs. Mary Carr, the Mrs. Carr of William Fox's *Over the Hill to the Poorhouse* fame, continued there, directing the movies which he himself wrote. After dinner each night he would roll back the tablecloth, reach for pad and pencil, and work out a story for his next movie.—Back to the dingy "A. B." for us.—Strange, even from the beginning we felt a sort of at-home feeling there. The casualness of the place made a strong appeal. What would happen if someone really got on the job down there someday? And so it came about shortly after *The Snowman* that the elder Mr. McCutcheon fell ill, and his son Wallace took over his job. He directed *When Knights Were Bold* directed Mr. Griffith in several pictures. But Wally was not ambitious to make the movies his life job. He soon made a successful debut in musical comedy. Some years later he married Pearl White, the popular movie star.

It began to look as though there soon might be a new director about the place. And there was. There were several. No offer of theatrical jobs came to disrupt the even tenor of the first two months at Biograph. It was too late for winter productions and too early for summer stock, so there was nothing to worry about, until with the first hint of summer in the air, my husband received an offer to go to Peaks Island, Maine, and play villains in a summer stock company there. Forty per, the salary would be, sometimes more and sometimes less than our combined earnings at the studio.—To go or not to go?—Summer stock might last the summer and might not. Three months was the most to expect. The Biograph might do as much for us. How trivial it all sounds now! Ah, but believe me, it was nothing to be taken lightly then. For a decision that affects one's very bread and butter, when bread and butter has been so uncertain, one doesn't make without heart searching and long councils of war. So we argued, in a friendly way. Said he, "*If I turn this job down, and appear to be so busy, they soon won't send for me at all. Of course, if this movie* thing is going to last and amount to anything, if anybody could tell you anything about it, we could afford to take chances. In one way it is very nice. You can stay in New York, and if I can find time to write too—fine! But you know you can't go on forever and not tell your friends and relatives how you are earning your living."

Then said she, "How long is Peaks Island going to last? What's sure about summer stock? What does Peaks Island mean to David Belasco or Charles Frohman? We've got this little flat here, with our very own twenty dollars worth of second-hand furniture, and the rent's so low—twenty. You don't know what's going to happen down at the Biograph, you might get to direct some day. Let's stick the summer out anyhow, and when fall comes and productions open up again, we'll see, huh?" So, we put Peaks Island behind us. Now it is as sure as shooting, *if* "Lawrence" Griffith had accepted the offer to play stock that summer he never would have become the David Wark Griffith of the movies. Had he stepped out then, someone else surely would have stepped in and filled his little place, and the chances are he would never have gone back to those queer movies. Of course, now we know that even in so short a time this movie business had gotten under his skin. David Griffith had tasted blood—cinema blood. And the call to stay, that was heard and obeyed when Peaks Island threatened to disrupt the scheme of things, was the same sort of call that made those other pioneers trek across the Plains with their prairie schooners in the days of forty-nine. With Peaks Island settled, we hoped there would be no more theatrical temptations, for we wanted to take chances with the movies.

☐☐☐☐☐☐☐☐☐☐

Considering the chaotic condition of things in the studio as a result of Mr. McCutcheon's illness, it was a propitious time to take heed and get on to the tricks of this movie business. To David Griffith the direction was insufferably careless, the acting the same, and in the lingering bitterness over his play's failure he gritted his teeth and decided that if he ever got a chance he certainly could direct these dinky movies. The studio was so without a head these days that even Henry Norton Marvin, our vice-president and general manager, occasionally helped out in the directing. He had directed a Mutoscope called *A Studio Party* in which my husband and I had made a joint appearance.

With the place now "running wild," Mr. Marvin wondered whom he'd better take a chance on next. He put the odds on Mr. Stanner [Edward Varley] Taylor. In the studio, one day shortly after my initiation, Mr. Taylor approached me and asked if I could play a lead in a melodrama he was to direct. A lead in a melodrama with a brief stage career that had been confined to winsome ingenues! But I bravely said, "*Oh, yes, yes, indeed I can.*" What I suffered! I had a husband who beat and deserted me, I had to appear against him in court, and I fainted and did a beautiful fall on the courtroom floor. After my acquittal I took my two babies and deposited them on a wealthy doorstep, wandered off to the New Jersey Palisades, took a flying leap and landed a mass of broken bones at the bottom of the cliff. Selected for the fall was a beautiful smooth boulder which had a sheer drop on the side the camera did not get of possibly some fifteen feet to a ledge about six feet wide, from which ledge, to the bottom of the Palisades, was a precipitous descent of some hundred feet. There were so many rehearsals of this scene of self-destruction that the rock acquired a fine polish as "mother" slipped and slid about. That the cameraman's assistant might try the stunt for at least the initial attempts at getting the focus never occurred to a soul. But a suggestion was made that if "mother" removed her shoes she might not slide off so easily.—Which she did for the remaining rehearsals.—Then finally as the sun sank behind the Palisades, "mother" in her last emotional moments, sank behind the boulder. On that picture I made twenty-eight dollars, oh, what a lot of money!—The most to date.—If pictures kept up like that! And the whole twenty-eight was mine, all mine, and I invested it at Hackett, Carhart on Broadway and Thirteenth in a spring outfit—suit, shoes, hat, oh, everything. The picture—the only one Mr. Taylor directed—lacked continuity. Upstairs in his executive office, Mr. Henry Norton Marvin was walking the floor and wondering what about it. Why couldn't they get somewhere with these movies? Another man fallen down on the job. Genial Arthur Marvin, Henry Norton's brother, and Billy Bitzer's [Gottfried Wilhelm Bitzer] assistant at the camera, was being catechized as to whether he had noticed any promising material about the studio. "*Well,*" drawled the genial Arthur, "*I don't know. They're a funny lot, these actors, but there's one young man, there's one actor seems to have ideas. You might try him.*" "*You think he might get by, eh?*" "*Well, I don't think you'd lose much by trying him.*" "*What's his name? I'll send for him.*" "*Griffith. Lawrence Griffith.*" Later that day a cadaverous-looking young man was closeted with the vice-president in the vice-president's dignified quarters. "*My brother tells me you appear to be rather interested in the pictures, Mr. Griffith, how would you like to direct one?*"

Mr. Griffith rose from his chair, took three steps to the window, and gazed out into space. "*Think you'd like to try it, Mr. Griffith?*" No response—only more gazing into space. "*We'll make it as easy as we can for you, Mr. Griffith, if you decide you'd like to try.*"—More gazing into space.—And finally this, "*I appreciate your confidence in me, Mr. Marvin, but there is just this to it. I've had rather rough sledding the last few years and you see I'm married, I have responsibilities and I cannot afford to take chances, I think they rather like me around here as an actor. Now if I take this picture directing over and fall down, then you see I'll be out my acting job, and you know I wouldn't like that, I don't want to lose my job as an actor down here.*" "*Otherwise you'd be willing to direct a picture for us?*" "*Oh, yes, indeed I would.*" "*Then if I promise that if you fall down as a director, you can have your acting job back, you will put on a moving picture for us?*" "*Yes, then I'd be willing.*"

It was called *The Adventures of Dollie*. Gossip around the studio had it that the story was a "lemon." Preceding directors at the studio had sidestepped it. "Dollie," in the course of the story, is nailed into a barrel by the gypsies who steal her, the barrel secreted in the gypsy wagon, the horses start off at breakneck speed, the barrel falls off the wagon, rolls into the stream, floats over a waterfall, shoots the rapids, and finally emerges into a quiet pool where some boys, fishing, haul it ashore, hear the child's cries, open the barrel, and rescue "Dollie." Not a very simple job for an amateur. But David Griffith wasn't worried. He could go back to acting were the picture no good. Mr. Arthur Marvin was assigned as cameraman. There were needed for the cast, "Dollie," her mother and father, the gypsy man, the gypsy man's wife, and two small boys. Upstairs in the tiny projection room pictures were being run for Mr. Griffith's enlightenment. He was seeing what Biograph movies looked like. Saw some of old man McCutcheon's, and some of Wally McCutcheon's, and Stanner Taylor's one and only. That evening he said to me, "You'll play the lead in my first picture—not because you're my wife—but because you're a good actress." "Oh, did you see Mr. Taylor's picture?" "Yes." "How was it?" "Not bad, but it don't hang together. Good acting, you're good, quite surprised me. No one I can use for a husband though. I must have someone who 'looks' like a 'husband'—who looks as though he owned more than a cigarette. I heard around the studio that they were going to hand me a bunch of lemons for actors." So, dashing madly here and there for a father for little "Dollie," Mr. Griffith saw coming down Broadway a young man of smiling countenance—just the man—his very ideal. Of course, he must be an actor. There was no time for hesitation. "Pardon me, but would you care to act in a moving picture? I am going to direct a moving picture, and I have a part that suits you exactly." "Moving pictures, did you say? Picture acting? I am sure I don't know what you are talking about. I don't know anything about picture acting." "You don't need to know—just meet me at the Grand Central Depot at nine o'clock tomorrow morning." And so Arthur [Vaughan] Johnson became a movie actor.

To my mind no personality has since flickered upon the screen with quite the charm, lovableness, and magnetic humor that were his. He never acquired affectations, which made him a rare person indeed, considering the tremendous popularity that became his and the world of affectation in which he lived. For the gypsy man Mr. Griffith selected Charles Inslee, an excellent actor whom he had known on the Coast. Mr. Inslee was a temperamental sort but Mr. Griffith knew how to handle him. So with Mrs. Gebhardt [Madeline West] for the gypsy wife, Mr. Griffith completed his cast without using a single one of the "lemons" that were to have been wished upon him, and as there were only outdoor sets in *The Adventures of Dollie* he did not have any of the "lemons" around to make comments.

Even the business of the barrel proved to be no insurmountable difficulty. Yards and yards of piano wire were attached, which, manipulated from the shore, kept the barrel somewhat in focus. The one perturbed person was our cameraman, who even though middle-aged and heavy, time and time again had to jump about, in and out of the stream, grabbing tripod and clumsy camera, trying to keep up with the floating barrel. We went to Sound Beach, Connecticut, to take *The Adventures of Dollie*. It was a lovely place, I thought.

The Black-Eyed Susans were all a-bloom, and everywhere was green grass although it was nearly midsummer. We spent almost a week working on *The Adventures of Dollie*, for the mechanical scenes took time, and—joy!—between us we were making ten dollars a day as long as the picture lasted. And then who could tell! "*If the photography is there, the picture will be all right, if it looks as good on the negative as it looked while we were taking it, it ought to get by,*" opined the director. From out of the secrecy of the darkroom came Arthur Marvin, nonchalantly swinging a short strip of film. "*How is it?*" "*Looks pretty good—nice and sharp.*"—"*Think it's all right?*" "*Yeah, think it is.*" Hopeful hours interspersed with anxious moments crowded the succeeding days. By the time the picture was developed, printed, and titled, we were well-nigh emotionally exhausted. What would they say upstairs? What *would* they say? In the darkened little projection room they sat. On the screen was being shown *The Adventures of Dollie*. No sound but the buzz and whir of the projection machine. The seven hundred and thirteen feet of the *Adventures* were reeled off. Silence. Then Mr. Marvin spoke, "*That's it—that's something like it—at last!*" Afterwards, upstairs in the executive offices, Mr. Marvin and Mr. Dougherty talked it over, and they concluded that if the next picture were half as good, Lawrence Griffith was the man they wanted. The next picture really turned out better. The world's premiere of *The Adventures of Dollie* was held at Keith and Proctor's Theatre, Union Square, July 14, 1908. What a day it was at the studio! However did we work, thinking of what the night held. But as the longest day ends, so did this one. No time to get home and pretty-up for the party. With what meager facilities the porcelain basin and makeup shelf in the dressing room offered, we managed, rubbed off the grease paint and slapped on some powder, gave the hair a pat and a twist, at Silsbee's on Sixth Avenue and Fourteenth Street, we picked up nourishment, and then we beat it to Union Square.—A world's premiere indeed, a tremendously important night to so many people who didn't know it.—No taxis—not one private car drew up at the curb. The house filled up from passersby—frequenters of Union Square—lured by a ten cent entertainment. These were the people to be pleased—they who had paid out their little nickels and dimes. So when they sat through *The Adventures of Dollie* seven hundred feet, interested, and not a snore was to be heard, we concluded we'd had a successful opening night. The contract was drawn for one year. It called for forty-five dollars per week with a royalty of a mill a foot on all film sold. Mr. Marvin thought it rather foolish to accept so small a salary and assured my husband the percentage would amount to nothing whatever right off. But David was willing—rather more than willing—to gamble on himself. And he gambled rather well this time. For, the first year his royalty check went from practically nothing to four and five hundred dollars a month—before the end of the year.

Wonderful it was—too good to be true. Although, had he known then that for evermore, through weeks and months and years, it was to be movies, movies, nothing but movies, David [Wark] Griffith would probably then and there have chucked the job, or keeping it, would have wept bitter, bitter tears.

☐☐☐☐☐☐☐☐☐☐

"Well, we're in the movies—we're working in the moving pictures." "Moving pictures? You're working in moving pictures? What do you mean you're working in moving pictures?"

"We're working at a place—they call it a studio—acting in little plays, dramas, and comedies—a camera takes pictures while we act, and the pictures are shown in those five and ten cent theaters that are all around the town, mostly on Third and Ninth Avenues and Fourteenth Street—such high-class neighborhoods." "Those dreadful places? I wouldn't be seen going into one of them." Yes, that was the attitude in those dark and dismal days when David signed that contract with the Biograph Company. For one year now, those movies so covered with slime and so degraded would have to come first in his thoughts and affections. That was only fair to the job. But only one who had loved the theater as he had, and had dreamed as he had of achieving success therein, could know what heartaches this strange new affiliation was to bring to him. Times came, agonizing days, when he would have given his life to be able to chuck the job. Mornings when on arising he would gaze long, long moments out the window, apparently seeing nothing—then the barely audible remark, "*I think I'll phone and say I cannot come.*" On such days he dragged heavy, leaden feet to 11 East Fourteenth Street. And there was an evening when, returning home after a drab day at the studio, and finding his modest menage festive with ferns and wild flowers, he became so annoyed that with one swoop he gathered up nature and roughly jammed her into the wastepaper basket.

A visiting relative who'd helped gather the flowers worried so over the strange procedure that I had to explain—"*It's those pictures, you know they're just the fringe of acting.*" The emotions that would sweep over us at times! How our pride was hurt! How lacking in delicacy people could be! With what a patronizing air the successful and prosperous actor friend would burst into the studio! Mr. Griffith would say, "Well, how about it? If you're hanging around this summer, how would you like to work with me a bit?" Polite and evasive the reply, "Well, you see, I'm awfully busy just now, have several offers and—well—when I'm signed up I'll *drop around again.*" But we, in the know, understood that all the King's horses and all the King's men could not induce such to join our little band of movie actors. We were always conscious of the fact that we were in this messy business because everything else had failed—because nobody had seemed to want us, and we just hadn't been able to hang on any longer. But David buckled to the job like a true sport. It was *his job* and he would dignify it. The leaden mornings came to be quite the exception to the rule. Many days were greeted with bright and merry song. And so, firm and unshakeable in our determination to do the most with what we had, we dismissed the silly sensitive business and set to work. What we had to work with was this, a little studio where interior scenes were taken, and exteriors also, for there was little money for traveling expenses—Fort Lee, Greenwich, and the Atlantic Highlands comprised our early geographical horizon. A few actors, a willing and clever cameraman, a stage carpenter, and a scenic artist, comprised the working force. Funny studio! Interesting old workshop! The "Last Leaf's" ballroom! The outer doors of the building opened into a broad hall from which on the left as one entered, a door gave into Mr. Dougherty's office, on the right was another door—the entrance to the bookkeeping department. An old colonial stairway on this same side led up to the projection room and other offices. The spacious hall of the main floor ended with double doors opening into the studio. There, first to meet the eye—unless one stumbled on it before seeing it—for it completely blocked the entrance—was a heavy rolling platform on which the camera, poised atop of its tripod, was set. So, if the studio doors chanced to invite you during the taking of a scene, you would have to remain put in the few feet of space between the platform and the doors until the scene was finished. Usually there would be someone to keep you company in your little niche. It was an easy matter in those days to get into the studio. No cards of announcement were needed—no office boy insulted you, no humiliation of waiting, as today. A ring of the bell and in you'd go, and Bobby Harron would greet you if he chanced to be nearby. Otherwise, any one of the actors would pass you the glad word. On an ordinary kitchen chair a bit to one side of the camera, Mr. Griffith usually sat when directing. The actors when not working lingered about, either standing or enjoying the few other kitchen chairs. During rehearsals actors sat all over the camera stand—it was at least six feet square—and as the actors were a rather chummy lot, the close and informal intimacy disturbed them not the least. A "scene" was set back center, just allowing passage room. What little light came through the few windows was soon blocked by dusty scenery.

On the side spaces of the room and on the small gallery above, the carpenters made scenery and the scene painters painted it—scenery, paint pots, and actors were all huddled together in one friendly chaos. We always had to be mindful of our costumes. To the smell of fresh paint and the noise of the carpenter's hammers, we rehearsed our first crude little movies and in due time many an old literary classic. Rolls of old carpet and bundles of canvas had to be climbed over in wending one's way about. To the right of the camera a stairway led to the basement where there were three small dressing rooms, and no matter how many actors were working in a picture those three dark little closets had to take care of them all. The developing or "dark" room adjoined the last dressing room, and all opened into a cavernous cellar where the stage properties were kept. Here at the foot of the stairs and always in everyone's way, the large wardrobe baskets would be deposited. And what a scramble for something that would halfway fit us when the costumes arrived! We ate our lunches in the dingy basement, usually seated on the wardrobe baskets. Squatted there, tailor fashion, on their strong covers, we made out pretty well. On days when we had numbers of extra people, our lunch boy, little Bobby Harron, would arrange boards on wooden horses, and spread a white cloth, banquet fashion. Especially effective this, when doing society drama, and there would be grande dames, financiers, and magnates, to grace the festive board. In a back corner of the studio reposed a small, oak, roll-top desk, which the new director graced in the early morning hours when getting things in shape, and again in the evening when he made out the actors paychecks. When the welcome words came from the darkroom, "*All right, everybody, strike!*" the actors rushed to the roll-top, and clamored for vouchers—we received our "pay" daily. Then the actor rushed his "makeup" off, dressed, passed to the bookkeeper's window in the outer office, presented his voucher, and Herman Bruenner gave him his money. And then to eat, and put away a dollar towards the week's rent, and to see a movie for ten cents! A little group of serious actors soon began to report daily for work. As yet no one had a regular salary except the director and cameraman.

"Principal part" actors received five and "extras" three dollars. In August this first year Mr. Griffith began turning out two releases a week, usually one long picture, eight to eleven hundred feet, and one short picture, four to five hundred feet.

The actors who played the principal parts in these pictures were Eddie Dillon, Harry Salter, Charles Inslee, Frank Gebhardt, Arthur Johnson, Wilfred Lucas, George Nichols, John Cumpson, Owen Moore, Mack Sennett, Herbert Prior, David Miles, Herbert Yost, Anthony O'Sullivan, and Daddy Butler. Of the women Marion Leonard, Florence Lawrence, and myself played most of the leading parts, while Mabel Stoughton, Florence Auer, Ruth Hart, Jeanie MacPherson, Flora Finch, Anita Hendrie, Dorothy West, Elinor Kershaw (Mrs. Thomas Ince), and Violet Mersereau helped out occasionally. Gladys Egan, Adele DeGarde, and Johnny Tansey played the important child parts. Though I speak of playing "principal parts," no one had much chance to get puffed up, for an actor having finished three days of importance usually found himself on the fourth day playing "atmosphere," the while he decorated the backdrop. But no one minded. They were a good-natured lot of troupers and most of them were sincerely concerned in what they were doing. David had a happy way of working. He invited confidence and asked and took suggestions from anyone sufficiently interested to make them. His enthusiasm became quite infectious. In the beginning Marion Leonard and I alternated playing "leads." She played the worldly woman, the adventuress, and the melodramatic parts, while I did the sympathetic, the wronged wife, the too-trusting maid waiting, always waiting, for the lover who never came back.

But mostly I died. Our director, already on the lookout for a new type, heard of a clever girl out at the Vitagraph, who rode a horse like a western cowboy and who had, had good movie training under Mr. Rainous. He wanted to see her on the screen before an audience. Set up in a store on Amsterdam Avenue and 160th Street was a little motion picture place. It had a rough wooden floor, common kitchen chairs, and the reels unwound to the tin-panny shriek of a Pianola. After some watchful waiting, the stand outside the theater, the sort of thing sandwich men carry—finally announced *The Dispatch Bearer*, a Vitagraph with Florence Lawrence. So, living nearby, after dinner one night we rushed over to see it. It was a good picture. Mr. Griffith concluded he would like to work with Mr. Rainous for a while and learn about the movies. For one could easily see that besides having ability Florence Lawrence had, had excellent direction. Well, David stole little Florrie, he did. With Harry Salter as support in his nefarious errand, he called on Miss Lawrence and her mother, and offered the Vitagraph girl twenty-five dollars a week, regular. She had been receiving fifteen at Vitagraph playing leading parts, sewing costumes, and mending scenery canvas. She was quite overcome with Mr. Griffith's spectacular offer, readily accepted, and by way of celebrating her new prosperity, she drew forth from under the bed in the little boardinghouse room, her trombone or was it a violin?—And played several selections.—As a child, Miss Lawrence, managed by her mother, and starred as "Baby Flo, the child wonder-whistler" had toured the country, playing even the "tanks." Immediately she joined the Biograph, Florence Lawrence was given a grand rush. But she never minded work. The movies were as the breath of life to her. When she wasn't working in a picture, she was in some movie theater seeing a picture. After the hardest day, she was never too tired to see the new release and if work ran into the night hours, between scenes she'd wipe off the makeup and slip out to a movie show. Her pictures became tremendously popular, and soon all over the country Miss Lawrence was known as "The Biograph Girl." It was some years before the company allowed the names of actors to be given out—hence "Biograph Girl" was the only intelligent appellation. After Miss Lawrence left Biograph, Mary Pickford fell heir to the title. Miss Lawrence's early releases show her versatility. Two every week for a time, *Betrayed by a Handprint*, *The Girl and the Outlaw*, *Behind the Scenes*, *The Heart of Oyama*, *Concealing a Burglar*, *Romance of a Jewess*, *The Planter's Wife*, *The Vaquero's Vow*, *The Call of the Wild*, *The Zulu's Heart*, *The Song of the Shirt*, *Taming of the Shrew*, *The Ingrate*, and *A Woman's Way*. Like Mary Pickford, Miss Lawrence was an awfully good sport about doing stunts. One day a scene was being filmed with Miss Lawrence thrown tummy-wise across a horse's saddled back.

As the horse dashed down the roadway he came so close to the camera that we who were watching breathlessly, for one moment closed our eyes, for Miss Lawrence's blond head just missed the camera by a few inches. Rainy August days forced us to work in the studio. Mr. Griffith had read a story by Jack London called *Just Meat*. He changed the name to *For Love of Gold* and let it go at that. We had no fear of lawsuits from fractious authors those days. The story was about two thieves, who returned home with the latest spoils, get suspicious of each other and each, unknown to the other, poisons the other's coffee and both die. The big scenes which were at the table when the men become distrustful of each other could be told only through facial expression. "Ah," puzzled Mr. Director, "*how can I show what these two men are thinking? I must have the camera closer to the actors—that's what I must do—and having only two actors in these scenes, I can.*" Up to this time, every scene had been a long shot, that is, the floor—the carpet—the greensward—showed yards in front of the actors feet. But Mr. Griffith knew he couldn't show nine feet of floor and at the same time register expression. So to his cameraman he said, "*Now don't get excited, but listen. I'm going to move the camera up, I'm going to show very little floor, but I'm going to show a large, full-length figure, just get in the actors feet—get the toes—one foot of foreground will do. Well, we've* never done anything like that—how do you think that's going to look?—A table with a man on each side filling up the whole screen nearly." "We'll do it—we'll never get anywhere if we don't begin to try new things." The burglars were screened so big that every wicked thought each entertained was plainly revealed.

Everybody came to like the idea afterwards, especially the actors. Along in November, Mr. Griffith began work on a series of domestic comedies—the "Jones Pictures." Florence Lawrence played "Mrs. Jones," and John Cumpson, "Mr. Jones." Their movie marital debut was in *A Smoked Husband*. The "Jones" movies were probably the first to achieve success as a series.

☐☐☐☐☐☐☐☐☐☐

In Biograph's story, quite a few who stuck to the ship in these first days are big names in the movies today. In the town of Erie, Pennsylvania, in the early nineteen hundreds flourished a little newspaper, on the staff of which was Frank Woods. Besides reporting "news," Frank Woods [also] sold advertising. Erie, Pennsylvania, not long satisfying his ambitions, Mr. Woods set out for the journalistic marts of New York City, and shortly after found himself selling advertising for the *New York Dramatic Mirror*. The idea of getting ads from the picture people came to him when he noticed that pictures were not mentioned in the *Dramatic Mirror*. Writers on the paper were told that any reference to the movies would be promptly blue-penciled.

Mr. Woods figured that if he could interest the movie people he might get ads from them and the *Dramatic Mirror* wouldn't mind that. But the picture people turned deaf ears.

Why pay money for an ad in a paper that was all too ready to crush them? Besides, the *Mirror* didn't circulate among the exhibitors and those interested in the movies. The movie people would stick to the more friendly, *Billboard*, thank you kindly—it could have their ads. Another idea came to Frank Woods. How about pictures being reviewed? He put the plan before Lee Dougherty, for Lee was always genial and had time to listen. Lee said, "Fine, give us real serious reviews—tell us where we are *wrong—but don't expect an ad for your effort."* The result of this conversation was that three reviews appeared in the *New York Dramatic Mirror*, June, 1908. On a rear end page captioned "The Spectator," Frank E. Woods dissertated through some columns on the merits and demerits of the movies, and thus became their first real critic. We were very grateful for the few paragraphs. It meant recognition—the beginning. How gladly we parted with our ten cents weekly to see what "Spec" had to say about us. But Mr. Woods didn't get an ad from the Biograph. So, he had another heart-to-heart talk with Mr. Dougherty, and Doc said, *"Never mind, keep it up—but as I told you, the reviews aren't going to influence us about ads."* But in August the Company came across and bought a quarter-page ad for the Biograph movies.

The active mind of Frank Woods was not going to stop with critical comments on moving pictures. His new duties necessitated his seeing pictures, and, looking them over and analyzing them for his reviews, he said to himself, *"Oh, they're terrible—I could do better myself—such stories!"* So he wrote three "suggestions"—that's all they were—and that's what they were then called. With great aplomb, he took them to Mr. Dougherty, and to his amazement Mr. Dougherty turned the whole three down. Sorry, but he didn't think them up to scratch. But Mr. Woods would not be fazed by a turn-down like that. He wrote three more "suggestions." The studio had a sort of nominal supervisor, a Mr. Wake, whose job was to OK little expenditures in the studio and to pass on the purchase of scenarios. One day, not long after our American Biograph affiliation, just as I was entering the main foyer, Mr. Griffith coming from the projection room seemed more than usually lighthearted. So I said, *"You're feeling good—picture nice?"* "Oh, yes, all right, but"—this in a whisper—*"Wake's been fired."* I wondered how I could wait all that day, until evening, to hear what had happened. But I did, and learned that Mr. Wake with Biograph money had purchased silk stockings for Mutoscope girls, and then had given the girls the stockings for their own. However, during a temporary absence from the studio before Mr. Wake's dismissal, Frank Woods came down with three more suggestions which were shown to Mr. Griffith direct. He bought the whole bunch, three at fifteen dollars apiece, *nine five-dollar bills, forty-five dollars*. Around the *Dramatic Mirror* offices Mr. Woods was already jocularly being called "M. P. Woods." And this day that he disposed of his three "suggestions," Moving Picture Woods with much bravado entered the *Mirror's* office, went over to the desk, brushed aside some papers, cleared a place on the counter, and in a row laid his nine five-dollar bills. In the office at the time were George Terwilliger (many scenarios he afterwards wrote), Al Trahern (he continued with his stock companies and featuring his wife Jessie Mae Hall), and Jake [Jacob] Gerhardt, now in the business end of the movies. The trio looked—and gasped—and looked—and in unison spoke, "Where did you get all that?" "Moving Pictures!" "Moving Pictures? For heaven's sake, tell us about it." "How did you do it?" queried George Terwilliger. "Forty-five dollars for three stories, good Lord, and they gave you the money right off, like that." So Mr. Woods told his little story, and as the conversation ended, George Terwilliger reached for paper and pencil, for five dollar bills were beckoning from every direction. Maybe he could put it over, too. He did—he sold lots and lots of "suggestions."

Frank Woods wrote thirty movies for Biograph. Frank Woods now set about to criticize the pictures with the same seriousness with which he would have criticized the theater. He bought books about Indians and let the producers know there was a difference between the Hopi and the Apache and the Navajo. With a critical eye, he picked out errors and wrote of them frankly, and his influence in the betterment of the movies has been a bigger one than is generally known outside the movie world. Mr. Woods is really responsible for research. And Mr. Dougherty gives him credit for turning in the first "continuity." The picture that has that honor is a version of [Alfred] Tennyson's *Enoch Arden*, called *After Many Years*. Scenarios that reached the Biograph offices, due to lack of organization, were sometimes weeks in reaching the proper department, but Mr. Griffith got first chance at *After Many Years*. Both he and Mr. Dougherty thought it pretty good stuff, but the obvious emotional acting that had prevailed somewhere in every picture so far, was here entirely lacking. Quiet suppressed emotion only, this one had. But Doc said he'd eat the positive if it wouldn't make a good picture. So, it was purchased. But *After Many Years*, although it had no "action," and some of us sat in the projection room at its first showing with heavy hearts, proved to write more history than any picture ever filmed and it brought an entirely new technique to the making of films. It was the first movie without a chase. That was something, for those days, a movie without a chase was not a movie. How could a movie be made without a chase? How could there be suspense? How action? *After Many Years* was also the first picture to have a *dramatic* close-up—the first picture to have a cutback. When Mr. Griffith suggested a scene showing Annie Lee waiting for her husband's return to be followed by a scene of Enoch castaway on a desert island, it was altogether too distracting. "*How can you tell a story jumping about like that? The people won't know what it's about.*" "*Well,*" said Mr. Griffith, "*doesn't Dickens write that way?*" "*Yes, but that's Dickens, that's novel writing, that's different.*" "*Oh not so much, these are picture stories, not so different.*" So, he went his lonely way and did it, did *After Many Years* contrary to all the old established rules of the game. The Biograph Company was very much worried—the picture was so unusual—how could it succeed? It was the first picture to be recognized by foreign markets.

When one recalls the high class of moving pictures that Pathe and Gaumont were then putting out, such as *The Assassination of the Duc de Guise*, this foreign recognition meant something. *After Many Years* made a change in the studio. All "suggestions" now came directly to Mr. Dougherty's office. He selected the doubtful ones and the sure bets and with Mr. Griffith read them over the second time. They threshed out their differences in friendly argument. So Lee Dougherty became the first scenario editor. And of the sad letters and grateful ones his editing jobs brought him, this letter from a newspaperman on a Dayton, Ohio, paper, now dead, he prizes most highly.

Lee E. Dougherty, Editor, Kinemacolor Company, Los Angeles, California, *Dear Sir*—Excuse me, but I can't help it. When I cashed the $25 check for *Too Much Susette*, the scenario of mine which you accepted, I took $5 of the money and put it on "Just Red" who won at Louisville at the juicy price of 30 to 1. I hope the film will bring your company as much luck as the script has brought me. *Yours very truly, George Groeber.* "Doc" was Mr. Griffith's friendly appellation for "the man in the front office," Lee Dougherty. It was going some for Mr. Griffith to give anyone a nickname. He never was a "hail fellow well met." It was Mr. "So and So" from Mr. Griffith and to Mr. Griffith with very few exceptions. Never once during all the Biograph years did he ever publicly call even his own wife by any other name than "Miss Arvidson." Only in general conversation about the movies, and in his absence, was he familiarly referred to as "Griff," or "DW," or the "Governor." Mr. Dougherty was the one man at 11 East Fourteenth Street before the Griffith regime who had more than a speaking acquaintance with the movies. In the summer of 1896 as stage manager of the old Boston Museum, he installed there the first projection machine of American manufacture, the Eidoloscope. When the season at the Boston Museum was over, Mr. Dougherty, who had become quite fascinated with this new idea in entertainment, went to New York City. The Biograph Company along about 1897 had just finished a moving picture of Pope Leo XIII taken at the Vatican. Pictures of the late Pope Benedict XV were announced as the first pictures made of a Pope, "approved by His Holiness." While they may be the first approved ones, Captain Varges of the International Newsreel, who claims the honor, brought the third motion picture camera into the Vatican grounds. The second film—Pope Pius X in the Vatican, and gardens, and the Eucharistic Congress, was released in 1912. Well, anyhow, Mr. Dougherty took a set of Biograph's Pope Leo XIII pictures to exhibit in the towns and cities of New Jersey and Pennsylvania on the old Biograph projection machine—one vastly superior to the Eidoloscope. The company exhibiting the picture consisted of an operator on the machine and Mr. Dougherty who lectured. And when he began his little talk (there was no titling or printed matter in the picture), the small boys in the gallery would yell "*spit it out, we want to see the picture.*" Numbers of motion picture directors today might well heed the sentiments of those small boys. From exhibiting Pope Leo XIII's picture, Mr. Dougherty became stage director of One Minute Comedies for the Biograph which at this time had a stage on the roof of a building at 841 Broadway. And sometimes in the midst of a scene the weather would pick up scenery and props and deposit them in Broadway. So came about experiments with electric lights, satisfactory results first being obtained with the Jeffries-Sharkey prize fight. The One Minute Comedies finally were given up, but the Mutoscopes, being Biograph's biggest source of revenue, were continued. The Mutoscopes were brief film playlets that were viewed in the penny-in-the-slot machines. One day, before Mutoscopes ended, my husband asked me to run over to Wanamaker's with him and help choose some pretty undies for the Mutoscope girls—photographically effective stuff—so we selected some very elegant heavy black silk embroidered stockings and embroidered pink Italian silk vests and knickers, last-word lingeries for that time. I felt rather ill about it. "*Oh dear,*" I thought, "*this is some business, but I'll be brave, I will, even though I die.*" Well, the parcel being wrapped, David took it and then handed it to me, and I thought, "*Why should I carry the bundle?*" So we reached Fourteenth Street. David started to the left without his parcel, I was continuing up Broadway, so handed it to him. But the lingerie wasn't for Mutoscopes at all—but for me—just a little surprise. So then with a light and happy heart, I took my way home to admire my beautiful present. After the Biograph had engaged David, Mr. Dougherty did not want them to make any more Mutoscopes. Mr. Griffith directed possibly six. In order to influence Biograph to cut out the Mutoscopes, Doc got very cocky, and he said to Mr. Kennedy and Mr. Marvin, "*You wait, you'll see pictures on Broadway someday, like you do plays.*"

But they gave him the laugh. "*Yes,*" Doc added, "*and they will accord them the same dignified attention that John Drew receives." They laughed some more at this, and said, "*Pictures will always be a mountebank form of amusement*," But Doc's prophecy came true. And David Ward Griffith did no more Mutoscopes.

The "Jones" pictures became very popular. Many persons well-known in the movies today, played "bits" in them. Jeanie MacPherson, author of *The Ten Commandments* was "principal guest" in *Mr. Jones at the Ball*. Miss MacPherson, who for many years has been and still is chief scenario writer and assistant to Cecil B. DeMille, got her first movie job on the strength of a pale blue crepe de chine evening gown. How funny we were when we moved in the world of brilliant men and beautiful women only we, who represented them, knew. Dress suits of all vintages appeared. Anyone with "clothes" had a wonderful open sesame. A young chap whom we dubbed "the shoe clerk'"—who never played a thing but "atmosphere"—got many a paycheck on the strength of his neat, tan, covert cloth spring overcoat—the only spring overcoat that ever honored the studio. (An actor could get along in the spring with his winter suit and no overcoat.) Clothes soon became a desperate matter, so Biograph consented to spend fifty dollars for wearing apparel for the women.

Harry Salter and I were entrusted with the funds and told to hunt bargains. We needed negligees, dinner dresses, ball gowns, and semi-tailored effects. The clothes were to be bought in sizes to fit, as well as could be, the three principal women.

In that day, on Sixth Avenue in the Twenties, were numbers of shops dealing in second-hand clothing, and Mr. Salter and I wandered among them and finally at a little place called "Simone," we closed a deal. We got a good batch of stuff for the fifty—at least a dozen pieces—bizarre effects for the sophisticated lady, dignified accoutrements for the conventional matron, and simple softness for young innocence. How those garments worked! I have forgotten many, but one—a brown silk and velvet affair—I never can forget. It was the first to be grabbed off the hook—it was forever doing duty. For it was unfailing in its effect. Arrayed in the brown silk and velvet, there could be no doubt as to one's moral status—the maiden lady it made obviously pure, the wife, faithful, the mother, self-sacrificing.

Deciding, impromptu, to elaborate on a social affair, Mr. Griffith would call out, "*I can use you in this scene, Miss Bierman, if you can find a dress to fit you.*" The tall, lean actresses and the short ones found that difficult, and thus, unfortunately, often lost a day's work. Spotting a new piece of millinery in the studio, our director would thus approach the wearer, "*I have no part for you, Miss Hart, but I can use your hat. I'll give you five dollars if you will let Miss Pickford wear your hat for this picture.*" Two days of work would pay for your hat, so you were glad to sit around while the leading lady sported your new headpiece. You received more on a loan of your clothes, sometimes, than you did on a loan of yourself. Clothes got five dollars always, but laughter and merrymaking upstage went for three. Jeanie MacPherson had recently returned from Europe with clothes the like of which had never been seen at Biograph. From the chorus of "Hello People" at the Casino Theatre little Jeanie entered the movies and even though she had a snub nose and did not photograph well, what could Mr. Griffith do but use her? Jeanie proved to be a good trouper, she was conscientious and ambitious. Though only extras and bits came her way, David encouraged her.

She was rather frail, and one time after remaining ill some days when on a picture up in the country, Mr. Griffith thought he should give her good advice. So, he told her to live on a farm for some months and drink milk and get strong, there being no future without health—he certainly could not use her in parts were she to faint on him thus. But Jeanie confided she'd have to overcome fainting without "months on a farm"—that luxury she couldn't afford. Since Biograph Miss MacPherson has carried on in every department of picture making except the acting. She early took stock of herself and recognized that her future would not be in the ranks of the movie stars. Just where it would be she did not then know—nor did anyone else. On a day in this slightly remote period Jesse Lasky and Cecil DeMille were lunching at

Rector's in New York—music, luscious tidbits, and Mr. Lasky casually remarking, "*Let's go into the moving picture business.*" "*All right, let's,*" answered Mr. DeMille with not the slightest hesitation. Mr. Lasky, thus encouraged, suggested more "*Let's,*" to each of which Mr. DeMille as promptly agreed "*Let's.*" Along came brother-in-law Sam Goldfish, married to Blanche Lasky, sister to Jesse. Mr. Goldfish (now Goldwyn) was in the glove business up in Gloversville, New York, and he was very grouchy this day because the Government had taken the duty off gloves and he was eager to listen in on this new idea of Mr. Lasky's.

By the time that lunch was finished this is what had happened, Mr. Goldfish had put up $5,000, Mr. Lasky $5,000, and Arthur Friend $5,000, and with the $15,000 Cecil DeMille was to go out to California to make movies. He begged his brother William to put up $5,000 and become a partner but William said, "*No, one of us had better be conservative and keep the home fires burning.*" So, when William later went into the movies, he went to work for his brother Cecil, and he has been doing so up to this time. Mr. Cecil DeMille became Director General of the new Jesse Lasky Pictures (Famous Players Company), and Mr. Oscar Apfel, General Manager. Out on Vine Street, Hollywood, Mr. DeMille took over a stable, and began to make movies. It was a crude equipment, but the company fell heir to some beer kegs from which they viewed their first picture *The Squaw Man* released sometime in 1913. The stable is still a part of the Hollywood, Famous Players-Lasky Corporation, but the beer kegs have vanished. Pictures kept on radiating from the stable with quite gratifying success. In time along came Jeanie MacPherson intent on an interview with Mr. Cecil B. DeMille. Jeanie now knew so much about the movies and Cecil B. so little, he just naturally felt the Lord had sent her. Miss MacPherson's presentation of ideas always got over to Cecil. So, Jeanie signed up with the new firm on that rather long ago day and now she gets one thousand a week, I understand, for writing Mr. DeMille's big pictures. We must go back now and rescue Jeanie from "Mr. Jones's" ball, for in *Mrs. Jones Entertains*, she has duties to perform. In that picture she was not "principal guest" but the "maid." Flora Finch was a guest. Miss Finch in another "Jones" movie becomes a book agent soliciting "Mr. Jones" in his office. In *Mr. Jones Has a Card Party*, Mack Sennett appears as one of husband's rummies, and in yet another *Jones*, Owen Moore, first husband of Mary Pickford is seen as "atmosphere" escorting a lady from a smart cafe.

So chameleon-like were our social relations in the *Jones* comedy series. A Flora Finch tidbit here comes to light. Though fifteen years have elapsed, they have not dimmed the memory of the one hundred and eighty-five feet of *Those Awful Hats*. The exhibitor was told, "*It will make a splendid subject to start a show with instead of the customary slides.*" The "set" represented the interior of a moving picture theater. The company was audience. Miss Finch was also "audience," only arriving late she had a separate entrance. Miss Finch wore an enormous hat. When she was seated, no one at the back or side of her could see a thing. But out of the unseen ceiling, soon there dropped an enormous pair of iron claws (supposedly iron) that closed tightly on the hat and head of the shrieking Miss Finch, lifting her bodily out of her seat and holding her suspended aloft in the studio heaven. How many times that scene was rehearsed and taken! It grew so late and we were all so sleepy that we stopped counting. But pay for overtime evolved from this picture. The members of the stock company that had grown up worked on a guaranty of so many days a week. Now with so much night work our director felt that the actors not on "guaranties" should be recompensed and it was ruled that after 7 PM they would receive three extra dollars. So when 6 PM would arrive with yet another scene to be taken, the non-guaranty actors became very cheery. More money loomed, and more sandwiches, pie, coffee, or milk, on the company. Frequently those not on the guaranteed list made more than those on it, which peeved the favored ones. Along about now Mr. Herbert Yost contributed some artistic bits. Once he was Edgar Allan Poe and he wrote *The Raven* while his sick wife, poor little Virginia, died. We were a bit afraid of being too classic. The public might not understand—we must go slowly yet awhile, but not all our days. Mr. Yost was one actor who used a different name for his picture work. He called himself "Barry O'Moore" in the movies. Not that he felt the movies beneath him but he was nervous about the future reaction. He showed good foresight. For as soon as the big theatrical producers got wind of the fact that their actors were working in moving picture studios, they decided to put a crimp in the idea. The Charles Frohman office issued an edict that any actor who worked in moving pictures could not work for them. But the edict was shortly revoked. Even so long ago had the power of the motion picture begun to be felt.

☐☐☐☐☐☐☐☐☐☐

One of our regular "extra" people was Mack Sennett. He quietly dubbed along like the rest, only he grouched. He never approved wholeheartedly of anything we did, nor how we did it nor who did it. There was something wrong about all of us—even Mary Pickford. Said the coming King of Comedy productions, "*I don't see what they're all so crazy about her for—I think she's affected.*" Florence Lawrence didn't suit him either—"*she talks baby talk.*" And to Sennett "baby talk" was the limit! Of myself he said, "*Sometimes she talks to you and sometimes she doesn't.*" Good-looking Frank Grandon he called "Inflated Grandon." But beneath all this discontent was the feeling that he wasn't being given a fair chance, which, along with a smoldering ambition, was the reason for the grouch. When work was over, Sennett would hang around the studio watching for the opportune moment when his director would leave. Mr. Griffith often walked home wanting to get a bit of fresh air. This Sennett had discovered. So, in front of the studio or at the corner of Broadway and Fourteenth Street he'd pull off the "accidental" meeting. Then for twenty three blocks he would have the boss all to himself and wholly at his mercy. Twenty-three blocks of uninterrupted conversation. "*Well now, what do you really think about these moving pictures? What do you think there is in them? Do you think they are going to last? What's in them for the actor? What do you think of my chances?*" To all of which Mr. Griffith would reply, "*Well, not much *for the actor, if you're thinking of staying. The only thing is to become a director. I can't see that there's anything much for the actor as far as the future is concerned."* Mr. Sennett had come to the movies via the chorus of musical comedy. It also was understood he had had a previous career as a trainer for lightweight boxers. If there was one person in the studio that never would be heard from—well, we figured that person would be Mack Sennett. He played policemen mostly—and what future for a movie policeman? His other supernumerary part was a French dude. But he was very serious about his policeman and his French dude. From persistent study of Max Linder—the popular Pathe comique of this day—and adoption of his style of boulevardier dressing, spats, boutonniere, and cane, Mr. Sennett evolved a French type that for an Irishman wasn't so bad. But even so, to all of us, it seemed hopeless. Why did he take so much pains? He got by pretty well when any social flair was unnecessary, when Mary Pickford and I played peasants, tenement ladies, and washwomen, Mack occasionally loved, honored, and cherished us in the guise of a laborer or peddler. He had a muscle-bound way about him in these serious roles, perhaps he was made self-conscious by the sudden prominence. But Mary and I never minded. The extra girls, however, made an awful fuss when they had to work in a comedy with Sennett, for he clowned so. They would rather not work than work with Sennett. How peeved they'd get! "*Oh, dear,*" they'd howl, "*do I have to work with Sennett?*" Now 'tis said he is worth five millions! In *Father Gets in the Game*, an early release, Sennett is seen as the gay Parisian papa, the Linder influence plainly in evidence. Mr. Griffith was more than willing, if he could find a good story with a leading comedy part suitable to Mr. Sennett, to let him have his fling. Finally, one such came along, quite legitimate, with plenty of action, called *The Curtain Pole*, venturesome for a comedy, for it was apparent it would exceed the five-hundred-foot limit. It took seven hundred and sixty-five feet of film to put the story over. Released in February, 1909, it created quite a sensation. The natives of Fort Lee, where *The Curtain Pole* was taken, were all worked up over it. Carpenters had been sent over a few days in advance, to erect, in a clearing in the wooded part of Fort Lee, stalls for fruits, vegetables, and other foodstuffs. The wreckage of these booths by Mack Sennett in the guise of Monsieur Dupont was to be the big climax of the picture. The "set" when finished was of such ambitious proportions—and for a comedy, mind you—that we were all terribly excited, and we concluded that while it had taken Mr. Sennett a long time and much coaxing to get himself "starred," it was no slouch of a part he had eventually obtained for himself. I know I was all stirred up, for I was a market woman giving the green cabbages the thrifty stare, when the cab with the curtain pole sticking out four or five feet either side, entered the marketplace. Monsieur Dupont, fortified with a couple of absinthe frappes, was trying to manipulate the pole with sufficient abandon to effect the general destruction of the booths. He succeeded very well, for before I had paid for my cabbage something hit me and I was knocked not only flat but considerably out, and left genuinely unconscious in the center of the stage. While I was satisfied he should have them, I wasn't so keen just then about Mack Sennett's starring ventures. But he gave a classic and noble performance, albeit a hard-working one. One other picture was released this same year with Mack Sennett in a prominent part—*The Politician's Love Story*. New York's Central Park awoke one February morning to find her leafless trees and brush all a-glisten with a sleet that made them look like fantastic crystal branches. When the actors reported at the studio that morning, they found Mr. Griffith in consultation with himself. He did not want to waste that fairyland just a few blocks away. A hurried look through pigeon-holed scripts unearthed no winter story. "*Well,*" announced our director, "*make up everybody, straight makeup. Bobby [Harron], pack up the one top hat, the one fur coat and cap, I'll call a couple of taxis, and on the way we'll change this summer story into a winter one.*" So was evolved *The Politician's Love Story* in which were scenes where lovers strolled all wrapped up in each other and cuddled down on tucked-away benches. Well, lovers can cuddle in winter as well as summer, and we were crazy to get the silver thaw in the picture, and we got it, though we nearly froze. But we had luxurious taxis to sit in when not needed, and afterwards we were taken to the Casino to thaw out, and were fed hot coffee and sandwiches in little private rooms. *The Curtain Pole* and *The Politician's Love Story* started the grumbling young Mack Sennett on the road to fame and fortune. Like the grouchy poker player who kicks himself into financial recuperation, Mack Sennett grouched himself into success.

☐☐☐☐☐☐☐☐☐☐

Before the first winter drove us indoors there had been screened a number of Mexican and Indian pictures. There was one thriller, *The Greaser's Gauntlet*, in which Wilfred Lucas, recruited from Kirke La Shelle's *Heir to the Hoorah* played the daring, handsome, and righteous Jose. And Wilfred Lucas, by the way, was the first real g-r-a-n-d actor, democratic enough to work in our movies. That had happened through friendship for Mr. Griffith. They had been in a production together. For a mountain fastness of arid Mexico, we journeyed not far from Edgewater, New Jersey. No need to go further. Up the Hudson along the Palisades was sufficiently Mexico-ish for our needs. There were many choice boulders for abductors to hide behind and lonely roads for holdups. New Jersey nearby was a fruitful land for movie landscape, it didn't take long to get there, and transportation was cheap. Small wonder Fort Lee shortly grew to be the popular studio town it did. In those days, movie conveyance for both actors and cargo was a bit crude. We had no automobiles. When Jersey-bound, we'd dash from wherever we lived to the nearest subway, never dreaming of spending fifty cents on a taxi. We left our subway at the 125th Street station.

Down the escalator, three steps at a bound, we flew, and took up another hike to the ferry building. And while we hiked this stretch we wondered [aloud]—for so far we had come breakfastless—if we would have time for some nourishment before the 8:45 boat. A block this side of the ferry building was "Murphy's," a nice clean saloon with a family restaurant in the back, where members of the company often gathered for an early morning bite. We stuffed ourselves until the clock told us to be getting to our little ferry boat. Who knew when or where we might eat again that day? "Ham," Mr. Murphy's best waiter, took care of us. As the hungry breakfasters grew in number and regularity Mr. Murphy became inquisitive. Mr. Murphy was right, we didn't work on the railroad and we didn't drive trucks. So, who, inquired Mr. Murphy of Ham, might these strange people be who ate so much and were so jolly in the early morning?

And Ham answered, "*Them is moving picture people.*" And Mr. Murphy replied, "*Well, give them the best and lots of it.*" We needed "the best and lots of it." We needed regular longshoremen's meals. Outdoor picture work with its long hours meant physical endurance in equal measure with artistic outpourings. Ham is still in Mr. Murphy's service, but his job has grown rather dull with the years. No more picture people to start the day off bright and snappy. Now he only turns on the tap to draw a glass of Mr. Volstead's less than half of one percent. "*But I want to ask you something,*" said Ham as I started to leave. "*Yes?*" "*Would you tell me*"—hushed and awed the tone—"*did Mary Pickford ever come in here?*" "*Oh, yes, Ham, she came sometimes.*" "*I told the boss so, I told him Mary Pickford had come here with them picture people.*" Whether Mary had or hadn't, I didn't remember, but I couldn't deny Ham that little bit of romance to cheer along his colorless todays. Ham's breakfast disposed of, we would rush to the ferry, seek our nook in the boat, and enjoy a short laze before reaching the Jersey side. At one of the little inns along the Hudson we rented a couple of rooms where we made up and dressed. Soon would appear old man Brown and his son, each driving a two-seated buggy. And according to what scenes we were slated for, we would be told to pile in, and off we would be driven to a "location." "Old Man Brown" was a garrulous, good-natured Irishman who regaled us with tales of prominent persons who, in his younger days, had been his patrons. How proud he was to tell of Lillian Russell's weekly visit to her daughter Dorothy who was attending a convent school up the

Hudson! Speaking of "Old Man Brown" brings to mind "Hughie." Hughie's job was to drive the express wagon which transported costumes, properties, cameras, and tripods. In the studio, on the night preceding a day in the country, each actor packed his costume and makeup box and got it ready for Hughie.

For sometimes in the early morning darkness of 4 AM. Hughie would have to whip up his horses in front of 11 East Fourteenth Street so as to be on the spot in Jersey when the actors arrived via their speedier locomotion. Arrived on location, Johnny Mahr and Bobby Harron would climb the wagon, get out the costumes, and bring them to the actor. And if your particular bundle did not arrive in double quick time and you were in the first or second scene, out you dashed and did a mad scramble on to the wagon where you frantically searched. Suppose it had been left behind! Hughie had a tough time of it trucking by two horsepower when winter came along. So, I was very happy some few years later, when calling on Mr. Hugh Ford at the Famous Players old studio in West Fifty-sixth Street, New York, now torn down, to find Hughie there with a comfortable job "on the door." David Griffith was always overly fastidious about "location."

His feeling for charming landscapes and his use of them in the movies was a significant factor in the success of his early pictures. So we had a "location" woman, Gene Gauntier, who dug up "locations" and wrote scenarios for the princely wage of twenty-five dollars weekly. Miss Gauntier will be eternally remembered as the discoverer of Shadyside. Shades of Shadyside! With never a tree, a spot of green grass, or a clinging vine, only sand, rocks, and quarries from which the baked heat oozed unmercifully. Miss Gauntier's aptitude along the location line, however, did not satisfy her soaring ambition, so she left Biograph for Kalem. Under Sidney Olcott's direction, she played Mary in his important production *From the Manger to the Cross*, and was the heroine of some charming Irish stories he produced in Ireland. *The Redman and the Child* was the second picture Biograph's new director produced, and his first Indian picture.

Charles Inslee was the big-hearted Indian chief in the story and little Johnny Tansey played the child. The picture made little Johnny famous. He had as much honor as the movies of those days could give a child. Jackie Coogan was the lucky kid to arrive in the world when he did. When the New Theater (now the Century), sponsoring high-class uncommercial drama opened, Johnny Tansey was the child wonder of the company. Here he fell under the observant eye of George Foster Platt and became his protege. And so our Johnny was lost to the movies. We went to Little Falls, New Jersey, for *The Redman and the Child*, which, at the time, was claimed to be "the very acme of photographic art." I'll say we worked over that Passaic River. Mr. Griffith made it yield its utmost. As there was so little money for anything pretentious in the way of a studio set, we became a bit intoxicated with the rivers, flowers, fields, and rocks that a munificent nature spread before us, asking no price. My memories of working outdoors that first summer are not so pleasant. We thought we were going to get cool, fresh air in the country, but the muggy atmosphere that hung over the Hudson on humid August days didn't thrill us much. I could have survived the day better in the studio with the breeze from our one electric fan. On Jersey days, work finished, back to our little Inn in a mad rush to remove makeup, dress, and catch the next ferry.

Our toilet was often no more than a lick and a promise with finishing touches added as we journeyed ferrywards along the river road in old man Brown's buggy. Were we ever going anywhere but Fort Lee and Edgewater and Shadyside? I do believe that first summer I was made love to on every rock and boulder for twenty miles up and down the Hudson. Well, we did branch out a bit. We did a picture in Greenwich, Connecticut.

Driving to the station, our picture day finished, we passed a magnificent property, hemmed in by high fences and protected with beautiful iron gates. Signs read "Private Property. Keep Out." We heeded them not. In our nervous excitement (we were not calm about this deed of valor) we kept away from the residence proper, and drove to the outbuildings and the superintendent's office. Told him we'd been working in the country nearby and would appreciate it much if we could come on the morrow and take some scenes, slipped him a twenty, and that did the trick. There was nothing we had missed driving around Milbank, which, we learned later, was the home of Mrs. Abraham Archibald Anderson (Elizabeth Milbank Anderson), the well-known philanthropist who passed away some few years ago. So, on the morrow, bright and early, we dropped anchor there, made up in one of the barns, and were rehearsing nicely, being very quiet and circumspect, when down the pathway coming directly toward us, with blood in her eye, marched the irate Mrs. Anderson. Trembling and weak-kneed we looked about us.

Could we be hearing alright? Was she really saying those dreadful things to us? Weakly we protested our innocence. Vain our explanation. And so we folded our tents and meekly and shamefacedly slunk away. Before the summer was over we went to Seagate and Atlantic Highlands. It wasn't very pleasant at Atlantic Highlands, for here we encountered the summer boarder. As they had nothing better to do, they would see what we were going to do. We were generally being lovers, of course, and strolling in pairs beneath a sunshade until we reached the foreground, where we were to make a graceful flop onto the sandy beach and play our parts beneath the flirtatious parasol. Before we were ready to take the scene we had to put ropes up to keep back the uninvited audience which giggled and tee-heed and commented loudly throughout. We felt like monkeys in a zoo—as if we'd gone back to the day when the populace jeered the old strolling players of Stratford town. Mr. Griffith got badly annoyed when we had such experiences. His job worried him, the nasty publicity of doing our work in the street, like ditch diggers. So, he had to pick on someone and I was handy. How could *I* stand for it? Why was *I* willing to endure it? He *had* to, of course. So, thinking to frighten me and make me a good girl who'd stay home, he said, "*Something has occurred to me, it's probable this business might get kind of public—some day, you know, you may get in the subway and have all the people stare at you while they* whisper to each other, 'That's that girl we saw in the movie the other night.' And how would you like that?" One saving grace the Highlands had for us. We could get a swim sometimes. And we discovered Galilee, a fishing village about twenty miles down the coast, the locale of that first version of "Enoch Arden" *After Many Years*. But when winter came, though we lost the spectators we acquired other discomforts. Our makeup would be frozen, and the dreary, cold, damp rooms in the country hotels made us shivery and miserable. We'd hurriedly climb into our costumes, drag on our coats and then light our little alcohol stove, or candle, to get the makeup sufficiently smeary. When made up, out into the cold, crisp day. One of the men would have a campfire going where we'd huddle between scenes and keep limber enough to act. Then when ready for the scene Billy Bitzer would have to light the little lamp that he attached to the camera on cold days to warm the film so it wouldn't be streaked with "lightning." While that was going on we stood at attention, ready to do our bit when the film was. We weren't so keen on playing leads on such days as those, for when you are half frozen it isn't so easy to look as if you were calmly dying of joy, for which emotional state the script might be asking. What we liked best in the winter was to follow Mack Sennett in the chases which he always led, and which he made so much of, later, when he became the big man in Keystone films. The chase warmed us up, for Mack Sennett led us on some merry jaunts, over stone walls, down gulleys, atop of fences—whatever looked good and hard to do. Somehow we found it difficult to be always working with the weather.

Though we watched carefully it seemed there always were *summer* stories to be finished, almost up to snow time, and *winter* stories in the works when June roses were in bud.

Pink Swiss on a bleak November day beneath the leafless maple didn't feel so good, nor did velvet and fur and heavy wool in the studio in humid August. But such were the things that happened. We accepted them with a good grace.

☐☐☐☐☐☐☐☐☐☐

This story must now take itself indoors. We are terribly excited over Tolstoy's *Resurrection*. So even though it be May, we must to the studio where the carpenters and scene painters are fixing us a Siberia. As the days went by we produced many works of literary masters—Dickens, Scott, Shakespeare, Bret Harte, O. Henry, and Frank Norris. We never bothered about "rights" for the little one-reel versions of five-act plays and eight hundred page novels. Authors and publishers were quite unaware of our existence. Arthur Johnson, Owen Moore, and Florence Lawrence played the leading parts in our "free adaptation of Leo Tolstoy's powerful novel." And it so happened that just as "Prince Demetri" was ready to don his fur robes, and the poor exiles their woolen slips, for the trudge over the snow-clad steppes, a nice hot spell came our way, and we must have been the hottest Russians that ever endured Siberia. Owen Moore got so querulous with the heat—he was playing one of those handsome, cruel officers who poke bayonets at the innocent and well-behaved exiles—that he nearly killed us throwing tables and heavy furniture at us. I objected to the realism. We were all a bit peevish, what with the unseasonable heat and the last moment discovery that the costumer had sent our wrapper-like dresses in sizes miles too large. The scene being set and rehearsals finished, there were left just the few moments while the property man added the finishing touches to the salt and flour snow (we had graduated from sawdust), to make the costumes wearable. So another girl and I grabbed the lot and rushed into a little Polish tailor shop in the basement next door and borrowed the Polish tailor's sewing machines so that we could put in the necessary hems and pleats. Zip went the sewing machines—there was no time to lose—for we could not afford two days of Russian exiles at three dollars per day. Nine o'clock was the morning hour of bustle and busy "ness" at 11 East Fourteenth Street. But the actors in their eagerness to work were on the job long before nine sometimes. They straggled along from all directions. They even came by the horse-drawn surface car whose obliging and curious conductors stopped directly in front of number 11. And so curious became one conductor that he was not able to stand the strain, and he quit his job of jerking Bessie's reins, and got himself a job as an "extra."

Although the conductor's identity was never fully established, we had strong suspicions that it was Henry Lehrman, an extra who had managed in a very short time to get himself called 'Pathe,' which was good for an Austrian. "Actors" graduates from various trades and professions of uncertain standing, and actors without acting jobs, lounged all over the place, from the street steps where they basked on mild, sunny days, into the shady hall where they kept cool on hot days, and had they made acquaintance with studio life, they could be found in the privacy of the men's one (single) dressing room shooting craps—the pastime during the waiting hours. An especially busy hour 9 AM when we were to start on a new picture. What kind of a picture was it to be? The air was full of expectancy. Who would be cast for the leads? How keen we were to work! How we hoped for a good part—then for any kind of a part—then for only a chance to rehearse a part. In their eagerness to get a good part in a movie, the actors behaved like hungry chickens being fed nice, yellow corn, knocking and trampling each other in their mad scramble for the best bits. This Mr. Griffith did enjoy. He would draw his chair up center, and leisurely, and in a rather teasing way, look the company over. And when you were being looked at you thought, "*Ah, it's going to be me.*" But in a few minutes someone else would be looked at. "*No, it was going to be he.*" A long look at Owen, a long look at Charlie, a long look at Arthur, and then the director would speak, "*Arthur, I'll try you first.*" One by one, in the same way the company would be picked. There would be a few rough rehearsals, someone wouldn't suit, the chief would decide the part was more in Owen's line. Such nervousness until we got all set! Indeed, we put forth our best efforts. There was too much competition and no one had a cinch on a line of good parts. When we did *The Cricket on the Hearth*, Mr. Griffith rehearsed all his women in the part of "Dot," Marion Leonard, Florence Lawrence, Violet Mersereau, and then he was "nice" to me. Miss Mersereau, however, portrayed "May

Plummer," making her movie debut. Herbert Prior played "John Perrybingle," and Owen Moore as "Edward Plummer."

Sometimes after rehearsing a story all day our director would chuck it as "no good" and begin on another. He never used a script and he rehearsed in sequence the scenes of every story until each scene dovetailed smoothly, and the acting was OK. He worked out his story using his actors as chessmen. He knew what he wanted and the camera never began to grind until every little detail satisfied him. There was some incentive for an actor to do his best. More was asked of us than to be just a "type," and the women couldn't get by with just "pretty looks." We worked hard, but we liked it. With equal grace we all played leads one day and decorated the backdrop the next. On a day when there would be no work whatever for you, you'd reluctantly depart. Sometimes Mr. Griffith almost had to drive the non-working actors out of the studio. The place was small and he needed room. Sometimes when rehearsing a picture he liked a lot, it would be as late as 3 PM before a fainting, lunchless lot of actors would hear those welcome words, "*All right, everybody, get your lunches and makeup.*" Then Bobby Harron would circulate a child's menu card and the thirty-cent allotment would be checked off. Roast beef or a ham-and-egg sandwich, pie, tea, coffee, or milk usually nourished us. And it was a funny thing that no matter how rich one was, or how one might have longed for something different, even might have been ill and needed something special, none of us ever dreamed of spending a nickel of his own. While the actors ate and made up, and the carpenters were getting the set ready, Mr. Griffith, accompanied by three or four or five or six actors not on the working list that afternoon, would depart for a restaurant nearby. But no woman was ever invited to these parties. This social arrangement obtained only on days when a new picture was to be got underway. David Griffith was a generous host, but he always got a good return on his investment. For while being strengthened on luscious steak, steins of Pilsener, and fluffy German pancakes all done up in gobs of melted butter, lemon juice, and powdered sugar, ideas would sprout, and comments and suggestions come freely from the Knights of Luchow's Round Table, and when the party was over they returned to the studio all happy, and the director ready for a big day's work.

But the other actors, now made up and costumed but fed only on sandwiches, were wearing expressions of envy and reproach which made the returning jolly dogs feel a trifle uncomfortable. "*Well, let's get busy around here—wasting a hell of a lot of time—six o'clock already—have to work all night now—now come on, we'll run through it—show me what you can do—Bitzer, where do you want them? Come in and watch this, Doc.*" Mr. Griffith was back on the job all right. One such rehearsal usually sufficed. Then Johnny Mahr with his five-foot board would get the focus and mark little chalk crosses on the floor, usually four, two for the foreground and two for the background. Then Johnny would hammer a nail into each cross and with his ball of twine, tying it from nail to nail to enclose the set.—Now a rehearsal for "lines."—And when Bitzer would say it was OK and Doc beamed his round Irish smile, we would take the picture, and God help the actor who looked at the camera or at the director when he was shouting instructions while the scene was being photographed.

The old ways of doing were being revolutionized day by day with the introduction of the close-up, switchback, light effects, and screen acting that could be recognized as a portrayal of human conduct. Exhibitors soon began clamoring for American Biograph pictures, not only for the United States but for foreign countries as well, and as Mr. Griffith had a commission on every foot of film sold, it was an easy matter for us to judge our ever-increasing popularity. The Biograph Company readily acknowledged its young director's achievements, and the other companies soon took cognizance of a new and keen competitor. The first metropolitan showings began a rivalry with the other companies. Once in the race, we were there to win—and we did. Biograph pictures came to mean something just a little different from what had been. There was a sure artistic touch to them, the fine shadings were there that mark the line between talent and genius. David Griffith had found his place, found it long before he knew it. In ways, it was a congenial berth. Mr. Marvin, once he saw how the wind blew, seldom came into the studio. He was willing to let the new producer work things out his own way.

An occasional conference there was, necessarily—a friendly chat as to how things were coming along. Mr. Marvin was tall and dark, quite a handsome man—so approachable. The actors felt quite at ease with him. Had he not been one of us? Had he not directed even Mr. Griffith in a penny-in-the-slot movie? Years later I recalled the incident to Mr. Marvin. He had forgotten it completely, but with a hearty laugh said, "*No, did I really? Well, God forgive me.*" "*God forgive us all,*" I answered. Liking Mr. Marvin as we did, we did not quite understand or approve the sudden, unexpected intrusion of Mr. J. J. Kennedy, one day. "*Oh, our president? Why, do you suppose,*" the anxious actors queried, "*he's become suddenly so interested?*" What could poor movie actors be expected to know of politics and high finance? Everything had been so pleasant, we couldn't understand it. We were rather awed by Mr. Kennedy at first. Red-headed, pugnacious Irish Jeremiah—why, he never gave an actor a smile or the faintest recognition, and feeling ourselves such poor worms, as a result, we became nothing less than Sphinxes whenever his rare but awe-inspiring presence graced the studio. But we soon learned that "fighting J. J." was of some importance in this movie business. And other things about him we learned, that he was a big man in the world of engineering—a millionaire who lived in a lovely brownstone in Brooklyn. We soon discovered he was human, too. It seemed Mr. Kennedy had, had his affairs all settled to retire from the world of business activities, when, in the critical days resulting from the 1907 panic, he stepped into the breach and saved from impending disaster the American Mutoscope and Biograph Company. The little American Mutoscope and Biograph Company would have been terribly surprised had she been told that she was to become the organization that would develop some of the greatest of motion picture directors and stars—the Augustin Daly stock company of the movies. For while there is never the grind of its preposterous old camera to be heard in the length of the land today, while for years (at the time of writing this, nearly ten) all its wheels of activity have been silent, "The Old Biograph" remains as the most romantic memory, the most vital force in the early history of the American motion picture. The association with these two scholarly gentlemen Messieurs Kennedy and Marvin, unusual then as today in the picture business, helped to soften the crudities of the work, and tone down the apparent rough edges of our job. So considerate of our tender feelings were both Mr. Marvin and Mr. Kennedy, that when either desired to visit or bring interested friends into the studio, they would ask Mr. Griffith for a propitious moment, and then standoff in the background as though apologizing for the intrusion. Mr. Griffith, but not by way of retaliation, had reason to make intrusions on his bosses. He went pleading the cause of better screen stories.

For that was the ticklish point—to raise our artistic standard—not to depart too rapidly from the accepted—and to keep our product commercial. David Griffith began feeling his wings. He dared to consider a production of [Robert] Browning's *Pippa Passes*. If just once he could do something radical to make the indifferent legitimate actors, critics, writers, and a better class of public take cognizance of us! So, there resulted long discussions with the Biograph executives as to the advisability of Browning in moving pictures, and after much persuasion consent was eventually granted. There was no question in our minds as to whether *Pippa Passes* would be an artistic success. Had this classic writer fashioned his famous poem directly for the movies he couldn't have turned out a better screen subject. But might not the bare idea of the high-brow Robert scare away the moving picture public? In those days there were several kinds of motion picture publics. In sections of New York City, there was the dirty, dark little store, a sheet at one end and the projection machine at the other. It took courage to sit through a show in such a place, for one seldom escaped without some weary soul finding a shoulder the while he indulged in forty winks. Besides this there were the better-known Keith and Proctor Theaters on Fourteenth

Street, Twenty-Third, and 125th Street, the Fourteenth Street Theatre, and the old Academy of Music. In the smaller American cities, the motion picture public was of middle-class homey folks who washed their own supper dishes in a hurry so as to see the new movie, and to meet their neighbors who, like themselves, dashed hatless to the nickelodeon, dragging along with them the children and the dog. Things like this happened, when dinner hour was approaching, and mother was anxiously awaiting her child, the neighborhood policeman would casually saunter over to the picture house, poke his head in at the door, spy the wanted child, tap her little shoulder, gently, "*Jennie, your mother wants you*" whereupon Jennie would reluctantly tear herself away so that the family could all sit down together to their pot roast and noodles. Yes, Browning would need courage. *Pippa Passes* being ever in Mr. Griffith's mind these days, he scanned each new face in the studio as he mulled over the needed characters. The cast would be the best possible one he could get together.

☐☐☐☐☐☐☐☐☐☐

It was a bright May morning in 1909. When I came off the scene, I noticed a little girl sitting quietly in a corner near the door. She looked about fourteen. I afterwards learned she was nearing seventeen. She wore a plain navy blue serge suit, a blue and white striped lawn shirtwaist, a rolled brim Tuscan straw sailor hat with a dark blue ribbon bow. About her face, so fresh, so pretty, and so gentle, bobbed a dozen or more short golden curls—such perfect little curls as I had never seen. A timid applicant usually hugged the background. Bold ones would press forward to the camera and stand there, obtruding themselves, in the hope that the director would see them, like their look, and engage them for a day's work. But Mary Pickford tucked herself away in a niche, while she quietly gave us "the once over." The boss's eagle eye had been roving her way at intervals, the while he directed, for here was something "different"—a maid so fair and an actress to boot! Pausing a moment in his work, he came over to me and said, "*Don't you think she would be good for*

Pippa?" "*Ideal,*" I answered. Before we closed shop that day, he had Mary made up—gave her a violin, and told her to walk across the stage while playing it so that Billy Bitzer could make a test. Before she left the studio that day, every actor there had a "line" on Mary. In the dressing room, the word went around, "*There's a cute kid outside, have you seen her?*" "*No, where is she?*" "*She's been sitting out there in a corner by herself.*" "*Guess I'll take a look.*" "*She's cute all right, they're taking a test.*" Something was impending. There was excitement and expectancy in the air.

"America's Sweetheart" was soon to make her first screen appearance. The test was OK and Mary was told to come to the studio on the morrow. David promised her five dollars a day for her first picture, and were her work good, he'd talk business with her. That satisfied Mary. As "Giannina," the pretty daughter of "Taddeo Ferrari," in *The Violin Maker of Cremona* Mary Pickford made her motion picture debut. She was ideally suited to the part, and had good support from David Miles as the cripple "Filippo." The studio bunch was all agog over the picture and the new girl, long before the quiet word was passed to the regulars a few days later, "*Projection room, run 'The Violin Maker.'* " After the showing, Mr. Griffith had a serious conversation with Mary and offered her twenty-five dollars a week for three days work. This Mary accepted. She felt she might stay through the summer. Her second picture was *The Lonely Villa*, the brainchild of Mack Sennett, gleaned from a newspaper—good old-fashioned melodrama. Mary played a child of twelve with two younger sisters and a mother. They were nice people, and wealthy. Miss Leonard, playing the mother, would be beautifully arrayed in the brown-silk-and-velvet. But what could be done for Mary? She had no clothes fit for the wealthy little aristocrat she was to portray and there was nothing in the meager stock wardrobe for her. "*Oh, she's so pretty,*" I said to my husband, "*can't we dress her up? She'll just be darling in the right kind of clothes.*" So he parted with twenty dollars from the cash register and trusted me to dispose of it at Best's—then on Twenty-Third Street—for a proper wardrobe. Off I went on my joyful errand, and brought back to the studio a smart pale blue linen frock, blue silk stockings to match, and nifty patent leather pumps. What a dainty little miss she looked, her fluffy curls a-bobbing, when she had donned the new pretties. During the dreary waits between scenes, there being no private dressing rooms, actors would be falling all over each other, and they could find seclusion only by digging themselves in behind old and unused scenery. Owen Moore was especially apt in hiding himself. He had an unfriendly way of disappearing.—None of the herd instinct in him.—At times we had quite a job locating him. Cruising along the backdrop of a Coney Island Police Court, or perhaps a section of the Chinese wall, we'd innocently stumble upon him. But we didn't need to hunt him the day that Mary Pickford was all dressed up in Best and Company's best. That day he never left the camera stand, and his face was all one generous Irish smile. (How little we know when our troubles are going to begin.) Following *The Lonely Villa* came *The Way of Man* and then a series of comedies in which Mary was teamed with Billy Quirk, *Sweet and Twenty*, *They Would Elope* and *His Wife's Visitors*. Though Mary Pickford affiliated with the movies for twenty-five dollars weekly with the understanding that she would work three days a week and play "parts" only, she was a good sport and would come in as an "extra" in a scene if we needed her. So occasionally in a courtroom scene, or a church wedding where the camera was set up to get the congregation or spectators from the rear, Mary could attend with perfect safety as the Pickford curls, from the back of her head, would never have been recognized by the most enthusiastic fan of that day.

    Mr. Griffith would not have his "Mary" a "super." Considering the stellar position she has held for years, and her present-day affluence, many movie fans may think that Mary Pickford was kissed by the fairies when she was born. Not so. Life's hard realities—the understanding of her little family's struggles to make both ends meet when she was even as young as Jackie Coogan at the time of his first appearance with Charlie Chaplin in *The Kid*—that was her fairy's kiss—that and her mother's great love for her. Of course, such idolatry as Mrs. Smith gave her firstborn might have made of her a simpering silly, or worse. But Gladys Smith (as Mary Pickford was born) was pretty—and she had talent and brains. So, what wonder if Mother Smith often sat all through the night at her child's bedside not wanting to sleep but only to worship her beautiful daughter? Mary told me her story in our early intimate days together in the movies. With her little gang she was playing in the streets of Toronto where she was born, perhaps playing "bean bag'"—she was indeed young enough for that. In frock coat and silk hat an advance agent was looking over the prospects for business in the town, and at the same time looking for a few kids needed in his show. His eye caught pretty little Gladys Smith. Would Mama let her play at the opera house? *"Let's ask Mama."* Mama, the young Mrs. Smith, consented. Seeing that, a very few years afterwards, through an accident on the St. Lawrence River boat on which her husband worked, Mama was suddenly left a young widow with three tiny youngsters to support, her consent that day proved to be one of those things just meant to be. With the Valentine Stock Company in her hometown when only five, Mary played her first part, "Cissy" in *The Silver King*. In 1902, Mary was already a "star," playing "Jessie" in *The Fatal Wedding*. The season of 1904 found Gladys Smith, then twelve years old, playing leading parts, such as "Dolly" in *The Child Wife*, a play written by Charles Taylor, first husband to "Laurette" and the father of her two children.

The following season Gladys Smith created the part of "Freckles" in *The Gypsy Girl*, written by Hal Reid, father of the popular and much-loved Wallace Reid. Gladys Smith's salary was then forty dollars per week and she sent her mother, who was living in Brooklyn, fifteen dollars weekly for her support. In 1906 the Smith family toured with Chauncey Olcott in *Edmund Burke*. But it was as the little boy "Patsy Poor" in *New York Life* that Mary's chance came for better things. David Belasco had told Gladys he would give her a hearing. And so the day came when on the dark and empty stage of the Republic Theater, a chair her only "support," Gladys did "Patsy's" death scene for Mr. Belasco and he thought so well of it that she was engaged for Charlotte

Walker's younger sister "Betty" in *The Warrens of Virginia*. So *The Warrens of Virginia* with Gladys Smith, rechristened by Mr. Belasco "Mary Pickford" (a family name) came and went. The magic wand of Belasco had touched Mary, but magic wands mean little when one needs to eat. *The Warrens of Virginia* finished its run, and Mary, her seventeen years resting heavily upon her, was confronted with the long idle summer and the nearly depleted family exchequer. So, arrived the day in the late spring, when from the weary round of agencies and with faint hope of signing early for next season little Mary wandered to the old Biograph studio at 11 East Fourteenth Street. Such a freshly sweet and pretty little thing she was, that her chances of not being engaged were meager. Since that day when she first cast her lot with the movies—that day in June, 1909, when the Pickford releases so inauspiciously started, they have continued with only one interruption. That was in January, 1913, when in David Belasco's production of *The Good Little Devil*, she costarred with Ernest Truex. What an exciting day at the studio it was when it was discovered that Mr. Belasco was up in the projection room seeing some of Mary's pictures! Mary's return to the legitimate was a clever move. It made for publicity and afterward served her, despite the shortness of the engagement, as a qualification for becoming an Adolph Zukor Famous Player. Mr. Zukor established his "Famous Players" through the production of *Queen Elizabeth*, the first feature picture with a famous player, the player being no less a personage than the divine Sarah Bernhardt. This was in 1912. So, when Mary Pickford became a Famous Player, it caused considerable comment. However, she has become the most famous of all the Famous Players engaged by Mr. Zukor. And as for Famous Players, long before Adolph Zukor's day, they had been appearing before a movie camera. As far back as 1903 Joseph Jefferson played his famous *Rip Van Winkle* for the American Mutoscope and Biograph Company. And Sarah Bernhardt appeared as *Camille*, in the Eclair Company's two-reel production of the Dumas play in 1911. Mary Pickford did not reach the peak of fame and affluence without her "ifs." When the first fall came, and little Mary had not connected up with a legitimate job, she said to me one day, "*Miss Arvidson, we have just fifty dollars in the bank for all of us, and I'm worried to death. I want to get back on the stage. Of course, the pictures are regular, but if I had enough put away, I'd get out.*" Another day, "*If I stay in the movies I know I will just be ruined for the stage—the acting is so different—and I never use my voice. Do you think it will hurt me if I stay in the pictures any longer?*" "Well, Mary," I answered, "*I cannot advise you. We all just have to take our chances.*"

Good fortune it was for the movies, for her family and for her that she stayed. In the beginning she encountered practically no competition. Not until dainty Marguerite Clark left the field of the legitimate in 1913 and appeared in her first charming photoplay *Wildflower* did Miss Pickford ever need to bother her little head over anything as improbable as a legitimate competitor in a field where she had reigned as queen undisputed and unchallenged. It is often asked whether Mary Pickford is a good businesswoman. My opinion is that she's a very good businesswoman. And I am told that she had a head for business as far back as the days of *Patsy Poor*. She must have an understudy and no one but sister, Lottie [Pickford] was going to be that understudy. Lottie stayed the season even though no emergency where she could have officiated, presented itself.

I know Mary brought a business head with her to Biograph. Mr. Griffith had told her if she'd be a good sport about doing what little unpleasant stunts the stories might call for, he would raise her salary. The first came in *They Would Elope*, some two months after her initiation. The scene called for the overturning of the canoe in which the elopers were escaping down the muddy Passaic. Not a second did Mary demur, but obediently flopped into the river. The scene over, wet and dirty, the boys fished her out and rushed her, wrapped in a warm blanket, to the waiting automobile. It was the last scene of the day—we reserved the nasty ones for the finish. Mary's place in the car was between my husband and myself. Hardly were we comfortably settled, hardly had the chauffeur time to put the car in "high," before Mary with all the evidence of her good sportsmanship so plainly visible, naively looked up into her director's face and sweetly reminded him of his promise. She got her raise. And I got the shock of my young life. That pretty little thing with yellow curls thinking of money like that! Later, when Carl Laemmle had bucked the General Film Company with the organization of his independent company, the "Imp," he enticed Mary away from the Biograph by an offer of twenty-five dollars a week over her then one hundred weekly salary. Mary was still under legal age, so Owen Moore, to whom Mary had been secretly married, had to sign the contract. He, with several other "Biograph-ers" had gone over to the "Imp." Mrs. Smith with Lottie and Jack [Pickford] still clung to the Biograph.

Amid anguished tears Mrs. Smith showed me the contract, and in a broken voice said, *"What's to become of Mary at that awful 'Imp' with no one to direct her? How could she have been influenced to leave Mr. Griffith for only twenty-five dollars extra and not even consult her mother? What good will the twenty-five dollars do with her career ruined?"* But the break did not hurt Mary. It helped her. She soon sued the "Imp," claiming that her artistic career was being ruined as she was being forced to act with carpenters. That was the story according to the dailies.

Shortly afterward she was back at Biograph with another twenty-five dollar weekly advance in her salary.

☐☐☐☐☐☐☐☐☐☐

Through conflicting emotions and varying decisions and an ever-increasing interest and faith in the new work, Biograph's first movie actors stuck. With Mary Pickford pictures winning favor, David Griffith became ambitious for new talent, and as the right sort didn't come seeking, *he* decided to go seeking. He'd dash out of the studio while the carpenters were putting up a new set, jump into a taxi, call at the different dramatic agencies, and ask, had they any actors who might like to work in moving pictures at ten dollars a day! At one of these agencies—Paul Scott's—he arrived just as a good-looking manly sort of chap was about to leave. "*That's the type I want.*" Mr. Scott replied, "*Well, I'll introduce you.*" Mr. Griffith lost no time in telling the personable Frank Powell about the movies, and offering the new salary, secured his services. With his fair bride, Eleanor Hicks, who had been playing "leads" with Ellen Terry, while he stage managed, Mr. Powell had just returned from England. But Miss Terry and London triumphs were now of the past, and Mr. Powell was glad enough to end the tiresome hunt for a job, and his temporary money worries by becoming the first actor to be engaged by Mr. Griffith at the fancy price of ten dollars a day.

Mr. Powell was well-worth the ten for he had good presence, clean-cut features, and wore good clothes. He became our leading aristocrat, specializing in brokers, bankers, and doctors—the cultured professional man. David soon saw that he could take over little responsibilities and relieve him of many irksome details not concerned with the dramatic end. So, he became the first assistant, and then a director of comedies—the first—under Mr. Griffith's supervision. In time he went with William Fox as director. He discovered the screen's first famous vamp, Theda Bara. Against Mr. Fox's protests—for Mr. Fox wanted a well-known movie player—Frank Powell selected the unknown Theda from among the extras to play Mr. Kipling's famous lady in *A Fool There Was*, simply because she was a strange-looking person who wore queer earrings and dresses made of odd tapestry cloths. The picture made William Fox his first big money in the movies, and established his place in the motion picture world. *His Duty* was Frank Powell's first picture. In the cast were Owen Moore and Kate Bruce. *The Cardinal's Conspiracy*—the name we gave to "Richelieu"—marked Mr. Powell's first important screen characterization. It was taken at Greenwich, Connecticut, on Commodore [Elias Cornelius] Benedict's magnificent estate, Indian Harbor. Soon came, *The Broken Locket*, which had a nice part for Kate Bruce. Fortunate "Brucie," as her confreres call her! She seems never to have had to hunt a job since that long ago day when D. W. Griffith picked her as a member of the old Biograph Stock Company. Little bits or big parts mattered nothing to "Brucie" as long as she was working with us. David hunted movie recruits not only at the dramatic agencies, but also at the Lambs and Players Clubs of New York City. It was at the Lambs he found James Kirkwood Sr., and determined right off to get him down to the studio. He had to be subtle. He never knew what mighty indignation might be hurled at him for simply suggesting "movie acting" to a legitimate actor. But Jim Kirkwood made good his promise to come, and no effort was spared to make the visit both pleasant and impressive. I always thought we were a rather well-behaved lot—there was rather strict discipline maintained at all times.

But on this occasion we old troupers were told to "sit pretty," to be quiet and stay in the dressing room if there were no scenes being taken in which we were working, and if we were called upon to work, to please just "work" and not be sociable.

Our director seemed to be somewhat ashamed of his faithful old crew. So the studio remained hushed and awed—a solemn dignity pervaded it. In the dressing room, those who didn't know what was going on said, *"Why are you all so quiet?"* *"Oh, don't you know?"* we sang in unison, *"There's a Broadway actor out there, from the Henry Miller Company."* *"Oh, you don't say so!"* The effect was funniest on Mack Sennett. He wore a satirical smile that spoke volumes. For he had divined that these "upstage" new actors were to get more than five per day, besides, he was getting few enough parts as things were, now where *would* he be? "Lord Jim" was certainly treated with great deference. He was shown several scenes "in the taking," and then escorted upstairs to see some of Mary Pickford's pictures. The cook's tour over, Mr. Kirkwood agreed to appear in the movies. A slow, easy manner had Jim Kirkwood, which with underlying strength made for good screen technique. Early June was the time of his first release, *The Message*, in which picture as "David Williams" he portrayed the honest, big-hearted farmer.

Mr. Kirkwood, the diamond-in-the-rough type, was honest and big-hearted through all his movie career. He was the heroic Indian, as in *Comata, the Sioux*, the brave fisherman as in

Lines of White on a Sullen Sea—the latter one of Stanner Edward Varley Taylor's early classic efforts which was taken in the little fishing village of Galilee in October, 1909. Harriet Quimby, now established as a journalist, came down to visit. Thought it would be good fun to act in a [movie] scene, so she played a village fisher maiden and thus qualified as a picture actress for her other more thrilling performance two years later. I was with her that time, on the flying field at Dover, where [Louis] Bleriot had landed on the very first Channel crossing, and where she was to "take off" for France. Gaumont took a five-hundred-foot picture of the flight, titling it *The English Channel Flown by a Lady Aviator for the First Time*. The day Harriet Quimby flew the English Channel brought sad news to the world, for that appalling disaster—the sinking of the *Titanic*—occurred. It also brought a personal sadness to the Biograph, for Mr. Marvin's youngest son, [Daniel Warner Marvin] who was returning from his honeymoon, was lost. Before the happy couple had sailed, a moving picture of the wedding had been taken in the studio. It was not long after his initiation that Mr. Kirkwood brought a fellow "lamb," Mr. [Henry] Walthall, to the studio. He had been one of the three "bad men" with Mr. Kirkwood in *The Great Divide*, which play had just finished its New York run. Mr. Griffith, an Italian costume picture on the ways, was snooping around for an actor who not only could look but also act an Italian troubadour. When he met Henry Walthall of the dark, curly hair, the brown eyes, the graceful carriage, he rested content. *The Sealed Room* was the name of the screened emotion (movie) that put Mr. Walthall over in the movies. Wally's acting proved to be the most convincing of its type so far. He was very handsome in his silk and velvet, and gold trappings, with a bejeweled chain around his neck, and a most adorable little mustache. It was foreordained that the Civil War should have a hearing very soon. There was Kentucky, David Griffith's birth state, calling, and there in our midst was the ideal southerner, Henry Walthall. And so after just a few weeks the first—"Stirring Episode of the Civil War"—a little movie named *In Old Kentucky*—was rushed along. In the picture were Mary

Pickford, Owen Moore, Kate Bruce, and many lesser lights. It was a long time back that Mr. Walthall started on his career of "Little Colonels." He portrayed many before he climaxed them with his great "Little Colonel" in *The Birth of a Nation*.—A remarkable trio, Frank Powell, Jim Kirkwood, and Henry Walthall, such distinct types.—Though they all owned well-tailored dress suits, Frank Powell's was featured most often. Henry Walthall, suggestive of romance, had fewer opportunities, and rugged Jim Kirkwood only occasionally was permitted to don his own soup-and-fish and look distingue. With the acquisition of the ten-dollar-a-day actor, we seemed to acquire new dignity. No doubt about recruits fresh from Broadway lending tone—although the original five-per-day actors, who were still getting the same old five, looked with varying feelings of resentment and delight at their entrance.

We old ones figured that for all our faithfulness and hard work, we might have been raised right off to ten dollars, too. But at least there was hope in that ten per—the proposition looked better now with salaries going up, and actors coming to stay, and willing to forego the dazzling footlights and the sweet applause of the audience. Having reached ten-dollars-a-day, it didn't take so long to climb to twenty—undreamed extravagance—but good advertising along the Rialto and at the Lambs Club.—"*Twenty dollars a day?—It listens well—the movies must have financial standing, anyway,*" the legitimate concluded. Occasionally, Frank Craven, since famous as the author of many successful Broadway plays, came down and watched pictures being made. While he personally didn't care about the movies, through him, Jack Standing, came down and jobbed at twenty per. Through friendship for Mr. and Mrs. Frank Powell, with whom he had acted in Ellen Terry's company, David Powell entered the fold for twenty per. Even though money tempted, the high-class actor came more readily through friendship for someone already "in" than as a cold business proposition. Our movie money was talking just the same. But hard as it was to get men, it was much harder to get women. They would not leave that "drammer" (how they loved it!) to work in a dingy studio with no footlights, no admiring audience to applaud them, and no pretty "make-ups." Only occasionally did I accompany my husband on a tour of the dramatic agencies, for our manner to each other was still a most unmarried one. I'd wait in the taxi while he went up to the different offices to see if he could entice some fair feminine. But, after each visit, back he'd plump into the taxi so distressed, "*I can get men, but I cannot get women, they simply won't come.*" Well, if he couldn't lure ladies from the agencies, he'd grab them off the street. With Austin Webb, an actor friend who has since left the stage for promotion of oil and skyscrapers, he was strolling along Broadway one day when a little black-haired girl passed by accompanied by her mother. "*Now that's the kind of girl I'm looking for,*" said Mr. Griffith. Mr. Webb answered, "*Well, why not speak to her? She's an actress, you can bet your hat on that.*"

But the movie director having a certain position to maintain, and not wanting to be misunderstood, hesitated. Mr. Webb volunteered, stepped up to and asked the girl would she like to work in a moving picture. Prompt her reply, "*Oh, I'd love to, I just love pictures.*" The "girl" was Marion Sunshine of the then vaudeville team of Sunshine and Tempest. She was quite a famous personality to be in Biograph movies at this time.

Now Austin Webb, who during David Griffith's movie acting days had loaned him his own grand wardrobe, was one who might have become a big movie star. David implored him to try it, but he was skeptical. It took sporting blood to plunge "moviewards" in the crude days of our beginnings.

Who could tell which way the thing would flop?

I was not one of the select few who made the first trip to Cuddebackville, New York. I had been slated for a visit to my husband's folks in Louisville, Kentucky, and while there this alluring adventure was slipped over on me. A new picture was being started out at Greenwich, Connecticut, at Commodore Benedict's, the day I was leaving, and as I was taking a late train, I was invited out on a farewell visit, as it were. The picture was *The*

Golden Supper, taken from [Alfred] Tennyson's *Lover's Tale*. I arrived just in time for the princess's royal funeral. Down the majestic stairway of the Commodore's palatial home, the cortege took its way, escorting on a flower-bedecked stretcher, in all her pallid beauty, the earthly remains of the dead little princess. Now in the movies, if anywhere, a princess must be beautiful. I knew not who was playing this fair royal child until the actors put the bier down, and the princess sat up, when I was quite dumbfounded to see our own little Dorothy West come to life.

    Dorothy had done nicely times before as a little child of the ghetto and as frail Italian maids of the peasant class, and now here she was a full-fledged princess. So, in my amazement, I said to my husband, for it was a sincere, impersonal interest in the matter that I felt, "*Is Dorothy West playing the princess? Aren't you taking a chance?*" With great assurance he answered, "*Oh, with the photography we now have, I can make them all beautiful.*" Next day, as the lovely Shenandoah Valley spread out before me, I kept hearing those startling words, "*Oh, with the photography we now have, I can make them all beautiful.*" The Mended Lute was perhaps the first picture produced with the inspiring background of Cuddebackville scenery.—Florence Lawrence, Owen Moore, and Jim Kirkwood, the leading actors.—David wrote me to Louisville on his return to New York. "*Dear Linda, Well, I am back in New York. Got back at twelve o'clock last night.—I have accounts to make out for eight days, imagine that job, can you? Haven't had my talk with Mr. Kennedy as yet, as I have been away, but expect to on Tuesday or Wednesday as soon as I can see him. Lost six pounds up in the country, hard work, if you please.—And then I want to go back to that place again and take you this time because it's very fine up there. I am saving a great automobile ride for you—if I stay.*"

    "*If I stay,*" always that "*if.*" A year had now rolled by and in August Mr. Griffith would sign his second contract—*if* he stayed. The hegira (journey) to Cuddebackville had been undertaken to show Biograph officials what could be done by just forgetting the old stamping grounds adjacent to Fort Lee. Contract signing time approaching, Mr. Griffith wanted to splurge. A number of scripts had collected that called for wild mountainous country, among them *The Mended Lute*. Mr. Kennedy and our secretary, Mr. R. H. Hammer, Mr. Griffith and his photographer, Mr. Bitzer, sitting in conference had decided upon a place up in the Orange Mountains called Cuddebackville. It had scenic possibilities, housing facilities, and lacked summer boarders. Through an engineering job—the construction of a dam at one end of the old DL and W Canal, on whose placid waters in days gone by, the elder Vanderbilt had towed coal to New York—Mr. Kennedy had become acquainted with Cuddebackville. Unsuspecting sleepy little village, with your one small inn, your general store, and your few stray farms! How famous on the map of movie locations you were to become! How famous in many lands your soft, green mountains, your gently purling streams, your fields of corn!

The Mended Lute would be Mr. Griffith's catchpenny. The beauties he had crowded in the little one-reeler should suffice to bowl over any unsuspecting President. So this "Cuddebackville Special," along with several others that had collected awaiting Mr. Kennedy's pleasure, was projected for the authorities. And David signed up for another year at an increase in salary and a doubling of his percentage. And he could go to Cuddebackville whenever he so desired. Of course, the next time *she* went, and she had that "great automobile ride" that he was saving for her. Joy, but didn't they become delirious, the actors slated for a Cuddebackville week. A week in the mountains in August, with no hotel bill, and paychecks everyday! Few there were so ultra modern that they would take no joy in the bleating of the lambs but would prefer their city third floor back.—Much preparation for such a week.—We had to see that our best blouse was back from the laundry and our dotted Swiss in order for evening, our costumes right, and grease paint complete, for any of us might be asked to double up for Indians before the week was over.

It was a five-hour trip—a pretty one along the Hudson to West Point—then through the Orange Mountains. Our journey ended at a little station set in a valley sweet with tasseled corn and blossoming white buckwheat. In the distance—mountains nearby—beckoning roads lined with maples. It was the longest stop that an Ontario and Western train had ever made at Cuddebackville. Such excitement and such a jam on the little platform! No chance to slink in unnoticed as on the first unpretentious visit. "*Were we sure it was the right place?*" the conductor kept asking. "*Oh, yes, quite so.*" Damned if he could make it out. For we didn't look like farmers come to settle in the country, nor like fishermen come to cast for trout in the Neversink River—we had nothing with us that resembled expensive fishing rods and boots, nor did we look like a strange religious sect come to worship in our own way. No, nor might we have been one of a lost tribe of Cuddebacks who after years of vain searching had at last discovered the remote little spot where the first Monsieur Caudebec had pitched his tent so far from his own dear France. As the train steamed on its way, from the rear platform the conductor was still gazing, and I thought he threw us a rather dirty look. An express wagon was waiting for our load of stuff—big wads of canvas for the teepees, cameras, and costume baskets. A man in a red automobile was also waiting—Mr. [Charles] Predmore, who owned Caudebec Inn where we were to stop. Mr. Griffith and Mr. Bitzer and a few other of the important personages took their places in the automobile—the second in the county—the "Red Devil" we afterwards called it. The actors straggled along. Caudebec Inn was no towering edifice—just a comfy place three stories high, with one bathroom, a tiny parlor, rag-rugged, and a generously sized dining room whose cheerful windows looked upon apple orchards. It was neat and spotlessly clean. On two sides were broad piazzas. The inn faced the basin at the head of the old DL and W Canal, and the canal took its pretty way alongside for a mile or more until it spilled itself over a busted dam (Mr. Kennedy's I opined—it was the only one about), making lovely rapids which later we used in many a thriller. It was extremely fortunate that we were the only guests. We filled the place. Such a thing as an actor having a room to himself, let alone a bed, was as yet unheard of in those vagrant days. Mr. Powell doubled and sometimes tripled them. Some actors got awfully ritzy, resenting especially the tripling, and at night would sneak downstairs hoping to find a nice vacant hammock on the porch. But that had all been looked into. The hammock would be occupied by some lucky devil whose snores were being gently wafted on the soft summer breezes.—Three in a bed, two in a cot, or two in a hammock, the stringy old-fashioned kind of hammock, which would offer the better comfort?—Immediately after lunch, the boss and Billy Bitzer, with Mr. Predmore at the wheel, would depart in the "Red Devil" on a location hunt.

The carpenters must get right to work on their stockade. The actors were soon busy digging out costumes and grease paint boxes, and getting made-up and costumed, for as soon as the chief returned, he would want to grab a couple of scenes if the light still held. The making up was not a quiet process.

As the actors acquired brown grease paint and leather trappings, animal skins and tomahawks—what a powwow! When the Cuddeback farmer first met the Biograph Indian, "*Gad,*" thought he, "*what was the world coming to anyhow?—Moving picture people?—Smart folks to have found their Cuddebackville? Who'd have believed it? New York City actors riding up and down their roads, and stopping off to do wicked stage acting right in front of their best apple tree.*" "Hey there, Hiram, how'll five bucks suit you?" Hiram was a bit deaf. "*No? Ten? All right, here she is.*" Hiram we won completely. He hoped we'd come often. And the big Farmer's "help" were with us heart and soul. We sometimes used them for "extras" and paid them five dollars.—Back to the farm at five per week after that?—No, they'd wait and loaf until the "picture people" came again. The picture people nearly demoralized the farming business in Cuddebackville and environs—got the labor situation in a terrible mess. There was need for a stone house in *1776* or *The Hessian Renegades*, and for *Leather Stocking*—a genuine pre-revolutionary stone house.

Three saddle horses were also needed. For the moment we were stumped. Toward late afternoon when the light began to fail us, we would utilize the time hunting the morrow's locations. This fading hour found Billy Bitzer, David, and myself (myself still in "Janice Meredith" costume and curls of 1776) enjoying the physical luxury of the "Red Devil," but mentally disturbed over the stone house and horses. We happened to turn into a pretty road, we spied a beautiful gateway and beyond the gateway, grassy slopes and wonderful trees and pools of quiet water. *"Let's stop here a minute,"* said Mr. Griffith. *"Whose place is this?"* *"I'd never go in there, if I were you,"* answered Mr. Predmore. *"That place belongs to Mr. Godeffroy, he's the wealthiest man around here, won't have an automobile on his place and is down on anybody who rides in one, has fine stables and the automobiles are just beginning to interfere with his horseback rides. I don't know just how he'd receive you. Anyhow I can't drive you in, in this car of mine."* So, we parked outside in the roadway. *"We've got to work in here, that's all there is to it,"* said David, looking about.

But where did anybody live? The road wound up and up. Sheep nibbling on the velvet grass were mixed in with a few prize pigs taking their siestas beneath beautiful copper beeches. *"Certainly is some place,"* he continued. We had sauntered up the gravel road quite to the hilltop before we saw coming towards us across the lawn, a bright-eyed, pink-cheeked woman in simple gingham dress. She greeted us pleasantly. The situation was explained and the lady replied, *"Well, that is very interesting, and as far as I am concerned you are quite welcome to take some pictures here, but you must ask the boss first."* Over by his stables we found the "Boss." *"We'd like to take some pictures, please, on your beautiful place."* Stone houses and horses we had quite forgotten for the moment in the wealth of moving picture backgrounds the estate provided. *"We're stopping up at the Inn for a week—doing some James Fenimore Cooper stories, and we are looking primarily for a stone house and some horses."* "Have you seen the old stone house down below?" "Stone house?" I repeated to myself, then to be sure, whispered to Bitzer, *"Did he say a stone house?"* Bitzer replied, *"Yes, he said a stone house."* Mr. Griffith managed to pull himself together, but his answer came rather halting, "Why, why, no." "Come along and I'll show you. Maybe you can use it." Weak-kneed and still struggling for breath we trailed along—and when we saw it. Just built for us was the old stone house that had been on the place so long that no one knew when it had been built. But we hesitated. "*We'll have to bring horses, because the party leaves on horseback, and that would mess up your place too much.*" "*Oh, yes, I forgot, you haven't your horses yet. I wonder if some of ours would do,*" said Mrs. Godeffroy, who was none other than the gingham-clad lady.

Back to the stable we went, emotionally upset by now, but trying to appear calm. We'd been quite reconciled to take a stab at it with the rough work horses of the Cuddebackville farmer, had thought to groom them up a bit and let it go at that. But here were gentlemen's horses. Yes, gentlemen's horses, but neither Miss Leonard, nor myself rode, and these spirited prancing creatures of the Godeffroy stables filled us with alarm. I would look for something "gentle," and not too young and peppy, but with the characteristics of good breeding and training. And that is how "Mother" and I met. "Mother" is one of the treasured memories of my motion picture life. What a gentle old mother she was, healthy, so lazy, and so safe. How relieved I was—how at ease on her broad back. "Mother" ambled on the scene and "Mother" ambled off, she ate the grasses and the flowers on the canal bank, she was not a bit concerned over having her picture taken. I have always felt the credit was wholly hers that my uncle, my sister, and I made our journey safely until the bad Indians surprised us going through the woods. It was lots of fun being invited on these location-hunting expeditions. An automobile ride was luxury. These were the first and we were getting them for nothing. No, the picture business was not so bad after all.

Back at the Inn the Indians would be changing from leather fringes and feathered headdresses to their bathing suits. And when the location party returned, they'd have reached the green slopes of the Big Basin where, soap in hand, they would be sudsing off the brown bolamenia from legs and arms before the plunge into the cool waters of the Big Basin—a rinse and a swim "to onct." The girls who "did" Indians had the privacy of the one bathroom for their cleaning up. So they were usually "pretty" again, lounging in the hammocks or enjoying the porch rockers, a few would be over in the spring house freshening up on healthful spring water, a few at the General Store buying picture postcards. And then came dinner and in ones, twos, and threes, the company strolled in—a hungry lot. Frail little Mrs. Predmore wondered would she ever get the actors fed up. It took her the week usually, she afterwards confided. When the cook would let her, she'd go into the kitchen and make us lemon meringue pies. The actors were always hoping the cook would leave, or get sick, or die, so Mrs. Predmore could cook all the dinner. Sometimes we were very merry at dinner. When Arthur Johnson would arrive, bowing himself gallantly in, in a manner bred of youthful days as a Shakespearean actor with the Owen Dramatic Company, loud and hearty applause would greet him, which he'd accept with all the smiling, gracious salaams of the old-time ten, twenty, and thirty tragedian. Evening at Cuddebackville! The biggest thrill would be an automobile ride to Middletown, nine miles away.

If Mr. Predmore weren't busy after dinner, he'd take us. It was a joyful ride over the mountains to Middletown, quite the most priceless fun of an evening. Everyone was eager for it except the little groups of twos, who, sentimentally inclined, were paddling a canoe out on the basin or down the canal. There would be Mary Pickford and Owen Moore, and James Kirkwood and Gertrude Robinson, and Stanner Edward Varley Taylor and Marion Leonard, experiencing tense moments in the silence broken only by the drip, drip of the paddle beneath the mellow moon. Romance got well under way at Cuddebackville. The evening divertisements became more complex as we became better acquainted. [Henry] "Wally" Walthall, Arthur Johnson, and Mack Sennett became our principal parlor entertainers. "Wally" rendered old southern ditties as only a true southern gentleman from Alabama could. Arthur Johnson and Mack Sennett did good teamwork—they were our Van and Schenck. Arthur, who presided at the piano, had a sentimental turn he liked *The Little Gray Home in the West* kind of song, but the future producer of movie comedies was not so sentimentally disposed. As long as harmony reigned in the camp of Johnson and Sennett, there were tuneful evenings for the musically inclined. But every now and then Sennett would get miffed about something and never a *do re mi* would be got out of him, and when Arthur's nerves could stand the strain no longer, he'd burst forth to the assemblage, "*I wouldn't mind if he'd fuss with me, but this silence thing gets my goat.*" Those who cared not for the song festival could join Jeanie MacPherson who, out in the dining room, would be supervising stunts in the world of black magic. Here Tony O'Sullivan could always be found. He told hair-raising ghost stories and wound up the evening's fun by personally conducting a tour through the cemetery. The cemetery lay just beyond the apple orchard and along the canal bank to the back of the Inn. Now, were the moon bright, the touring party might get a glint of lovers paddling by. Arrived back at the Inn, they might greet the "Red Devil" returning with a small exclusive party from the Godeffroys—Mr. Griffith and Miss Arvidson, Mr. Powell and Miss Hicks. There was just one little touch of sin. Secluded in an outbuilding some of the boys played craps—sometimes losing all their salary before they got it. One of the men finally brought this wicked state of affairs to Mr. Griffith's attention, and there were no more crap games. In front of Caudebec Inn the "Red Devil" is snorting and getting impatient to be started on her way to the station, for the actors are strolling down the road ahead of her. Mr. Griffith and Mr. Predmore are just finishing the final "settling up" of the board bill. Mrs. Predmore looking tinier than ever, seemed to shrivel during our strenuous weeks is gratefully sighing as she bids us farewell. She was glad to see us come, and she was glad to see us go. Meanwhile, out in Hollywood, the Japs are still raising carnations, and a few bungalow apartment houses are just beginning to sprout on the Boulevard, but otherwise the foothills continue their undisturbed sleep beneath the California sunshine.

☐☐☐☐☐☐☐☐☐☐

There was a frictional feeling in our return to prosaic studio life after the glorious freedom of the country. But the new "projections"—the pictures that had been printed and assembled in our absence—would take the edge off and cheer us up some, we were all a-thrill about seeing the first run of the pictures we had taken in the country, and we were eager about the picture we were to do next. During our absence we would have missed seeing not only our own releases but those of the other companies, which, our day's work finished, we used to try to catch up on. Mondays and Thursdays had come to be release days for Biograph pictures. Then at some theaters, came whole evenings devoted to them. On these occasions exhibitors would put a stand outside saying "Biograph Night." After the first showing it was a difficult job to locate a picture. From Tenth Avenue to Avenue A, we'd roam, and no matter how hot, stuffy, or dirty the place might be, we'd make the grade in time. *Pippa Passes*, which was to make or unmake us, was all this time hanging fire. Mr. Griffith was getting an all-star cast intact.

The newly recruited James Kirkwood and Henry Walthall gave us two good men who, with Owen Moore and Arthur Johnson, were all the actors needed. For the women, there were Marion Leonard, Gertrude Robinson, and myself.—And little Mary Pickford whom our director had engaged with "Pippa" in mind.—When the day came to shoot Robert Browning for the first time, it was winsome Gertrude Robinson with black curls and dark blue eyes who was chosen for the role of the spiritual "Pippa." David thought Mary had grown a bit plump—she no longer filled his mental image of the type. When at last we started on *Pippa Passes*, things went off with a bang. Each of the four themes—Morn, Noon, Evening, Night—would be followed by a flash of "Pippa" singing her little song. It was "Morn" that intrigued. To show "daybreak" in her little room would mean trying out a new light effect. The only light effect so far experimented with had been the "fireside glow." The opportunity to try a different kind so interested Mr. Griffith that before he began to *shoot* "Pippa," he had a scheme all worked out. He figured on cutting a little rectangular place in the back wall of "Pippa's" room, about three feet by one, and arranging a sliding board to fit the aperture much like the cover of a box sliding in and out of grooves. The board was to be gradually lowered and beams of light from a powerful Kleig shining through would thus appear as the first rays of the rising sun striking the wall of the room. Other lights stationed outside "Pippa's" window would give the effect of soft morning light. Then the lights full up, the mercury tubes a-sizzling, the room fully lighted, the back wall would have become a regular back wall again, with no little hole in it. All this was explained to the cameramen Billy Bitzer and Arthur Marvin, for the whole technical staff was in attendance on the production of this one thousand foot feature—one thousand feet being the length of our features at this time.

    Bitzer didn't think much of the idea, but Arthur Marvin, who had seen his chief's radical ideas worked out successfully before, was less inclined to skepticism. But response, on the whole, was rather snippy. While David would have preferred a heartier appreciation, he would not be deterred, and he spoke in rather plain words, "*Well, come on, let's do it anyhow, I don't give a damn what anybody thinks about it.*" "Pippa" is asleep in her little bed. The dawn is coming—a tense moment—for "Pippa" must wake, sit up in her little bed, rise, cross to the window, and greet the dawn in perfect harmony with the mechanical force operating the sliding board and the Kleigs. All was manipulated in perfect tempo. The skeptical studio bunch remained stubborn until the first projection of the picture upstairs. At first the comments came in hushed and awed tones, and then when the showing was over, the little experiment in light effects was greeted with uncontrolled enthusiasm. *Pippa Passes* was released on October 4, 1909, a day of great anxiety. We felt pretty sure it was good stuff, but we were wholly unprepared for what was to happen. On the morning of October 10th, while we were scanning the news items in the columns of *The New York Times*, the while we imbibed our breakfast coffee, our unbelieving eyes were greeted with a column headlined thus—BROWNING NOW GIVEN IN MOVING PICTURES—*Pippa Passes* the Latest Play Without Words to be Seen in the Nickelodeons.—THE CLASSICS DRAWN

UPON—Even Biblical Stories Portrayed for Critical Audiences. Improvement Due to Board of Censors.—It was all too much, much too much. The newspapers were writing about us. A conservative New York daily was taking us seriously. It seemed incredible, but there it was before our eyes. It looked wonderful! Oh, so wonderful we nearly wept. Suddenly everything was changed. Now we could begin to lift up our heads, and perhaps invite our literary friends to our movies! This is what *The New York Times* man had to say, "*Pippa Passes is being given in the Nickelodeons and Browning is being presented to the average motion picture audiences, who have received it with applause and are asking for more. This achievement is the present nearest-Boston record of the reformed motion picture play producing, but from all accounts there seems to be no reason why one may not expect to see soon the intellectual aristocracy of the nickelodeon demanding [Immanuel] Kant's Prolegomena to Metaphysics with the "Kritik of Pure Reason" (Critique of Pure Reason) for a curtain raiser. Since popular opinion has been expressing itself through the Board of Censors of the People's Institute, such material as the Odyssey, the Old Testament, Tolstoy, George Eliot, DeMaupassant and Hugo has been drawn upon to furnish the films, in place of the sensational blood-and-thunder variety which brought down public indignation upon the manufacturers six months ago. Browning, however, seems to be the most rarefied dramatic stuff up to date. As for Pippa without words, the first films show the sunlight waking Pippa for her holiday with light and shade effects like those obtained by the Secessionist Photographers. Then Pippa goes on her way dancing and singing. The quarreling family hears her, and forgets its dissension. The taproom brawlers cease their carouse and so on, with the pictures alternately showing Pippa on her way, and then the effect of her "passing" on the various groups in the Browning poem. The contrast between the tired businessman at a roof garden and the sweatshop worker applauding Pippa is certainly striking. That this demand for the classics is genuine is indicated by the fact that the adventurous producers who inaugurated these expensive departures from cheap melodrama are being overwhelmed by offers *from renting agents. Not only the Nickelodeons of New York but those of many less pretentious cities and towns are demanding Browning and the other "high-brow" effects."* There certainly was a decided change in the general attitude toward us after this wonderful publicity. Directly we had phone calls from friends saying they would like to go to the movies with us, and they would just love to come down to the studio and watch a picture being made. Even our one erudite friend, a Greek scholar, inquired where he could see *Pippa Passes*. As the picture was shown for only one night, we thought it might be rather nice to invite the dead-language person and his wife to the studio.

They came and found it intensely interesting, met Mary Pickford and thought her "sweet." Besides the Greek professor, another friend, one of the big men of the Old Guard, an old newspaper man, and president and editor of *Leslie's Weekly* and *Judge* at this time began making inquiries. The night the Ritz Carlton Hotel in New York City opened, David thought it wouldn't be a bad idea to splurge a bit and invite Mr. Sleicher to dinner, he being the editor who had paid him six dollars for his poem, *The Wild Duck*. He'd surely think we had come a long pace ahead in the movies, dining at the Ritz, and doing it so casual-like. Talk there was at the dinner about newspapers and magazines, and then we got around to the movies, and the money they were making. Mr. Sleicher said, *"Well, there's more money in them than in my business, but I like my business better. Now in my game, twenty-four hours or even less, after a thing happens you can see a picture of it and read about it in the paper, and you can't do that in your movies."* (I understand that even before the time of this dinner, events of special interest occasionally found their way to the screen on the day they happened. In London, in 1906, the Urbanora people showed the boat race between Cambridge and Harvard Universities on the evening of the day they were held, but we did not know about that.) Mr. Griffith was not going to be outdone, so, with much bravado, for he was quite convinced of its truth, he said, *"Well, we are not doing it now, but the time will come when the day's news events will be regularly pictured on the screen with the same speed the ambitious young reporter gets his scoop on the front page of his newspaper. We'll have all the daily news told in moving pictures the same as it is told in words on the printed page. Now, I'm willing to bet you."* But John Sleicher was skeptical. Had he not been, he would then and there have invested some of his pennies in the movies. He regretted the opportunity many times afterward, for while the prediction has not been fulfilled exactly, the Newsreel of today gives promise that it will be. However, Mr. Sleicher lived to enjoy the Newsreel quite as much as he did his newspaper, and that meant a great deal for him. These little happenings were encouraging. Intelligent persons on the outside were taking interest. So again we'd buck up and go at the movie job with renewed vigor.

For a time we lived in the clouds—our habitat a mountain peak. But that couldn't last. No kind of mountain peak existence could. We should have known. Even after all the encouragement, down off our peak we'd slip into the deep dark valley again. We tried to keep an unswerving faith, but who could have visioned the great things that were to come? Doubts still persisted.

Yes, even after the Browning triumph, longings came over us to return to former ambitions. They had not been buried so deeply after all. We'd see a fine play and get the blue devils.

In this mood my husband would do the rounds of the movie houses and chancing upon a lot of bad pictures, come back utterly discouraged. *"They can't last. I give them a few years. Where's my play? Since I went into these movies I haven't had a minute to look at a thing I ever wrote. And I went into them because I thought surely I'd get time to write or do something with what I had."* "Well, anyhow, nobody's going to know I ever did this sort of thing when I'm a famous playwright. Nobody's ever going to know that David W. Griffith, the playwright, was once the Lawrence Griffith of the movies." So "Lawrence" continued on the next Biograph contract. The two names would get all balled up sometimes and I'd get peeved and say, *"Why don't you use your right name? I think you're so silly."* But David Griffith remained obdurate until he signed his third Biograph contract.

One thing was sure—the pictures were making money. The percentage told that story. What a thrill we got at the first peek at the royalty check each month. Made us nervous.—Where were we headed? Sometimes we almost wished that financially we were not succeeding so well, for then we would have quitted the movies. But wouldn't that have been a crazy thing to do? A year of fifty-two working weeks?—At the rate we were going, we could keep at it for three years, and quit with twelve thousand in the bank, then David could write plays and realize his youthful ambition. We lived simply. When the royalty check before the end of the second year amounted to nine hundred and a thousand a month, we still maintained a thirty-five-dollar a month apartment.—Never dreamed of getting stylish.—No time for it. So, each month there was a nice little roll to bank, and it was put right into the Bowery Savings Bank. The only trouble with a savings bank was they wouldn't accept more than three thousand dollars, so we secured a list of them and I went the rounds depositing honest movie money, with a rapidity [that was] quite unbelievable. The Griffiths were not the only thrifty ones. When Mary Pickford was getting one hundred a week, her mother wept because she wouldn't buy pretty clothes. At Mount Beacon this happened. One of the perky little ingenue-ish extra girls appeared in a frock decidedly not homemade. You could count on it that it had come either from Macy's or Siegel Cooper's Eighteenth Street store, and that it had cost a whole week's wages. Not much escaped Ma Smith's eagle eye, and so she wailed, "*I wish Mary would buy clothes like the other girls.*" But Mary, the same simple, unaffected Mary that a year since had said "thank you" for her twenty-five, was quite contented to continue wearing the clothes her mama made her, and at that a few would do. A few years after this time I met Mary in Macy's one summer day and hardly recognized her. She had grown thin and had acquired style. I admired her smart costume and said, "*Nice suit, Mary, I'm looking for one. Mind telling me where you found it?"* But Mary, with a note of boredom, so unlike the Mary I'd known, answered, *"Oh, my aunt brought me six from Paris." "Mary, you haven't forgotten how we used to strike bargains with the salesman at Hearn's on Fourteenth Street, have you?"*

"Oh," said Mary, quickly coming back to earth and proving greatness but a dream, *"wasn't it fun? Let's go over to the Astor and have tea."* Across from Macy's, Mary's first bus was parked and young brother Jack was chauffeuring. When we hopped into the car, we found a very disgruntled youth who, having waited longer than he thought he ought to have, gave me a stony stare and never spoke a word. As far as young Jack Smith was concerned, I'd never been on earth before. We wondered about Mack Sennett. Would he ever buy a girl an ice cream soda?

Marion Leonard said it would be his birthday if he ever did. But the day arrived when Mack Sennett did open up. He bought a seventy-five dollar diamond necklace for Mabel Normand, and then after some misunderstanding between himself and Mabel, proving he had a head for business, he offered it to different members of the company for eighty-five dollars. Spike Robinson, who used to box with Mr. Griffith and who now boxes with Douglas Fairbanks, looms up as the one generous member of the company, being willing always to buy the girls ice cream sodas or lemonade or sarsaparilla—the refreshments of our age of innocence. The fall of 1909 brought to the studio a number of new women who proved valuable additions to our company. Stephanie Longfellow, who was a *bona fide* niece of the poet Henry, was one of them. Her first pictures were released in August. They were *The Better Way* and *A Strange Meeting*.

Miss Longfellow was quite a different type from her predecessors and her work was delightful. She was a refreshing personality with unusual mental attainments. *"She's a lady,"* said the director. Some ten years ago Miss Longfellow retired to domestic life via a happy marriage outside the profession. Handsome Mrs. Grace Henderson became our grande dame of quality, breezing in from past glories of *Peter Pan* (having played Peter's Mother) and of the famous old Daly Stock Company.

Another grande dame of appearance distinguished, drawing modest paychecks occasionally, and with a cultural family background most unusual for a stage mother, was Caroline Harris. Miss Harris, otherwise Mrs. Barthelmess, and mother of ten-year-old Dicky Barthelmess, was one stage mother not supported by her child.—Only when home on a vacation from military school did Dicky work in a picture.—He made his debut with Mrs. Thomas Ince, and his little heart was quite broken when he discovered his only scene had been cut out. Miss Harris's first stage appearance had been with Benjamin Chapin playing "Mrs. Lincoln" in *Lincoln at the White House*, afterwards called *Honest Abe*. Her first part in the movies was in DeMaupassant's *The Necklace*, in which Rose King played the lead. Miss Harris had learned of Biograph through a girl who jobbed at the studio, Helen Ormsby, the daughter of a Brooklyn newspaper man. Mabel Trunnelle had a rather crowded hour at the Biograph.

She had had considerable experience at the Edison studio and was well-equipped in movie technique. She had come on recommendation of her husband, Herbert Prior, and she succeeded, even though a wife, which was unusual, for wives of the good actors were not popular around the studio. If an actor wanted to keep on the right side of the director, he left his wife at home, that meant a sacrifice often enough, for there were times without number when women were needed and a wife could have been used and the five dollars kept in the family, but the majority preferred not to risk it. Dell Henderson and George Nichols succeeded quite well with this "wife" business, but they seem to have been the only ones besides Mr. Prior. Florence Barker, a good trouper who had had stock experience in Los Angeles, her hometown, now happened along to enjoy popularity, and to become Frank Powell's leading woman. Through her Elinor Kershaw, sister to Willette [Kershaw], and wife to the late Thomas H. Ince, happened to come to the Biograph. Quite the most pathetic figure at the studio was Elinor Kershaw Ince. In deep mourning for her mother who had just been killed in an accident, and all alone, with a tiny baby at home she put in brave hours for her little five-dollar bills. When six o'clock came and her work was not finished, how she fretted about her little one. That baby, Thomas Ince's eldest child "Billy," is now a husky lad and he probably doesn't know how we all worried over him then. Miss Kershaw played sad little persons such as the maid in *The Course of True Love*, flower girls, and match girls, in wispy clothes, on cold November days, offering their wares on the streets of Coytesville and Fort Lee. There was the blond and lily-like Blanche Sweet, an undeveloped child too young to play sweethearts and wives, but a good type for the more insignificant parts, such as maids and daughters. David wanted to use her this first winter in a picture called *Choosing a Husband*, so he tried her out, but finding her so utterly unemotional, he dismissed her saying, "*Oh, she's terrible.*" Then he tried Miss Barker and had her play the part. But he directed Miss Sweet in her first picture, *All on Account of a Cold*. Mr. Powell liked Miss Sweet's work and so did Doc—and so Mr. Powell used her in the first picture he directed, *All on Account of the Milk*. Mr. Powell was rehearsing in the basement of number 11 while Mr. Griffith was doing the same upstairs. Mary Pickford played the daughter and Blanche Sweet, the maid, and in the picture they change places. On the back porch of a little farmhouse a rendezvous takes place with the milkman. It was bitterly cold, and even though the girls wore woolen dresses under their cotton aprons, they looked like frozen turnips. The scenes being of tense love, the girls were supposed to be divinely rapturous and to show no discomfort—not even know it was winter. But the breathing was a different matter, for as young Blanche uttered endearing words to her lover, a white cloud issued from her mouth. Now that would look dreadful on the screen. So in the nervousness of the situation Mr. Powell yelled at her, "*Stop talking, just look at him, this is supposed to be summer.*" She obeyed, when from her delicate nostrils came a similar white line of frosted breath at which the director, now wholly beside himself, yelled, "*Stop breathing, what kind of a picture do you think this will be, anyhow.*"—So, little Blanche proceeded to strangle for a few moments while we secured a few feet of summer.—In *The Day After*—four hundred and sixty feet of a New Year's party picture, showing what a youngster she was, Blanche Sweet played Cupid. Kate Bruce had become the leading character woman. Little [William] Chrystie Miller, frail, white, and bent, played the kindly old men, while Verner Clarges interpreted the more pompous, distinguished elderly ones. Daddy Butler was mostly just a nice kind papa, and George Nichols played a diversified range of parts—monks, rugged Westerners, and such. George Nichols had been a member of the old Alcazar and Central Theatres in San Francisco, where Mr. Griffith in his stranded actor days had worked. Of the children, little Gladys Egan did remarkable work playing many dramatic leading parts. Her performance in *The Broken Doll* should be recorded here. Adele DeGarde was another nine-year-old child wonder. These children were not comiques. They were tragediennes and how they could tear a passion to tatters! The Wolff children sufficed well in infantile roles. Their mother kept a dramatic agency for children. Boys were little in demand, and as Mary Pickford usually had her family handy, we came to use little Jack—he was at this time nine years old. He created quite a stir about the old American Biograph. He even managed to make himself the topic of conversation at lunch time and other off-duty hours. "*Had he a future like sister Mary?*" We were even then ready to grant Mary a future. Lottie was discussed too, but in a more casual way.

    No one was especially interested in Lottie. Mary was very hesitant in bringing her to the studio, she confided that Lottie was not pretty and she didn't think she'd be good in the movies. She was the tomboy of the family and she loved nothing better than to play baseball with the boys, and when later she did become a Biograph player she had her innings at many a game.

    For a year and a half that had winged its way, my husband and I had kept our secret well, although a something was looming that might make us spill it. There had been nervous moments. Only three people at the studio knew the facts of the case, Wilfred Lucas, Paul Scardon, and Harry Salter. But Wilfred Lucas whose hospitality we'd frequently enjoyed never betrayed us. Nor did Paul Scardon. I don't remember Mr. Scardon doing any work of consequence at the Biograph, but he eventually connected up with the Vitagraph, becoming one of its directors. He discovered Betty Blythe, developed her from an unknown extra girl to a leading woman of prominence. After the death of his first wife, he married her. Miss Blythe has been a big star for some years now and while Mr. Scardon has not been directing her, he travels with her to distant enchanting lands, to Egypt, the Riviera, and such places where Miss Blythe has been working on big feature pictures. It was under William Fox's banner that Miss Blythe first came into prominence. The picture was *The Queen of Sheba*. Lucas and Scardon were friends of ours before our marriage, but Harry Salter was the only person about the studio in whom David had confided. And I wasn't told a thing about it.

Helping to purloin Florence Lawrence from the Vitagraph, Mr. Salter had just naturally fallen in love with her and they had been secretly married, and no one knew it but Mr. Griffith.

A fellow-feeling probably had made David a bit confidential—an unusual thing for him. It was one day, on a little launch going to Navesink. My husband was in the front of the boat, his back to us. Harry and Florence and I were seated aft. We were quietly enjoying the ride, not a word being spoken, when Harry Salter, pointing to a hole in the heel of David's stocking, at the same time turned to me and with a knowing smile said, "Miss Arvidson, look!" The something that was looming that would make us reveal our well-concealed secret, was a trip to California to escape the bad eastern weather of January, February and March. Now I did not intend to spend three nights on the Santa Fe Limited in a Lower Eight, or an Upper Three, when there was the luxury of a drawing room at hand. Nor was it my husband's wish either. I felt I had earned every little five-per-day I'd had from the Biograph and had minded my own business sufficiently well to share comfort with the director. Yes, I would take my place as that most unwelcome person—the director's wife. So, when the tickets were being made up, Mr. Hammer was brought into the secret, but he just couldn't believe it. But Mr. Dougherty said, "*Well, that is bringing coal to Newcastle.*" Nobody could understand what he meant by this, but that is what he said.

☐☐☐☐☐☐☐☐☐☐☐

After shivering through one Eastern winter, trying to get the necessary outdoor scenes for our pictures, we concluded that it would be to our advantage to pack up the wardrobe, the cameras, and other paraphernalia, get a little organization together, and with a portmanteau of Western scripts hie (quickly get) ourselves to the city of Los Angeles. We weren't the first to go there. [William] Selig already had a studio there. Frank [Francis W.] Boggs had brought a little company of Selig players to Los Angeles in the early days of 1908. The next company that reached the coast was that of the New York Motion Picture Patents Corporation, making the Bison brand of pictures. They had arrived in Los Angeles about Thanksgiving, 1909—seventeen players under the command of Fred Balshofer. Kalem was taking pictures in Los Angeles, too. I felt very much annoyed one night, shortly before we left New York, to see a Kalem picture with Carlyle Blackwell and Alice Joyce having a petting party in Westlake Park. How we did buzz around, those last weeks in New York! Mr. Powell's company worked nights to keep up the two one-thousand-foot releases per week. News was already being broadcast that it was quite OK down at the Biograph if you got in right—that they were doing good things and were going to send a company to California for the winter, which would mean a regular salary for the time away.—And so arrived, Mr. Dell Henderson, who became leading man for the night company at five per night.—The demands for physical beauty that he had to fulfill certainly should have earned more than the ordinary five. He had to be so handsome that his jealous wife prevails upon thugs to waylay him and scar for life his manly beauty so that the admiring women will let him alone. This movie, *The Love of Lady Irma*, was one of the first pictures Mr. Powell directed. Florence Barker, who became the leading woman for the number 2 California comedy company, played "Lady Irma," the jealous wife. She had joined the company in December, her first picture being *The Dancing Girl of Butte*, in which she was cast with Owen Moore and Mack Sennett. It was in these days that Elinor Kershaw did her bit, also Dorothy West and Ruth Hart. Miss Hart, now Mrs. Victor Moore and the mother of two children, played the sweet domestic wife, a role Mr. Griffith felt she was a good exponent of, and which she has successfully continued in her private life. Frank [Francis] Grandon appears in his first leading part, playing the "Duke" in *The Duke's Plan*, and our atmospheric genial Englishman, Charles Craig, affiliated the same month, playing opposite Mary Pickford in *The Englishman and the Girl*. The studio was now a busy place.

A Civil War picture had to be rushed through before we could get away. Mr. Powell was busy engaging actors for it and had just completed his cast of principals when he bumped into an actor friend, Tommy [Thomas] Ince. It seems Mr. Ince at the moment was "broke." Apologetically, Mr. Powell said he couldn't offer anything much, but if Mr. Ince didn't mind coming in as an "extra" he would give him ten dollars for the day. This quite overcame Tommy Ince and he stammered forth, "*Glory be*"—or words to that effect—"*I'd be glad to get five.*" Only one part did Thomas Ince play with Biograph and that was in *The New Lid* with Lucille Lee Stewart, Ralph Ince's wife and sister of Anita Stewart. I happened to call on Eleanor Hicks Powell one evening in the summer of 1912 when our only Biograph baby, Baden Powell, had reached the creeping age. During the evening Mr. and Mrs. Thomas Ince dropped in. Of course, we talked "movies." Mr. Ince was worrying about an offer he'd had to go to California as manager and leading director of the 101 Ranch, Kay-Bee [Pictures] Company, for one hundred and twenty-five dollars per week, as I remember. He offered me forty dollars to go out as leading woman, but I couldn't see the Indians. Mr. Ince couldn't see them either—but it was the best offer that had come his way. Mr. Ince made a great success out of the 101 Ranch, but having ambitions to do "high-class," he moved on in quest of it. Took to developing stars like Charles Ray, Enid Markey, and Dorothy

Dalton, became one of the Triangle outfit with David Griffith and Mack Sennett, exploited dramatic stars like George Beban, Billie Burke, and Enid Bennett, did *Civilization*—but after *The Birth of a Nation*. Who was to go to California and who wasn't? Ah, that was the question! Some husbands didn't care to leave their wives, and as they couldn't afford to take them, they were out. Some didn't mind the separation. Some of the women had ties, if not husbands, mothers, and the California salary would not be big enough to keep up two homes. Some didn't want to leave New York, and some who should have known they didn't have a ghost of a chance wept sad and plentiful tears whenever the director looked their way. One of these was Jeanie MacPherson.

Jeanie didn't go along this first time. A few days after Christmas was the time of the first hegira to the land of the eucalyptus and the pepper tree. It was a big day. We were going to Los Angeles to make moving pictures, and Hollywood didn't mean a thing then. Pasadena, the company knew about. Like Palm Beach, it was where millionaires sojourned for two months during the Eastern winter. San Gabriel Mission they'd seen photos of, and counted on using it in pictures. They understood there were many beaches accessible by trolley, and residential districts like West Adams, even Figueroa, the home of Los Angeles's first millionaires, was a fine avenue then, and Westlake and Eastlake Parks which were quite in town. But they didn't know Edendale from the Old Soldiers's Home at Sawtelle. San Pedro? Yes, that was where the steamers arrived from San Francisco. San Fernando? Well, yes, there was a Mission there too, but it was rather far away and right in the heart of a parched and cactus-covered desert. Mt. Lowe was easy—there was the incline railway to help us to the top.—Four luxurious days on luxurious trains before we would sight the palms and poinsettias that were gaily beckoning to us across the distances.—Let us away! The company departed via the Black Diamond Express on the Lehigh Valley, which route meant ferry to Jersey City.

A late arrival in Chicago allowed just comfortable time to make the California Limited leaving at 8 PM. The company was luxurious for but three days. It was only Mr. R. H. Hammer, my husband, and myself who had been allotted four full days of elegance.—We *de-luxed* out of New York via the Twentieth Century Limited.—I had come into my own. Mr. Powell was in charge of the company and so he checked them off on arrival at the ferry—Marion Leonard, Florence Barker, Mary Pickford, Dorothy West, Kate Bruce, the women, George Nichols, Henry Walthall, Billy Quirk, Frank Grandon, Charlie [Charles] West, Mack Sennett, Dell Henderson, Arthur Johnson, Daddy Butler, Chrystie Miller, Tony [Anthony] O'Sullivan, and Alfred Paget, the men. There were three wives who were actresses also, Eleanor Hicks, Florence Lee (Mrs. Dell Henderson), and Mrs. George Nichols [Viola Alberti]. And there were two cameramen, Billy Bitzer and Arthur Marvin, a scenic artist, Eddie Shelter, a carpenter or two and two property boys, Bobby [Robert] Harron and Johnny Mahr. No theatrical job had come along for Mary Pickford, and the few summer months she had intended spending in "the pictures" would lengthen into a full year now that she had decided to go with us to California. Her salary was still small—it was about forty dollars a week at this time.

Frank Powell had a busy hour at the Ferry Building although Mr. Griffith was there also to see that all the company got on board. He had not anticipated too smooth an exit. Nor did he get it, even though he had taken well into account his temperamentalists. And sure enough, Arthur Johnson and Charlie West arrived breathless and hatless, fresh from an all-night party, just as the last gong rang. And while David was nervously awaiting them and while dear relatives were weeping their fond farewells, the Pickford family chose the opportune moment to put on a little play of their own. Ma Smith [Charlotte Hennessey Smith], it seems, had made up her mind that a last minute holdup might succeed in forcing Mr. Griffith to raise Mary's salary—I'm not sure whether it was five or ten dollars a week. So, they held a little powwow on the subject, right on the dock, in the midst of all the excitement, and Jack began to cry because he wasn't going along with his big sister, and Owen Moore between saying sad goodbyes to Mary, hoped the boss might relent and give him the ten extra he had held out for, for Los Angeles. For, much as Owen loved Mary and Mary loved Owen, he let a few dollars part them for the glorious season out in California. Well, anyhow, little Jack's tears and Mother Smith's talk and pretty Mary's gentle but persistent implorations did not get her the ten dollars extra. David had something up his sleeve he knew would calm the Smith family, and make them listen to reason, and he delivered it with a firm finality. "*Now I've got little Gertie Robinson all ready to come on at a moment's notice. Mary goes without the five (or ten) or not at all.*" Mary went. Then Jack began to bawl. It was a terrible family parting. So, Mr. Griffith compromised and said he'd take Jack and give him three checks a week, fifteen dollars. The company paid his fare, of course, for we had extra tickets and plenty of room for one small boy in the coaches at our disposal. It was a pleasant trip, especially for those who had not been to California before. Some found card games so engrossing that they never took a peek at the scenery. Some, especially Mary and Dorothy West, oh'd and ah'd so that Arthur Johnson, thinking the enthusiasm a bit overdone, began kidding the scenery lovers.

"*Oh, look-it, look-it,*" Arthur would exclaim when the gushing was at its height. The "Biograph Special" we were. We had rare service on the train. We had every attention from the dining car steward. Had we not been allowed three dollars per day for meals on the train? And didn't we spend it?

For the invigorating air breathed from the observation platform gave us healthy appetites. At San Bernardino (perhaps the custom still survives, I don't know, for now when I go to Los Angeles, I go via the Overland Limited to San Francisco instead) we each received a dainty bouquet of pretty, fragrant carnations. Flowers for nothing! We could hardly believe our eyes. At last we were there! Mr. Hammer gallantly suggested, although it was afternoon—that the women of the company go to a hotel at the Biograph's expense, until they located permanent quarters. So, the ladies were registered at the Alexandria, then but lately opened, and shining and grand it was. Although they made but a short stay there, they attracted considerable attention. One day Mary Pickford stepped out of the Alexandria's elevator just as William Randolph Hearst was entering. Seeing Mary, he said, "*I wonder who that pretty girl is.*" And one night at dinner, between sips of his ale, indicating our table which was but one removed from his, Mr. Hearst wondered some more as to who the people were. The players were quite overcome at the company's hospitality. It was quite different from traveling with a theatrical road show where you had to pay for sleepers and meals, and where you might be dumped out at a railroad station at any hour of the cold gray dawn, with a Miners Convention occupying every bed and couch in the town, and be left entirely to your own resources. I may be wrong, but I think Mr. Grey of the office force (but not the Mr. Grey of the present Griffith organization, it was years before his movie affiliation, and the Biograph's Mr. Grey has been dead some years now) went out to California ahead of the company to make banking arrangements and look around for a location for the studio. On Grand Avenue and Washington Street, hardly ten minutes by trolley from Broadway and Fifth, and seven by motor from our hotel, mixed in with a lumber yard and a baseball park, was a nice vacant lot. It was surrounded by a board fence six feet or so in height, high enough to prevent passersby from looking in on us. Just an ordinary dirt lot, it was. In the corners and along the fence edges the coarse-bladed grass, the kind that grows only in California, had already sprouted, and otherwise it looked just like a small boy's happy baseball ground. It was selected for the studio. A stage had to be rigged up where we could take "interiors," for while we intended doing most of our work "on location," there would have to be a place where we could lay a carpet and place pieces of furniture about for parlor, bedroom, but not bath. As yet modesty had deterred us from entering that sanctum of tiles, porcelain, cold cream, and rose water jars. Mr. Cecil B. DeMille was as yet a bit away in the offing, and Milady's ablutions (washing) and Milord's Gillette were still matters of a private nature—to the movies. A load of wood was ordered from our neighbor, and the carpenters set about to fix up a stage and some dressing rooms, we couldn't dress and make up in our hotels, that was sure, nor could we do so in the open spaces of our "lot." Our stage, erected in the center of the lot, was merely a wooden floor raised a few feet off the ground and about fifty feet square, of rough splintery wood, and when we "did" Western barrooms—*au naturel*—it was just the thing. Two small adjoining dressing rooms for the men soon came into being, then similar ones for the women. They looked like tiny bathhouses as they faced each other across the lot. They sufficed, however. There were no quarrels as to where the star should dress. When there were extras, they dressed in relays, and sometimes a tent was put up. Telegraph poles ran alongside the studio and after our business became known in the neighborhood, and especially on days when we were portraying strenuous drama and got noisy, up these poles the small boys would clamber and have a big time watching the proceedings and throwing us friendly salutations which didn't always help along the "action." A place had to be found where our cameramen could develop the film and we could see the results of our work, for when a picture left Los Angeles it must be complete and ready for release, so down on Spring Street and Second, a loft was rented for a few dollars a month. It was a roomy, though dingy, barn of a place, but it served our purpose well. A tiny darkroom was boarded off and fixed up for the developing, and a place set apart for the printing.

The huge wheels on which the prints were dried stood boldly apart in the room. There was a little desk for cutting and splicing. At the head of the room furthest from the windows a screen was set, and a sort of low partition about midway the length of the loft hemmed in the projection room.

When things had settled into a routine, and on rainy days, we rehearsed and worked out scenarios up in our loft. We also had the costumes delivered there. The loft was always accessible, and we spent many evenings seeing projections and getting our things together for an early morning start. Across the street from the loft was a famous old eating place, Hoffman's, where my husband and I dined when we returned late or too weary to dress for the more pretentious hotel dining room. It was a bit expensive for some of the company, but convenient to our headquarters was one of those market places, indigenous to Los Angeles, where violets and hams commingled on neighborly counters, that served good and inexpensive food on a long white enameled table where guests sat only on one side, on high, spindly stools.

It was patronized generously by the actors for breakfast and lunch, when we were working in the downtown studio.

Here Mary Pickford and brother, Jack, and Dorothy West were regular patrons. While the studio was being put in shape, the members of the company had been scouting about looking for suitable places to live. Salaries were not so large, but that economy had to be practiced, even with the fourteen dollars a week, expense money allowed every member of the company. Mary Pickford had brother Jack to look after, and she decided that if she clubbed in with some of the girls and they all found a place together it would be cheaper and also not so lonely for her. So Mary, with Jack, and two of the young girls—Dorothy West and Effie Johnson—thirty-dollar-a-weekers, found shelter in a rooming house called "The Lille." It was on South Olive and Fifth Streets, but it is there no more. The four had rooms here for three and a half per week per person. But the quartette didn't stay long at "The Lille"—decided they needed hotel conveniences. So they scurried about and located finally for the winter at the New Broadway Hotel on North Broadway and Second Streets. Here they lived in comfort, if not in style, with two rooms and a connecting bath, for five fifty per week per person. When we got going, Mr. Griffith was rather glad Jack Smith was along, for with the two companies working we found we could use a small boy quite often. So Jack earned his fifteen a week regularly that first California winter. The men of the company were all devoted to little Jack. He would sit around nights watching them play poker, sometimes until 3 AM—he didn't want to be forever at the movies with his big sister. Mary allowed Jack fifty cents a night for his dinner—he'd connect up somewhere or other with his pals, in any event with his big brother Dell Henderson, and they would make a night of it. We were to be no proud owners of an automobile, but rented one by the hour at four dollars for car and chauffeur. The director and his cameraman and persons playing leads would travel by motor to location while the others would trolley.

As Los Angeles had, even then, the most wonderful system of trolleys in the world, there were few places, no matter how remote, that could not be reached by electric car. Sunday came to be a big day for the automobile, for on that day we scouted for the week's locations—that is, after David had made out his weekly expenses—his Sunday morning job.

□□□□□□□□□□

We would not have been true to the traditions of the Golden State had we not used a Mission in our first picture. We meant to do our very best right off and send back a knockout. So to San Gabriel we went to get the lovely old Mission atmosphere in a picture called *Threads of Destiny*. We spread ourselves, we took the Mission front, back and sideways, inside and out, we used the worn old stairway, shaded by a fragrant pepper tree, that led to the choir loft, we even planted lilies—or rather, Mary Pickford as "Myrtle," the orphan girl of San Gabriel, planted lilies—along the adobe wall of the old cemetery where slept baptized Indians and Mexicans. It was pleasant sprawling about in the lazy sunshine. We who were "atmosphere" wandered about the cemetery, reading the old tombstones, and had the priest guide us through the Mission showing us its three-hundred-year old treasures. And across the way we visited the curio shop where we bought pretty postcards and ate *tamales*, real Mexican *tamales*. We would experiment on this Mission picture.

We wanted a dim, religious light, and here it was, and we wanted to get it on the screen as it looked to us, the real thing.

One little window let in an afternoon slant of soft sunshine that fell directly upon the pulpit where Chrystie Miller, playing an old priest, was to stand and bless the congregation. If we could light up Chrystie, the devout worshipers could be mere shadows and it would look fine—just what we wanted. Billy Bitzer would "get" it if it could be got, that we knew. So, while Billy was tuning up his camera, Bobby Harron came and gathered in the congregation from the curio shop and cemetery, and we quietly took our places in the chapel and did our atmospheric bit. We did pray—we prayed that it would be a good effect. We rather held our breath at the picture's first showing until his tricky scene was flashed on the screen. Then we relaxed, it was all there! Spanish California was not to be neglected this trip, and our next picture, a romance of the Spanish dominion, called *In Old California* is historical as the first Biograph to be taken in Hollywood.

The Hollywood Inn was at this time the only exclusive winter resort between the city and the ocean. We needed rooms where we could makeup and dress, and Mr. Anderson, the genial young proprietor, welcomed us cordially. Marion Leonard was playing the beautiful Spanish senorita in this movie and Frank Grandon the handsome young lover who afterwards became the governor of California. As we came out of the hotel in our makeup and Spanish finery and quietly drove off into the foothills, guests were lolling on the broad front porch. With a start they came to. Whatever in the world was happening! "*Did you see those people? What is it? What's going on? Let's get our motor and follow them and see*," said they. We had selected what we thought a remote and secluded spot in the foothills, but soon in ones and twos and threes the guests appeared. For a time they seemed well-behaved spectators, they kept quiet and in the background. But Miss Leonard's dramatic scenes proved too much for them. They resented the lovemaking and began making derogatory comments about movie actors, and one "lady" becoming particularly incensed, shouted loudly, "*Well, I wouldn't dress up like a fool like that woman and act like her, no, not for all the money in the world.*" That off her chest, she turned on her heel, and left us flat. Paul de Longpre, the famous flower artist, lived only a few blocks from the Inn on Hollywood Boulevard. Many years ago he had left his native France and built a lovely chateau in the broad stretches of young Hollywood. In his gardens he had planted every variety of rose. A tangled profusion of them covered even the walls of his house. We offered fifty dollars a day for the use of the gardens. Mr. de Longpre went us one better. He offered to let us work if we'd buy a corner lot for three hundred dollars. But what could we do with a corner lot?

We had no idea we would work six days and pay the three hundred dollars just in rental. But that we did. What we didn't do, was, take title to the corner lot. Had we done so we would have laid a foundation for fortune. I recall Mr. de Longpre as the first person we met on location in California who seemed to appreciate that we were at least striving for something in an art line. To him we were not mere buffoons as we were to the ladies of the Hollywood Inn. *Love Among the Roses* we aptly called the picture in which Marion Leonard played a great lady residing in the Kingdom of Never-Never Land. Monsieur de Longpre's lovely house and gardens—a show place for tourists some twelve years ago—has long since been cut up into building lots on which have been erected rows of California bungalows. For when motion picture studios began to spring up like mushrooms in this quiet residential district, actors had to be domiciled and the boulevard was no longer desirable as a restful home locality. Also, the financial return on property thus manipulated was not to be lightly regarded. The town council voted a memorial to the kindly French artist. So Hollywood has a de Longpre Avenue.

The day we lunched at the Hollywood Inn marked an event for Hollywood. Few motion picture actors had desecrated the Inn's conservative grounds until that day. A few years later only motion picture actors lived there, and they live there now, though the old maid regime is coming along rapidly. Aside from the movie intrusion, Mr. Anderson foresaw changes that were to come. In due time, he built the now famous Beverly Hills Hotel. But the movie actor, who has now achieved a social and financial standing that equals that of other professions, he still has with him. Goodness gracious, how could we ever get all the scenic beauty on the screen! It was too distracting, what with Missions, desert, mountains, ocean, beaches, cliffs, and flowers. We wanted to send enough of it back in our pictures to ensure our coming again next winter. We had a scenario that called for a wealthy gentleman's winter home. We hied (quickly got) ourselves out to Pasadena, to Orange Grove Avenue, Hillside Avenue, Busch's Sunken Gardens, Doheny's, and other famous show places. We found a place with gardens and pergolas, just the thing. Asked permission to use the house and grounds, from very charming ladies wintering within, possibly a bit bored, for they seemed delighted with the idea. It was not the custom in those days to explain the nature of the story for which one desired a place, and the ladies being so keen on seeing moving pictures being made, the matter ended right there.

The scenario which had been selected for our pioneer work in Pasadena was called *Gold is Not All*. The day came to start work on the picture. We were all packed up in our motor car outside the Alexandria Hotel getting an early start, for the earlier we got to work, the fewer the days we would need to trespass on the borrowed property. *Gold is Not All* was a story of contrasts. There were very wealthy people in it and very poor people. And the poor faction was so poor that mother, little mother, had to take in washing to help out, which washing she returned to the rich people's houses. Like many other fallacies that have become identified with motion picture characterization, rich people are invariably represented as being unkind, selfish, penurious, and immoral—oh, always immoral. And the poor are loving, kind, true, surfeited with virtue. The poor mother idolized her children, worked and slaved for them, father always loved mother, never strayed from home. But the rich man, drat him, ah, he had sweethearts galore, he was dishonest on the stock market, he put marble dust in the sugar, his wife was something merely to be exploited, and his children were always "poor little rich boys and girls." So, we were primed for action and quite ready to make our wealthy gentleman sojourning in his winter mansion an utter rake, a miserable specimen of the middle-aged debauchee who treated cruelly a long-suffering wife. But the little poor families were such models of all the virtues, they hadn't missed one, and their days were full of happiness. The hostess of this charming home with some friends watched our performances. There was no limit to their hospitality. They brought out tables and a tea service and they loaned us their "bestest" butler—there was a lawn party in the story. When the picture was finished, Mr. Griffith invited the owner and his family and their friends to the studio to see the picture. The projection over, we noticed a strange lack of enthusiasm, and then Monsieur took Mr. Griffith aside and asked him if it would be absolutely necessary for him to release the picture. "*Really*," said the gentleman, "*we are a very happy family, my wife and I and the children, we like each other a lot. All my friends have been told about the picture and they'll watch for it—and I just don't like it, that's all. You know a person can have money and still be a respectable citizen in the community.*" And that was that. But we learned something. And here comes little Jack Pickford in his first leading part, a comedy directed by Frank Powell, and called *The Kid*. It was full of impish pranks of the small boy who does not want his lonely daddy to bring him home a new mama, but he comes across in time and soon is all for her. Two more pictures, *The Converts*, and *The Way of the World*, finished us at San Gabriel. Both were Christian preachments, having repentant "Magdalenes" as heroines, and were admirably suited for portrayal against the Mission's mellow walls. Sleepy old San Gabriel, where dwelt, that first winter, but a handful of Mexicans and where no sound but the mockingbird was heard until the jangling trolley arrived and unloaded its cackling tourists! Mission atmosphere got under the skin, so we determined on San Fernando for *Over Silent Paths*, an American desert story of a lone miner and his daughter who had come by prairie schooner from their far away Eastern home. San Fernando Mission was twenty-two miles from Los Angeles, with inadequate train service, and the dirt road, after the first winter rains had swelled the "rivers" and washed away the bridges, was often impassable by motor. The desertion and the desecration of the picturesque place was complete. For more than two hundred years the hot sun and winter rain had beat upon the Mission's adobe walls. It boasted no curio shop, no lunchroom, not even a priest to guard it. A few Japs were living in the one habitable room—they mended bicycles. We were as free to move in as were the swallows so thickly perched on the chapel rafters.

An occasional tourist with his Kodak [camera] had been the only visitor until we came. Then all was changed. It was in San Fernando that we first met up with the typical California rancher. This man, whose name I recall as "Boroft" had been one of the first settlers in the valley. On a "location hunt" we had spied Mr. Boroff's interesting looking place with its flowers and its cows, and had decided to pay our respects and see if we could get the ranch for a picture, sometime. One of the "hands" brought Mr. Boroff to us. Rangy and rugged, oh, what health-in-the-cheeks he had! He swung us about the place and then suddenly we found ourselves in a huge barn drinking tall glasses of the most wonderful buttermilk. "*Do you know*," said Mr. Boroff, downing his, "*I drink a quart of whiskey every day to pass the time away, and a gallon of buttermilk so I'll live long.*" Squatted one afternoon on the edge of the roadway in front of the Mission, I began idly scratching up the baked dirt with an old Mexican stiletto we were using in a picture. A few inches below the surface I noticed funny little round things that did not seem to be rocks. I picked up a few, broke off pieces of dry dirt, cleaned the small particles on my Mexican shawl, and found them to be old Indian beads, all colors, blue, red, and yellow. Through the leisure hours of that day I dug beads until I had an interesting little string of them. The Indians from whose decorated leather trappings the beads had fallen had been sleeping many years in the old cemetery back of the Mission. Now there are grass and flower beds growing over my little burial place of the beads, for the Mission has been restored, but even were it not so, the movie actress of today would surely rather lounge contentedly in her limousine than squat on old Mother Earth, digging up Indian beads. The third and last of the Missions we visited was romantic San Juan Capistrano, seventy miles south of Los Angeles, nestling in the foothills some three miles from the Pacific. Our scenario man, Mr. Taylor, had prepared a Spanish story of the padre days, and this lovely rambling Mission with its adjacent olive ranches, live oak groves, silvery aliso [sycamore] trees, and cliffs along the seashore, was to afford stacks of local color. Our one automobile deposited its quota—Mr. Griffith and party—in San Juan Capistrano in the late afternoon. The evening train brought the rest of the actors. There was one little Inn, the Mendelson [Mission Inn]—now fixed up and boasting all modern conveniences, then merely an airy wooden structure evidently built under the prevailing delusion that Southern California has a tropical climate. There was a tiny office, the only parlor, the proprietor's personal one, which he was kind enough to let us use. He had a stove and it felt mighty good to get warmed up nights before turning in. The bedrooms were upstairs. To reach them you had to go out in the yard, the backyard, climb the rickety stairs to the porch, on to which each little bedroom by means of its own little door, opened.

The bare-floored bedrooms were just large enough to hold a creaky double bed, wash bowl and pitcher, and a chair. We must see the Mission before dinner. The idea of dinner didn't thrill us much, and the thought of going to bed thrilled us less. But why expect the beauty of old things and modern comfort too? The thought of seeing old San Juan in the dim light of early evening should have sufficed. Beautiful old ruin! The peace and the silence! We might have been in the Sahara. Every member of the company was to work in this picture. There were no more than ten little bedrooms in the hotel. Actors slept everywhere, two and three in a bed, even the parlor had to be fixed up with cots. Miss Leonard and others of the women had been domiciled in a neighborly Spanish house—the only other available decent quarters. Dell Henderson, who had put himself wise to the arrangement of sleeping partners, had copped little Jack Pickford as his bedfellow. Dell was one of our very largest actors and Jack being about as big as a peanut, Dell had figured that with the little fellow by his side he might be able to catch forty winks during the night. Few of us managed to get unbroken winks.

Between the creaking of one's own bed and the snores from other rooms down the line (the walls were like paper) and the footsteps on the shaking porch, of actors going from room to room looking for something better than what had been allotted them, it was a restful night! All through it, at intervals, Charlie Craig kept calling to his bedfellow, "*Don't squash me—don't squash me.*" But the most disgruntled of all was Sennett. To every room he came calling "*Hey, how many in this bed? Who's in there? Got three in my bed, I can't sleep three in a bed.*" But responses were few and faint, and from Dell Henderson's room came only silence. So, after waiting in vain for help in his difficulty, and thoroughly disgusted, Mack returned to what must have been very chummy quarters. There had been engaged for this picture a bunch of cowboys, rough riders, headed by Bill Carroll, for we were to pull some thrillers in the way of horse stuff.

    The riders with their horses were leaving Los Angeles on the midnight train, due to reach Capistrano at 2 AM. It was all so weird and spooky that midnight had arrived before I had summoned sufficient courage to let myself go to sleep. No sooner had I dozed off than out of the black and the silence came, a terrific roar, yells, and loud laughter, and pistol shots going zip, zip, zip. These hot-headed Mexicans! Things happened here, and something dreadful was going to happen right now. I heard horses, and soon horses and riders galloped madly into the backyard, right to the foot of our stairs, it seemed. But it was only our cowboys who had arrived, feeling good, and full of the joy of life. Old Colonel [Theodore] Roosevelt knew all about this sort of thing, and would have appreciated the celebration. No thought had been given the "boys" slumber places, and so after a look around they docilely crawled up into the barn and were soon asleep in the sweet smelling hay. *The Two Brothers*, the picture we were to do—told the story of the good and bad brother. Good brother marries the pretty senorita in the Mission chapel. An experienced and cultured gentleman was the French priest in charge of this Mission. He was most obliging and told us we could use whatever we liked of the wedding ceremonial symbols, which we did, but which we shouldn't have done on this particular day of days, Good Friday. The wedding was some spread. There were

Spanish ladies in gay satins and mantillas, and Spanish gentlemen in velvets and gold lace, and priest and acolytes carrying the sacred emblems. They paraded all over the Mission grounds. Then the camera was set up to get the chapel entrance. While all was going happily, without warning, from out the turquoise blue sky, right at the feet of the blushing bride and the happy groom, fell the stuffed figure of a man! Right in the foreground the figure landed, and, of course, it completely ruined our beautiful scene. On Good Friday in these Spanish-Mexican towns of California a ceremonial called "burning Judas" used to take place (and may still, for all I know). Old carts and wheels and pieces of junk in the village are gathered in a heap outside the Mission grounds, and old suits of clothes are stuffed with straw, making effigies of Judas. The villagers set fire to this lot of rubbish and to the Judases as well, and the evil they have brought during the year is supposed to disappear in the smoke from their burning bodies. The handsomest Judas, however, is saved from the conflagration for a more ignominious finish. A healthy young bull is secured and to his formidable horns this Judas is strapped. Then the bull is turned loose, so annoyed by this monstrous thing on his horns that he madly cavorts until Judas's clothes are torn to shreds and his straw insides are spilled all over the place, and he is done for, completely. Now, while we had been rehearsing and taking the wedding scenes, the sacristan, a little old man to whom life meant tending the Mission and ringing the bells at the appointed hour, had been covertly taking us in, and when he saw our gay though holy processional start into the very sanctum of the Mission on Good Friday, his soul revolted. No, that he would not stand for!—Something even worse than riding the bull's horns could happen to Judas, and that was to be thrown at movie actors.—So the sacristan picked the prize Judas, and at the climactic scene he dropped him on us, and then broadcasting a roar of Mexican oaths he went on his way, his soul relieved and his heart rejoicing. But we felt differently. There was no telling now what these San Juan hotheads might do to us. But the seeming lack of reverence of our procession was explained to the little sacristan by the understanding priest. The next day we did the abduction. We took ourselves miles from the Mission. We chose a treacherous-looking road along the ocean cliffs. In a ramshackle buggy the bride and groom were speeding on their honeymoon, but bad brother and his band of outlaws were hot on the trail to steal the bride. Our cowboys bringing up the rear were cavorting on their horses, the horses were rearing on their hind legs, and the director was yelling, "*A dollar for a fall, boys, a dollar for a fall!*" The boys fell, on all sides they fell, they swung off their horses, and they climbed back on, and they spilled themselves in the dust, their horses riding on without them. Some of the boys made ten and some twenty dollars that day, just for "falls." And not one was even scratched. The next day was Easter Sunday, and our work being finished, in the gray dawn we folded our tents and silently slunk away. But the curse of Judas was upon us.

When the picture was projected, all was fine—scenic effects beautiful—and photography superb, until—we came to the wedding procession! Judas, to our surprise, was nowhere to be seen, he had fallen out of focus evidently, but the effect of his anathema was all there. The scene was so streaked with "lightning" we could not use it. At San Gabriel we retook it later, but it never seemed the same to us. Sierra Madre was another of our choice locations this first trip. Here were wonderful mountains with fascinating trails and canyons deep and long.

From Sierra Madre, Mount Wilson was climbed, by foot or donkey, for no magnificent motor road then led to its "five thousand and something foot" summit. At the quarter-mile house we did *The Gold Seekers*, a story of California in the days of 1849, with Henry Walthall striking pay dirt in the west fork of the San Gabriel Canyon. Mary Pickford did one of her Indians here, *A Romance of the Western Hills*. David thought Mary had a good face for Indians on account of her high cheekbones, and usually cast her for the red-skinned maid or young squaw. A smear of brown grease paint over her fair face and a wig of coarse straight black hair made a picturesque little Indian girl of "our Mary." Curls and Mary Pickford were not yet synonymous. She played, besides

Indians, many character parts with her hair smacked straight back, and she "did" young wives with her hair in a "bun" on the top of her head to make her look tall and married. When Mary wore curls, it meant an hour of labor at night. The curls necessitated three distinct kinds of "curlers," the ones for the wave on top, others for the long curls, and little curlers for the shorter hair around the face. I often thought Mary Pickford earned her slim salary those days for the time and effort she spent on her hair alone. It was an unhappy Mary on that first trip to Los Angeles, Owen Moore having passed up his little sweetheart on account of the weekly ten dollars he thought Mr. Griffith should have added to his salary. The day's work over, came her lonesome hour. On the long rides home from location, cuddled up in her seat in the car, she dreamed of home and dear ones. And one day passing the eastbound Santa Fe Limited, out of a deep sad sigh the words escaped, "*God bless all the trains going East and speed the one we go on*"—the Irish in her speaking. An urge to do *Ramona* in a motion picture possessed Mr. Griffith all the while we were in California, for the picturesque settings of Helen Hunt Jackson's deep-motived romance were so close at hand. Several conferences had been held on the subject in New York, before we left. But in order to make a screen adaptation of this story of the white man's injustice to the Indian, arrangements would have to be made with the publishers, Little, Brown and Company. They asked one hundred dollars for the motion picture rights and the Biograph Company came across like good sports and paid it, and *Ramona* went on record. It was conceded to be the most expensive picture put out by any manufacturer up to that time. To Camulos, Ventura County, seventy miles from Los Angeles, we traveled to do this production of *Ramona*. For Camulos was one of the five homes accredited to the real "Ramona" that Mrs. Jackson picked for her fictional one. She picked well. What a wealth of atmosphere of beautiful "old Spain," Camulos's far-famed adobe offered! Scenes of sheep shearing and scenes in the little flower-covered outdoor chapel where "Ramona's" family and their faithful Indian servants worshiped, love scenes at "Ramona's" iron-barred window, scenes of heartache on the bleak mountain top but a few miles distant where "Alessandro" and "Ramona" bury their little baby, dead from the white man's persecutions, and finally the wedding scene of "Ramona" and "Felipe" amid the oranges and roses and grass pinks of the patio. Even bells that were cast in old Spain rang silently on the screen. The Biograph Company brought out a special folder with cuts and descriptive matter. The picture was Mr. Griffith's most artistic creation to date. Nor did we neglect the oil fields, for oil had its romance. So, at Olinda, that tremendous field, we "took" plungers innumerable and expensive oil spilling out of huge barrels into little lakes, all black and smooth and shiny. The picture, called *Unexpected Help*, had Arthur Johnson and little Gladys Egan as star actors. One other oil picture we did, *A Rich Revenge*, a comedy of the California oil fields, with Mary Pickford and Billy Quirk. We had located a picturesque oil field. A crabbed-looking man in dirty blue jeans seemed the only person about. We asked him would there be any objection to our working, and he gruffly answered in the negative. So we "set up," and got our scenes, and, work finished, looked about for our man, wishing to thank him. Feeling sorry for him, we went one better and tendered him a twenty-dollar gold piece. When he saw that money, he began to curse us so hard that we were glad when we hit the highway. At the garage in the village we made inquiries and were enlightened. The man of the dirty blue jeans was none other than the millionaire owner of the oil well, an oil well that was gushing one fair fortune per day.

And though he refused our money as though it were poison, three times a week that man walked to Santa Ana, ten miles distant, where he could buy a ten-cent pie for five cents. Still more atmosphere we recorded in a picture called *As it is in Life*—the famous old pigeon farm located near the dry bed of the San Gabriel River. Shortly after the time of our picture, the winter storms washed away this landmark and we were glad then that we had so struggled with the thousands of fluttering pigeons that just wouldn't be still and feed when we wanted them to, and insisted upon being good, quiet little pigeons when we wished them to loop the loop. It seems we paid little attention to sea stories. Perhaps because we had our own Atlantic waiting for us back home, and we had done sea stories. We produced only one, *The Unchanging Sea*, suggested by Charles Kingsley's poem, *The Three Fishers*. Charlie [Charles] Stanton Ogle, who had worked in a few old Biographs but had been signed up with Edison before Mr. Griffith had a chance to get him, said to me one day out at the Lasky lot last winter—1924. "*What was that wonderful sea picture you played in? My, that was a picture, and you did beautiful work. I'll never forget it.*" "*You couldn't remember a sea picture I played in, Mr. Ogle. Heavens, that was so long ago you must mean someone else.*" "*No, I don't, and I remember it very well. What was the name?*" "*Enoch Arden?*" "*No.*" "*Fisher Folk?*" "*No, now what was that picture?*" And at that moment we were interrupted in our game of guess as Leatrice Joy, whom we had been watching, came off the scene to revive from the heavy smoke of a cafe fire, before doing it over again. "*I've got it—'The Unchanging Sea.'*" "*That's it, that's the one. I'll never forget that picture.*"

"*As I remember, it was considered quite a masterpiece.*" The fishing village of Santa Monica was the locale of this story.

At this time there was but a handful of little shacks beyond the pier, places rented for almost nothing by poor, health-seeking Easteners. No pretentious Ince studio as yet meandered along the cliffs some nine miles beyond. The road ran through wild country on to Jack Rabbit Lodge where a squatter had a shack that tourists visited occasionally and for twenty-five cents were shown an old Indian burial ground. The only fellow movie actors we met this first winter in Los Angeles were two members of the Kalem Company, beautiful Alice Joyce and handsome Carlyle Blackwell, who often on fine mornings trotted their horses over Santa Monica's wet sands. Occasionally, we met Nat [Nathaniel Carl] Goodwin, who had cantered (rode a horse) all the way from his home in Venice-by-the-Sea.

Now we must pack up our troubles in our little black bag and go home. They must be lonesome for us at 11 East Fourteenth, for the studio has been dark and silent in our absence.—Mr. Dougherty especially will be glad to see us.—And others—the jobless actors. For things were coming along now so that Mr. Griffith didn't have to dig so hard for new talent.—Much talk there'll be about the pictures we did—how the public is receiving them—which ones are most popular—how worthwhile the trip was—how economical we were—and how hard we worked. When once again we had donned our working harness, how stuffy and cramped the studio seemed! Four months in the open had ruined us, four months with only a white sheet suspended above our heads when we did "interiors" on our lot and the sun was too strong. We felt now like toadstools in a dark cellar, with neither sun nor fresh air. There was so much to keep Mr. Griffith busy—cutting and titling of pictures, and conferences upstairs. But the blossoming pink and white apple orchards must be heeded, so we deserted a few days, hied (quickly got) ourselves to New Jersey's old stone houses and fruit trees and friendly hens, and did a picture *In the Season of Buds*. Dorothy West played a leading part in *A Child of the Ghetto*, in which was featured more Eastern atmosphere—the old oaken bucket. For a time we stayed indoors. We acquired a new actor, Joseph Graybill, and a few old ones returned, Verner Clarges and Mrs. Grace Henderson, Jim Kirkwood and Gertrude Robinson. They now played leading parts. The public must not get fed up with the same old faces—Mr. Griffith always saw to that—so it was "go easy" on the California actors for a while. The feeling of the old actors towards the new ones, this spring, was largely a jealous one. "*Gee, Griff likes him all right, what are we going to do about it?*" said Charlie West and Arthur Johnson when Joe Graybill was having his first rehearsals and the director was beaming with satisfaction and so happy that he was singing lusty arias from *Rigoletto*. "*We'll fix him,*" they decided. So this day Charlie and Arthur returned from lunch with a small brown bottle containing spirituous liquor, with which they would ply Joe Graybill surreptitiously in the men's dressing room in the hope that they might incapacitate him. But Joe drank up, rehearsed, and Mr. Griffith's smile only grew broader. Better than ever was the rehearsal. So Charles went out for another little brown bottle and Joe disposed of it, and rehearsed—better still. Another bottle, another rehearsal—better than ever—until in a blaze of glory the scene was taken and Joe Graybill stood upon the topmost rung of the ladder, leaving Charles and Arthur gazing sadly upward.

There was another reason why Mr. Griffith welcomed new faces. He had a way of not letting an actor get all worked up about himself. When that seemed imminent, new talent would suddenly appear on the scene to play "leads" for two or three weeks so that the importance of the regular could simmer down a bit. Now that they had developed an affection for their movie jobs, the actors didn't like this so well. They'd come down to the studio, sit around and watch, get nervous, and after drawing three or four weeks's salary without working (things had come along apace), they wouldn't know what to make of it. They'd carry on something awful. They'd moan, "*When am I going to work? I don't like this loafing—I wonder if Griffith doesn't like me anymore—I'd like to know if he wants me to quit and this is his way of getting me to make the overture.*" Finally, Eddie [Edwin] August, after suffering three weeks of idleness, on pay, got very brave and told Mr. Griffith he wished he'd fire him or else, for God's sake, use him. Mr. August was quite relieved to have Mr. Griffith's explanation that in his case he was merely trying out new people, and didn't want him to quit at all, would be very glad to have him stay. When the Black-Eyed Susans had reached full bloom, we went back to Greenwich, Connecticut, and did a picture called *What the Daisy Said*, with Mary Pickford and Gertrude Robinson. We visited Commodore Benedict's place again, and again he brought out boxes of his best cigars. A good old sport he was. To the Civil War again, in the same old New Jersey setting, with Dorothy West playing the heroine in *The House with the Closed Shutters*. In her coward brother's clothes she takes his place on the battlefield, breaks through the lines, delivers a message, and is shot as she returns. And, forever after, inside the darkened rooms of the house with the closed shutters the brother pays through bitter years the price of his cowardice. All our old stamping grounds we revisited this summer. At the Atlantic Highlands we did two pictures, one, *A Salutary Lesson*, with Marion Leonard, and the other, *The Sorrows of the Unfaithful*, with Mary Pickford. At Paterson, New Jersey, we found a feudal castle. It belonged to one Mr. [Catholina] Lambert, a silk manufacturer. Here we did *The Call to Arms* where little Mary donned tights for the first and only time, playing a page, and looking picturesque on a medieval horse, but being a very unhappy Mary for a reason that none of us knew. How she fussed about those tights—nearly shed tears. She sat on the lawn all wrapped up in the generous folds of her velvet cape, and wouldn't budge until she was called for her scene, and she talked so strangely.—For Owen was there, and all the other actors were to see her in the tights, and Mary and Owen had a secret—a secret that made such a situation quite unbearable.—She had confided it only to "Doc," but the rest of us had been wondering. What a miserable, hot, muggy day it was. Tolerable only sitting on the grassy slopes of the Lambert estate, but how awful in the rooms of the little frame hotel over by the railroad tracks where we had made up and where some of the actors were still awaiting orders as to how they should dress. Dell Henderson, who was assisting Mr. Griffith on this picture, was laboring back and forth from the castle to the hotel bringing orders to the waiting actors as they were needed. Sennett was one of the waiting ones, and he was all humped up in his pet grouch when Dell entered and said, "*Here, Sennett, the boss says for you to don this armor.*"—"Armor, in this heat? Armor? I guess I won't wear armor."—Then a short pause, "*Are you going to wear armor?*" "Yes, I'm no teacher's pet," said Dell, as he gathered to himself the pieces of his suit of metal and began to climb into them. So, the doubting Mack Sennett could do naught but imitate him, for no matter how balky his manner, one word from the boss and he became a good little boy again. In August we were once more back in Cuddebackville. The O and

W's conductor was no longer skeptical of our visits. We brought so many actors sometimes that we not only filled the little Inn but had to find neighboring farmhouses in which to park the overflow. We met all the old Cuddebacks again. We never realized what a tribe they were until we had to do a scene in a cemetery, and every grave we picked made trouble for us with some Cuddeback or other still living. How to get away with it we didn't know until we hit upon the idea of simultaneously enacting a fake but intensely melodramatic scene down by the General Store. That did the trick. All the villagers missed their lunch that day and were unaware of the desecration of their dead. "Wally" [Henry] Walthall gave his famous fried chicken luncheon at the minister's house. Talent was versatile. We'd worked through our lunch hour this day, so it was either go lunchless or beg the privilege of slaughtering some of the minister's wife's tempting spring chickens and cooking them in her kitchen. That's how "Wally" had the opportunity to prove his fried chicken the equal of any Ritz Carlton's. We met up with old Pete again. Although nearly ninety, he was worrying his faithful spouse into a deep and dark melancholia. Pete drove the big bus, rigged up for our use out of one of his old farm wagons. It was usually filled with "actresses"—wicked females from the city who wore gay clothes and put paint on their faces. What a good time old Pete did have once out on the highway! What a chatter, chatter, chatter, he did maintain! Never had he dreamed of such intimacy with ladies out of a theater! But a wife was ever a wife. So, no matter how old and decrepit Pete was, to Mrs. Pete he still had charm, so why wouldn't he be alluring to these city girls? Every night Mrs. Pete was Johnny-on-the-spot, when the bus unloaded its quota of fair femininity at the Inn, waiting to lead her errant swain right straight home. Our friends the Godeffroys still held open house for us. Dear old Mr. Godeffroy told us of the disquieting notes that had crept into Cuddebackville's former tranquil life, due to our lavish expenditures the first summer—told Mr. Griffith he was "knocking the place to hell." But they still loved us. In a smart little trap they'd jog over to location bringing buckets of fresh milk and boxes of apples and pears. Toward late afternoon of a warm summer day, when working close to their elaborate "cottage," the "Boss" would appear with bottles of Bass Ale, and bottles of C & C Ginger Ale, both of which he'd pour over great chunks of ice into a great shining milk bucket—shandygaff (diluted beer). Was it good? For the simple moving picture age in which we were living we seemed to get a good deal out of life.

We enjoyed the other social diversions of the year before—canoeing, motoring, table-tipping. But one night, the night on which the MacPherson magicians broke up Mr. Griffith's beautiful sleep, nearly saw the end of table-tipping. Retiring early after a hard day David was awakened by noisy festivities downstairs and getting good and mad about it he rapped a shoe on the floor. The group on an occult demonstration bent, thinking how wonderfully their spooks were working, instead of quieting down became hilarious. The morning found them much less optimistic about spirit rapping. We did an Irish story of the days when the harp rang through Tara's Hall—the famous "Willful Peggy" in which pretty Mary never looked prettier nor acted more willfully. But the something that had happened to Mary since our first visits to Cuddebackville made her a different Mary now. One day we were idling over by the Canal bank when, with the most wistful expression and in the most wistful tone, Mary spoke, "*You know, Mrs. Griffith, I used to think this canal was the most beautiful place I'd ever seen, and now it just seems to me like a dirty, muddy stream.*" What had happened to her love's young dream to so change the scenery for her? Early that fall we went to Mount Beacon to do an Indian picture. The hotel on the mountain top had been closed, but we dug up the owner and he reopened parts of the place. At night we slid down the mountainside in the incline railway car to the village of Fishkill where we dined and slept at a regular city hotel. We nearly froze on that mountain top. Playing Indians, wrapped up in warm Indian blankets, and thus draped picturesquely on the mountainside, saved us.

Mrs. Smith, not yet Pickford, did an Indian squaw in this picture, which featured a picturesque character, one, Dark Cloud

[Elijah Tahamont], for years model to the artist [Frederic] Remington. Dark Cloud was sixty years old, but had the flexible, straight, slim figure of nineteen. How beautifully he interpreted the Harvest Festival dance! There were other actor-Indians on this Mount Beacon picture, present-day celebrities who were thanking their stars they were being Indians with woolly blankets to pose in. There were Henry Walthall and Lily Cahill and Jeanie MacPherson and Jim Kirkwood and Donald Crisp, among others. Donald Crisp had crept quietly into the Biograph fold as Donald Somebody Else. Occasionally, he authored poems in *The Smart Set*—reason for being Donald Somebody Else in the movies. Of late, Mr. Crisp has rather neglected poetry for the movies. He gave the screen his greatest acting performance as "Battling Burrows" in Mr. Griffith's artistic *Broken Blossoms*. The night that *Way Down East* opened in New York in 1920 (September 3) Donald was radiant among the audience saying his farewells, for on the morrow he was to sail for England to take charge of the Famous Players studio there, where he put on among other things *Beside the Bonnie Brier Bush*. Claire McDowell and her husband, Charles Hill Mailes, joined Biograph this season. Stephanie Longfellow returned to play in more pictures—Alfred Paget began to play small parts, as did Jeanie MacPherson—also beautiful Florence LaBadie, who afterwards became a fan favorite through [Edwin] Thanhouser's startlingly successful serial *The Million Dollar Mystery*. As one of the four principals, along with James Cruze of *The Covered Wagon* fame, Sidney Bracey and Marguerite Snow, she attracted much attention. A job as model to Howard Chandler Christy had preceded her venture into the movies. Her tragic death, the result of a motor accident, occurred in 1917. Edwin August came, to look handsome in costume, playing his first part with Lucy Cotton (recently married (1924) to Edward Russell Thomas) in *The Fugitive*, taken on Mount Beacon. Mabel Normand, who had "peeked" in on us the year before, returned after a winter spent with Vitagraph. Mabel, as everyone knows, had been responsible for the lovely magazine covers by James Montgomery Flagg, and had also been model to Charles

Dana Gibson, before she came to pictures, which had happened through friendship for Alice Joyce, who had also been a model but was now leading lady at the Kalem Company.

It was at Kalem, playing extras that Mabel Normand began her rather startling movie career. Dorothy Bernard made a screen debut, as did the other Dorothy who afterward became the wife of Wallace Reid. I recall Dorothy Davenport at the Delaware Water Gap where we took some pictures that fall. She was a modish little person—she wore brown pin-check ginghams and a huge brown taffeta bow on the end of a braid of luxurious brown hair that fluttered down her back. She looked as though she came direct from Miss Prim's boarding school for children of the elite—and so was distinctive for the movies. Fair Lily Cahill of the tailored blue serge, plain straw "dude," and lady-like veil worked intermittently that summer, she was always immaculately bloused in "sun-kissed linen." Not long after the days of the Water Gap and Mount Beacon Indian pictures, Miss Cahill became a Broadway leading woman in support of that longtime matinee idol—Brandon Tynan—and somewhere along in this period she married him. Henry Lehrman, alias "Pathe," hung about. How he loved being a near actor! How he adored getting fixed up for a picture! He was satisfied by now that his "make-ups" were works of art. From the dressing room he would emerge patting his swollen chest, with the laconic remark, "*Some makeup!*" Eddie Dillon returned, to smile his way through more studio days. He often engaged me in long converse. Eddie was quite flabbergasted when he learned my matrimonial status.

He need not have been. For in Los Angeles on Mr. Griffith's busy evenings he often suggested my taking in a movie with Eddie. But Eddie never knew about that. And there was Lloyd Carlton, who went all around the mulberry bush before he landed in the movies. He first heard of them in far-off Australia in 1908, when as stage manager for *Peter Pan* he met a Mr. West, who was "doing" Australia and the Far East with a "show" that consisted of ten and fifteen-foot moving pictures, toting the films and projection machine and the whole works along with him.

Back on home soil, Mr. Carlton bobbed up at Biograph where instead of Mr. [Charles] Frohman's one hundred and fifty dollars weekly he cheerfully pocketed five dollars per day for doing character bits. Followed Thanhouser, [Siegmund] Lubin, and Mr. [William] Fox. Mr. Carlton says he directed the first five reel picture ever released—*Through Fire to Fortune*—written by Clay Greene and released March 2, 1914, by the General Film Company. Mr. Carlton also says his picture contained the first night scene. Through crude lighting manipulations Mr. Carlton secured it in the quarry at Betzwood (Pennsylvania) where rocks were painted black and properties arranged to represent the interior of a mine. And so from near and far, and from diverging avenues of endeavor, came the new recruits to Biograph, but in the late fall Mary and Owen, and the Smith family sailed for Cuba one fine day to produce some "Imp" pictures there. When safe aboard the steamer, Mary and Owen decided to brave mother's tears and anguish. They told her of the secret marriage.

☐☐☐☐☐☐☐☐☐☐

There were no social engagements during these Biograph years. Our dinner parties, which were concerned with nourishment mostly, were with our co-workers. As we never knew when we would be allowed to eat, it was impossible to dine with friends. There was no time for anything but work—a good, hard steady grind it was, and we liked it. The one, lazy, lenient affair of the week was breakfast on Sunday morning. From ten to twelve it stretched, and it was so restful to eat at home and not have to look at a menu card or talk to a waiter, even though the conversation would be all about the movies. "*What are people interested in?*" said he, one Sunday. "Well, men like to make money, and women want to be beautiful." "That would make a good movie. Why don't you write it?" "Glad to, if you think it's any good." So she wrote it, the part about the women wanting to be beautiful, and called it *How She Triumphed*, and in it Blanche Sweet evolved from an ugly duckling with no beau to a very lovely bit of femininity with sighing swains (suitors) all around her. In the picture she did calisthenics according to Walter Camp as one way of getting there. After the leisurely Sunday morning hours had crept their way, to the studio David would hie (hasten) himself to read scripts with Mr. Dougherty. And Sunday night would mean a movie show somewhere. And Monday morning it began all over again. From "Wark," to "work," only the difference of a vowel, so what an appropriate middle name for David Griffith! What infinite patience he had. If we got stuck in the mud when going out to location—we were stuck, and we'd get out, so why worry? No cursing out of driver or car or weather. No "*What the—? Why the—? Couldn't you have taken another road?*" Instead would suddenly be heard baritone strains of *Samson and Delilah* or some old plantation Negro song while we waited for horses or another car to pull us out.—And it did happen once when on location perhaps twenty miles out in the wilds, that the leading man suddenly discovered he had brought the wrong pair of trousers.—Nothing to do but send back for the right ones.

Mr. Griffith was not indifferent to the time that would be lost, but getting himself all worked up would not make the picture any better. He'd sing, perhaps an Irish come-all-you, or, were he out in the desert, get out the automobile robe and start a crap game. Arthur Marvin never ceased to marvel at his chief's agility and capacity for hard work. Mr. Marvin had a sort of leisurely way of working. Up and down a stubble field Mr. Griffith was tearing one day—getting a line on a barn, a tree and some old plows. Arthur was having a few drags on his pipe—the film boxes being full and everything in readiness to put up the tripod wherever the director should decide. David's long legs kept striding merrily all over the cut harvest field—most miserable place to walk—Arthur musing as he looked on. "*There goes Griffith, he'll die working.*" In a few moments Mr. Griffith right about faced and with not a symptom of being out of breath said, "*Set her up here, Arthur.*" That winter we lost our genial Arthur Marvin, but David Griffith is still hitting the stubble field. Well, he took good care of himself. He did a daily dozen and he sparred with our ex-lightweight, Spike Robinson. The bellboys at the

Alexandria Hotel called him "the polar bear" because he bought a bucket of cracked ice every morning to make the Los Angeles morning bath more tonic-y. One could not have better equipment for the trying experiences of movie work than patience, and a sense of humor. And the "polar bear" is well equipped with both. But there were times when even a sense of humor failed to sustain one. Nothing was funny about the uncertain mornings when we'd gather at the 125th Street ferry for the 8:45 boat, having watched weather since daylight through our bedroom window, only to cross and re-cross the Hudson on the same boat, the cumulus clouds we delighted in for photographic softness having turned to rain clouds even as we watched from the ferry slip. Back to the studio then to begin another picture and to work late. And oh, how we'd grouch!

But when it rained while we were registered at some expensive place like the Kittatinny at the Delaware Water Gap, there was need for anxiety, with the actors's board bill mounting daily and nothing being accomplished. Yes, we had worries. But we were getting encouragement too. The splendid reviews of our pictures in *The Dramatic Mirror* helped a lot. The way our pictures were going over was a joy. With their first announcement on the screen, what a twitter in the audience! A great old title page Biograph pictures had. Nothing less than our National Emblem, our good old American eagle, sponsored them. He certainly looked a fine bird on the screen, his wings benignly spread, godfathering the Biograph's little movie children. Exhibitors were certainly getting keen about "Biographs"—the public was too. People were becoming anxious about the players as well, and commencing to ask all sorts of questions about them.

Stacks of mail were arriving daily imploring the names of players, but of this no hint was given the actor. How surprised I was that time my husband said to me, "*You know we are getting as many as twenty five letters a day, about Mary Pickford?*"

"*Why, what do you mean letters about her?*" "*Every picture she plays in brings a bunch of mail asking her name and other things about her.*" "*You're not kidding?*" "*Of course not.*" "*Did you* tell her?" "No. I don't want her asking for a raise in salary." Biograph found it a difficult job sticking to their policy of secrecy. Letters came from fans asking about their favorites, the pretty girl with the curls—the girl with the sad eyes—the man with the lovely smile—the funny little man—and the policeman. What tears of joy Sennett would have wept had he known!

In bunches the postman soon began to leave the "who" letters at 11 East Fourteenth Street. *Who played the tall, thin man in 'The Tenderfoot?'* " "*Who played the little girl in the Colonial dress and curls who danced the minuet in the rose garden at midnight in 'Willful Peggy?'* " "*Who was the handsome Indian who did the corn dance on the mountain top in 'The Indian Runner's Romance?'* " Other picture concerns than Biograph had not as yet made the actor's name public.—But they did give him his mail when addressed with sufficient clarity. Arthur Mackley, the famous "Sheriff of Essanay," was receiving, those days, ten letters a day. They came addressed. Some boy, "the Sheriff," getting ten letters a day! It remained for English exhibitors first to name the Biograph players. For Biograph, long after all the other picture companies had made the actor's name public, still refused to come out into the open. Over in London the fans were appeased with fictitious names for their favorites.

Beautiful names they were, so hero-ish and so villain-ish, so reminiscent of the old-time, sentimental, maiden-lady author. I recall but one and a half names of our players. Dell Henderson was given the beautiful soubriquet of "Arthur Donaldson" and Blanche Sweet became "Daphne" something or other. But the yearning American youths and maidens continued to receive the cold, stereotyped reply, "*Biograph gives no names.*" The Biograph was not thinking as quickly as some of its players. Our friends from Cuddebackville, the Godeffroys, being in New York one time this summer, Mr. Griffith thought it would be rather nice to arrange an evening. They were interested in our California pictures, as they were planning a trip there. We fixed up the projection room and ran the better of the Western stuff. Afterward with our guests and a few of the leading people we repaired to Cavanagh's on West Twenty-Third Street. Busy chatter about the pictures, everyone raving over Mary Pickford's work in *Ramona*, when Mary, quietly, but with considerable assurance said, *"Someday I am going to be a great actress and have my name in electric lights over a theater."* I turned pale and felt weak. We all were shocked. Of course, she never meant the movies—that would have been plumb crazy. No, she meant the stage, and she was thinking of going back. The thought of losing Mary made me very unhappy. But just how had she figured to get her name in electric lights? What was on her mind, anyway? This summer of 1910 Mr. Griffith signed his third Biograph contract.

This contract called for a royalty of an eighth of a cent a foot on all film sold and seventy-five dollars per week, but the name "Lawrence" which had been signed on the dotted line the two preceding years, was this time scratched out and "David" written in. "David" had gone into the silence and decided that the movies were now worthy of his hire, and couldn't dent his future too badly, no matter what that future might be. David W. Griffith and Mary Pickford were certainly growing bold.

□□□□□□□□□□□

Though the licensed picture companies—The General Film Group—kept a watchful eye on one another, each had pride in its own trademark and was satisfied with the little company of actors bringing it recognition. But the independent companies, now beginning to loom on the horizon, were looking with envying eyes on the rich harvest the licensed companies were reaping, and they figured that all they'd need, to do as well, would be some of their well-trained actors, especially those of Mr. Griffith's quite famous little organization. Surely D. W. Griffith had less to do with Mary Pickford's success than Mary Pickford herself! She, it was the public came to see, so they were out, red-hot for Mary, and offering publicity and more money. The "little" war was started. Actors in the companies that comprised the General Film Company could not be bargained for except by the "Independents." For instance, if an actor of the Biograph

Company were discovered offering his services to Lubin or Edison or any of the General Film, that company promptly reported the matter to Biograph and the ambitious actor found himself not only turned down by Edison or Lubin or any other but his nice little Biograph job would be gone as well. That had happened to Harry Salter and Florence Lawrence. An actor in one of the General Film Group would have to resign his job before he could open negotiations with any other company in that group.

We did grind out the work this fall and early winter. The promise of California again was a big incentive. We might stay longer and have a new studio, a regular place. While there was no more excitement pervading the studio than there had been the year before, a more general willingness was noticed among the leading people and more tears and anguish on the part of the beseeching extras. Jeanie MacPherson sat on the steps leading to the basement of the studio, and cried, until Mr. Griffith felt remorseful and took her. But such conduct hadn't availed pink cheeked lanky "Beau," the year before, when he was the one property boy left behind. Then that unhappy youth's tearful parting shot, "*All I ask, Mr. Griffith, is that some day you take me to California,*" kept intruding and spoiling the complete satisfaction of our days. Another year Mr. Griffith harkened to his pleading. For nearly ten years now "Beau" as William Beaudine has been directing pictures in Los Angeles. And so, while some of the old guard would not be with us, a goodly number would. To the "Imp" had gone Mary and Owen, and while Ma fussed terribly about it, there was nothing for her and Lottie and Jack to do but follow suit. David Miles and Anita Hendrie, his wife, were already with "Imp" and they, with [William] King Baggot and George Loane Tucker, Joe [Joseph] Smiley, Thomas Ince, Hayward Mack, and Isabel Rae [also Rea], made a fair number of capable people. But even so, Mary's "Imp" pictures fell far short of her Biograph pictures, and she wasn't very happy and she didn't stay so very long. As a member of the "Imp" Company, the silence and mystery that had surrounded her when with Biograph instantly vanished. She now received whole pages of advertising for that was how the "Imp" would put the pictures over. One of her first independent pictures was *The Dream* of which a reviewer said, "*The picture got over on account of Miss Pickford. Our feelings were somewhat sentimental when we saw 'Our Mary' as a wife arrayed in evening gown and dining with swells. In other words, we have always considered Mary a child. It never occurred to us she might grow up and be a woman someday.*" Marion Leonard and Stanner Edward Varley Taylor had taken their departure. I believe it was "Reliance-Ward" they went, as did Mr. Walthall, Mr. Kirkwood, and Arthur Johnson. Arthur had become not so dependable, and Mr. Griffith being unable to stand the worry of uncertain appearances, reluctantly parted with his most popular actor, and his first leading man. He never found anyone to take his place exactly. For even so long ago, before he and Mr. Griffith parted, 'twas said of Arthur Johnson, "*His face is better known than John Drew's.*" Mary gone, Mr. Griffith located Blanche Sweet somewhere on the road and telegraphed an offer of forty dollars weekly to come with us to California, which Miss Sweet accepted. He was willing to take a chance on Blanche, being in need of a girl of her type. If she didn't work out right (he hardly expected her to set the world a-fire) the loss would be small, as he was getting her so cheaply. Wilfred Lucas also received a telegram, but his tenderly implored him to come for one hundred and fifty dollars—a staggering offer—the biggest to date. He also accepted. Dell Henderson had been commissioned by Mr. Griffith to dispatch the Lucas-one-hundred-and-fifty-dollar telegram, and the high salary made him so sore that he promptly told it everywhere, causing jealous fits to break out all over the studio. We had also in our California cast, Claire McDowell, Stephanie Longfellow, Florence Barker, Florence LaBadie, Mabel Normand, Vivian Prescott, and Dorothy West for the more important parts, Grace Henderson, Kate Toncray, and Kate Bruce for the character parts, and little Gladys Egan for important child roles. And of men—as memory serves me—there were Frank Powell, Edwin August, Dell Henderson, Charlie [Charles] Craig, Mack Sennett, Joe [Joseph] Graybill, Charlie [Charles] West, Donald Crisp, Guy

Hedlund, Alfred Paget, Eddie [Edward] and Jack Dillon, Spike Robinson, Frank Grandon, Tony O'Sullivan and "Big" Evans, and George Nichols. And some wives, Mrs. Frank Powell, Mrs. Dell Henderson, Mrs. George Nichols, and Mrs. Billy Bitzer.—And one baby, Frank Baden Powell.—At Georgia and Girard Streets, Los Angeles, a ten-minute ride from the center of the city (downtown), on a two-and-a-quarter-acre plot adjoining some car barns, the carpenters were building our grand studio. An open air studio—no artificial lighting—we could get all the light effects we desired from the sun—and could begin to work as early as 8:30 and continue until late in the afternoon. We had not yet reached the stage where we felt that "Mr. Electric Lamp" could compete with the sun. How joyful we were when we first beheld the new studio! The stage was of nice smooth boards and seemed almost big enough for two companies to work at the same time. The muslin light diffusers were operated on an overhead trolley system. There was even a telephone on the stage. The studio was then indeed the last word in modern equipment. An elongated one-story building contained the office, projection room, rehearsal room, for nights and rainy days, and two large dressing rooms for the men. In order to save wear and tear on the women's clothes, they were given the two dressing rooms in the rear of the building which opened directly onto the stage.

    To tell the world how secure our position—how prosperous financially—at the street entrance to our studio there now waited through the day one, and often two big, black, seven passenger touring cars—rented by the month, at six hundred dollars per. Now between sets in the studio we could dash out in the car and grab an exterior. In our dressing rooms we had makeup tables, mirrors, lockers, and running water. And oil stoves to keep us warm. For in the early mornings, before the sun had reached our room, it was a shivery place. Our cold cream and grease paints would be quite as stiff as our fingers. So now, with the new studio, a larger company, and our knowledge of the surrounding country, there was nothing to it but that we must get right on the job and do better and bigger pictures. With the one exception already noted we had neglected the sea the year before, and as yet we had attempted nothing important that had to do with "*Ol' davil Sea*," as Eugene O'Neill calls it. The sea was trickier than the mountains, and more expensive if one needed boats and things. But this year we would go to it right, with a massive production of Tennyson's *Enoch Arden*—a second production of the poem that had written history for us in our screen beginnings. The first time we had taken most of it in the studio, with only one or two simple shots of the sea. Now we would do something g-r-a-n-d. *Enoch Arden* was such good movie stuff, and Mr. Griffith was wondering how he could get it all into one thousand feet of film. An exhibitor in those days would accept eleven hundred feet of film, but that was the limit. The programs were arranged only for the thousand-foot picture, a thousand foot Biograph being shown Mondays and Thursdays. How could two thousand feet be shown on Monday and none on Thursday? Even could the exhibitor have so arranged it, would the people sit through two thousand feet without a break? Well, now, we could do this, we could take the picture in two reels, each of a thousand feet, show one reel Monday, the second Thursday, and take a chance on the people becoming sufficiently interested in the first reel to come back for the second—the only logical way of working out the problem. Mr. Griffith fully realized his responsibility. Again he would chance it. Santa Monica would be the ideal place for this big production, so every day for a week—for a whole week was given to exteriors alone—we motored out to Santa Monica in the cold early morning. The place had changed little in the year that had passed. The row of tiny shacks was now occupied by Japs and Norwegians who caught and dried fish and fought with each other at all other times.

    One friendly Norwegian loaned his shack as a dressing room for the women. We "shot" the same shack for Annie's bridal home. The men made up in a stranded horse car of bygone vintage that had been anchored in the sand. We sent out an SOS for a sailing vessel of "Enoch's" day, and we heard of one, and had it towed up from San Pedro. What would we do next? We did

Enoch Arden in two reels. Wilfred Lucas played "Enoch," Frank Grandon, as "Philip," and I played "Annie Lee." Well, Jeanie MacPherson said I had "sea eyes," whatever that meant. Mrs. Grace Henderson kept the Inn to which Enoch returns, Annie's and Enoch's babies grew up to be Florence LaBadie and Bobby Harron (one of Bobby's first parts), and Jeanie MacPherson powdered her hair and played nurse to the little baby that later came to Philip and Annie. George Nichols departed via the *Owl* for San Francisco to get the costumes from Goldstein and Company. There was so little to be had in costumes in Los Angeles. Mr. Nichols had also journeyed to San Francisco for costumes for *Ramona* the year before. The exhibitors said they would accept *Enoch Arden* in two reels, show the first on Monday, and the second reel Thursday. And so it was first shown. And those who saw the first reel came back in all eagerness to see the second half. And that was that. The picture was so great a success, however, that it was soon being shown as a unit in picture houses, also in high schools and clubs, accompanied by a lecturer. And so *Enoch Arden* wrote another chapter of screen history. Sustained by its success Mr. Griffith listened to the call of the desert. With two thousand feet of celluloid to record a story, he felt he now could do something with prairie schooners, pioneers, and redskins, and so he answered the desert call with a big epic of pioneer romance, *The Last Drop of Water*. We set up camp in the San Fernando desert, two huge tents, one for mess, with a cook and assistants who served chow to the cowboys and extra men. Two rows of tables, planks set on wooden horses, ran the length of the tent—there must have been at least fifty cowboys and riders to be fed hearty meals three times a day. The other tent contained trunks and wardrobe baskets, and here the boys slept and made up. The hotel in the village of San Fernando, three miles or so from the camp, accommodated the regular members of the company and all the extra women, to whom the director, as he dashed off for his camp in the morning, gave this parting advice, "*Girls, stay together when you're not busy, for you're likely to hear some pretty rough stuff if you don't.*"

Prairie schooners to the number of eight made up our desert caravan, and there were the horses for the covered wagons, the United States soldiers, and the Indians, dogs, chickens, and a cow, for this restless element from a Mississippi town, making the trek across the land of the buffalo and the Indian to gather gold nuggets in the hills of California, brought with them as many familiar touches from their deserted homes as they reckoned would survive the trip. Of course, conflicts with Indians, and the elements, resulted in a gradual elimination of the home touches and disintegration of the caravan, but there was a final triumphant arrival at their destination for the few survivors. The picture was expensive—but quite worth it—we were at least headed the right way in those crude days of our beginnings. We were dealing in things vital in our American life, and not one bit interested in close-ups of empty-headed little ingenues with adenoids, bedroom windows, manhandling of young girls, fast sets, perfumed bathrooms, or nude youths heaving their muscles. Sex, as portrayed in the commercial film of today, was noticeable by its absence. But if, today, the production of clean and artistic pictures does not induce the dear public to part with the necessary spondulics so that the producer can pay his rent, buy an occasional meal and a new lining for the old winter overcoat, then even Mr. Griffith must give the dear public what it wants. And for the past year or two it has apparently wanted picturizations daring as near as possible the most intimate intimacy of the bedroom. The season closed with another "Covered Wagon" masterpiece called *Crossing the American Prairies in the Early Fifties*. The picture was taken at Topanga Canyon. There were hundreds of men and women and cowboys and a hundred horses from ranches nearby, as well as eleven prairie schooners. In the picture, guards had been posted at night, but being tired, they fell asleep, so the Indians pounced upon the emigrants, slaughtering some and taking some prisoners, to be burned at the stake. The few survivors who escaped left numbers of dead pioneers behind. The shifting desert sands would soon cover the bodies and remove all trace of the massacre. The dead bodies were represented by the living bodies of members of the company who had to be buried deep in the alkali waste, and the getting covered up was going to be a dirty job for the living corpses. So those scenes had to be taken last. Little grains of sand gently falling upon one from out the property boys's cornucopias, while unpleasant, could be silently endured but when the property boys got the storm really started and the sand was being poured upon one thick and heavy, getting into hair and ears and eyes, no matter how protective the position one had assumed, there were heard smothered oaths from the dead people that no wild cowboy had ever excelled. Dell Henderson, dying with little old Chrystie Miller, was all humped up and writhing in the desert sands. And while Dell was just about to be featured as the far-famed gambler of the West in a line of showy parts, and while he felt that Mr. Griffith had a friendly feeling for him, his ardor for his movie job was beginning to cool. And when, after being extricated from his earthy grave, he found the boss, he lost all restraint. "*Old man,*" said Dell to David, "*this is too much, I quit pictures—I'm through.*" But the next day when all bathed and barbered up, he felt differently about it.

But Dell hadn't had it as rough as the atmospheric members of the company. Even the wives had been called upon for atmosphere, and were to makeup and dress as men. They didn't like the old trousers and the greasy felt hats that were passed out to them, and they weren't keen on being recognized on the screen, in the unflattering costumes. So Mr. Griffith compromised, "*All right, I'll put you in the background and you can sit down.*" At that the women became more amiable and agreed to help out the perspective. And in the last few hundred feet of the second reel, they joined the dead emigrants and were covered up in the whirlwind. The final scenes were reserved for the days immediately preceding our departure for the East. As soon as they were taken, the company would be dismissed to make the necessary preparations prior to leave-taking.

So, to their pet establishment the women beat it to have their hair beautifully and expensively washed and lemon-rinsed and were all in readiness for the California Limited, when a retake was announced. Static in the film! To their burial places once more they were rushed, and again the boys stood by and again poured the cornucopias of sand over them, ruining completely the crop of nice clean heads. Few got a chance at another fashionable shampoo. The majority had to be contented with just a home wash—or to take the sand along with them.

□□□□□□□□□□

We fell to the lure of the Bret Harte story this winter. We advanced to the romances of the hardy Argonauts, and the "pretty ladies" of the mining towns. What a wealth of picturesque cinema material the lives of the rugged forty-niners afforded! Dell Henderson was featured as the handsome gambler, "Jack Hamlin," and Claire McDowell as the intriguing lady of uncertain virtue, Stephanie Longfellow as the rare, morally excellent wife. Blanche Sweet was still too much the young girl to interpret or look the part of Bret Harte's halo-ized "Magdalenes." Mr. Griffith, as yet unwilling to grant that she had any soul or feeling in her work, was using her in "girl" parts. But he changed his opinion with *The Lonedale Operator*. That was the picture in which he first recognized ability in Miss Sweet. The outdoor life of the West had "plumped" up the fair Blanche, and Mr. Griffith felt at this stage in her development she typified, excellently well, buxom youth. Why wouldn't Blanche have "plumped" up when she arrived on location with a bag of creampuffs nearly every day and had her grandmother get up at odd hours of the night to fry her bacon sandwiches? She soon filled out every wrinkle of the homemade looking tweed suit she had worn on her arrival in Los Angeles.

Way, way up on the Santa Monica cliffs we built a log cabin for Blanche Sweet to dwell in, as the heroine of *The White Rose of the Wilds*. The location was so remote, the climb so stiff, that once having made it no one was going down until the day's work was over. It was a heavenly day. Gazing off into the distances quite sufficed, until, whetted by clean, insistent breezes, little gnawings in the tummy brought one back to realities. It took more than dreamy seas and soft blue skies to deter a hungry actor from expressing himself around lunchtime. And so, in querulous accents soon were wafted on the sage scented air such questions as, "Gee, haven't they sent for the lunch yet? Gosh, I'm hungry. Hasn't the car gone? It'll take a couple of hours to get food way up here. Hope they bring us enough—this air—I'm starved." Sooner or later lunch would be on the way. The car had to go for it as far as Venice. It was nearly three o'clock when the car returned and by that time everyone was doggone hungry. Mr. Griffith had tipped his two "leads" and Mr. Bitzer and myself to get off in a little group, for hot juicy steaks had been ordered for those select few—leading players must be well nourished—and it was just as well to be as quiet and unobtrusive about it as possible. For while it wasn't exactly fair—sandwiches and coffee was all the lunch the company usually afforded for the extra people. Mack Sennett, who always had a most generous appetite, was wild-eyed by now, for he was just an "extra" in *The White Rose of the Wilds*. And he was on to the maneuvers of the "steak" actors and so resentful of the partiality shown that he finally could contain himself no longer, and in bitter tones, subdued though audible, he spoke, "Steaks that way," with a nod of his head indicating Griffith and the leading people, "and sandwiches this way"—himself and the supers. And though Mack sat off on the side, and from his point of vantage continued to throw hungry glances, they brought him no steak that day.

This winter it was that Mr. Sennett invested in a "tux" and went over to the Alexandria Hotel night after night, where he decorated the lobby's leather benches in a determined effort to interest Messieurs [Adam] Kessel and [Charles] Baumann. (The Kay-Bee Company) His watchful waiting got him a job. *The Battle of Elderberry Gulch* was a famous picture of those days. The star was a pioneer baby all of whose relatives had been killed by Indians. During the time the baby's folks were being murdered another party of pioneers, led by Dell Henderson, was dying of thirst nearby. With just enough life left in them to do it, they rescued the baby from its dead relations, staggered on a few miles, and then they, too, sank exhausted in the sand and cacti. Another cornucopia sandstorm blew up. Kindhearted Dell Henderson, now sunk to earth, had protectingly tucked the baby's head under his coat. But the tiny baby hand (in the story, and it was good business) had to be pictured waving above the prostrate figures of the defunct pioneers, to show she still lived. Otherwise, she might not have been saved by the second rescuing party, and saved she had to be for the later chapters of the story. For though in the end of the story the baby became the lily-white Blanche Sweet, it was, as matter of fact, a tiny, lightly colored, colored baby from a Colored Foundling Home, whom we often used for the photographic value of its black eyes, and Dell must see to it that the tiny pickaninny (black child) was in no way hurt, even though he had surreptitiously to wave the baby hand from under his rough outer garments. Having succeeded so well at Santa Monica, we decided to work other beaches this year.

We became acquainted with them all—Redondo, Long Beach, Venice, and Playa del Rey. The number 2 company became especially familiar with the beaches, for they did numbers of bathing pictures. Frank Powell was still directing the comedies, with Dell Henderson and Mack Sennett occasionally trying their hands at it. It was in these bathing pictures that Mabel Normand began winning admirers both on the screen and off. Even Mack Sennett began to take an interest in the beautiful and reckless Mabel, a slim figure in black tights doing daredevil dives or lovely graceful ones. Mabel was always ready for any venturesome aquatic stunt. But her work was equally daring on land, for she thought nothing of riding the wildest bucking bronco bareback. It took more than bucking broncos to intimidate the dusky-eyed Mabel. All of this Sennett was noting—clever kid was Mabel—and if he ever should be a director on his own! On the beach by the old Redondo Hotel, which the passing years had changed from a smart winter resort patronized by Easterners to a less stylish summer one patronized by Angelenos, one balmy winter day, some bathing scenes were being taken. This type of stuff was new to me and I was all eyes. Working only with the

Griffith "company," there were lots of things I didn't see. But this day there were two companies working on the same location, and that was how I first saw Marguerite Loveridge (Marguerite Marsh), of lovely Titian (red) hair and fair of face, sporting the most modern black satin bathing suit, and high-heeled French slippers. Imagine, right in the seashore sand! I was interested in this Loveridge girl, for she was pretty, and had a rather professional air about her. Sometimes when rehearsing we'd suddenly find ourselves in need of a little two-or three-year-old, which need would be supplied by Mr. Griffith or Mr. Powell or Dell Henderson calling right out at rehearsal, "*Who's got a kid?*"

Marguerite Loveridge on one such occasion had replied affirmatively.—And so we came to use her small son occasionally, and when Marguerite was working and we needed the child, and Marguerite couldn't bring it or take care of it, she'd press her little sister into service.—For Miss Loveridge had also a little sister. And it was some such situation that led little sister to the movies and to Redondo at this time. Little sister was a mite—most pathetic and half-starved she looked in her wispy clothes, with stockings sort of falling down over her shoe-tops. No one paid a particle of attention to the child. But Mr. Griffith popped up from somewhere and spied her, and gave her a smile. The frail, appealing look of her struck him. So he said, "*How'd you like to work in a picture?*" "*Oh, you're just fooling—you mean me to work in a picture?*" "*Yes, and I'll give you five dollars.*" No stage bashfulness in the hanging head, the limp arms, and the funny hop skip of the feet. "*Oh, you couldn't give me five dollars.*" "*Oh, yes I can.*" "*You sure you're not fooling?*" "*No, you come around some time, and you'll see, I'll put you in a scene. What's your name?*" "*Mae Marsh.*" "*I'll remember, and I'll put you in a movie someday.*" Right about now Dell Henderson was directing a picture in which Fred Mace was playing the lead and Marguerite Loveridge had a part. It was understood about the studio that Mr. Mace was quite taken with the charms of the fair Marguerite. Now Marguerite couldn't get out on location, and she wanted to send a message to Fred Mace, so she sent little sister, and little sister looked so terrible to Mr. Mace that he said to her, "*Don't let Griffith see you or your sister will lose her job.*" When Mace saw Margaret again he said, "*Don't have your sister come around the studio looking like that.*" And Margaret answered, "*Well, I will, for Mr. Griffith is going to use some children at San Gabriel and she is going to be one of the children.*" "*All right,*" answered Mace, "*take your chance.*" And at San Gabriel Mae did a little more of the funny hop skip, and she talked up rather pert to the director, "*You think you're the King*" sort of thing, and he liked it, and he said to Dell, "*The kid can act, she's great, don't you think so?*" Dell answered "yes," but he didn't think so. No one thought so but Mr. Griffith. A few weeks later when little Mae Marsh came to the studio carrying a book and the boys made jokes about it, Dell said to himself, "*When she puts that down, I'm a-going to see.*" The book was Tennyson's poems. The boys knew when a new actress came with such literature that Mr. Griffith was already seeing her bringing home the cows, or portraying some other old-fashioned heroine of the old-fashioned poets. As intended, our stay in California this second year was much longer than the first.

The three months lengthened to five, and it was May when the company returned East. It did seem a pity to close up the new studio, for it was the last word in organization. Why, we'd even a separate department for finances. The money end of things had grown to such proportions that David could no longer handle it as he had the first year. And Mr. Dougherty was along too, in charge of the front office. With Mabel Normand and Blanche Sweet well-started on their careers, the second winter's work in California ended. Another milestone had been passed, the birth of the two-reeler, which having been tried was not found wanting. What otherwise came out of the winter's work as most important was Biograph's acquisition of the little hop-skip girl, Mae Marsh. She played no parts this season, made very few appearances even as an insignificant extra girl, and when the company returned to New York they left Mae behind them.

☐☐☐☐☐☐☐☐☐☐

The serious students of the motion picture, for they had arrived, were at this time writing many and various articles in the trade papers. Epes Winthrop Sargent was a-saying this, *The Moving Picture World* more than advocates the ten cent theater. It looks forward to the time when the dollar photoplay theater will be an established institution following the advance in quality of the films. But there will always be five cent theaters in localities that will not support the ten cent houses and ten cent houses for those who cannot afford fifty cents or a dollar. It is the entertainment for the whole family. And W. Stephen Bush, the reviewer, said this, of a Biograph, "*The Battle* is a perfect picture in a splendid frame. I cannot close without a well-deserved word of praise regarding the women's dresses and coiffures of the wartime period. It is in the elaboration of such details that the master hand often betrays itself as it does here to the last chignon on the young girls's heads." And an unsigned article is headlined, "*Will Moving Pictures Save Madison Square Garden?*" And the late Louis Reeves Harrison in his "Studio Saunterings" in *The Moving Picture World*, "*I did not meet the mighty Griffith until after I had had an opportunity to study some examples of his marvelous work—he is the greatest of them all when he tries—but I found him to be keenly alive to the future possibilities of the new art to which he has so materially contributed. His productions show lofty inspirations mixed with a desire to help the world along, a trend of thought that is poetic, idealistic with a purifying and revivifying influence upon the audience that can best be excited through tragedy.*" The inquiry department of magazines published replies of this sort almost every week, "*Since the lady is in the Biograph, we premise her name is Jane Doe. Tis the best we can do.*" Or this, "No, John Bunny is not dead, report to the contrary notwithstanding.—Miss Turner, Miss Lawrence, Miss Pickford, Miss Gauntier, and Miss Joyce are all alive, and there have been no funerals for Messieurs Costello, Delaney, Johnson, Moore, or others." Or this, "Questions about tall, thin girls two years old are barred. Keep up to date." Or this, "All Biograph players are either John or Jane Doe." So, while Biograph players were still nameless, Vitagraph, Lubin, Kalem, Edison, Essanay, Melies, and Selig not only gave out players names but offered exhibitors trade photos at twenty cents each, and stereopticon slides of all players. Ambitious actors were getting out postcards with their photos to send [out to] the fans. The flow of Biograph players into the ranks of the Independents left the Biograph Company temporarily weakened. So much so that when *His Daughter* was released in the spring of 1911 a critic said, "*The picture has something of the spirit and character of the old Biograph stock company's work.*" And another speaking for an open market said, "*The best argument that I can offer for an open market is the well known fact that when Biograph was supreme, a mere sign of "Biograph today" would draw the crowd. Yes, folks would rather pay a ten cent admission and be satisfied with only two reels as long as there was a Biograph than to visit the neighbor house with three reels and four vaudeville acts and no Biograph. Everybody knows what a magnet was the word 'Biograph.'* " But other good actors were coming to the front and the loss of the old ones made but a brief and shallow dent in the prestige of Biograph.

On a June day in 1912 arrived little Gertrude Bambrick. She came on pretty sister Elsie's [Elsie Bambrick] invitation—just to look. Sister Elsie liked the movies, liked it at Biograph, but to get Gertrude down to the place had required considerable coaxing. Gertrude didn't like the place when she finally got there. "*How terrible*," said she, "*why, they haven't even chairs, what an awful place!*" She was almost ready to beat it before she had, had a good look around. A tall, angular man had noticed the pretty little girl, and he kept passing and repassing before her, giving her a searching look each time. Then, one time, when directly in front of her he made an abrupt stop and a significant beckoning of his right forefinger plainly said, "*Youngster, I would speak with thee.*" But Gertrude paid no attention to the beckoning finger.

She only thought what a funny thing for anyone to do. If the man wanted to speak to her, why didn't he speak? Sister Elsie gave her a poke and whispered to her secretly that it was the "great Griffith" who was beckoning, and when he beckoned the thing to do was to follow. So, somewhat in a daze, Gertrude started off and as she did so the actors and others in the studio cleared a way for her much as they might for a queen. Mr. Griffith led the way into the ladies dressing room, which, when the actresses were out on the stage, was the only place of privacy in the studio. There his eagle eye scrutinized the girl some more. Gertrude now figured, being in the studio and having no business there, she was in for a call down, and quick on the defensive she let it be known she was only visiting her sister, she didn't want to work in the pictures, she had a good job as a dancer in vaudeville with Gertrude Hoffmann—dancing was what she loved most of all, and, well, "*Well, who are you?*" asked Gertrude.

"*I'm the director down here, I'm Mr. Griffith.*" As far as Gertrude was concerned, Mr. Griffith was entirely without honor even in a picture studio. "*So you dance,*" said he, "and *you don't want to work in pictures. Well, come down tomorrow anyhow, I want to make a test of you. And I am going over tonight to see your show.*" "*Well, all right,*" said Gertrude with tolerance, "*but I must get on home now. I have to have dinner with my family.*" (If one so young could be bored, Gertrude Bambrick was just that thing.) "*I'll send you home in my car,*" said Mr. Griffith, which frightened little Gertrude almost to pieces and which would have frightened her more had she known that the car was a gorgeous white Packard lined with red leather. But in she hopped, nevertheless, and when she arrived home, and her mother opened the door, and saw a huge touring car of colors white and red, in the days when any kind of a touring car was a conspicuous vehicle, mother said, "*Now don't you ever do that again—come home here in a car like that for all the neighbors to talk about.*" Gertrude promised she wouldn't. That evening she went to her show like a good little girl and did her bit, and Mr. Griffith and Eddie Dillon sat out front. To show how much he liked her work, D. W. Griffith's big white touring car next morning, entirely unexpected, drove up again to the Bambrick home. Gertrude had to forego her morning sleep that day—the neighbors must not see that rakish motor car outside the house again any longer than was necessary. "*What kind of girls will the neighbors think I have, anyhow?" said Mrs. Bambrick, very much annoyed at the insistent person who had sent the car. To such extremes Mr. Griffith went to land a new personality—particularly if that personality was so wholly indifferent to him and his movies as Miss Gertie was. But Gertie was pretty and graceful, and pictures were just arriving at the place where it was thought dancing could be photographed fairly well and cabaret scenes might be introduced to liven things up, now that picture production was advancing toward the spectacle. The next day little Gertrude had her "test" and sat around, and looked on, and felt lonesome, until she suddenly spied an old friend who had been with her in Gertrude Hoffmann's dancing chorus. Gertrude called out, *Oh, hello, Sarah*." But Sarah [Blanche] Sweet, since become Blanche Sweet, only looked blankly at the new girl. Oh, the fear that gripped at the possibility of a new rival! Mr. Griffith was "getting it (noticed her behavior)," and he wasn't going to stand for it, so he spoke, "*Blanche, you know Gertie Bambrick,*" at which Blanche capitulated.

"Little Mary" returned to Biograph. From "Imp," in the fall of 1911 she had gone over to the Majestic, where she and Owen put in a brief season. Then back to Biograph she came, but without Owen. He went to Victor with Florence Lawrence.

Mary Pickford was now so firmly entrenched that she had no fear of bringing other little girls to the studio. And so, on her invitation, one day came a-visiting two sisters, one, decidedly demure, the other, decidedly not. Things were quiet in the theater and Mary saw no reason why, when they could find a ready use for the money, her little friends shouldn't make five dollars now and then as well as the other extra people. Mr. Griffith rather liked the kids [Dorothy and Lillian Gish] that Mary had brought—they were little and slinky. He liked the elder [Lillian Gish] the better of the two, she was quiet and reserved. Dorothy was too forward. She even dared call the big director "a hook-nosed kike," disregarding completely his pure Welsh descent. The little Gish sisters looked none too prosperous in mama's homemade dresses. I'll say for the stage mamas of the little Biograph girls that they did their bit. Mrs. Smith would sometimes make her child a new dress overnight, and Mary would walk in on a bright morning sporting a new pink frock of Hearn's best gingham, only to make Gertrude Robinson feel so orphaned, her mama seemingly the only one who had no acquaintance with a needle. Lillian and Dorothy Gish just melted right into the studio atmosphere without causing a ripple. For quite a long time they merely "extra-ed" in and out of the pictures. Especially Dorothy—Mr. Griffith paid her no attention whatever, and she cried because he wouldn't, but he wouldn't, so she just kept on crying and trailed along. But she let out an awful howl when Gertie Bambrick was put on a guaranty and she wasn't. Their introduction to Biograph had happened the very same day. Lillian didn't mind so much, as she was still full of stage ambitions. When the company left for California, Lillian went back to the stage as a fairy in *The Good Little Devil* with Mary Pickford. Dorothy paid her own fare to the coast. That was how popular she was just then. It was going to be a "big time" for Gertie Bambrick and Dorothy Gish in Los Angeles, away from home and mothers. They ducked to the Angelus Hotel to be by themselves, and not to be bothered by elders and fuss-budgets. They had an idol they would emulate, and wanted to be alone where they could practice. The idol was Mabel Normand.

Could they be like Mabel Normand, well, then they would be satisfied with life. So bright, so merry, so pretty, oh, could they just become like Mabel! Perhaps cigarettes would help. They bought a box. And at a grocery store, they bought—shush—a bottle of gin. Almost they would have swallowed poison if it would have helped them to realize their youthful ambition. But their light had led them only as far as gin, and this they swallowed as a before-dinner cocktail, a whole teaspoonful which they drank right out of the teaspoon. Yes, Mabel Normand was the most wonderful girl in the world, the most beautiful, and the best sport. Others have thought of Mabel Normand as these two youngsters did. Daring, reckless, and generous-hearted to a fault, she was like a frisky young colt that would brook no bridle. The quiet and seemingly demure little thing is the one who generally gets away with things. The gay life of Dorothy and Gertrude was short-lived. Their first night of revelry on Los Angeles's Gay White Way was their last. Up in their room, the night of arrival, they had planned their evening, dinner in the grill, the movies afterward, the grill again as a finish. They put up their hair, they slipped their skirts to the hip, the jacket just covering the lowered waistline, and the lengthened skirt the legs. So they sallied forth. Their program was well-nigh fulfilled, they finished with two-thirds of it. As they were leaving Clune's Auditorium they were apprehended by two men, David Griffith and Dell Henderson, who, having been out scouting for the youngsters all evening, were just beginning to get seriously worried over their disappearance. Mr. Griffith had made Mr. and Mrs. Henderson responsible for the girls, and at his suggestion they had already found an apartment for them—not only in the same house with themselves, but on the same floor, and, adjoining. All the fun was gone out of life. This arrangement would be worse than boarding school. But it got worse still. Sister Lillian, at Mary Pickford's suggestion, decided she'd return to the movies, and so she and mother came on to Los Angeles. That meant Dorothy and Gertrude would be transferred to Mother Gish's care, where their bubbling spirits and love of noisy innocent fun would be frowned upon by the non-approving eyes of the more sober elder sister.

Things became more complicated when Marshall Neilan began paying ardent attentions to little Gertrude. Marshall had fallen in love with Gertrude from seeing her on the screen, and he told Allan Dwan with whom he had worked at the American Film Company in Santa Barbara that he was going to marry the cute little kid. In the fall of 1912 the funny little hop-skip girl [Mae Marsh] had arrived on the scene in New York. When he got back to the city, Mr. Griffith had found need for her, and he fussed, and finally Mr. Hammer told him to send for her. Two tickets were accordingly rushed west to Los Angeles, one for Mae and one for Mae's mama. In due time two members of the Marsh family arrived. The day they reached the East the company was working outside at some place with a meaningful name like "Millville," where we took small country-town stuff. The two Marshes were so excited when they got off the train in New York and dashed to the studio at 11 East Fourteenth Street and found the company working outdoors that they departed immediately for "Millville." They must get right on location. So to "location" they hied (went quickly). And when they had fluttered onto the scene, and Mr. Griffith looked up and saw his Mae, and not his Mae's mama, but the fair Marguerite, Mae's sister, he was pretty mad about it. Marguerite Loveridge, as soon as sister, Mae's star began to rise in the movie heavens, changed her name to "Marguerite Marsh" but to her intimates she became "Lovey Marsh." Little Mae Marsh back on the job did a lot of extra work before she got a part. Mr. Griffith worked hard with her, especially when a scene called for a sudden transition from tranquility to terrible alarm. But a bright idea came to him. He had noticed in battle scenes that young Mae became terribly frightened, so when he didn't have war's aid to get the needed expression of fright, without her knowledge he would have a double-barreled shotgun popped off a few feet from her head, and the resultant exhibition of fear would quite satisfy the exacting director. Mae Marsh's first hit was in *Sands O' Dee*, a part that Mary Pickford had been scheduled to play, and there was quite a to-do over the change in cast. But it was the epochal *Man's Genesis* that brought her well to the front, as it did also Bobby Harron. In the parts of "Lilly White" and "Weak Hands" their great possibilities were discerned, with no shadow of doubt. *Man's Genesis* was produced under the title *Primitive Man*, and Mr. Griffith and Mr. Dougherty had an awful time because Doc said he couldn't see the title and he couldn't see the story as a serious one—as a comedy, yes! But Mr. Griffith was determined it should be a serious story, and he did it as such, although he changed the animal skin clothing of the actors to clothes made of grasses. For if the picture were to show the accidental discovery of man's first weapon, then the animal skins would have had to be torn off the animal's body by hand, and that was a bit impossible. So, Mae and Bobby dressed in grasses knotted into a sort of fabric. *Man's Genesis* wrote another chapter in picture history. It *was* taken seriously by the public, as was meant, and every picture company started right off on a movie having some version of the beginning of man. For Mr. Griffith it was the biggest thing he had yet done, and one of the most daring steps so far made in picture production. Again, against great opposition David had put it over, not only on his studio associates, but on the entire motion picture world. Besides *Man's Genesis*, our most talked of picture of the winter—our biggest spectacle—was *The Massacre*. It was taken at San Fernando. There were engaged for it several hundred cavalry men and twice as many Indians. A city of tents, as well as the two large ones, similar to the ones of the year before, was built outside the borders of the town. There was so much preparation, due to the magnitude of the production, that the secrecy usually attending a Biograph picture did not hold in this case, and the village of San Fernando, two miles away from the place of the picture, declared a holiday. The townspeople having found out just when the raid on the Indian village and the slaughter of the men and women of the tribe was to take place, closed up shop and school, and swarmed out to within a safe distance of the riding and shooting incidental to Custer's Last Fight, and spent the day in the enjoyment of new thrills. There was a two weeks's fight over a subtitle in *The Massacre*—by the scrappers Mr. Griffith and Mr. Dougherty. David never used a script, and a subtitle never was written until he was convinced that one was necessary to elucidate a situation. A picture finished, at its first running we would watch for places where the meaning seemed not sufficiently clear, where we doubted if the audience would "get" it. And in such a place in the film, a title would be inserted.

So, *The Massacre* finished, and being projected, this scene was reached.—Horses with riders dashing madly down the foreground, the enemy in pursuit, then the riders dismounting and using the horses as a barricade, shooting over them.—Here arose the disagreement about the subtitle. Mr. Griffith wanted to insert a caption "Dismounting for Defense." Mr. [Lee] Dougherty said, "*The audience will know that is what they are doing.*" But Mr. Griffith was not so sure about it, so he said "*Now I think, I'd just like to have the title, they may not know what I am trying to show.*" "*Yes, they will,*" said Doc. Even Mr. Kennedy was swept into the debate. As the argument continued his morning greeting became, "*Well, are you still at it, you Kilkenny cats?*" The title went in. How it would improve some pictures in these days to have two weeks of conversation over a subtitle. How a good old row with the whole force would perk things up for some directors, for too many of them, poor things, have had their pictures "yes-ed" to death by the fulsome praise of their assistants, the "yes-sirs" who, grouped in friendly intimacy about their director, have only one answer when he says, "*Do you like that scene?*" "*Oh, yes, sir, the scene is wonderful.*" "*Do you like that title?*" "*Yes, sir, the title is great.*" But that is how the "yes sirs" hold their jobs! Before the year 1912 ended, Lionel Barrymore had been acquired. His plunge movie-ward was inauspicious. "*Who's the new man?*" "*That's John Barrymore's brother.*" "*Never heard of him—is he an actor?*" "*No, he's an artist, just back from Paris, been studying painting,*" answered the wise guys. On the return trip east this winter, a stopover was made at Albuquerque to secure legitimate backgrounds for some Hopi Indian pictures. One, especially atmospheric, was *A Pueblo Legend* with Mary Pickford.

□□□□□□□□□□

It was being hinted in the spring of 1913 that Biograph was having a change of heart about the secrecy regarding their players, and that they might end it. Contrary to the policy of other companies, their scheme was not to give the popular players the first publicity—but the directors and cameramen.

D. W. Griffith would thus head the honor list—his name to become identified with a certain class of strong and highly artistic drama, Dell Henderson, farce comedies, Tony O'Sullivan, melodrama, Billy Bitzer, photography, lastly—the actors. The Biograph had always held to the policy that they were an "institution," and as such, the value of their pictures did not depend on an individual. Sufficient, that it was a "Biograph." Apparently, they now felt they had reached a place so firmly fixed in public esteem through the fine quality of their pictures, that giving credit to individuals could not in any way react on them. So D. W. Griffith became the first Biograph star. Biograph's policy he afterwards took to himself. He is still the "star" of his productions. His actors continue as "leading people" as long as they stay with him. And when they go on to bigger money and names in bigger type with other companies and under other directors, some succeed and some do not. Mary Pickford was one who did. In the picture world, especially abroad, big things were now happening. *Quo Vadis*, a great spectacle, splendidly acted, had been produced in Italy by the Societa Italiana Cines, in three acts of four reels. It came to America and had a run in a Broadway theater. From France, this same time, April, 1913, the steamer *La Touraine* arrived in America bringing *Les Miserables* in four sections and twelve reels. *The Miracle*, which Morris Gest presented in the year of 1924 in the Century Theatre, New York, as a pantomime, had been filmed by Joseph Menchen and was shown at the Park Theatre, New York, in February, 1913. It was a "filmed pantomime" (not a moving picture drama), based on the Wordless Mystery Play which, under the direction of Max Reinhardt, had had a wonderful run at the Olympic Theatre in London. A reviewer said of it, "*What was seen and heard last night only went to emphasize that the moving picture under certain conditions, conditions like those that prevailed last night, may be capable of providing entertainment to be taken seriously by audiences which have never seen the inside of an electric theatre.*" Then Eugene Sue's *Wandering Jew* came over, the work of the Roma Film Company. In our own country, Helen Gardner in her own productions was appearing as *Cleopatra* and like characters. The Vitagraph started on a trip around the world with Clara Kimball Young to do a picture in each country visited, but that rather fell by the wayside, Miss Young, however, had somewhat contented herself with having charming "still" photos taken in costume in each country on their route, when the company reached Paris, Vitagraph cabled for the actors to come home. Kalem had already made some beautiful pictures in Ireland, and in Egypt had made *From the Manger to the Cross*, under Sidney Olcott. Vitagraph answered an inquiry as to when they made *Macbeth* by saying they "*made it so long ago they wanted to forget it in these days (1913) of high art production.*"

Keystone Comedies were coming along, directed by Mack Sennett, featuring the two famous detectives, Mack Sennett and Fred Mace. In these comedies Mabel Normand began to daredevil. Henry Lehrman joined Sennett. Hal Reid, Wally Reid's father, was directing Reliance Pictures, *Traffic in Souls*, written by Walter MacNamara and directed by George Loane Tucker, opened at Weber's Theatre, Twenty-Ninth Street and Broadway, at twenty-five cents the seat. People clamored for admission, with thousands turned away. So Biograph, concluding to get into the march of things, ordered posters for twelve of their players whose names they would make public. "David Belasco Griffith" became Mr. Griffith's nom-de-moving-pictures. It was a time of tremendous ambitions to him. In California, during that winter, was filmed his "masterpiece"—*Mother Love*—seven hundred feet over one reel. Mr. Griffith refused to have it the conventional length, refused to finish it in a stated time, refused to consider expense, introducing a lavish cabaret scene, costing eighteen hundred dollars exclusive of salaries. Miss Bambrick arranged the dances and coached the dancers. Mr. Griffith said of it, "*If it serves no other use, it will teach cafe managers in the interior how to run a cafe.*" There was also *Oil and Water* in which Blanche Sweet surprised both exhibitors and fans by her splendid work in an unfamiliar role. It was strange that the one woman in whom Mr. Griffith had seen the least promise came to play the most important roles in his Biograph pictures. Strange also that Mary Pickford, who had played in so many more pictures than any of his stars, and was by far the most popular of them all, never played in a big Griffith picture. Before the end of the season much curiosity was abroad as to what David Griffith was up to.

Way out to the wilds of Chatsworth he was beating it day by day—this remote spot having been chosen to represent the plains of Bethulia. For the story told in a book of the Apocrypha of "Judith" and "Holofernes" was the big thing Mr. Griffith was doing, and being so secretive about it, he had aroused everybody's curiosity. Blanche Sweet played the lead in this picture—*Judith of Bethulia*—Mr. Griffith's most pretentious movie so far, and his "Old Biograph" swan song. Henry Walthall and the late Alfred Paget were the male leads. How hard and how patiently the director worked with the temperamental Miss Sweet. For hours one day he had been trying to get some feeling, some warmth out of her, until the utter lack of response got his goat. So, with bended knee he went after the fair lady and he gently but firmly kicked her off the stage—just politely kneed her off. Then, as was his wont, he burst forth in song, apparently oblivious of the situation. It was now Blanche's turn to worry. She backed up on to the stage and over to her discouraged director. He escaped her—stretching his arms and singing louder than ever he took large strides away from her. Finally, the penitent reached him, and on her bended knees begged, "*Please, Mr. Griffith, please take me back.*" When he thought she had begged hard enough he took her back, and he got results for the rest of that day. *Judith*, owing to expensive sets, cost thirty-two thousand dollars, but that was not advertised as a point of interest in the picture. Much excitement prevailed over *Judith*—D. W. Griffith's first four-reeler. It was shown to financiers. Wall Street was to be brought into intimate conversation. The old days and the old ways of 11 East Fourteenth Street, how brief they had been! Those vital Biograph days under the Griffith regime, how soon to pass! For when, late in the winter of 1912, the company left for the West Coast studio, they said goodbye to the nursery, and to the intimate days and the pleasant hours of their movie youth. The big new studio up in the Bronx was now finished, with two huge stages—one artificially lighted, and one a daylight studio. There was every modern convenience but an elevator. Of course, one director couldn't utilize so much studio, so while Mr. Griffith was still in California and without saying anything to him about it, the Biograph Company made a combine with Klaw and Erlanger by which all the Klaw and Erlanger plays were to be turned over for Biograph production in three, four, and five-reel pictures.

Mr. Griffith didn't fancy the idea—he felt also that Biograph might have consulted him before closing the deal. There was nothing to interest David in supervising other directors's movies or in giving them the "once over" in the projection room. After watching the other fellow's picture for a while, even though he'd be considering it very good work, he'd yawn and declare, "*Well, it's a hell of a way to earn a living.*"

But that slant never occurred to him when watching his own pictures. But a growing restlessness was noticeable, threats to leave were in the air, rumors floated all about. However, he lingered through the summer, a busy one, as in those introductory months the new studio had to be got thoroughly into a moving and functioning affair. Among the many to whom it gave opportunities was Marshall Neilan. For his years young Mr. Neilan hadn't missed much. At the age of fourteen he had run away from Los Angeles, his home, to Buffalo. There he washed cars for a living—which he probably didn't mind much, for it enabled him to satisfy somewhat his fascination for mechanics. Then, back in Los Angeles once more, he got a job as chauffeur for a kindly person, a Colonel Peyton, who also sent him to the Harvard school in Los Angeles. From chauffeuring to the movies was then but a natural step. For Marshall, a nice-looking Irish boy with Irish affability soon had a "stand" at the Van Nuys Hotel, which was a wonderful way to meet the movie people. Alice Joyce it was who inveigled him. She kept asking him, "*Why don't you come on in?*" It was just like an invitation to go swimming.

So, he took the plunge via Kalem, but not until after he had become manager of the Simplex Automobile Company in Los Angeles. When the Biograph Company returned east after that winter in which young Neilan had met his heart's desire, he wrote to New York to ask Mr. Griffith for a job. Mr. Griffith asked Miss Bambrick if it was her wish to have Marshall come on, but

Gertrude wasn't so anxious. David had him come just the same. The Klaw and Erlanger pictures, especially *Men and Women* and *Classmates*, gave Marshall Neilan his big chance. He soon fell into the producing ranks, where recognition came quickly. And he married his Gertrude. Marshall Neilan Jr., is now nine years old. But they didn't live happily forever after. Many years ago they parted. Just recently Mr. Neilan married Blanche Sweet.

By fall, with four and five companies working, there were so many actors that it wasn't interesting at all anymore. There was Millicent Evans and Georgie [Georgia] O'Ramey, Louise Vale, Travers Vale, Louise Orth, Jack Mulhall, Thomas [Lockyer] Jefferson, Lionel Barrymore, Franklin Ritchie, Lily Cahill, Donald Crisp, Dorothy Bernard, Edwin August, Alan Hale, William [Winter] Jefferson—oh, slews and slews of new ones, besides the old guard minus Mary Pickford. From Chatsworth's lonely stretches and prehistoric atmosphere to the spic-and-span-ness and atmosphere-less Bronx studio came *Judith of Bethulia* to receive its finishing touches. *Judith* was about the last of Blanche Sweet in anything as pretentious directed by Mr. Griffith. Mae Marsh was coming along and so was Lillian Gish. Lillian was beginning to step some, and it was interesting to watch the rather friendly rivalry between the three, Blanche, and Mae, and Lillian. Dorothy Gish was still a person of insignificance, but she was a good sport about it, a likable kid, a bit too perky to interest the big director, so her talents blushed unnoticed by Mr. Griffith. In *The Unseen Enemy* the sisters made their first joint appearance. Lillian regarded Dorothy with all the superior airs and graces of her rank. At a rehearsal of *The Wife*, of Belasco and De Mille fame, in which picture I played the lead, and Dorothy the ingenue, Lillian was one day an interested spectator. She was watching intently, for Dorothy had, had so few opportunities, and now was doing so well, Lillian was unable to contain her surprise, and as she left the scene she said, "Why, Dorothy is good, she's almost as good as I am." Many more than myself thought Dorothy was better—for she was that rare thing—a comedienne, and comediennes in the movies have been scarcer than hen's teeth.

She proved what she could do when she got her first real chance as the bob-haired midinette (seamstress) in *Hearts of the World*. Four or five companies working on the big stage these days made things hum like a three ring circus. From the dressing rooms a balcony opened that looked down on the studio floor, and here Blanche Sweet could often be seen, her feet poked through the iron rails of the balcony, her elbows resting on the railing, her chin cupped in the hollow of her hands, her eyes bulging as she watched every move the director made. For Blanche was worried. Would Lillian or Mae be chosen to play in the next big picture? Mr. Griffith kept all the girls worried.—All but Mary Pickford.—She was the only one who dared demand.

With Mother, Mary came up to the new studio to see what she could put over in the way of a job. She'd now a legitimate reason for making herself costly. In January, 1913, Miss Pickford made a second appearance on the dramatic stage under David Belasco's wing. On her opening, the papers said that the success of Miss Pickford as the little blind princess was so marked that it practically precluded her return to the screen. Adolph Zukor had followed up his first Famous Players picture, the four-reel *Queen Elizabeth*—with James K. Hackett in *The Prisoner of Zenda*—and Mrs. Fiske [Minnie Maddern Fiske] in *Leah Kleschna*. Astute business man that he was, as soon as *The Good Little Devil* closed, he secured the play for the screen with the dramatic company intact and Mary as a Famous Player. No, her dramatic success would not preclude her return to the screen. It would merely fortify her with great assurance in making her next picture contract. I am told it happened thus, Mother and Mary bearded the lion in his den. "*Well, what are you asking now?*" queried Mr. Griffith. "*Five hundred a week,*" answered Mrs. Smith. "*Can't see it. Mary's not worth it to me.*" "*Well, we've been offered five hundred dollars a week and we're going to accept the contract, and you'll be sorry someday.*" They could go ahead and accept the contract as far as Mr. Griffith was concerned. Indulging in his old habit of walking away while talking, he brought the interview to an end, calling back to the insistent mother, "*Three hundred* dollars is all I'll give her. Remember, I made her." And so the Famous Players secured Mary Pickford for a series of features, the first of which was *In the Bishop's Carriage*. But whether Mr. Griffith has ever been sorry, nobody knows but himself. Kate Bruce, the saintly "Brucie" to so many, pillowed in her lap or on her shoulder by turns, all the feminine heads of sufficient importance, and at times, with her arm about me, it was even "Oh, dear Mrs. Griffith." But Miss Bruce was thoughtful, indeed, for her little room often made night lodging, when we had an early morning call, for the girl whose home was distant.

Dorothy West, who lived in Staten Island, often accepted Miss Bruce's hospitality. For Lillian Gish, "Brucie" had an especially tender heart. Miss Gish, at this time, affected simple, straight, dark blue and black dresses. She had long ago reached the book-carrying stage, being one of Mr. Griffith's most ambitious girls. Many times she'd arrive at the studio an hour or more ahead of time and have Billy Bitzer make tests of her with different make-ups. With a tight little hat on her head, and a red rose on the side of it from which flowed veils and veils, and a soulful expression in her eyes, Miss Gish was even then, so long ago, affecting the Madonna.—But reclining in the arms of "Brucie," purring *"Brucie, do you still love me?"*—that was the perfect picture of the fair Lillian those days. And Brucie's reply came in honeyed words, *"Oh, you sweet, little innocent golden haired darling."* Then turning to the girl sitting next her on the other side, she'd say, *"You know this girl needs to be protected from the world, she's so innocent and so young."* She had a strong maternal complex, had the maidenly Kate Bruce.—In need of a gown for a picture at this time (the Biograph was just beginning to spend a little money on clothes for the women), Miss Gish spied Louise Orth one day wearing just the very thing her little heart craved.—*"Oh, what a lovely gown you have on. Where did you buy that?"* Madame Frances (Frances Spingold) then had a tiny shop on Seventh Avenue, near the Palace Theatre, Polly Heyman had Bon Marche gloves on one side and Frances had gowns on the other. Frances had just made some thousands of dollars worth of gowns for Valeska Suratt's show, *The Red Rose*, which were so beautiful they won Madame Frances prestige and recognition from Al Woods. Miss Orth had been a member of the Eltinge show for which Madame Frances had made the dresses, which is the long story of how Lillian Gish got her first Frances gown. The Klaw and Erlanger Pictures were going to be "dressed up," and we were being allowed about seventy-five dollars for gowns. Miss Gish's selection at Madame Frances's was price tagged eighty-five dollars, so back to the studio flew Miss Gish.

With as much pep as she had, which wasn't so much, she slunk up to her director and coaxingly said, "*Mr. Griffith, I must have that dress, it's just beautiful, it's just what I must have for the part, and it costs eighty-five dollars.*" "Who in the world ever heard of eighty-five dollars for a dress?" "I don't care—now—I've got to have it." "Don't bother me—it's too expensive—we cannot afford it." Then growing bolder, as she followed him about she reached for his coat tail, and twisting it and shaking it she implored, "*Oh, please, Mr. Griffith, buy me that dress.*" "Will you get away?" "Well, I won't play in the picture if you don't get me that dress—I've got to have it." "All right, for heaven's sake, get the dress—but don't bother me." Lillian got the dress. Occasionally, Miss Gish took advantage of a beauty sleep. On such occasions she seldom arrived before eleven in the morning. And when she went to a party she played the role of the sphinx, and all evening long never spoke. But little Mae Marsh made up for her, she chattered incessantly. Lillian's hope was to come and go without being noticed. She appeared one time at a midnight performance of *Shuffle Along* done up in black veils to the tip of her nose and a fur collar covering her mouth, with only little spots of cheek showing. Dorothy, on the other hand, acting like a real human being, was calling out to her friends, "*Hello there, hello, hello,*" but Lillian, passing an old acquaintance, merely said, "*Forgive me for not stopping and speaking, I don't want anyone to know I am here.*"

But as everybody was awfully busy having a good time and no one seemed to be particularly disturbed by Miss Gish's hiding away, she finally took her hat off and revealed herself. But she came out of her seclusion that time (1920s) she preached in answer to the Reverend John Roach Straton at his church on Fifty-Seventh Street. Someone was needed to answer the Reverend Mr. Straton's knocks on the theatre and its people. Lillian came forward, and she so impressed her brother-in-law, James Rennie, Dorothy's husband, that he arrived late at a Sunday rehearsal of a George M. Cohan show. In perfect Sunday morning outfit, striped pants and gloves and cane he burst upon the rehearsal and quite breathlessly spluttered, "*Please forgive me for being late, but I have just heard my sister-in-law preach a sermon, and never in my life have I heard anything so inspiring in a church. Don't go very often. More in Lillian than one suspects.*"

Mr. Cohan gave himself time to digest Mr. Rennie's outburst, and then went on with the rehearsal.—Inevitable the parting of the ways. Though the last word as to modern equipment, the new studio merely chilled.—That atmosphere of an old manse that had prevailed at 11 East Fourteenth Street, did not abide in the concrete and perfect plumbing and office-like dressing rooms at East 175th Street. The last word in motion picture studios brought Biograph no luck. For as a producing unit, after a few short years they breathed their last, and quietly passed out of the picture. When the doors at the old studio closed on our early struggles, when Biograph left its original nursery of genius, was the proper time for Mr. Griffith to have left the company. In the fall, less than a year later, he did.

□□□□□□□□□□

From the old Biograph Stock Company they graduated, scenario writers as well as actors, and here and there they went, filling bigger jobs in other companies, as actors, directors, and scenario editors. And as manager and head director of the Kinemacolor Company went David Miles. Directly upon leaving Biograph, Mr. Miles had spent a short time at the "Imp" with Mary Pickford and her family, [William] King Baggot, George Loane Tucker, Gaston Bell, Isabel Rea [Isabel Rae], and Thomas Ince. Leaving "Imp," he had gone over to Reliance. While at

Reliance, and in need of a handsome young juvenile, there came to mind his friend Gaston Bell. Mr. Bell already was signed up for a ten weeks's stock season in Washington DC with *Caught in the Rain* by William Collier and Grant Stewart, as the opening bill, Julia Dean, the leading lady, Mr. Bell's part that of the dapper Englishman, the [writer] Grant Stewart part. Mr. Miles suggested that Gaston play the needed juvenile in the Reliance Company's movie while rehearsing the opening bill of his Washington stock season in New York, and promised a good movie job when the Washington season ended. Said he'd rush him through at odd hours, so as not to interfere with rehearsals, and finish with him in time for the opening. Well, everything went along fine, and for the last scene Gaston reported beautifully arrayed in a new spring suit purchased especially for his stock opening. Suavely spoke the director, "*Now, Gaston, we have saved this scene for the finish, we must take you out somewhere and run you over.*" "*Take me out and run me over—in my beautiful new suit? Oh, no, you can't.*"

But no one heeded Gaston's distress. Everybody piled in the automobile—after a couple of turns it landed on a quiet street. "*All out.*" The car emptied—camera was soon set up and Mr. Bell shown the place where he was to be run over. These were amateur days in fake auto killings and injuries, but they did the "running over" to the director's satisfaction and Gaston's, as he escaped with no damage to his clothes or himself. But Gaston had reckoned without a thought of static. How many hours of anguish "static" caused us—static, those jiggly white lines that sometimes danced and sometimes rained all over the film. Early next morning his phone rang—Mr. Miles on the wire. "*Awfully sorry, Gaston, but we'll have to take you out and run you over again because there was static.*" So they did it again, and again was Gaston dismissed as finished. It came close on to train time, another phone—ye gods, static again! He'd be bumped from juvenility to old age in this one running over scene, first thing he knew, and hobble onto the stage with cane and crutch, which would never do for his precious little Englishman in *Caught in the Rain*. Well, they ran him over again. This was Saturday.

The following Sunday the company was to leave for Washington. Thinking to cinch things, Mr. Miles offered, should anything be wrong with the scene this last time, to pay Mr. Bell's fare to Washington and his expenses if he would stay in New York over Sunday. "*Wildly extravagant, these picture people,*" thought Mr. Bell, as he departed for Washington with the company. But no sooner was he nicely settled in his hotel, "static" and "being run over" quite forgotten, and all set for his opening—when a long distance came. Mr. Miles on the wire, "*Awfully sorry, Gaston, but there was more static and we will have to take you out and run you over again.*" And before Gaston had time to recover from the shock, the movie director and his camera man were right there in Washington! "*Good night,*" said Gaston, despairingly, to himself. But to Mr. Miles he said, "*Now I'll tell you what you have to do, you must have another actor handy to go on for me tonight, for I cannot take any more chances.*" Well, they took the scene another time, ruining neither Mr. Bell nor his grand new suit, and as this time the scene was static-less, the day was saved for Gaston. But "never again" vowed he. And "never again" vowed the director. David Miles kept good his promise and when Gaston's season in Washington closed, he joined Reliance. There he and George Loane Tucker soon became known as the "Hall Room Boys." For in an old brownstone they shared a third floor back—also a dress suit. And if both boys happened to be going out into society the same night, whoever arrived home first and got himself washed up and brushed up first, had the option on that one tuxedo.

The hall room days of George Loane Tucker were brief. *Traffic in Souls*, the white slave picture that he produced for Universal, put him over. An unhappy loss to the motion picture world was Mr. Tucker's early death, for that truly great picture, *The Miracle Man*, his tribute to the world's motion picture library de-luxe, promised a career of great brilliance. Mr. Tucker had come rightfully by his great talent, for his mother, Ethel Tucker, was an actress of note and a clever stage director also. As leading woman in stock repertoire at Lathrop's Grand Dime Theatre of Boston, she had a tremendous popularity in her time.

And long years afterward, she too went into "the pictures" in Hollywood, for a very brief period. Mr. Tucker's *Miracle Man* brought stardom to its three leading players, Lon Chaney, Betty Compson, and Tommy [Thomas] Meighan. Tommy Meighan's leap to fame was surprising to both friends and family.—For Tommy had been considered not exactly the black sheep of the family, but rather the ne'er-do-well.—During the run of *Get Rich Quick Wallingford*, both being members of the cast, Frances Ring, sister to the lustrous Blanche [Ring] of *Rings on My Fingers* and *In the Good Old Summertime* fame, had married Mr. Meighan, Tommy becoming through this matrimonial alliance the least important member of the Ring family of three clever sisters, Blanche, Frances, and Julie [Ring]. An obscure little Irishman, Tommy trailed along, with a voice that might not have taken him so very far on the dramatic stage. Like weaving in and out the paper strips of our kindergarten mats is the story of the Ring sisters and Tommy. For Los Angeles beckoned, with Blanche headlined at the Orpheum, Frances in stock, and Tommy playing somewhere or other. Blanche and her husband, Charles Winninger, a member of her company, were invited by Louise Orth for a weekend out Las Palmas way. The weekend proved very significant in results, for through their hostess, who was leading woman at the Elko Studios, a meeting between Mr. Winninger and Mr. Lehrman was arranged the next week which led directly to Charlie's signing on the dotted line at the fabulous salary of two hundred and fifty dollars a week—to do comedies. But Charlie's pale blue eyes did not register well enough on the screen, and the comedy note in his characterizations thus being lost, the good job just naturally petered out. Then Miss Ring, who had now taken over one of Los Angeles's show places, on the Fourth of July gave a party—a red, white, and blue party at which were gathered more notables than had as yet ever been brought together at a social function in Los Angeles. It was Broadway transplanted. There were David Belasco, Laura Hope Crews, Charlie Chaplin, Edna Purviance, Julian Eltinge, Geraldine Farrar, Jesse Lasky, Mr. Goldwyn, Wallace and Mrs. Reid, Mr. Morris

Gest, then representative for Geraldine Farrar and Raymond Hitchcock, who viewing from the back piazza the distant lights of Los Angeles was supposed to have said something when he remarked, "*This reminds one of a diamond bar pin.*" It was an illustrious and patriotic party. Before the festivities were over, Mr. Gest unwound the maline (stiff net) scarf from Miss Orth's neck while Charlie Chaplin sang the Spring Song, and Mr. Gest danced on the lawn waving the scarf and crushing the slimy snails that in droves were slowly creeping up to the house. The party was illustrious in that it was here voted that Tommy Meighan would photograph well in pictures, and Mr. Lasky invited him to the studio and offered him, perhaps, fifty dollars a week and he made a hit in his first picture with Geraldine Farrar and was then given a substantial raise. At which Blanche, the astounded sister-in-law said, "*And to think that at times I've had to support that Irishman.*" There had been enough job uncertainty to discourage her, so that she had wondered sometimes whether she would have him on her hands for the rest of her life. Even after Mr. Tommy Meighan's advent into pictures, sister Blanche rather expected, every now and then, that he would be "canned." And so Tommy evolved from a liability into an asset, and became the idol of innumerable feminine hearts. It was a colorful paper mat the Ring family wove. While out at the Elko studio Charlie Winninger, with all his brilliant and sustaining background, had so disastrously flopped, at Mack Sennett's studio another Charlie was very busy thinking out stunts that would make people laugh. For the more people laughed, the more dollars could Charlie Chaplin add to the savings for the rainy day, against which, if he ever got the chance, he would make himself foolproof. For, so I have been told, Charlie Chaplin had known rainy days even when a youngster.

He was only seven when, in a music hall sketch, he made his first theatrical appearance. Later, he toured for some time through the United Kingdom as one of the "Eight Lancashire Lads." There was an engagement with *Sherlock Holmes*, and then the association with Fred Karno in *The Mumming Birds*. To America with Mr. Karno he came, appearing as "Charlot" in the now famous *A Night in an English Music Hall*. When he debarked he was far from being the richest man on the boat. The movies claimed him. He was discovered by Mack Sennett in this way.

Mr. Sennett at this time was busy on the lot out in Los Angeles. He heard of a funny man in an act called *A Night in an English Music Hall* playing at [Oscar] Hammerstein's Victoria Theatre, which used to stand at Broadway and Forty-Second Street, now replaced by the Rialto Motion Picture House. Mr. Adam Kessel and Mr. [Charles] Baumann, the firm for whom Mack Sennett had nightly warmed the Alexandria's leather benches in the hope of landing a job, and for whom he was now producing comedies, were both in California, and so in September, 1913, a wire was sent to Charles Kessel, brother of Adam, to go over to Hammerstein's and get a report on the comedian about whom Mr. Sennett was so anxious. Mr. Charles Kessel, the secretary of the company, heartily approved of the comedian, who was none other than Charlie Chaplin. He thought so well of him that he sent a letter asking Chaplin to come in and see him. This Mr. Chaplin did. Mr. Kessel asked him how he'd like to go into moving pictures. Mr. Chaplin answered that he had never given them any thought. Said Mr. Kessel, "*I've seen you act and like you, but you needn't make any assertions now, nor any answers, but go out and make inquiries as to Kessel and Baumann and if you think well enough of them, well then we'll talk.*" Mr. Chaplin found out that the firm was OK. So Mr. Kessel said, "*I'll give you a contract for a year and gamble with you—I'll give you the same salary that you're getting on the stage.*" "*One hundred and fifty dollars,*" said Mr. Chaplin quickly. He really was getting sixty dollars. "*All right,*" said Mr. Kessel so quickly that Charles as quickly swallowed his Adam's Apple, and regretted he hadn't said more. "*But I don't think I care to change from the stage to the pictures.*" "*Well, our contracts are for fifty two weeks, no Sunday work, no intermissions between pictures, in vaudeville you get thirty-two weeks and you pay your own traveling expenses.*"

Mr. Chaplin said he'd make up his mind and let Mr. Kessel know. So, in about six weeks a letter came from Mr. Chaplin from

Omaha saying he was ready to start. The contract was mailed December 19, 1913, and signed January 2, 1914. *Mabel's Predicament*, a one-reeler, was Charlie Chaplin's first picture. *Dough and Dynamite* the first two-reeler. Mr. Chaplin's success was instantaneous. It also must have been tremendous, for the Keystone Company (Kessel and Baumann) within five months dared to do a comedy five reels in length. When the five-reel comedy was announced, there were many who thought that now surely the picture people were going cuckoo. No one believed an audience would stand for a *five-reel comedy*. They did.

The picture was *Tillie's Punctured Romance*, adapted from the Marie Dressler play, *Tillie's Nightmare*. Marie Dressler was engaged for the picture and for fourteen weeks she received the unbelievable salary of one thousand dollars weekly and fifty percent of the picture, which, released in June, 1914, was one of the sensations of the picture world. All sorts of offers now began coming to Mr. Chaplin. Carl Laemmle was one who was keen to get Charlie under contract, he kept himself informed of Mr. Chaplin's activities even to the social side of his life so that he would know when and where best to set the bait. Out at Sunset Inn, a place by the ocean where movie people then made merry, Charlie Chaplin was to be one of a party. Mr. Laemmle being wised up to it, gave a party of his own the same night, a most expensive and grand party. Well, he would have Charlie's ear for a moment anyhow, and one never could tell. The party in full swing, Mr. Laemmle invited Mr. Chaplin over to his table, and after a few social preliminaries said, "*Let's talk business, I want you to come and work for me.*" But Mr. Chaplin, always a clever business man, answered, "*I'm enjoying myself—I don't want to talk business tonight, I'm on a party.*" Mr. Laemmle was all set to secure the services of the rising young comedian, so he would not be daunted. Charles could talk "party," but *he* would talk "business." Mr. Laemmle offered a little better salary, promised to advertise Chaplin big, and make him a tremendous star. But Mr. Chaplin was too clever for Mr. Laemmle. With a most sweet smile he turned to one of Mr. Laemmle's guests, Louise Orth of the corn yellow hair, and said, "*Gee, that's great music, I like blondes, and I am going to dance with a blonde, may I?*"

It *was* great music, about the first syncopated music with a saxophone heard in that neck of the woods. There was a great horn into which the dancers, if they desired an encore, threw a silver dollar. There needed to be five particularly anxious dancers to get the expensive orchestra to repeat an orchestration.

The dollars clicked down the horn into a sort of tin bucket on the floor below, and the loud jangle of the silver money could be easily heard by the dancers who would listen attentively for jangle number five, and then "On with the dance." As the music finished for the first dance this night, the dancers stopped and with much excitement waited for the click of the silver dollars.

Charlie Chaplin was out for a big time, also he wanted to worry Mr. Laemmle and one thing sure—he was not going to talk business this night. So, he was the first to say, "*This dance is worth an encore,*" and he threw a silver dollar into the horn. It was perhaps the first time Mr. Chaplin had been known to spend money in public either for food or music, for everyone was so tickled and flattered to have him as a guest that he never was given a chance to spend money. So Charlie's Chaplin's silver dollar nearly caused a riot on that dance floor. The guests hooted and screamed and those who knew him well-enough and had been given stray bits of confidence, called out, "*You cannot plant your first dollar now because you've spent it.*" And Mr. Chaplin answered, "*Oh, don't you worry I planted my first dollar some time ago.*" Mr. Chaplin could never squander money—memories of lean days inhibited him from doing that. But he must hold off Mr. Laemmle, and he was enjoying the dance. Two other dollars had joined Charlie Chaplin's first one and clicked their way down the yawning chasm of the brass horn, and then a pause, but just for a second. Grabbing his blonde partner, Mr. Chaplin threw the two needed dollars into the horn's hungry maw, and the moaning saxophone started off again while Mr. Laemmle looked sadly on. He never did secure the screen's greatest funny man. In six months Charlie Chaplin's rise to fame and fortune was phenomenal. Not only had a kind Providence richly endowed him, but he worked very hard, as genius usually does. Even back in those days, Mr. Chaplin often began his day making excursions with the milkman. From the cold gray morning hours of three and four until seven, the two would ramble through the poor districts, and while the milkman would be depositing his bottle of milk, Mr. Chaplin would hobnob with drunks and derelicts, and in the later hours, talk with the little children of the slums, drawing out a story here, getting a new character there, and making the tragic humorous when finally the story was given life on the screen. The story of *The Kid* as Mr. Chaplin and Jackie Coogan told it was nearer the truth than any audience ever guessed. The ups and downs of the movie world! Mack Sennett all dressed up and grouching on a leather settee in the hotel lobby, waiting for his prey! He would not be handed dry, old sandwiches all his days. He was out for steak, red and juicy. He got there and has stayed put. Henry Lehrman patting his inflated chest! He got there, but stayed put the littlest while. Charlie Chaplin, who topped them all, working while others slept, out on excursions with the milkman!—Tommy Meighan of the genial smile and Irish red bloodedness. He got a chance, and the ladies liked him. Nice personality, and good actor, even so. Not alone in the movies is it easier to get there than to stay there. Chance sometimes enters into the first, but to stay there means ears attuned, feet [firmly planted] on the ground, and heaps and heaps of hard work.

◻◻◻◻◻◻◻◻◻◻◻

Late in the summer of 1912 the Kinemacolor Company of America, a subsidiary of the English company, started the production of movies in color at a studio in Whitestone, Long Island. The year of Kinemacolor's endeavor also marks Mr. Griffith's last year with Biograph, for he went to the Mutual with Harry Aitken while I became leading woman with Kinemacolor. Messieurs [Charles] Urban and [George Albert] Smith had rather startled the world with their color pictures of the Coronation of George the V of England, and the Durbar Imperial at Delhi, and even though their pictures were a bit fringy, they were becoming ambitious for honors in color movies along dramatic lines. Great things were achieved in America in the movies, and great things might have been achieved in America in Kinemacolor, but it was destined otherwise. Kinemacolor was fated to be but a brief though fruitful interlude in color photography in the movies, which, for some seemingly mysterious reason, is so long in arriving. Sunshine being imperative for Kinemacolor, Southern California's staple brand could not be denied, and soon the company left its studio in Whitestone and repaired to the modest little town of Hollywood where it took over the Revier Laboratory [Reliance-Majestic Studios] at 4500 Sunset Boulevard. That the place had been used as a studio was not discernible from the front. It was a pretty corner on which, some distance apart, stood two simple cottages, Middle Western in character.

They represented office and laboratory. Dressing rooms and stages of a crudeness comparable to the original Biograph studio were at the back. No fence gave privacy from passersby, but a high board fence, decorated with pictures of foxes and the words "Fox Pictures," protected the lot in the rear. It was not the William Fox of today who thus sought to advertise his trademark and his wares. Another Mr. Fox it was of whom we seem to hear nothing these days. Here Kinemacolor moved in, with David Miles at its head, Jack [Edward] Le Saint, director of the number 2 company, and our old friend Frank Woods making his movie directing debut as teacher to the actors of the number 3 company. For Mr. Woods having tasted movie blood through his little Biograph scenarios and his position as chief reviewer of the movies had grown anxious to plunge more deeply into the swiftly moving waters of reel life. So Mr. Miles opened the way for him. And although Kinemacolor opened up financially to a salary of only seventy-five dollars a week, the Woodses made the most of it, for from that humble beginning in less than ten years they have come to own a town near Barstow, California. They have named it "Lenwood." Charles H. Fleming, who was assistant to David Miles, afterwards became a director and tastefully executed a number of pictures. When the Kinemacolor Company was gathering in what youth and looks and talent it could afford, Mr. Miles, remembering a little deed of kindness, recalled Gaston Bell and took him to Hollywood, and when the much-loved and generous-souled Lillian Russell came out to do some pictures in Kinemacolor, Mr. Bell was rewarded by being made her leading man. Mahlon Hamilton loaned his good looks to the same films. The Russell pictures were used to illustrate "Beauty Talks" in an act in which Miss Russell was headlined on big vaudeville time throughout the United States. Mahlon Hamilton and Gaston were the company's two best "lookers." As to "acting," Mahlon made not a single pretense. He and the company quite agreed as to his dramatic ability. To be so perfectly Charles Dana-ish, and histrionic also, was not expected of one man in those days.

We had not reached the [Rudolph] Valentino or Neil Hamilton age. Mr. Mahlon Hamilton, of late, not quite so Gibsonesque, has become a surprisingly good actor. So, do the years take their toll and yield their little compensations.

The wonderful possibilities of Kinemacolor had not even been scratched when the American subsidiary was formed, for the foreign photographers—English, French, and German—who had "taken" the Coronation and also some picture plays that were produced in southern France, insisted that the close-up was impossible in color. But Mr. Miles, having had Biograph schooling, insisted contrariwise, and after a long and hard scrap with his photographers, he succeeded in inducing them to do as he said. The result proved his contention. The Kinemacolor close-ups were things of great beauty. During its short life, Kinemacolor made some impression, for Dan Frohman after seeing some of the pictures said that *The Scarlet Letter* was the most artistic movie he had seen up to that time. Many distinguished visitors stopped at its Hollywood studio to see the new color pictures.

Madame [Luisa] Tetrazzini, the opera singer, among many others, was tremendously enthusiastic. It has been stated in error that the Kinemacolor pictures were never released. They were very much released, being shown at the New York Theatre

Roof, besides many other theatres in New York, and contracts for their service all through the country were made by the Kinemacolor Company. Things started off with such a bang, we never did get over the shock of the sudden closing. It was one exciting year with Kinemacolor, but it ended suddenly and tragically with the death of the president, Mr. [Henry J.] Brock. While preening our wings for a flight to southern France, a telegram arrived from the New York office announcing the finish of picture production in Kinemacolor. The sudden disruption of the Kinemacolor Company sent a flock of actors and a few directors scouting for new jobs. Frank Woods took up with Universal, only to suffer a six weeks's nightmare. Being unable to turn out the class of stuff wanted, and anticipating what was coming, he resigned, dug up the return half of his Kinemacolor roundtrip ticket, and was not long in New York before he got busy as a freelance, and not so long after that a telephone from D. W. Griffith asked him to become his scenario writer. With great joy he accepted, filling the position with Mr. Dougherty, who was now back at Biograph after a short spasm with Kinemacolor. Right away Mr. Woods and Mr. Griffith got busy on *Judith of Bethulia*, for having produced such a classic, Mr. Griffith wanted some special titling for it. He turned it over to Frank Woods, who phrased the captions in the style of language of the day—the first time that was done. However, it proved too much of a strain for the exhibitors, for they afterward fixed the titles up to suit themselves in good old "New Yorkese." Mr. Griffith's connection with the Mutual Film organization and his association with Harry E. Aitken resulted in the production of such eventful and popular pictures as *The Tell Tale Heart*, *Home, Sweet Home*, *The Escape*, *The Avenging Conscience*, and *The Battle of the Sexes*. The Clara Morris home out on Riverdale Road served as a studio until the 29 Union Square Place was acquired. Billy Bitzer, D. W.'s photographer, went with him in his new affiliation, as also did Frank Woods and Christy Cabanne. As Mr. Griffith's work with the Mutual became organized, one by one he took over his old actors, but he left them working with Biograph until he could put them directly into a picture. So they trailed along, Henry Walthall, Blanche Sweet, James Kirkwood, Mae Marsh, Lillian and Dorothy Gish, Eddie Dillon, and many others. After a short time at the Mutual studio, Mr. Griffith and his company went to California.

At the old Kinemacolor lot they encamped, the Mutual having taken over that studio. The carpenters got busy right away, and soon little one-story wooden buildings crowded to the sidewalk's edge, and the place began to look like a factory. The sprinkling can that had given sustenance to red geraniums and calla lilies was needed no more. Now before the Kinemacolor Company had started work at Whitestone they had held a contract with George H. Brennan and Thomas Dixon for the production in color of Thomas Dixon's *The Clansman*.

The idea was that the dramatic company touring through the Southern States in *The Clansman* would play their same parts before the camera. In these Southern towns all the Southern atmosphere would be free for the asking. Houses, streets, even cotton plantations would not be too remote to use in the picture. And there was a marvelous scheme for interiors. That was to drag the "drops" and "props" and the pretty parlor furniture out into the open, where with the assistance of some sort of floor and God's sunshine, there would be nothing to hinder work on the picture version of the play. But the marvelous scheme didn't work as well as was expected, and eventually the managers decided that trying to take a movie on a fly-by-night tour of a theatrical company was not possible, so the company laid off, to take it properly. They halted for six weeks and notwithstanding the sum of twenty-five thousand dollars were spent—it was a poor picture and was never even put together. Although Thomas Dixon's sensational story of the South turned out such a botch, it was to lead to a very big thing in the near future. Frank Woods, after several others had tried, had written the continuity of this version of *The Clansman*, and had received all of two hundred dollars for the job. That the picturizing of his scenario had proved such a flivver (failure) did not lessen his faith in *The Clansman*'s possibilities. Mr. Griffith was doing some tall thinking. His day of one-and two-reelers having passed, and the multiple-reel Mutual features having met with such success, he felt it was about time he started something new. So, one day, he said to Frank Woods, "*I want to make a big picture. What'll I make?*" With his Kinemacolor experience still fresh in mind Mr. Woods suggested *The Clansman*. With the Dixon story and the play Mr. Griffith was quite familiar as he had heard from his friend Austin Webb, who had played the part of the mulatto "Silas Lynch," about all the exciting times attending the performance of the play—the riots and all—and more he had heard from Claire McDowell, who was also in the show—and more still from Mr. Dixon himself. So David Griffith said to Frank Woods, "*I think there's something to that. Now you call Mr. Dixon up, make an appointment to see him, and you talk it over, but say nothing about my being the same actor who worked for him once.*" So, the meeting was arranged, the hour of the appointment approached, and as Mr. Woods was leaving on his important mission Mr. Griffith gave final parting instructions, "*Now remember, don't mention I'm the actor that once worked for him, for he would not have confidence in me.*" So while Thomas Dixon nibbled his lunch of crackers, nuts, and milk, Mr. Woods, without revealing his little secret, unfolded the mighty plan, "*We are going to sell Wall Street and get the biggest man in the business.*" "*Who?*" "*D. W. Griffith.*" "*Oh, yes, I've heard a lot about him—he used to work for me.*" Mr. Dixon was greatly interested and evinced no hesitation whatever in entrusting his sensational story of the South to his one-time seventy-five dollars a week actor. He'd already taken one sporting chance on it, why not another? Yes, Mr. Griffith could have his *Clansman* for his big picture. Harry E. Aitken, who had formed the Mutual Film Company, had had on his Executive Committee Felix Kahn, brother of Otto Kahn, and Crawford Livingston. They had built the Rialto and Rivoli Theatres. The Herculean task of financing the "big picture," Mr. Aitken presented to Mr. Kahn, and he genially had agreed to provide the necessary cash—the monetary end was all beautifully settled—when the World War entered the arena and Mr. Kahn felt he could not go on. So Mr. Aitken had to finance the picture himself. He financed it to the extent of sixty thousand dollars, which was what *The Birth of a Nation* cost to produce. With legal fees and exploitation, it came to all of one hundred and ten thousand dollars. Mr. Felix Kahn and Mr. Crawford Livingston afterwards offered to help out with fifteen thousand dollars but there were fifteen directors on the executive committee of the Mutual Film, and they overruled the fifteen thousand dollars tender, leaving Mr. Aitken as sole financier.

Mr. Dixon received two thousand five hundred dollars cash and twenty-five percent of the profits. He wanted more cash—wasn't so interested in the profits just then. But afterwards he had no regrets. For it happened sometimes in later days, when the picture had started out to gather in its millions, that Mr. Dixon casually opening a drawer in his desk, would be greeted by a whopping big check—his interest in *The Birth of a Nation*, and one of these times, happening unexpectedly on one such check, he said, "*I'm ashamed to take it*"—a sentiment that should have done his soul good. Well, Mr. Dixon is one who should have got rich on *The Birth of a Nation*, but the one whose genius was responsible for the unparalleled success of the epoch-making picture says he fared like most inventors and didn't get so rich. However, it probably didn't make Mr. Griffith so very unhappy, for so far he has seemingly got more satisfaction out of the art of picture making than out of the dollars the pictures bring. Had the Epoch Company not sold State Rights on the picture when they did, Thomas Dixon's interest would have been fabulous. But as the State Rights privilege was not for life, only for a term of years, now soon expiring, or perhaps expired now, and as up to date the picture has brought in fifteen million dollars, it seems as though there's nothing much to be unhappy about for any of those concerned. One of the State Rights buyers who took a sporting chance on the picture was Louis B. Mayer, who had begun his movie career with a nickelodeon in some place like East or South Boston, borrowing his chairs from an undertaker when they weren't being used for a funeral. Mr. Mayer managed to scrape together enough money to buy the State Rights for New England

and he cleaned up a small fortune on the deal after the owners had figured they had skimmed all the cream off Boston and other New England cities. Oh, well, what's money anyway?

A little while and we all will rest in good old mother earth and if we're lucky perhaps pink and white daisies may nod in the soft spring breezes overhead. Or we may be grand and have a mausoleum, or a shining shaft of stone, or a huge boulder to mark our spot, or perhaps we may just rest in a neat little urn—a handful of ashes.—And what then of the feted days of Mary [Mary Pickford] and Doug [Douglas Fairbanks]?—Of the peals of laughter that rocked a Charlie Chaplin audience?—Of the suspenseful rescue of a persecuted Griffith heroine on the ice blocked river?—Of the storm-tossed career of Mabel Normand? Of the magic city of Hollywood?—And the Hollywooders?—Of the exotic and hectic life of the beautiful stars?—Of the saner careers of the domestically happy?—Who was greatest? Who produced the best pictures? Who was the most popular? Who made the most money? All this will be told of in books reposing on dusty library shelves. Possibly a name alone will be left to whisper to posterity of their endeavor, or tinned celluloid reels shown maybe on special occasions, only to be greeted by roars of laughter—even scenes of tender deathbed partings—so old fashioned will the technique be. But David Wark Griffith's record may yet perhaps shine with the steady bright light of his courage, of his patient laboring day by day, of his consecration to his work, and of his faithful love for his calling, once thought so lowly. And so eventually *The Birth of a Nation* was finished. At the Liberty Theatre in West Forty-Second Street, New York—1915 was the time—it had its premiere—one wholly novel for a moving picture—for it was the first time a movie was presented bedecked in the same fashion as the more luxurious drama, and shown at two dollars per seat. It was not the first picture to be given in a legitimate theatre, however, for Mr. Aitken had previously booked at the Cort Theatre *The Escape*, the picture made from the Paul Armstrong play of the same name. At this first public projection of *The Birth of a Nation*, an audience sat spellbound for three hours. The picture was pronounced the sensation of the season. From critics, ministers, and historians came a flood of testimonials, treatises, and letters on the new art and artists of the cinema. *The Birth of a Nation* remains unique in picture production. It probably never will be laid absolutely to rest, as it pictures so dramatically the greatest tragedy in the history of America, showing the stuff its citizens were made of and the reason why this nation has become such a great and wonderful country. Through the success of *The Birth of a Nation* the two dollar movie was born. But here let there be no misunderstanding, the two-dollar-a-seat innovation in the movies was Harry E. Aitken's idea. He was opposed in it by both, Mr. Griffith and Mr. [Thomas] Dixon, Mr. Dixon becoming so alarmed that he type-wrote a twelve-page argument against it.

However, Mr. Aitken persisted and the result proved him right. The public will pay if they think your show is worth it. Through the success of *The Birth of a Nation*, the sole habitat of the movies was no longer Eighth Avenue, Sixth Avenue, Avenue A and Fourteenth Street—the movies had reached Broadway to stay. D. W. Griffith had achieved that, and had he stopped right there he would have done his bit in the magical development of the motion picture. For though "Bagdad Carpets" fly, and "Ten Commandments" preach, and "Covered Wagons" trek—miles and miles of movies unreel, and some of them awfully fine, they must all acknowledge that the narrow trail that led to their highway was blazed by Mr. Griffith. Whoever might have had a dream that the degraded little movie would blossom into magnificence, now was beginning to see that dream come true. The two-dollar movie was launched, tickets were obtainable at the box office for what future dates one pleased, there were surroundings that made the wearing of an evening dress look quite inconspicuous, serious criticism and sober attention were to be had from the high minded—these were the first stages of the dream's fulfillment. But little we then dreamed that today's picture world was to be like an *Arabian Nights* tale! Kings and Queens and Presidents interested! A University proposed for the study of the motion picture alone!—James M. Barrie consenting to *Peter Pan* in the movies and selecting the "Peter" himself. Anyone who had made such suggestions then would have been put where he could have harmed no one! The wildest flights of fancy hardly visioned a salary of one thousand dollars a day for an actor.—But it came, as everyone now knows, and with the approach of dizzy salaries departed the simple happiness and contentment, and the fun of the old days, when thirty or fifty dollars weekly looked like a small fortune. We had to grow up. It was so written. I, for one, am glad I served in a day when we could afford to be good fellows, and our hearts were young enough and happy enough to enjoy the "gypsying" way of things.

Comments made by Linda Arvidson in her autobiography of news being broadcast like movies across screens began coming true during her lifetime in the form of newsreels, starting in the 1920s. The practice became even more popular in the coming decades, of where events of the day would be shown before screening of movies. Although Arvidson didn't live to see the television era of broadcast news, she seemed to know it was going to happen eventually. Imagine what her reaction would be to present-day streaming of news within seconds after it occurs *or* as it is actually happening around the world.

Afterword

As with the pioneers who braved Western America in covered wagons for decades before trains bridged the gap between the east and west areas of the United States, pioneers from New England traveling to Hawaii had one choice of travel available to them in 1819—the open ocean. How scary must it have been for Lucy Thurston and so many others like her who braved the dangers of traveling for months on the open ocean never knowing if one rogue wave would capsize their world?

It must have seemed ludicrous to many at the time why anyone would do such a thing, but though he lived only a short time among the New England Missionaries, a native from the Hawaiian Islands, Henry Obookiah, inspired courage and despite his death they forged ahead with completing his dream of converting his people to Christianity. Among arriving in the tiny strip of islands in the middle of the vast Pacific Ocean, the hardy group from New England set upon achieving their goal of making sure Obookiah's dreams became reality. Decades later as Lucy Thurston looked back at her life in preparation of writing her memoir she must have marveled at the life she lived which at the time seemed destined to be brief and uneventful. Today, her legacy continues with many descendants, of which several were notable for their own achievements. Her eldest daughter Persis Thurston Taylor was an accomplished artist, her grandson (from her son Asa Jr.) Lorrin Andrews Thurston earned infamy being associated with the 1893 overthrow of Queen Liliuokalani, ending the short-lived Hawaiian Monarchy, and her great-great grandson, (Lorrin's grandson) Thurston Twigg-Smith turned the *Honolulu Advertiser* newspaper into a successful outlet for quality journalism. Lucy's memoir has been reprinted twice (in 1921 and 1934) and featured in many historical volumes about the Hawaiian Islands. Considered one of the most important accounts of nineteenth century Hawaii (before the 1893 overthrow) and of the impact American missionaries attempt to convert native Hawaiians to Christianity—while destroying parts of their history in the process, lessons can still be learned from the mistakes made by missionaries despite their belief they were making the lives of native Hawaiians better. Throughout the Pacific and Africa, attempts to convert native peoples to Christianity were aggressively followed regardless of the consequences. In many cases such behavior led to uprising and tragedy. From what can be observed from Lucy's writings, she genuinely had warm feelings toward native Hawaiians despite eying them with caution initially after being told "stories" from other visitors who had been to the Hawaiian Islands previously. In the end I believe that unlike many so-called Christians today, Lucy was truly trying to follow the teachings in the Bible and not pretending to follow its writings with cherry-picked passages that appealed to her.

    Lucy Thurston passed away in October 1876 and was buried in the Thurston family plot at Oahu Cemetery in the same grave as her late husband. Two of her children and several grandchildren are buried in the Andrews family plot nearby.

    As the era of silent movies began to dominate Hollywood in the late 1910s and early 1920s, many of those who had founded the industry such as Linda Arvidson, retreated to private lives in New York and Pennsylvania. The Griffiths separated during the 1910s and officially divorced in 1936. They had no children. Changes in the silent movie industry continued for a period of ten years, when finally in the late 1920s the arrival of sound spelled the end for many actors who had become successful. Several years before the end of the silent era in 1925, Linda Arvidson penned one of the first accounts of the silent movie industry.

Considered by film historians to be a behind-the-scenes tell-all of the lives of those who created the motion picture industry at the turn of the twentieth century, it couldn't be further from the truth. *When the Movies Were Young* was actually an account of entertainment history being made as seen through the eyes of someone who actually witnessed firsthand events that became the stuff of film lore decades later. Linda Arvidson chose to ignore the gossip and scandalous stories that filled many books of the era, instead focusing on what she saw, not what appeared regularly in newspapers and magazines. So, were there scandals surrounding some of the people mentioned in Linda Arvidson's book? Look on the Internet and you'll see plenty. But seriously, is anyone, famous or not, really able to point fingers at others when their own lives probably has plenty that should never be known of talked about in a book or played out as back street gossip among neighbors. Linda Arvidson should be congratulated in writing a book from her point of view that captured historic events as she saw them taking place at the beginning of the silent movies era—not what she may have heard through idle gossip or accidentally overheard in private conversations among friends.

Linda Arvidson died in July 1949 in New York City at the age of 65 and was buried at Cypress Lawn Memorial Park, at Colma, in San Mateo County, just outside of San Francisco.

Additional Notes

Below are some mini biographies of notable people from the silent movie era mentioned within the pages of *When the Movies Were Young*.

John Barrymore (John Sidney Blythe) was born in February 1882 and died in May 1942. He was a successful actor on screen, radio and stage for most of his life. Barrymore battled an addiction to alcohol from the age of 14 which ruined his career toward the end of his life. Following his death he was buried at Calvary Cemetery in East Los Angeles, but was cremated and later reburied near some of his relatives at the Mount Vernon Cemetery in Philadelphia on the orders of his son in 1980.

Lionel Barrymore (Lionel Herbert Blythe) was born in April 1878 and died in November 1954. He appeared many films from the silent era until the early 1950s. He also appeared on stage and radio during his long career. He is best known as the villainous "Potter" in the classic 1946 film, *It's a Wonderful Life*, directed by Frank Capra. He was a member of famous Barrymore family, of which his siblings Ethel Barrymore and John Barrymore were equally well-respected. He is buried at the Calvary Cemetery in the East Los Angeles area of Los Angeles, California.

Richard Barthelmess was born in May 1895 and died in August 1963. He began his career as a child appearing mostly in stage productions. He later appeared in two well-known movies directed by D. W. Griffith, *Broken Blossoms* and *Way Down East*. With the end of silent films at the close of the 1920s, his career went the way of most of his contemporaries. Barthelmess is also known for being one of the founders of the Academy of Motion Picture Arts and Sciences in 1927. He is buried at the Ferncliff Cemetery and Mausoleum in Westchester County, New York.

Gaston Bell (George Gaston Bell) was born in Boston in September 1877 and died in Woodstock, New York in December 1963. He was a stage actor who also was featured in silent movies during the 1910s. He worked with several film companies, among them the Majestic, Kinemacolor, Lubin and General Film companies before returning to working on stage. He eventually retired to a small town in New York where he managed an inn.

Billy Bitzer (Gottfried Wilhelm Bitzer) was well-known for his association with director D. W. Griffith. He was born in Massachusetts in April 1872 and died in Los Angeles in April 1944. Once the silent movies were replaced by sound movies Bitzer's career reached a standstill like most of his contemporaries, including Charlie Chaplin and Mary Pickford. His autobiography was posthumously published in 1973. Bitzer was buried at the Cedar Grove Cemetery in Flushing, Queens, New York City.

Charlie Chaplin (Charles Chaplin Jr.) was born in April 1889 and died in December 1977. Chaplin was one of the silent movie era's biggest stars. He was extremely talented but dealt with many controversies with sidelined his brilliant career later in his life. He wrote several books about his experiences in the movie industry and was the subject of numerous trashy tell-all biographies as well. In 1992 a movie version of his life (based on his autobiography) was made starring Robert Downey Jr.

Dorothy Gish was born in March 1898 in Ohio and died in Italy in June 1968. She portrayed characters in silent movies that were unlike her, as Gish led somewhat of an adventurous life. Very outspoken in her views, her comments sometimes caused issues with others. Gish married a Canadian actor in December 1920 but the marriage ended in 1935 without children. Unlike her sister Lillian Gish, Dorothy's movie career ended with the end of the silent film era and for the remainder of her life focused mostly on stage acting. Gish is buried at the Saint Bartholomew's Episcopal Church in Manhattan, New York City, New York.

Lillian Gish was born in October 1893 in Ohio and died in New York in February 1993. She had one of the longest film careers in the entertainment industry and continued working right up to the last years of her life. She successfully transitioned from silent movies into sound pictures and made numerous television movies in the 1970s and 1980s. She was mentioned by Mary Astor in Astor's 1959 autobiography for helping Astor get into the movie business during the early 1920s. Gish wrote two accounts of her life as well was the subject of numerous biographies. Lillian Gish is buried at the Saint Bartholomew's Episcopal Church in Manhattan, New York City, New York.

D. W. Griffith (David Wark Griffith) was born in Kentucky in January 1875 and died in California in July 1948. Notable for being one of the most distinguished film directors from the silent movie era, Griffith was a hard act to follow. Originally starting his career as an actor he transitioned to directing and never looked back. Griffith married actress Linda Arvidson in 1906 and later briefly married actress Evelyn Baldwin in the 1930s. His career slumped once the silent movie era ended but he remained a respected member of the film community until his death. His most famous movie *The Birth of a Nation* (1915) was heralded as an achievement of excellent filmmaking while also being criticized for its sanitized depiction of the hate group, Ku Klux

Klan. He is also credited with being one of the founders of United Artists in 1919. Griffith is buried at the Mount Tabor Methodist Church Graveyard in Kentucky just outside of Louisville.

Robert Harron was born in April 1893 in New York City and died in September 1920 in the same city. Often referred to as Bobby, he gained acclaim as one of D. W. Griffith's favorite actors throughout the 1910s. Harron started working for Griffith as an errand boy but eventually venturing into acting, appearing in countless films over a short period of time. He worked often with Mae Marsh and Lillian Gish, alongside other established stars of the time. Harron endured much tragedy in his short life but somehow managed to overcome it all to become quite successful in a time when silent movies constantly were adapting to changes in the industry. Having appeared in *Enoch Arden*, *Birth of a Nation*, *Intolerance*, and *True Heart Susie* among many—his future seemed bright—but it was not to be. Exactly what happened on September 5, 1920 remains a mystery to this day. Harron had traveled from Los Angeles to New York to attend the premiere of *Way Down East* and checked into the Hotel Seymour as soon as he arrived. Various accounts of his death were reported, but none proven. The standard account was that as he was unpacking his suitcase inside his hotel room his gun fell from a jacket pocket and hit the floor—firing a bullet into his chest. From reports given at the time, Harron called for help and was taken to the hospital where he told several people what had happened. Nevertheless stories began circulating that Harron had tried to kill himself over his fading career. No viable proof has ever been found to verify he was depressed or intended to kill himself. Exactly how and why Harron obtained the gun remains a mystery. One version told was that he brought the gun with him because of family troubles at his home in Los Angeles. Another version of the story has Harron buying a gun from a homeless man at some point after arriving in New York City. Actresses Miriam Cooper, Dorothy Gish and her sister Lillian Gish, all denied Harron attempted to kill himself. His friend, Victor Heerman, who attended the premiere of *Way Down*

East with Harron, also denied the claims. It should be noted that after being shot, Harron was still conscious, so, if he truly had intended to kill himself, he certainly could have shot himself yet again, this time in the heart or head. For that reasoning, the suicide narrative seems questionable. For most, what happened was possibly one of two scenarios. The gun fell out of his jacket as he unpacked his suitcase and he was shot accidentally or he was depressed over his fading career according to tabloid gossip and planned to take his own life at some point—but it accidentally discharged as he was cleaning the gun while he held it close to his chest. In the autopsy report, the coroner stated there was gunpowder residue on his clothing. If that statement is accurate it would verify the "bullet accidentally discharging as he was cleaning the gun" story. Harron was a devout Catholic and told a family priest he had not tried to kill himself when asked. Those who knew him said he wouldn't lie about something like that because of his upbringing. Other theories that circulated implied his friend Victor Heerman actually shot Harron in a scuffle and then he and Harron tried to cover up what happened to avoid a scandal. But that scenario sounds like it was created from a present-day sleazy tabloid reporter's mind. Harron died shortly afterwards from his wound and was buried in his family's plot at the Calvary Cemetery in Queens, New York City, New York. He was fondly remembered by close friend Lillian Gish decades later in taped conversations about her long-ago silent film career.

Dell Henderson (George Delbert Henderson) was born in July 1877 in Canada and died in December 1956 in California. He enjoyed a long association as an actor with D. W. Griffith and as a producer for Keystone Studios. Henderson later worked as a director during the late 1910s and resumed his acting career in sound movies at the end of the 1920s and worked into the 1940s He is buried at Valhalla Memorial Park in North Hollywood, Los Angeles, California. The date of his death is stated as 1956 but on his grave marker 1957 is listed. The reason remains unknown.

Thomas Ince was born in November 1880 in Rhode Island and died in November 1924 of which the location is unknown due to the suspicious circumstances of his demise. Ince worked with D. W. Griffith and later ventured out on his own in California in the early days of the movie industry. His death remains uncertain based on different accounts of what occurred on board a yacht owned by William Randolph Hearst. Most accounts indicate he was shot by Hearst after being mistaken for Charlie Chaplin. To this day the truth about what actually occurred remains a guarded mystery. Ince was cremated and his ashes scattered.

Florence LaBadie (Florence Russ) was born in April 1888 in New York City and died in October 1917 in Westchester County, New York. She spent her early years in Canada and moved back to New York City where she worked as a fashion model for a while before being introduced to silent movies by Mary Pickford. LaBadie would later work with noted silent film producer Edwin Thanhouser where she achieved her greatest acclaim as a film actress. LaBadie died from injuries received in a car accident at 29. She was buried at the Greenwood Cemetery in Brooklyn, New York in an unmarked grave. Trashy tabloid-like stories about her "accidental" death surfaced decades later from questionable accounts linking her death with Woodrow Wilson. Nevertheless all supposedly-factual eyewitness accounts were later debunked and proven false when thoroughly researched by credible film historians. In 2014, Ned Thanhouser, a grandson of Edwin Thanhouser, paid for a headstone which was installed on LaBadie's 126th birthday. Some of LaBadie's movies still exist and can be seen presently on YouTube and Internet sites.

Mae Marsh (Mary Wayne Marsh) was born in November 1894 in the New Mexico territory and died in February 1968 in Hermosa Beach, a suburb of Los Angeles in California. She was discovered in 1910 while D. W. Griffith was shooting the movie *Ramona* with Mary Pickford in the Los Angeles area and from that point forward she worked steadily in movies with Griffith. Marsh was one of few actors who successfully transitioned into sound pictures after the demise of silent movies and continued working into the mid 1960s. Mae Marsh wrote one of the first books about her experiences (first published in 1921) in the movie business and of her notable co-stars. She is buried at the Pacific Crest Cemetery in Redondo Beach, Los Angeles, California. The year of birth on her headstone is incorrectly stated as 1895. According to the census of 1900, the date of her birth is listed as 1894.

Jack Mulhall (John Joseph Francis Mulhall) was born in October 1887 New York and died in Los Angeles in June 1979. He began his career in theater and worked as a model for magazine illustrators for a while. Mulhall was successful in silent movies and continued into sound pictures, working until the 1950s where he then worked for the Screen Actors Guild until 1974. He is buried at Holy Cross Cemetery in Culver City, Los Angeles, California.

Mabel Normand (Amabel Ethelreid Normand) was born in November 1893 in Staten Island, New York City, New York and died in February 1930 in Monrovia, Los Angeles, California. She worked with legends such as Mack Sennett and Charlie Chaplin, nevertheless, her career was tainted with scandal in association to the notorious 1922 unsolved murder of director William Desmond Taylor—and it led to an early retirement in 1926. She is buried at the Calvary Cemetery in East Los Angeles, Los Angeles, California. The year of her birth is incorrect on the front of her crypt. Other sources list her birthdate as 1892 but it is 1893.

Jack Pickford (John Charles Smith) was born in August 1896 in Toronto, Canada and died in January 1933 in Paris, France. Pickford was the younger brother of Mary Pickford who seemed destined for a long career in the motion picture business after catching the eye of director D. W. Griffith. But despite his obvious talents, Pickford was a troubled young man who seemed intent on self-destruction at any cost possible. His marriage to film star Olive Thomas ended in tragedy in September 1920 which led to further problems with alcoholism resulting in an early death at 36. He is buried at Forest Lawn Memorial Park in Glendale, Los Angeles, California in the Pickford family vault.

Mary Pickford (Gladys Marie Smith) was born April 1892 in Toronto, Canada and died in May 1979 in Santa Monica, Los Angeles, California. Considered to be America's first real movie star, she had intended a career on stage but after catching the eye of D. W. Griffith her life changed forever. Pickford is also credited as having introduced Dorothy and Lillian Gish to her mentor Griffith, who then turned them both into major movie stars of the silent era. She was also one of the founders of United Artists in 1919 with Griffith, Douglas Fairbanks, and Charlie Chaplin. United Artists would go on to release many classic films including the popular *James Bond* series beginning in the 1960s. Mary Pickford is buried at Forest Lawn Memorial Park in Glendale, Los Angeles, California in the Pickford family vault.

Wallace Reid (William Wallace Halleck Reid) was born in April 1891 in St. Louis, Missouri and died in January 1923 in Los Angeles, California. He was considered the first matinee idol in the movie industry once female fans discovered his presence on the movie screen—but in reality Reid preferred to work behind the camera when given a chance. He was hurt on the set of a movie in 1919 and prescribed morphine to ease his pain—but of which led to addiction and alcohol abuse. Reid attempted to overcome his health issues with morphine and alcohol but died in a sanatorium while attempting to recover. His mother wrote a memoir about her son and his career in the motion picture business. It was published in 1923 shortly after his death. He was cremated and buried in an urn at Forest Lawn Memorial Park (in the Great Mausoleum) in Glendale, Los Angeles, California.

Mack Sennett (Michael Sinnott) was born in January 1880 in Quebec, Canada and died in November 1960 in Woodland Hills, Los Angeles, California. Sennett began working in films through the American Biograph Company and later created Keystone Studios where he made a star out of Mabel Normand as well many other well-known actors such as Harold Lloyd, Marie Dressler, Gloria Swanson and W. C. Fields. Though successful at first, he encountered several setbacks as silent movies faded and sound productions began to take hold. By 1933 his career was over and his remaining years were mostly of tributes. He is buried at Holy Cross Cemetery in Culver City, Los Angeles, California.

Blanche Sweet (Sarah Blanche Sweet) was born in June 1896 in Chicago, Illinois and died in September 1986 in New York City, New York. She was discovered by D. W. Griffith and was considered a rival of Mary Pickford for most of their careers in silent movies. With the end of the silent pictures era, her career faltered and eventually she was forced to work in a department store in Los Angeles. Toward the end of her life she was honored for her pioneering work in the movie industry and appeared in several documentaries about the early years of silent movies. She died from a stroke at 90 and her ashes were scattered at the Brooklyn Botanical Gardens in New York City, New York.

George Loane Tucker was an actor, director and writer during the silent film era of the movie industry. He born in June 1872 in Chicago, Illinois and died in June 1921 in Los Angeles, California. He continued working until his death at 49 and was laid to rest at Hollywood Forever Cemetery in Los Angeles.

About the Series Editor

Gary Brin was born in 1965 and has lived in the United States Virgin Islands, Hawaii and California. He has edited numerous original literary works over the years—both new and revised. In 2019 he established Standish Press to bring forth interesting fictional and historical material usually ignored by mainstream publishers because of specific views or content. In addition to publishing books, he also created the Nancy Hanks Lincoln Public Library (named after the mother of Abraham Lincoln) in 2014 to make available hard-to-find books to a worldwide audience.

Production Notes

Written by Lucy Thurston and Linda Arvidson
Manuscripts edited by Gary Brin
Front cover design and book layout by Gary Brin
Cover layout and additional design by Victoria Valentine
Additional help provided by Carlton J. Young
Series created by Gary Brin

For free public domain books please visit
www.nancyhankslincolnpubliclibrary.org

Marie Laplace
February 13, 1892
August 16, 1981

Robert J. Questel
June 22, 1911
August 4, 1990

Marie Anicia Berry Questel
January 13, 1912
April 9, 1997

Eugene Albery Brin
March 21, 1932
May 26, 1977

Lucille Questel Brin
February 21, 1940
December 10, 2000

They never got to have the dreams they wanted or expected but their lives were important nevertheless.

**Lucy Thurston
and
Linda Arvidson**

Published by
Standish Press